THE BOOK ANN RU...
WRITE—THE RIVETI...
FOR THE G...

Be Sure to Read
GREEN RIVER, RUNNING RED

"Ann Rule once again validates her standing as one of the pre-eminent chroniclers of modern serial murder.... [This is her] definitive narrative of the brutal and senseless crimes that haunted the Seattle area for decades.... A nuanced and easily comprehensible account of the hunt for the man responsible for at least 48 killings.... Perhaps her greatest achievement is bringing Ridgway's victims to life as distinct individuals.... Her eventual realization that the murderer had attended some of her lectures and book signings will give readers the creeps."

—*Publishers Weekly*

"Rule infuses her case study with a personally felt sense of urgency.... She sketches the uniformly short, sad lives of the victims with poignancy. But her most riveting portrait is of Ridgway...."

—*People*

"Rule eschews the 'police procedural' style, focusing instead on Ridgway's victims with carefully constructed profiles.... It is Rule who best conveys the emotional truth of the Green River case. She has an eye for the telling anecdote and schoolgirl poem, mining interviews and police documents, especially Ridgway's confession and his interview by an FBI psychiatrist. She's also good at conveying the terror that gripped her community as so many girls disappeared off crowded streets."

—*Los Angeles Times*

"Rule is a veteran true-crime author. . . . Rule skillfully handles the personal angle to bring the reader closer to the victims, the crimes, the investigation, and the long-awaited arrest and conviction. . . . She is particularly adept at profiling the victims and their families."

—Associated Press

"Perhaps Rule's finest work to date. . . . Her mastery of words holds the reader in a firm grip . . . as the full horror that is Ridgway becomes clear. . . . This book is an act of compassion for the known victims and a paean of gratitude for the multiple law-enforcement officers who didn't give up until they had their man. And it doesn't take long while reading this amazing book to realize just how much information those dogged lawmen had and how complex the puzzle was that they faced."

—Statesman Journal (Salem, OR)

And Don't Miss These Stunning Bestsellers

HEART FULL OF LIES

"A convincing portrait of a meticulous criminal mind."

—The Washington Post

"Rule knows a good drama when she finds one. . . . A real-life soap opera. . . . [It will] keep readers turning pages."

—Publishers Weekly

"Fascinating and strange. . . . The sheer weight of [Ann Rule's] investigative technique places her at the forefront of true-crime writers."

—Booklist

EVERY BREATH YOU TAKE

"Affecting, tense, and smart true-crime. . . . A case study of the classic American con man crossed with the more exotic strains of the sociopath."

—*Washington Post Book World*

"Troubling but absolutely riveting. . . . A sober, nonsensational account. . . . As usual, Rule excels at painting psychologically perceptive portraits of all the characters in this stranger-than-fiction but nevertheless real-life drama."

—*Booklist*

. . . AND NEVER LET HER GO

"Most people like to think they recognize evil when they see it. But as this gripping story makes clear, most people are wrong. Much more than the profile of a handsome, insidious killer and the young woman he murdered, . . . *And Never Let Her Go* is also the story of three close-knit families and how thirty-year-old Anne Marie Fahey's death strengthened or destroyed them. . . . In Rule's capable hands, [this is] the raw material for a modern-day tragedy."

—*Publishers Weekly* (starred review)

"Truly creepy. . . . This portrait of an evil prince needs no embellishment."

—*People*

BITTER HARVEST

"A must-read story of the '90s American dream turned, tragically, to self-absorbed ashes."

—*People*

"Impossible to put down. . . . A tour de force from America's best true-crime writer."

—*Kirkus Reviews*

Books by Ann Rule

Green River, Running Red
Without Pity: Ann Rule's Most Dangerous Killers
Every Breath You Take
. . . And Never Let Her Go
Bitter Harvest
Dead by Sunset
Everything She Ever Wanted
If You Really Loved Me
The Stranger Beside Me
Possession
Small Sacrifices

The I-5 Killer
The Want-Ad Killer
Lust Killer

Ann Rule's Crime Files:
Vol. 9: Kiss Me, Kill Me and Other True Cases
Vol. 8: Last Dance, Last Chance and Other True Cases
Vol. 7: Empty Promises and Other True Cases
Vol. 6: A Rage to Kill and Other True Cases
Vol. 5: The End of the Dream and Other True Cases
Vol. 4: In the Name of Love and Other True Cases
Vol. 3: A Fever in the Heart and Other True Cases
Vol. 2: You Belong to Me and Other True Cases
Vol. 1: A Rose for Her Grave and Other True Cases

ANN RULE

EMPTY PROMISES

AND OTHER TRUE CASES

ANN RULE'S CRIME FILES: Vol. 7

POCKET BOOKS
New York   London   Toronto   Sydney

The names of some individuals in this book have been changed. Such names are indicated by an asterisk (*) the first time each appears in the narrative.

An *Original* Publication of POCKET BOOKS

POCKET BOOKS, a division of Simon & Schuster, Inc.
1230 Avenue of the Americas, New York, NY 10020

ISBN: 978-0-671-02533-5
ISBN: 0-671-02533-3

This Pocket Books paperback edition August 2005

20 19 18 17 16 15 14 13

POCKET and colophon are registered trademarks of
Simon & Schuster, Inc.

Front cover illustration and design by James Wang

Manufactured in the United States of America

For information regarding special discounts for bulk purchases, please contact Simon & Schuster Special Sales at 1-800-456-6798 or business@simonandschuster.com.

To all the women trapped in abusive and
tragic relationships,
with the sincere hope that *Empty Promises*
may help you
find a way to be free and to be safe at last.

Acknowledgments

Sometimes I tell myself that I can turn in a perfect manuscript the first time out, but I know I'm just whistling into the wind. *Empty Promises* needed far more talent and expertise than I possess. The skill of editors, the canny knowledge of detectives, the brilliance of prosecutors, lawyers and judges all combine to make a book. And always, always, there are the victims' families who are willing to share their stories with me.

I thank my publisher, Judith Curr, and my very encouraging editor, Mitchell Ivers—who had some editing assistance from Amanda Ayers and Emily Heckman—as we put together the many cases in *Empty Promises*. No writer can manage without an able production staff and I was lucky to have Donna O'Neill and Penny Haynes. As he always does, Paolo Pepe designed a cover that embodies the essence of my book.

My literary agents, Joan and Joe Foley, have been with me for three decades and we are like family now.

I'd also like to thank my theatrical agent, Ron Bernstein.

My all-time first reader, Gerry Brittingham Hay,

Acknowledgments

somehow managed to read my manuscript in planes, trains and automobiles as she headed east for a family wedding. Gerry read the end of the book as she drove up to the church!

For the *Empty Promises* book-length feature, I am indebted to Lt. J.W.B. Taylor and Detectives Greg Mains and Mike Faddis of the Redmond Police Department. *They* solved an unsolvable case with the help of Detectives Lon Shultz, Brian Tuskan, Anne Malins, Rob Bunn, Glenn Rotton, and Detective Secretary Sandy Glynn, who transcribed a tower of notes and tape recordings. Officers Christine Penwell and Kristi Roze and Victims' Advocate Linda Webb were vital to the probe. The Redmond crew was headed by Commander Chuck Krieble and Commander Gail Marsh.

King County Senior Deputy Prosecutors Marilyn Brenneman, Hank Corscadden, and Kristin Richardson took on a murder case that few prosecutors would have attempted—and won. Val Epperson kept all their files in order, a gargantuan job. I also admire King County Superior Court Judge Anthony P. Wartnik for his ability and calm as he oversaw a trial with inflammatory possibilities. And thanks as well to his very helpful assistants, Pam Roark and Barbara Tsuchida, and to King County Court Deputies Andre Tuttle and Richard Clements.

I especially appreciated Judy and Jerry Hagel's kindness as they shared memories of their daughter with me, and I admire their courage and commitment.

Without exaggerating, I have interviewed thousands of detectives in my life, and they have taught me a great deal and have shared their feelings and their philosophies with me to the point that I sometimes feel a little like a detective myself. My gratitude for the cases in

Acknowledgments

Empty Promises goes to Don Cameron, Wally Hume, the late Don Dashnea, Arnold Hubner, Jim Byrnes, John Boatman, Walt Stout, Terry Murphy, John Nordlund, Mike Tando, Danny Melton, Gary Fowler, George Marberg, William Dougherty, George Vasil and Darryl Stuver.

Many thanks to former Oregon Attorney General Bob Hamilton, Kent and Kim Smith, Bob Grau, C.N. "Nick" Marshall, Trilby Jordan, Ila Birkland, and to my own office staff: Leslie, Mike and Don.

Contents

Contents

Foreword

Sometimes it's hard for me to believe that, over the last three decades, I have researched and written about more than 1,400 actual felony cases. Most of them dealt with homicide, but many were also about sexual predators, arsonists, bank robbers, and con artists. As I leaf through some of the fact-detective magazines for which I was a correspondent early in my career, I come across cases that once captured my attention for weeks, or even months, and I'm back in a kind of true-crime time tunnel. How many times I sat on hard benches in a stuffy courtroom, and how many hours I spent interviewing detectives or friends and families of victims.

Each case comes back to me as though it is my first. Out of those 1,400 cases, there are probably 300 whose stories might well have happened yesterday; I can recall every detail. Initially, some seemed almost impossible to solve, and others involved human aberration that still shocks me. Sadly, the way humans respond to their needs, wants, desires, and compulsions has not changed, although in many cases it would be fortunate for society if they did.

While I was working on the older cases in this book, I was also writing about and attending the trials of two recent cases that came to court. With an intense rush of déjà vu, I found myself in the same courtrooms I'd visited years ago, where nothing but the faces had changed. After thirty years, a certain philosophy has burned itself into my mind: Bereft of honesty, empathy, trust, concern for other human beings, and any sense of guilt, there are those among us who seem destined to commit the kinds of crimes that make headlines. There are certain rules of human interaction that, when broken, will lead to tragedy, if not violence. The era in which we live doesn't change that. But sometimes we can only understand the people who break these rules with the clear vision that comes with hindsight.

Then we can see that long before relationships escalated to a point where murder was committed, there were lies. There are people, both men and women, who pretend to be someone they are not. They make commitments, agreements, assurances, pledges, and vows—promises— to get what they want. When they abuse the trust of those who believe in them, those empty promises often lead to violent death.

This is the seventh volume of the crime files series I began in 1993. *Empty Promises* focuses on cases where all manner of victims were betrayed by killers who were adept at making pledges that they never intended to honor. The naïveté of the victims often led to chilling endgames. As I looked for cases for this volume, I wasn't surprised to find an inordinate number of homicides that were spawned by broken love affairs, where one partner "loved" too much. I found many hollow vows made to victims who were kind and trusting—so trusting that their lives ended at the hands of the devious schemers who ensnared them. For many, the promises were implicit in a friendly smile. Innocents—who failed to recognize the danger in those smiles—died.

Two disturbing categories of homicide keep appearing in the letters and calls I receive from readers and detectives. One has, I fear, always been with us and is finally surfacing because the victims are no longer ashamed to come forward to ask for help. Many years ago I responded to domestic violence calls when I was a policewoman, but there was nowhere for battered women to go for help in those days. Even though there are now shelters and help, many women live with abuse, both mental and physical, until it is too late. The second murder genre that has accelerated alarmingly in the last decade may well reflect the violent images our children are routinely exposed to: homicides committed by teenagers. Cases representative of each category appear in this volume.

I often say that what real people do can be so heroic, bizarre, savage, and completely unpredictable that no fiction writer could have pulled it out of her imagination. The characters in *Empty Promises* won't disappoint you as you read their incredible stories.

As many of you know, in the seventies and eighties my territory as a correspondent for five fact-detective magazines was the Northwest: Washington, Oregon, Idaho, and western Montana. In my fifteen years as a stringer, I wrote about the same detectives from big-city police departments dozens of times. Readers of my true-crime files may recognize the names of these investigators. The names are the same; the cases are unique. If I were producing a television series, it would be along the lines of *NYPD Blue, Homicide: Life on the Street,* and *Hill Street Blues.* But the series would be called *Seattle: Murder in the Emerald City* or *Portland: Cops and Roses.* Another, far more important, difference would be that every one of my cases would be absolutely true.

Most of the stories in this collection are companion pieces. They show slightly different views of similar motivation on the part of the killers. The first book-length case deals with the bleak mystery of wives and mothers who vanish inexplicably from their homes. In "Empty Promises" you will learn about a lovely young woman, trapped and seduced by a world that was completely alien to the atmosphere in which she was raised. Her marriage was a nightmare. It's necessary only to turn that story a few degrees to find a tragically similar puzzle.

"Bitter Lake" and "Young Love" demonstrate that not being loved at all can be preferable—and much safer—than being loved too much.

"Love and Insurance" and "The Gentler Sex" seem at first to be quite different from one another. And yet they both deal with charming con artists who actually seem to savor the elaborately deceptive plots they have concocted more than the sex and money that appear—at first—to be their motivation.

"The Conjugal Visit" and "Killers on the Road" explore the mindless kind of murder that we all fear in our deepest hearts. Why would an absolute stranger set out to earn our trust—and at the same time be coldly willing to destroy us? These predators are out there, prowling our streets and highways, looking for a perverted and deadly thrill.

"A Dangerous Mind" and "To Kill and Kill Again" explore the phenomenon of socially alienated youthful murderers whose motivation is more difficult to understand than any I have encountered. Teenage killers inspire shocking headlines as their number increases in our society. We have to wonder how someone so young can be so full of rage.

"The Stockholm Syndrome" stands alone. This is the case on which I based my only novel, *Possession*. This Oregon case may be a lesson for anyone who has ever said that he or she could never be brainwashed. Think again; it is only a matter of how long it would take.

Empty Promises

The disappearance of Jami Hagel Sherer has many chilling similarities to the vanishing of a half-dozen wives and mothers who were listed as missing in western Washington in the nineties, so many women gone with no explanation that it seemed epidemic in the Northwest.

Jami was twenty-five when she disappeared. She would be thirty-five today—if she is still alive. Jami grew up only blocks from where I raised my four children in the sixties and seventies. Young families moved to the Seattle suburb of Bellevue as it burgeoned in the early fifties because it seemed the safest, best place to raise children. Then it was a world where crime and drugs and ugliness seemed far away.

1

It was a Sunday afternoon, the last day of September 1990, when Judy Hagel began to feel uneasy. Usually she grew annoyed and exasperated when her son-in-law, Steve Sherer, phoned constantly to check on her daughter, Jami. He kept such close tabs on Jami that she seemed to move on an invisible tether. If she left home to visit her parents, he called to be sure she arrived within fifteen minutes, and then he kept calling to ask what she was doing, and very soon, of course, to insist that she come back home to their house in Redmond. If he had his way, Jami would never visit her family at all.

But *this* afternoon, Steve didn't call—not for five hours. It was a record for him, and Judy found herself jumpy not at the ringing of her phone but because of the silence. She had expected Jami all day, and Jami never showed up. Judy was baby-sitting with Jami's little boy, Chris,* and it wasn't like her daughter to stay away when she had promised Chris she would be back soon.

Bellevue was once as far removed from Seattle in lifestyle and population as any of a number of small towns that dot the state of Washington. Fifty years ago it was a rustic hamlet on the other side of Lake Washington, where farms and blueberry bogs could be found just outside town. Before the first floating bridge con-

3

necting Mercer Island and Bellevue to the mainland in Seattle was completed in 1940, the little town was far off the beaten path. No one ever imagined Bellevue would become the third largest city in the state with its own mirror-windowed skyscrapers and upscale malls. After World War II, it became a bastion of affordable three-bedroom, bath-and-a-half houses that young marrieds could afford, and they flocked to the neighborhoods of Lake Hills and Eastgate. Returning veterans and recent college graduates found jobs at the Boeing Airplane Company. Young husbands went off to work and young wives stayed home and raised four children per family, long before anyone had heard about the population explosion. Appliances were avocado green, carpets were an orange shag that had to be raked as well as vacuumed, and tile floors were waxed faithfully once a week.

It was a world of kaffeeklatsches, where wives shared recipes for frozen strawberry jam, onion soup dip, and complicated casseroles whose main ingredient seemed always to be Cheez Whiz. Yards sprouted gardens, and wives traded seedlings as frequently as they took turns baby-sitting. It was a time long before day care and two-income families. Bellevue seemed to promise that after the long dark war, everything was going to be all right. It was an ideal community in a halcyon era.

But the decades that followed brought a tragic tumbling-down for many of the children whose future had seemed so bright. Bellevue, Washington, wasn't unique; drugs and more wars and assassinations and rock and roll and XXX-rated movies and videos and the erratic vicissitudes of fortune eroded family-based towns all over America. As Bellevue became a little grittier and far less inviolate, Jami Hagel's desolate destiny began to take shape, despite her family's struggle to save her.

Judy and Jerry Hagel left tiny Carrington, North Dakota, in 1967 and headed for Washington State; Judy's two brothers lived there, and they said the job prospects were good. Judy and Jerry's oldest child, Randy, was five then and Jami Sue was almost three. A year later, Judy gave birth to twin boys, Rob and Rich.

Rather than resenting all the attention the twins got, Jami was enthralled with them, and their birth gave her a tighter bond with her mother. Even though she was only three, she took care of the twins for her mother. "I wasn't expecting twins," Judy recalls. "I had no help, and Jami was there to help me. We had a little rocker, and I couldn't feed two babies at one time, so I'd hand one baby to her and she'd rock it to sleep. And I'd get the other baby and hand it to her. She was very helpful for me. She was always holding them—they were so little."

And so was Jami. She was so petite as a child that she wore only size zero or size one. Her mother would seek out little specialty stores where there were clothes small enough to fit tiny Jami.

Growing up in Bellevue as the only daughter in a family with three sons, Jami was in the thick of whatever her brothers were doing, despite her size. Randy was three years older than Jami, and her twin brothers, Rich and Rob, were three years younger. Jami looked like a little doll with bright brown eyes, luxuriant dark hair, and a "lovely smile," but she could give as good as she got from her brothers, who teased her, as all brothers do. Even when she was grown, Jami weighed only 95 pounds and stood just a smidgen over five feet tall. Jami was sweet-natured, but she wasn't afraid of anything. Judy and Jerry had raised her to be self-confident.

Jerry Hagel and all of his children were involved in softball competitions early on. The whole family played in local leagues, and Jami was a tomboy. "She was small but feisty," her brother Rob recalled.

Judy Hagel stayed at home to raise her children. She was the mother who was always available to drive her children and their friends to Lake Sammamish to swim or to the movies or to go horseback riding. Jami loved horses even more than baseball, and she and her friend Lori Stratton also loved to climb trees.

Besides playing softball together, the Hagels spent their vacations together. They usually traveled back to North Dakota to visit their extended family during summer vacations. Christmas and all holidays and birthdays were special for them, and the Hagels' family album grew thick with photos of various celebrations. Judy loved her boys, but she delighted in her only daughter and the feeling was mutual. Judy and Jami shared secrets and discussed problems together.

Judy couldn't imagine that life would ever be any other way. Jami was close to her father, Jerry, too. In photographs she is usually sitting near him. He treated her as if she were made of porcelain, and Jami always expected to marry a man like her dad.

Jami Hagel was a nice girl who grew up to be a kind woman. A friend several years younger remembers how she idolized Jami. "She had a wonderful bedroom," the woman says, "with a rainbow theme. I thought it was so beautiful. Jami used to let me come in and look at her things, even though I was probably a little pest."

As a teenager, Jami Hagel went to Sammamish High

School, near Lake Hills in Bellevue. When she was a sophomore, she began going steady with Greg Coomes, who was very handsome and a year older than she was. They went together for five or six years, all through high school and beyond. Jami's family approved of Greg. The young couple had a monogamous, "very serious" relationship and eventually became lovers. "She was my first love," Greg would recall one day. "She was the first woman I was ever intimate with."

Jami's high school world would have been the envy of any teenager. She had her own car, but she wasn't spoiled. She worked hard at her studies, and she was confident. Greg described her as having a strong sense of self. Most of her friends used the word "bubbly" or "outgoing and friendly" when they described her then—and later.

Jami Hagel was unfailingly happy and never moody. While some teenagers go through angst and self-doubt, no one recalled that Jami was ever depressed. She was certainly not suicidal. She remained close to her family, particularly to her mother, a special relationship that Judy Hagel cherished.

Jami and Greg's relationship did not, however, survive the changes that inevitably come with maturity. He graduated a year ahead of Jami and went to work for a hotel chain in Portland, Oregon, for six months. After that, he came back to the Seattle area to work at the Boeing Company. There was no big emotional breakup, but they simply saw each other less and less. "By 1986," Greg said, "we were down to just phone calls."

Nevertheless, they remained friends, just as Jami kept her friendships going with most of the people who were part of her school years. June Young, a beautiful

7

brunette, met Jami when they were in the ninth grade. "We were best friends. We were from the same background—we both had brothers," June remembers. "She had a great self-image," June says. "She was outgoing, happy, bubbly. Jami was a T-shirt-and-jeans girl."

Jami and June continued to be best friends for a dozen years, even though they both encountered tragedies and problems. June went off to Western Baptist Bible College for a year after high school. When she lost her sister in a traffic accident, she came home to help her family bear the loss and took a job at an insurance company. June got married in 1988.

Right after Jami graduated from high school, she found a job in the computer industry and moved into an apartment with another girl. She came home to live briefly when that living arrangement ended. After that, Jami got an apartment by herself in Redmond, about six miles from her parents' home.

Jami Hagel's bond with her family remained strong; she called her mother three or four times a week and spent most weekends with them. Unlike many girls her age who can't wait to grow up and go through a period of proving how independent they are, Jami often dropped by to talk with her mother. If Judy was out in her garden or in the kitchen, Jami sat with her and talked about what was going on in her life. There were no secrets, and Judy could always find Jami when she needed to talk with her.

But sometime in the mid-eighties, while Jami was living in her own apartment in Redmond, she met a man who was nothing like Greg Coomes. He was nothing like anyone Jami had ever dated, and her family and friends were a little surprised that Jami was attracted to him.

Judy Hagel remembers the first time she ever saw

Steve Sherer. He and Jami "drove up on a motorcycle," Judy says, "and he was very proud of the motorcycle because he had bought it from his winnings at the race-track."

Every other boyfriend that Jami had brought home to meet her parents had made an effort to be polite and friendly, but Steve seemed completely uninterested in them. The first time he met the Hagels, he strutted around as if he thought they should be impressed with him and his shiny new motorcycle. Almost as soon as Jami and Steve arrived, he was anxious to leave. Jami climbed on the bike behind him and they roared off, leaving the Hagels puzzled and worried. They told themselves that Jami couldn't really be interested in such a man.

At twenty-four, Steven Frank Sherer was two years older than Jami. Despite his small stature, he had a powerful personality, more abrasive than pleasant much of the time, but he could also be completely charming. Steve told Jami early on that he was the son of a very wealthy family, and she noticed that he always seemed to have money. The money didn't matter that much to her; Steve's personality did. In the beginning, she liked his take-charge attitude.

No one can predict the chemistry between two people, and for whatever reason, Jami Hagel and Steve Sherer soon began to date steadily.

Steve claimed to be five feet nine, but he was closer to five seven. He carried himself like a much taller man. He often bleached his thick light brown hair so it turned blond in the sun and then combed it in a pompadour. His knife-like profile, while not handsome, was striking. He had a solid, muscular body, and he drove new cars, although he seldom seemed to work.

Judy and Jerry Hagel saw nothing about Steve that erased their first impression of him, but they were smart enough not to voice their feelings to Jami; finding fault with Steve would just have made him seem more appealing.

To a parent, Steve was anything but appealing. He was a spoiled rich kid whose rap sheet was longer than his job résumé, although Judy and Jerry Hagel didn't know about that when Jami first brought him home. He was also possessed of a truly ugly temper and just about every bad habit and addiction available. He drank, used marijuana and cocaine, gambled at racetracks and card rooms, and believed that women were basically chattels. When Jami answered his questions about men she had been with before she knew him, Steve was furious.

Greg Coomes, her high school boyfriend, received a call in 1986 that at first seemed to be a wrong number. A man on the phone started swearing at him, using the worst gutter language. "He said he was going to kill me," Coomes recalled. "I had no idea who he was."

Finally, Coomes heard a woman's voice and recognized Jami. She apologized for the caller and said he was her "lover" and the "person she lived with."

In the beginning, shocked as she was by Steve's need to possess her, she also saw it as a sign that he was very much in love with her. Steve's jealousy made her feel happy and secure.

Steven Frank Sherer was born at 6:57 A.M. on November 4, 1961, at Our Lady of Perpetual Help Hospital in Santa Maria, California. His father, David Kent Sherer, was twenty-two years old and worked as a bricklayer. Like Jami's parents, David Sherer came from North Dakota. His mother, Sharon Ann Bleiler

Sherer, known as Sherri, who was born and raised in California, was only seventeen when she gave birth to Steven. She and David would have two more children—Saundra and Laura.

Sherri was a very pretty petite brunette. David Sherer was five feet six and had blue eyes. His son would grow to resemble him physically and be genetically predisposed to some of his father's weaknesses, but he didn't inherit David Sherer's strengths. From his early days as a bricklayer, the elder Sherer worked his way up with business savvy and hard work.

The Sherers left California and moved to Lynnwood, Washington, where the building boom had just begun. Their younger daughter, Laura, was born there. David Sherer started a construction company—Sherer Quality Homes—in Everett. He caught the wave of the Northwest's construction boom in the seventies. He bought acreage cheap where no one but his partner saw any promise. Some of that land became Mill Creek, which would soon be one of the most desirable suburbs of Seattle.

The Sherers were soon richer than they could ever have envisioned. They had a house in Lynnwood as well as vacation homes in Scottsdale, Arizona, and Palm Desert, California, near Rancho Mirage.

Steve drove a new blue Ford pickup truck when he was still in high school. One of his school friends, David Harrington, recalled that the Sherers were a very nice family. "Things were pretty darn good in his house," David said. Sherri Sherer had invited him to live with them for the last half of his senior year in Alderwood High School, and he was amazed at the good life that Steve took for granted.

After they graduated, David and Steve rented a

"dumpy little house" together in Montlake Terrace. They were eighteen then and far more interested in partying than in education. For a year, the two of them held a full-time open house and enjoyed having liquor and marijuana available with no one to stop them. They also did some cocaine, although that was mostly light experimentation. There were girls and discos, but eventually David and Steve vacated their rental house. "We might have gotten tossed out because of the parties," David said later, looking back to that time.

In 1982, David Harrington joined the Marine Corps and his close association with Steve Sherer ended. He saw Steve occasionally on leaves, but Steve hadn't changed. He was still involved in the same kind of life they had shared when they were eighteen—girls and booze and drugs. It was as if time had stood still for Steve Sherer. When David saw Steve in 1987 after his own discharge from the marines, they had virtually nothing left in common.

It wasn't that Steve hadn't faced tragedy in his life; he had—but tragedy seemed not to affect him. The month that Steve turned twenty-two, his father died under unusual circumstances. David Sherer had become a multimillionaire by the time he was forty-four. He never got to enjoy his wealth, however.

During 1983, Sherri and David Sherer had many arguments over his drinking. All his wealth and business acumen had not made David Sherer happy. Maybe he had too much time on his hands and liquor was always around; maybe he was genetically predisposed to alcoholism. In November of that year, David Sherer packed up and left Lynnwood, reportedly headed for their Palm Desert home so he could "get himself together" and stop drinking. The Sherer vacation home in Palm

Desert was in the exclusive Lakes Country Club, a gated community with private security guards. Friends who lived there played golf with David Sherer almost every day and saw how distraught he was about the disintegration of his marriage.

November 24 was Thanksgiving Day, a sad day for anyone to be all alone and thousands of miles from family. One of Sherer's neighbors saw him in the clubhouse drinking around five or six o'clock on Thanksgiving afternoon. Sherri called him later that day and could tell that he was inebriated. They had the same old argument and when she called her husband again at 1:00 A.M., they reportedly exchanged angry words.

Reportedly, David Sherer told his wife that she would be "better off without him" and informed her he had a gun and "was going to do something about [their situation]." Sherri told authorities later that she wasn't particularly worried because she didn't believe him. The only gun her husband had was an old .32 caliber automatic given to him by her grandfather, and she was sure that was someplace in their Washington home.

But his threat must have niggled at Sherri Sherer because she immediately booked a flight to California. It was almost 11:00 P.M. when she arrived at their Palm Desert house, but the place was oddly silent. When she walked north from the front door into the den, she found her husband. David Sherer was sitting on the couch. He was dead, his head tilted back unnaturally. A .32 caliber automatic, with an empty shell casing beside it, lay on the carpet next to the couch and just below Sherer's right arm. The phone was on the floor next to his leg.

Sherri called the country club security office for help, asking them to call the police and fire department.

Paramedic Jay Manning from the Indio Fire Department arrived first, and pronounced forty-four-year-old David Sherer dead. He had obviously been dead for some time; his body was frozen with rigor mortis, and lividity—the staining of the skin caused when the heart no longer pumps blood and it settles in lower body parts—was also advanced.

An Indio police officer named Coillet notified the Riverside County Coroner's Office at three minutes to midnight that David Sherer appeared to have committed suicide. Investigator Sabas Rosas from the coroner's office tended to agree. There was a bullet hole in the north wall of the den with blood spatter and what appeared to be bone fragments staining the wall nearby. The bullet itself was missing, but Rosas concluded it had probably dropped to the floor between the studs of the wall rather than penetrating the next wall.

Sherri Sherer and two of the Sherers' friends told Rosas that the dead man had been drinking heavily over the past few days. The house showed no signs of forced entry or burglary; it was neat and clean and nothing was ransacked or missing. David Sherer was fully dressed and had no defense wounds on his hands. The only signs of violence were the entrance wound of a bullet in his right temple, the exit wound in the left temple, and blood on his shirt. There were gunpowder burns around the entrance wound. Even though he had left no suicide note, the circumstances suggested that David Sherer had died by his own hand. His blood alcohol was .10 percent—legal proof of intoxication in most states.

"Based on the physical evidence, statements made by the spouse and friends, the findings of the Indio Police Department, the victim's psychological condition, his alcohol disease, and the findings of the pathologist," Rosas wrote, "the death was classified as suicide."

His body was sent home to Washington State for burial in Green Lawn Cemetery. At age thirty-nine, Sherri was a widow, but she would remarry the next year.

There is no information about Steve accompanying his mother to Palm Desert that day after Thanksgiving, nor is there any record of his whereabouts at the time. For a while there were rumors that Steve had killed his father, but that is unlikely. There is only a thin file relating to the elder Sherer's death; it contains the coroner's report and autopsy findings that showed the deceased was in good health before the bullet traversed his brain. One way or another, however, Steve had surely added to his father's depression. The Sherers' daughters didn't cause their parents heartache, but Steve had been in more trouble than any three ordinary young men. From the time he was born, he was indulged, and he grew up with a tremendous appetite for all things forbidden and with a stubborn insistence that he should have whatever he wanted.

He usually got it. David Sherer left his family well provided for, and Sherri always had trouble saying no to her only son. At first she gave him what he wanted because she loved to see him happy. Later she may have been afraid of his temper and what he might do if she refused to grant his requests.

Sherri sold the Palm Desert house, purchased another southwestern vacation spot in Scottsdale, Arizona, and one on Lake Chelan, Washington. All of the homes that might have brought back sad memories of her late husband were sold.

Steve Sherer jumped from job to job and from girl to girl. By July 4, 1987, he was with Jami. David Harrington, Steve's high school buddy and first roommate, remembered that holiday, and a bizarre incident that ended their friendship. Steve, then twenty-five, invited David and his girlfriend to join him, Jami, Jami's brother Rich, and Rich's girlfriend, Timarie, at the Sherers' resort home on Lake Chelan in eastern Washington. David was annoyed to see how Steve picked on Jami when he was drinking, but he never saw him hurt her physically. "I wouldn't have tolerated that," he said.

"It was the usual Steve holiday celebration," David continued. "Big house, very nice—on the lake. Illegal fireworks, drinking, cocaine. And then Steve commented that my girlfriend was very attractive. He asked me, 'You want to swap girlfriends?' I asked him, 'You kidding?' and he said he'd enjoy watching Jami get fucked by another guy. He said, 'I'd enjoy watching, but if she ever cheated on me with another guy, I'd kill her.' "

After that, David avoided Steve, still unsure if he was serious about his offer to exchange girlfriends. "But I never introduced Steve to my current wife," he said later.

Steve seldom worked, but he always had a new car and plenty of spending money. Sherri had tried desperately to help Steve grow up, alternately indulging him and banishing him. He was moody and unpredictable, and she worried about him. Still, his main activities were partying and breaking the law. Sherri was always waiting for the other shoe to drop.

Steve's police contacts were initially limited to his own fairly circumscribed neighborhood. In November 1981, shortly after his twentieth birthday, he and a girlfriend were at a Lynnwood pizza parlor. Steve, who was drunk, stared at two attractive women; one was with her husband, and the other was with a boyfriend. Emboldened by alcohol, Steve pinched one woman's buttocks. When she whirled in disbelief and dismay,

Steve threatened her male friends. Lynnwood police responded and found Steve argumentative and uncooperative. When they moved to handcuff him and take him into custody, he ran. He was charged with simple assault and resisting arrest.

Steve Sherer's troubles with the law seemed always to be sparked by alcohol or women—or both. His attraction to Jami Hagel wasn't surprising when one looked at the women he dated before—and after—his relationship with her. He had a preferred type and he often found women who fit it. He was never without a fabulous-looking petite woman at his side.

Steve was unfailingly attracted to women who were tiny, large-breasted, and blond. He would send roses and romantic cards to them during his courting phase. He could be charming and exciting—at first. But almost every girl who dated Steve for any length of time eventually came to regret she ever met him. Beyond emotional and verbal abuse, they were subjected to threats, choking, and beatings. Steve seemed to have an almost Svengali-like power over certain women that kept them captive long after common sense would have dictated that they leave.

Two months after his father's suicide—in January 1984, long before he met Jami Hagel—Steve began to date Bettina Rauschberg.* Bettina was a prototype for Steve's ideal woman, and she found him fun and loving when she first met him. Entranced, Bettina moved with Steve to Balboa Beach, California, in early 1984. They lived in an apartment there, but Bettina soon learned that Steve could erupt into violence whenever he imagined that she was unfaithful. She never considered being with another man and was upset when Steve wouldn't trust her.

17

Even so, when one of his friends dropped by their apartment, she didn't think twice before telling the man he could wait for Steve. The friend was lying on the living room carpet watching TV and Bettina was in the kitchen making pizza when Steve came home half an hour later. He was agitated to begin with—she didn't know why— and the sight of another man in the apartment threw him into a maniacal rage. Steve grabbed a bottle and smashed it over his friend's head. The man ran, and Bettina raced for the bathroom, slamming it and locking it against Steve. She was scared to death of him when he was angry.

"He broke down the door, broke through glass," she said. "He hit me in the face and put his hands around my throat until I passed out."

Someone in a neighboring apartment called for an ambulance, and when Bettina came to, she was in the hospital. "Steve was sitting beside my bed, saying he didn't know why he'd done that to me. He said he was sorry. He begged me not to leave him . . . I called his mother and she said she didn't want to hear about it. So I stayed with him."

It was always like that; after he hurt her, Steve was contrite and seemingly horrified at his own violence. Nobody is as pitiful as a batterer when he swears he will never, ever, hit a woman again. For a while, during their second honeymoon period, Steve kept his word, but inevitably something set him off again.

Bettina wasn't encouraged to have friends of her own, but she met a couple at work who sensed that something was wrong in her life. When she confided in them about Steve's abuse and how frightened she was sometimes, they told her that no one had to live in fear. The next time Steve blew up at her, she accepted the couple's offer to move in with them.

When they knew Steve was away, they took Bettina back to the apartment she'd shared with Steve so she could pack some of her clothing and belongings. Her key still worked in the front door, but when they walked in, they gasped in horror. All of Bettina's stuffed animals and dolls lay on the carpet, and they had been neatly decapitated.

There was a note that read "That's what I'm going to do to you."

Bettina moved out, but only for a short time. She soon moved back in with Steve, convinced that he really would kill her if she stayed away too long.

Bettina stayed with Steve through a number of other brutal incidents, relenting each time when he sobbed that he couldn't get along without her. His promises meant nothing at all. By May 1985 they were back in Lynnwood when police were called to a fitness club where they worked out. They found Bettina bruised and scratched. Tearfully, she told them that Steve had hit her in the face several times and kicked her car. She had made the mistake of trying to break up with him. He was arrested on May 29 for simple assault and malicious mischief.

Bettina continued down the predictable path of a victim of domestic violence: She got a temporary order of protection against Steve on June 2 and a permanent order two weeks later. As far as the police knew, the couple went their separate ways. But orders of protection are about as strong as the paper they're written on.

Bettina tried to stay away from him, but breaking up with a man like Steve Sherer was not easy. Even though he began to date Jami Hagel, he continued to harass and threaten Bettina. He was far from out of her life. On March 4, 1986, Steve hit her hard enough to knock her unconscious. Bettina didn't call the police, deciding to bide her time in the hope that she could get away from Steve without angering him further. She'd called the police before, but they couldn't be there every time Steve beat her. She was running scared.

Steve had Jami now, Bettina figured, and perhaps he would let her go. Oddly, both women lived in the same apartment building; Steve had arranged that. Sometimes he was with Jami; sometimes he wanted to come back to Bettina. He hit them both when they got out of line. He was short, but he prided himself on his muscles and he honed them at health clubs so that his biceps bulged. He often appeared in police reports because he got into fights at parties with other men. He seemed unable to go more than five or six months without exploding in one way or another.

Bettina went back to Steve; she couldn't resist him when he was sweet. It appeared to the Lynnwood police who responded to a call for help on March 6, 1986, that Sherer intended to own both Bettina and Jami. Bettina told them she wondered why Jami stayed with Steve, and yet she couldn't see that her own situation was a mirror image of Jami's.

"Jami was always crying that spring," Bettina remembered, adding that Jami was fiercely loyal to Steve even though she knew he was really with Bettina. Apparently he had told Jami that it was Bettina who caused all the problems. Maybe Jami thought that *she* could make Steve happy. *Let her try,* Bettina thought wearily.

On that rainy night of March 6, Steve showed up at the apartment he shared with Bettina in Alderwood in the wee hours of the morning, only to find her packing her bags to leave him again. She couldn't share him any longer, she said, and she was sick of having him gone all night, even when she knew he wasn't with Jami. Despite his growing interest in Jami, Steve wouldn't allow Bettina to walk away from him—not until *he* said it was over.

It was a terrible time for both young women. "There were a lot of bad memories," Bettina said, trying to sort out one single incident from a string of abuse.

But this was the night when she finally decided to leave. Steve didn't come home. Bettina was worried about how she would get to work by seven the next morning. "I had no ride and Steve had the car," she recalled. "He'd been out all night long. He kept calling and saying he was on his way home, but he never got there. When he finally walked in, I picked up my bags to leave."

She told the officers who responded to her 911 call that she was almost at the door when something slammed into the back of her head. Blood streamed down her neck from a deep gash in her scalp. Steve had thrown a heavy shot glass at her, and it had shattered on impact. She was lucky to have only a concussion.

Bettina was taken to the ER to have her wound stitched up, and then police accompanied her back to her apartment to ensure her safety. That was a prudent decision; when they searched the premises, they found Steve Sherer hiding under a blanket in the bedroom closet. When he was arrested and led past Bettina, he turned to her, shouting, "Fuck off! I'm going to kill that bitch!"

The officers noted his remark in the police report; it would come back to haunt him.

This time, Steve was convicted—but only of second-degree assault. He filed his own complaint, accusing the arresting officers of using excessive force. His charges were judged to be unfounded.

Within two days, Steve transferred his affections to Jami Hagel. Although there were a few more legal skirmishes, Bettina had finally succeeded in extricating herself from a punishing alliance. She would, however, never completely get over her fear of Steve Sherer. More than a decade later, she was still afraid of him.

2

Bettina Rauschberg was only one woman among more than a million in 1986 who had suffered injuries in what the U.S. Justice Department calls intimate partner abuse. Most of the physical attacks were, like hers, deemed simple assaults. Ten years earlier, 1,600 women and slightly fewer men had died in domestic disputes; ten years later, 1,320 women and 510 men were killed by "intimate partners." Through sheer luck or a final desperate decision to run, Bettina got away. Experts on domestic violence have a rule of thumb; it takes seven beatings before a woman or a man will find the strength and the courage to leave.

Some don't make it that far.

The man Bettina escaped from was the same man that Jami Hagel took home to meet her family. Steve had a way with women, a power that only those who fell in love with him could explain—if even they could put it into words. He wasn't that good-looking, he wasn't that affluent unless his mother helped him out, and he had demonstrated an explosive temper. Still, he never lacked for female company.

From the beginning, Jami Hagel was mesmerized by Steve, and her parents and brothers carefully held their breath, reminding each other that they mustn't criticize him or she would be even more attracted to him. But they didn't want to give him a stamp of approval either. Perhaps it wouldn't have mattered; Jami was in love with Steve and determined to marry him. The Hagels watched in horror as they saw their feisty, bubbly, self-assured daughter and sister become more and more submissive to a stranger in their midst. They had no idea how to stop her frightening metamorphosis.

As he did with every woman in his life, Steve set out to "customize" Jami to meet his specifications. She was the right size and had a lovely face, but that wasn't good enough. Although Jami's thick brown hair was one of her best features, Steve told her he much preferred blondes. Jami lightened her hair, but it reacted oddly to the bleaching process, which left it orange-yellow.

True to the profile of the abusive male, Steve systematically distanced Jami from her family. He complained about how close she was to them and was annoyed by family get-togethers. When he did go to holiday dinners or ball games with her, Jami constantly darted glances at Steve to see what his reaction was. His mood was more important to her than anything else. She was no longer the confident young woman she had been; her whole life seemed dedicated to making Steve happy, even when his demands were excessive and selfish. She was very tentative, looking to Steve to determine what he wanted her to do and say.

Steve didn't want Jami to see her women friends, her family, or anyone else who took her attention away from him. His was the classic posturing of the possessive male. To make the situation worse, as he had done with Bettina, Steve convinced Jami that they should move to California.

"They came to our house," Judy Hagel recalled, "and said they were going to California, supposedly for a vacation for a week. I think that was in May 1986. But I just sort of had a feeling it wasn't going to be just a week, and so I waited all week long, just waited for Sunday so she could come home. She didn't come home. The next thing I know I get a phone call from her saying they've decided to stay in California . . . I kept in close touch with her. She called me often, and I called while she was there."

Judy and Jerry Hagel had watched their precious daughter drive away from everyone she had always counted on as she and Steve headed off to Palm Desert, California. She was an adult; there was nothing they could do. She had yet to marry Steve and they hoped she never would. Judy Hagel had seen purple bruises and the marks of fingers on Jami's arms and legs. Jami always had an explanation about falling, banging her elbow on a doorway, or hurting herself in some other way.

Steve had good reason to want to leave the state of Washington. He had been bombarding Bettina with phone calls and letters, and she was frightened enough of him to call the police to record each violation of her order of protection.

More dangerous to him was a recent burglary in Bellevue. In the late afternoon of April 7, 1986, someone had broken into a residence and taken stereo equipment, jewelry, and a small-caliber handgun. Without a job, with his mother cutting down on loans and handouts, and with his prodigious appetite for drugs and gambling, Steve was hungry for money.

Bellevue detectives were able to lift latent fingerprints but AFIS (Automatic Fingerprint Identification System) was not yet in wide use. (In October 1988, AFIS matched the burglary prints to Steven Frank Sherer, but that was two years after the fact.)

In California, Steve continued his spotty work history; he had worked occasionally for his father's construction firm, but he didn't have any particular skill as a builder. Sometimes he got sales jobs, but they never lasted long. He still liked to gamble and he still liked drugs; he was more than dabbling in cocaine by this time. And he always drove like a bat out of hell.

Steve spent some time in jail on traffic warrants in San Bernadino in September 1986. While he was there, he flooded Jami with romantic cards:

> *I miss you, baby! When I get out, will you spend the rest of your life with me? I hope so, because your [sic] what I want in life. Your what I'm living for! Please wait for me. Wait and spend the rest of your life in my arms. I love you so much and it just gets stronger every day. Please have faith in our love. . . . Things will never be bad. Just better each and every day. . . . Life is only worth the love that one can share with another and I'd like to make mine worth billions with you!*
>
> *Love forever,*
> *Steven*

Steve always called Jami his little rose. "To the flower of my life," he wrote. "Soon to be future wife with all the love in my heart. I care for you with my life, giving it up for you at any moment. I can't stand not having you within my sight. Forever I will love you, no matter what the future holds, you'll never leave my heart and I'll always see you as my *ROSE!"*

Jami was working, trying to keep up with their bills. She missed Steve too, and no woman could ask for more romantic mail.

But it was easy for a man in jail to feel romantic. The bruises and scratches that were always with Jami when she lived with Steve began to heal. Her faith began to blossom. Of course, when Steve came home, he lost much of his romantic veneer. His mother was trying tough love, so they had money problems. Steve couldn't live the way he wanted to.

Judy Hagel didn't know about most of Jami's problems, but Jami called her one night and she was crying. "They were down around a swimming pool somewhere and he was not being nice to her," Judy said. "I told her to leave, and she said that he had threatened to kill himself with a knife if she left him, and I told her she *had* to come home. I said, 'I will catch a flight to Los Angeles and I will get you and we'll pick up your car and we'll come home.' And she says okay. . . . The next morning I call her and of course everything was okay and she wasn't coming home."

Worried, Judy and Jerry Hagel arranged to meet Jami and Steve in Las Vegas in October 1986. It was the first time they had seen Jami's shocking metamorphosis. "I walked into this casino," Judy recalled in a hushed voice. "Jami was just a very small person. She weighed probably all of ninety pounds dripping wet. . . . All I saw was cheekbones and big brown eyes and blond hair. She had dyed her hair blond. . . . She was so thin it was awful. I could not believe this was Jami, but it was. And we tried to go have a talk, but we just couldn't be left alone [by Steve] and so we left and she went back to California with Steve, and Jerry and I went home."

Empty Promises

Judy and Jerry Hagel had no idea the kind of life Jami was living or the terror that she felt more and more often. They didn't care for Steve, but if he made Jami happy, they respected her right to choose a mate.

By November 1986, Jami and Steve were living in a double-wide mobile home on Portola Avenue in Palm Desert, California. They were secretly engaged, and Steve gave Jami an heirloom ring. It was a size four, yellow gold with three round full-cut diamonds. The center stone was perfect and over a carat in weight; the side stones were .24 carats each, and it was appraised at $13,500. Steve suggested they take out insurance on it and their other expensive possessions. The policy, which went into effect in October, was written by Farmers' Insurance for a year.

Steve called the Riverside County Sheriff's Department on November 4 to report that someone had broken into the mobile home and stolen a number of items, including Jami's ring. Their claim form listed computers, cameras, miscellaneous jewelry, silver dishes, and a Colt .357. They estimated that their total loss, allowing for depreciation, was well over $32,000. They had paid only the first quarter of the premiums due on their renter's policy, and their coverage was due to expire on January 2, 1987. The claim agent for Farmers' was uneasy about the timing, but the insurance company decided eventually to pay off Steve and Jami's claim.

They should have used the insurance money for something practical, but it didn't last long. Steve still had expensive tastes—and more expensive habits. Although he had been raised in a wealthy family, he was nowhere near the entrepreneur his father had been. Soon Steve and Jami were barely able to pay the rent on the mobile home on Portola Avenue. It was a far cry from the posh country club home his parents had once owned in Palm Desert, the house where his father died.

Steve may have consciously or unconsciously hoped to recapture that splendor in his own life. But he was failing miserably. Finally, Jami placed an ad in a local paper seeking someone to move in and share the rent. Sally Kirwin,* a twenty-six-year-old woman from Wisconsin, found herself in a situation where she had to move in a hurry. Her landlord was an alcoholic and she was afraid of him. She answered the ad and arranged to meet Jami.

"Jami was about twenty-two then," Sally remembered. "She was very, very small." Sally liked Jami and was relieved to learn that she could move into the extra bedroom in the mobile home without putting down a deposit or paying first and last months' rent. Later she met Steve Sherer, Jami's boyfriend. He seemed pleasant enough. He had long hair, and she wasn't sure what he did for a living. It didn't really matter, though, because Sally wasn't looking for roommates with whom she had a lot in common; she just needed a place she could afford where her cat would be welcome, too. Jami and Steve said a cat would be fine with them. They occupied the master bedroom at the back of the mobile, they used one bedroom for their exercise equipment, and said Sally could have the extra one for only $300 a month.

Sally had a job as a publicist for famous and wannabe famous people, and it kept her so busy that she wasn't home much. However, she accepted Jami and Steve's invitation to join them for Thanksgiving dinner. The three of them posed for photos around a heavily laden buffet. She didn't really know them, but she liked Jami, and Steve had a good sense of humor. Sally was planning to stay in the mobile home only long enough to build a nest egg so she could get her own apartment.

There was nothing at all to warn Sally Kirwin that she had walked into a volatile situation. She had never been exposed to domestic violence and the thought never occurred to her.

A few days before Christmas 1986, Sally was packing to head home to Wisconsin for the holidays. She was terribly afraid to fly, trying to psyche herself up for the next day. She accepted a beer Jami offered her and sat down with Jami and Steve, trying to relax and convince herself that flying was a perfectly safe mode of transportation.

As they visited, she realized how little she knew about her housemates. She'd had a drink with Jami just that once, but Jami hadn't confided in her; they had simply discussed the possibility of Sally's moving in.

Now Steve seemed to be on edge. He and Jami were arguing listlessly about something at his work, when he suddenly turned to Sally and said, "You think you're too good for us, don't you, Sally? You never bring your friends over to meet us."

She stared at him, sure that he must be kidding. She worked with a number of celebrities, but there was no reason to introduce them to Steve. She didn't socialize with them very much herself. She just worked for them.

Jami looked embarrassed and told Steve to mind his own business. As Sally watched them, stunned, the couple's comments grew louder until they were yelling at each other.

"It very, very quickly escalated into a fight—an all-out brawl," Sally recalled. "They were screaming and shouting at each other. Glass was breaking."

As small as she was, Jami stood up to Steve. "This is it!" she screamed. "This is it. It's over!"

Steve made a move toward Jami and said, breathing heavily, "Shut the fuck up! I'll kill you."

Horrified, Sally ran to grab the phone in her bedroom, but first she pushed Jami behind a table in the hallway to give her a little protection from Steve, who was trying to get to her, swinging his arms and swearing.

Sally did manage to connect with 911 and let out a cry for help, but then she rushed out of her room to see that Steve was holding a kitchen knife. He had an odd, almost vacant look on his face. "Shut the fuck up," he snarled at Jami. "I'll kill both of you." He was either drunk or crazy—and it had happened so rapidly.

Sally believed him, but she could hear sirens approaching the mobile home park. She grabbed her cat and tossed it into her room. She didn't know how she could help Jami, but she was going to try. For the moment, Steve couldn't reach Jami where she huddled behind the table.

With a sharp flick of his wrist, he turned the knife so that it pointed toward his own belly.

"Steve!" Jami cried. "Don't!"

There was no expression on Steve's face as he slid the knife into his flesh. Sally thought it must have been some sleight of hand until she saw blood burst from his belly. She was amazed that he was still on his feet, and then he disappeared. She wasn't sure just how he got out of the trailer. By that time, both she and Jami were screaming and hysterical.

Jami talked to the police. They found Steve, put him in an ambulance, and took him away.

Sally Kirwin was so shocked that all she could think of was getting away from the madness. She went to a friend's house. "I came back in the wee hours of the morning," she recalled. "No one was there."

Now she could see the damage. The bedroom door was broken, and she could see that Steve had knocked the glass out of several windows. The desert wind blew through the mobile home, the only sound left after all the crashing and splintering of glass and wood.

Sally didn't know Steve Sherer well enough to know if he'd had some kind of psychotic break or if this was how he behaved when he was drunk or mad, or both. One minute they had been having a routine conversation and the next, he was white with rage.

Around dawn, Jami came home. She had dark circles under her swollen eyes, and she seemed very contrite. "This wouldn't have happened," she told Sally, "if Steve didn't love me so much."

Sally stared at Jami, dumbfounded. "Aren't you going to leave him?" she asked.

Jami shook her head. "He just loves me so much— we can work it out. It will never happen again."

Sally tried to reason with Jami, and she suggested places she could go where she would be safe. Sally said her friend had volunteered to take Jami in until she could get home to her family. Jami looked at her as if Sally didn't understand. She was adamant that she could never leave Steve, because he needed her. She was sure that things were going to be fine. He wasn't badly hurt, but he had shown her how devastated he would be if Jami ever left him, and she could never do that to him. People just didn't understand how sensitive he was.

Jami and Steve spent Christmas 1986 in Washington. On Christmas Eve, he was arrested by a Snohomish County sheriff's deputy for driving under the influence, driving with no valid license, and violating a protection order from his old girlfriend, Bettina.

Sally flew home to Wisconsin and spent Christmas with her family. Her friend fed her cat while she was gone. When she returned to Palm Desert a week later,

Sally saw the mobile home at 99 Portola Road for the last time. She was "too afraid of Steve" to press charges for her financial loss. By the time she got back, neither Jami nor Steve was at the mobile home. They were still in Washington when she moved her things out, and that was fine with her. She never expected to see them again.

Steve's temper tantrums over the holiday season had been expensive. Beyond the new fines he'd racked up in Washington, the mobile home on Portola was heavily damaged. He had broken four wall panels so badly they had to be replaced and other walls had to be repainted. That came to $981.40. He had shattered the bedroom and closet doors trying to get to Jami with a knife. That cost another $497.00. And then there were all the broken windows. The landlord was not happy.

Jami was the one who kept track of their expenses. She saved every estimate, receipt, bank statement, and stub from the bills she paid each month. Years later it would be easy to look at her life with Steve simply by thumbing through her meticulous records.

3

Steve's attempts to make big money in California didn't work out. The money from the insurance payoff on their burglary was dwindling. Once again he headed back to Washington State. The Hagels were relieved to know that Jami was going to be living close to them again, although they continued to be stunned at how she had changed, as were Jami's friends. She wasn't the dark-haired bundle of energy they all remembered. She was very thin and very blond. "Steve likes me blond," Jami confided. "And he likes me really thin."

Shortly after they came back to Washington, Steve told Jami that she was too flat-chested to really please him. He had always preferred women with very large breasts, and he insisted that Jami agree to breast augmentation surgery. She went along with it reluctantly. Her mother took care of her after the surgery, which was much more painful than Jami had expected.

Jami regretted the plastic surgery almost at once. The implants left her top-heavy and out of proportion for a woman as petite as she was. Steve, however, was delighted with the results and made a point of showing her off. Where Jami had always worn clothes with clean, sporty lines, she now wore clothes that were so feminine they were almost ridiculous—flowered silk dresses, tiny miniskirts with tight tops, revealing bikinis. She showed her girlfriends lingerie in her drawer that looked to be straight out of a Frederick's of Hollywood catalog: tiny thong panties that were hardly more than G-strings.

There were spates of calm in her relationship with Steve, but inevitably there were also arguments and temporary breakups. Jami visited her family as often as Steve would let her, and when she was with them it seemed as though everything was going to be all right after all. At one point, Jami broke off with Steve completely; she had enough strength to stop being a "Stepford Barbie girlfriend" as one of her friends called her changed persona.

The separation didn't last.

Concurrent with his return to the Northwest, Steve

Sherer's Washington State rap sheet sprouted new entries. He already had the arrest on Christmas Eve 1986, when the Bellevue police found him at the Hagels' home. Judy had seen a strange car driving by their house at all hours of the day and night and wondered about it. It was Steve's bail bondsman, who figured Steve and Jami might come home to spend Christmas with their families. When Steve showed up, the bail bondsman spotted him. He'd skipped out on the bond posted the time he laid open Bettina's scalp with the shot glass. Bail bondsmen who have been stiffed are notoriously dedicated to finding their quarry, and Steve was arrested where he hid in Jami's family's home.

He was anathema to the Hagels. Never in a million years could they have imagined that Jami would align herself with a man like Steve or that they would have the police coming into their home at Christmas to arrest him.

It only got worse. Two months later, Steve was identified as the person seen fleeing a just-burglarized home in a posh neighborhood near Lake Sammamish in Bellevue. The Bellevue police found his truck parked nearby, and Jami Hagel walked up as police were checking it. She refused to say who owned the truck, but by now the Bellevue police knew Steve. They knew him as Steven Sherer a.k.a. Steven Frank Sherer a.k.a. Steven Jeffrey Sherer a.k.a. Steven Christophe Michaels. He used aliases and reversed his Social Security number just enough so his name wouldn't draw a hit on police computers. But this time they had his fingerprints, and they matched them to the prints in the house that had been burglarized. He was arrested a week later and sentenced to sixty days in the county jail.

In May 1987 Steve Sherer was spending his days

and nights in jail, and Jami was desolate without him. Even though he was locked up, and she was free and working at her new job at Microsoft, Steve was still manipulating her. He had groomed her carefully to be totally dependent on him and to accept the blame for whatever went wrong in their lives.

A letter she wrote to him on May 24 is a classic example of the thought process of an emotionally abused woman: "Dear Steve, I have done so much thinking since last night after I left you. I have been so selfish and stupid . . . feeling sorry for myself lately and taking it out on you. I have this bad habit of holding everything inside for too long. I just didn't want to burden you with my problems when you're in jail, and instead you think I don't care about you."

Jami wrote that she was miserable because he was the only person she could trust enough to talk to: "My whole problem is that I miss you *so* much. Nobody (especially you) can believe that I am not out enjoying myself while you are in jail. . . . I should be fine because I'm not locked up, right? Wrong, because actually, Steve, I am locked up too. The only difference is that somebody else is holding the key to your cell and you're holding the key to my heart. . . . Every time we are apart, I want to crawl into a hole until you come home."

Again and again, Jami reiterated that Steve was "all I have." It was clear that she was filled with anxiety because he had suggested it might be better if they broke up:

> But you said something the other day about us being too dependent on each other and that was the first time you actually talked to me about a problem with us. I only wish you would write me a

*letter regarding your feelings. Because sometimes
I feel more like just your "friend" visiting you in
jail. Have your feelings changed to friendship? . . . Please don't hold back on me. On three
occasions since you have been in jail, you have
told me we are over. I used to convince myself you
feel that way because you're in jail, but you have
done a lot of things to me when I should [have]
ended us, but I never could say it was over, and I
still couldn't—which makes me realize I have only
been thinking about me and my feelings because
you are always telling me I don't love you anymore, but you are the one always trying to end
us. . . . It is you who doesn't love me the way you
used to. I get the feeling you're hoping I will give
you the strength to get rid of me. Is that true? Are
you just afraid of hurting me?*

It was obvious that Steve had been dangling Jami
like a puppet, pretending that he wanted to leave her—
an idea difficult to give much credence to because it
seemed only a sadistic game with which he could oc-
cupy himself while he was in jail.

*I would never leave you, so you aren't threat-
ened. . . . It is my fault for being so in love with
you. . . . Honey, I don't want us to end. God, you
hurt me so much last night when you said you
thought of me as your enemy.*
*I know I can be moody and bitchy . . . that is
what makes me want to be more spontaneous and
easy going (and positive) like you. Because I see
how depressing it is to be around a negative person everyday. I know that is why I love to be with*

you, because you are positive and full of life.

*I love to think back to the day we first met up
until now. I only have a few minor regrets, but the
rest of it has been the most exciting time of my life.
You have shown me things and places I never
thought I would see. When I think of marrying you,
all I think about is a life full of excitement and
love. . . . I don't know what you see in me since I
was and still am a boring, unexciting person, while
you are such an adventurous and fun-loving person. You must have just felt sorry for me, huh? And
wanted to show me what life really had to offer.
Because there is no comparison to that life I had
before as to that life you have given me and hope-
fully still want to give me.*

Jami's "minor regrets" probably involved bruises
and suicide threats and being terrorized at knifepoint,
but she had grown adept at denial. The bad things paled
as Steve drew her deeper and deeper under his control.

To those who loved Jami, it was unthinkable that she
should stay with Steve. But his pleas were convincing
to her, and when he withheld his love, he was even
more convincing.

Trilby Jordan, whose daughter, Lori, was Jami's
oldest friend, recalled how relieved she had been to
hear about a time when Jami had broken away from
Steve and was saying that she would never go back to
him. "I remember telling Jami," Trilby said, " 'I'm so
glad you've broken up with Steve. You know, Jami, that
statistics show that if he hits you before your wedding,
he'll hit you after.' "

Jami smiled and nodded. But later Trilby heard that
Jami and Steve were not only back together; they had

set a wedding date. Her heart sank. Like Judy and Jerry Hagel, Trilby had wished so much more for Jami.

It was as if her family and friends saw an entirely different man than Jami did when they looked at Steve. There was no reasoning with her. Even her friend June Young begged her to reconsider. When Jami introduced June to Steve in a bowling alley in Bellevue, June saw that her bubbly friend had changed drastically. After that, Jami just drifted away. "He was pretty much in control," June recalled. "I might have seen them together five times after that—mostly, I saw Jami alone. Steve would talk to other girls in the bowling alley and I commented to Jami about it, but she said, 'That's just Steven.' "

Jami felt that her destiny lay with Steve—that he needed her and loved her so much that she had no choice but to marry him. It was as if her innate kindness was much stronger than the part of her that had once been confident and outgoing. Steve always came first. Quite simply, he orchestrated her life, told her what to think, what to wear, and even when to speak.

"He created what he wanted," one of Jami's friends remembered. "Eventually he did manage to turn Jami into a Barbie doll."

The Hagels' friends and Jami's peers recalled that Steve never complimented her, no matter how hard she tried to please him. "He was always demeaning her," said Jeff Daniels, a longtime friend of the Hagels. "Jami was bright and cheerful and pleasant, but Steve put her down a lot. She was on edge and she lost her spark. She was very guarded around him."

Daniels recalled one night when he visited the Hagels and they played the board game Balderdash with Jami and Steve. "It wasn't a fun evening. . . . Steve kept calling Jami useless and stupid for the way she played."

Jami had always loved M&M's. Judy Hagel usually kept a bowl of the multicolored candies on the table when company came over. "Jami would go to pick them up, and Steve said, 'You put those back. *You put those back!*' And she would put them back in the dish. [He was concerned] that she would gain weight."

Because the Hagels had always included their four children not only in holidays but also in bowling, cards, dancing, and, of course, softball, they tried to include Steve, too. Judy bowled on a team with Steve and Jami. Bowling was one sport he was interested in.

Jami's brothers and their girlfriends often went places with Jami and Steve. Rich Hagel's girlfriend, Timarie, whom he dated for ten years, remembered what an effort it was to plan an evening or a trip with Steve. Rich was one of Jami's twin brothers and he was protective of her. "She and Rich were very close," Timarie said. She described Jami as "fun, sweet, nice, and caring.

"We met Steve when they came up from California," Timarie recalled. "We tried to hang out with them. We went to Lake Chelan with them and we tried to go out to the movies, but we always ended up trying to find cocaine for Steve instead."

It wasn't just the drunk driving, reckless driving, and burglaries that drew police attention to Steve. Cocaine was what drove him and made him lose control: cocaine and alcohol and sex and card rooms and power. Anyone who accepted an invitation to go on a trip or to double-date with Steve and Jami learned that much of their time would be spent in a frenzied search for a dealer when Steve ran out of cocaine. There was no question of talking to him about it; he always wanted more. Jami learned early on that if she could hold back at least some of his coke supply, Steve wouldn't spiral completely out of control. But he soon figured out she was hiding some of his stash.

"If he didn't get all of it from her," Timarie explained, "he'd yell at her and pester her until there was a huge fight."

Steve's mother, Sherri, often loaned her vacation home on Lake Chelan to Steve. Timarie remembered one trip to the lake, a four-hour journey across Snoqualmie Pass from Seattle, when Steve's addiction ruined the weekend. He drank from two-liter bottles of Coors beer as he drove the winding roads of the mountain pass. He refused to let either Jami or Timarie take over the wheel. Despite his intoxication, they arrived at the luxurious cabin safely, only to have another fight when Steve accused Jami of once again hiding cocaine from him. He stormed out of the lakefront residence and walked to the small downtown section of Chelan, threatening to catch a bus back to Seattle.

"Rich went to get him and brought him back to the lake," Timarie said. The Hagels' sons tried to hide a good many of Jami's activities from their parents. The elder Hagels already felt bad enough. Jami's brothers hoped she might still free herself from Steve. In the end, however, Steve's persuasive powers drew her brothers into the world of drugs, although they never got in as deep as he did.

"The next day, Steve's mother arrived and he stopped his tantrums about finding more cocaine. Steve could put on a good act for his mother, who naturally didn't approve of his drug use. She put him through drug rehabilitation programs, but none of them took. Since his mother could be a significant source of money for him, Steve often fooled her. Despite his frequent arrests and the numerous charges against him, Steve spent comparatively little time in jail and slid free of most of the consequences of his lifestyle. He laughed at the justice system, bragging to Rich Hagel once that "The first two DWIs are the hardest, and after that, they lose you [in the system]."

Steve certainly had the experience to comment on that. Between May 1982 and January 2000, Steve racked up twenty-one arrests in Washington State alone, and there was a steady exacerbation of the seriousness of the charges against him. Many of his confrontations with police resulted in fines or probation. He was the consummate rich kid who always ended up avoiding jail time and getting what he wanted.

What Steve wanted in the summer of 1987 was Jami Hagel. And Jami desperately wanted to marry him.

4

There was nothing that Judy and Jerry Hagel could do to keep Jami from marrying Steve, so they gave her the best wedding they could afford. Steve's sisters gave Jami a wedding shower, and she listed her china and silver patterns at a local department store. Many of her relatives gave her place settings for her china, Imperial Blossom. Jami was always sentimental; she saved all the minutiae, including the cards and the guest lists, just as any old-fashioned bride would. She wrote thank-you notes for shower and wedding gifts. She wanted to relegate all the bad scenes with Steve to the past and make a fresh start.

"It was a nice wedding," Judy remembered. "We did as much as we could for her. It was in a park and there were a lot of family and friends."

Jami and Steve's wedding in July 1987 was a formal affair at Robinswood Park, with its gloriously landscaped grounds that had once been a multimillionaire's estate. Steve wore a white tux with a swallowtail coat and white shoes. He had bleached his hair so blond that he resembled a California beach boy. No one could ever have guessed he was only two months out of jail on burglary charges. He looked like the handsome scion of a wealthy family—which indeed he was.

Jami looked lovely, but shockingly unlike the girl many of the guests recalled. Steve's sister Saundra was with her when she picked out her wedding dress. Far from the demure, simple style Jami had always preferred, the wedding gown she chose was cut so low that, given Jami's enhanced breasts, it verged on indecent.

"Steve loved it," a friend said. "He enjoyed the way men were staring at Jami; it was as if she was the prize and he was the one who owned her. . . . He said the guys there all had hard-ons because of the way Jami looked."

A few months after their wedding, Steve was arrested for drunken driving. At the Bellevue police station, Officer Bernard Molloy brought Steve out of the holding cell for questioning. Steve had been so combative earlier when he was booked that he had to be restrained. Now he pleaded with Molloy to remove his handcuffs because they hurt him, and Molloy—noting that Sherer wasn't a very large man—took the cuffs off. While there were other officers in the room, Steve was well behaved and cooperative. But when the others left,

Steve leaped at Molloy, choking him with both hands and threatening to kill him.

Remembering that night, Officer Molloy said, "Many times as a police officer, I guess we all have times when you feel like you're gonna die. This time, I really thought I *was* going to die. I was beginning to black out; the guy was strong and there was a look in his eyes. His eyes . . . his *eyes* . . . It's hard to describe the look that came into them. I'm not exaggerating. I was moments from dying when someone came in and pulled him off me."

Steve was convicted of felonious assault, but he didn't serve much time. As usual, he walked away with "community supervision."

Steve owned Jami now.

But marriage didn't make Jami feel any more confident. If anything, she deferred to Steve's wishes even more than she had when they were only living together. When he was sober, he could be nice to her, but she was the main target of his derision when he was under the influence of drugs or alcohol. "She just went into a shell then," one of Steve's friends said.

Jami had gone into the marriage with full awareness of Steve's faults, despite the pleas of her parents and her friends. Before her wonderful career at Microsoft, she had lost jobs because of him, and she was cut off from her friends because of him. But she still made excuses for him. Whatever Steve said or did remained gospel to her.

"I never, ever, *ever* would have believed in brainwashing," Judy Hagel said. "But I sat and watched it before my very eyes. I watched my daughter change. She got depressed. She was not happy anymore."

Judy was most shocked to realize that Jami had

begun blaming others for anything that went wrong in her marriage. Jami had always been totally honest and had a strong conscience, but that had changed too.

"She wasn't the daughter I raised," Judy said, as she related her suspicions after talking with an insurance investigator about the burglary claim Steve and Jami had filed in Palm Desert. "The investigator asked me about a couple of different items [that Steve and Jami] said I had given her, and I told them, 'Yeah, [I gave them] a couple of the things.' They called me back and kept conversing with me on it. The insurance company guy said, 'I know this is a fraud, but I can't prove it. Can you help me?' I told him, 'No, I don't know what they had.' "

But Judy Hagel did remember her daughter's engagement ring, the ring worth almost $14,000 which was supposedly lost in the burglary. Sometime after Jami's marriage, she was sitting at her mother's table and Judy felt a chill: "I looked at the ring [Jami had on], and I said, 'Jami, you know that is the same ring you've always had.' And she looked at me sort of funny, and I said, 'You know, that insurance, that was a fraud. Jami, that *is* your ring!' "

"How do you know, Mom?"

"That is the same ring," Judy repeated.

"Yes," Jami said, "it is."

"How could you do something like that? You've been brought up to know better."

Jami looked away. "I didn't know at the time what was going on," she said quietly. "Then it was too late."

Judy felt sick, but she didn't turn her daughter in. How could she? It wasn't Jami who had thought up the scam; she was sure of that. It was Steve; Jami did anything he asked of her.

She did anything, that is, except abandon her family. When Jami visited Judy and Jerry, she could put on a happy face, even if it was often a mask. Steve seldom accompanied her, but Jami was a frequent visitor and her parents were always delighted to see her. Still, Jami rarely enjoyed an undisturbed visit; Steve called constantly to ask when she was coming home. Wherever Jami went without him, Steve's phone calls were sure to follow, as if he had her on an invisible leash. He demanded that she account for every minute of each day.

There was, however, one side of Jami that didn't buckle under to Steve. When she and Steve returned from Palm Desert in 1987 and she went to work for Microsoft, she was a valuable employee from the very beginning. Since Steve's employment record was so spotty, it helped a lot that Jami had a position with Bill Gates's booming software company, whose campus was located on the east side of Lake Washington. The complex was bigger than many towns, and Gates by then was well on his way to being the richest man in America.

Jami was highly thought of at Microsoft. She had worked her way up steadily, eventually finding a secure niche in the human resources department. Jami was responsible for setting up offices for new hires, ordering the software they needed, and helping them adjust to the unique ambience of Microsoft. Her outgoing personality and natural friendliness made her a natural in her job. No one she dealt with at work even imagined the smothering atmosphere she faced in her marriage.

"She had a fantastic work ethic," a co-worker recalled, also noting that Jami never talked about Steve until the time she broke off her engagement to him. Jami and Steve, of course, reconciled and many of her co-workers were invited to the wedding. The Jami at Microsoft was totally different from the Jami who sat silently beside Steve when they went to clubs or bowling or out with his friends. On the job, she was confident and competent, and she made life so much easier for newcomers lured to Seattle by the exciting new company. Jami was always punctual and rarely missed a day's work because of illness.

The newlyweds moved continually, usually from one apartment to another. Jami longed to have her own home, and finally they rented a little house. It wasn't long after that when Jami learned she was pregnant. She was elated; motherhood was something she had always longed for. As tiny as she was, she carried her pregnancy proudly.

Steve seemed pleased that he had demonstrated his virility, but a baby wasn't the first thing on his list. He was still interested in the bar scene and in bowling, where he won a number of tournaments. He had begun to gamble on football games, and he worked out a schedule with several of his friends, charting professional sports wins and losses. Cocaine and alcohol mattered more than ever to him, often igniting his already short fuse. Steve was a man whose own needs always came first, and he was constantly looking for ways to enhance his sex life as well as his ability to party.

Steve baffled many of Jami's co-workers, when they finally met him. Like her family and friends, they wondered why a woman with so much going for her would stay with a man who attempted to control every facet of her life. Jami seemed to love him, but it was difficult for anyone to understand why. They had virtually no common interests: Jami hated to bowl and it made her uncomfortable to hang out at the bowling alleys with him. For some reason, he was meaner to her at the alleys than anywhere else in public. Even Steve's friends wondered why he picked on her.

Janet Gilman, who for three years worked closely with Jami at Microsoft, came to learn a great deal about

Steve Sherer. She and Jami often ate lunch together, although never anywhere extravagant. Jami's favorite spot was Taco Time.

Jami once commented to Janet that she hated going bowling. Steve loved it and had special shirts made up with his nickname, "Sparky," on his and "Jami" on hers. On the back, Steve's sponsor's name—All But Here's Traveling Software—was embroidered.

Steve was adamant that Jami had to bowl with him. "But I hate it," Jami told Janet.

"Well then, don't go," Janet said. "It can't be comfortable for you when you're pregnant."

"Steve wouldn't allow that," Jami said quietly.

The women continued their lunches at Taco Time. When Jami was pregnant, she had a craving for McDonald's and they went there also.

One day when Jami was nearing the end of her pregnancy, Janet walked into Jami's office to find her doubled over in pain. Janet got Jami to the hospital and the doctors said she was in premature labor.

"I called Steve," Janet remembered. "He was watching something or other on TV and he said he'd come to the hospital when it was over."

Steve eventually made it to the hospital two hours later, but Janet found his attitude "indifferent," far from the way most fathers-to-be acted. It was as if the baby was no part of him and he was a little annoyed to have his plans interrupted. Jami's labor turned out to be false, however, and her obstetrician sent her home.

As she neared childbirth, Jami wanted her mother around, but Steve had made it clear that if Judy came to the hospital when Jami was in labor, he wouldn't be there. He had long since stopped being a real member of the Hagel family, and he resented Judy the most.

"I had been told numerous times," Judy said, "that if I didn't stay out of their business, I wouldn't see Jami."

When Jami went into labor a few weeks later, Judy wanted so much to be with her, but she forced herself to stay home. Jami called her mother at about 11:30 that night, but Judy said, "I was scared to go." She didn't want to cause trouble in Jami's marriage, and Steve was so volatile. However, when Jami was in hard labor and near delivery, Steve himself called Judy at 1:00 A.M. and said that Jami wanted her.

"So then I said okay," Judy recalled. "I did go, and I was with her while she was in labor. I was with her when she gave birth."

After hours of hard labor, Jami gave birth to a baby boy. Chris* Sherer was to be the most important thing in her life.

Jami's life grew happier after the birth of her wonderful, healthy baby boy. She was a devoted mother and very careful with Chris. Although Steve enjoyed showing him off, Jami didn't really trust him to stay with the baby. Steve was not a caregiver and she feared he would get distracted by something he wanted to do and forget about the baby. She didn't complain about that, but she only rarely left Steve alone with Chris. Luckily, Judy Hagel was happy to baby-sit when Jami had to go out. Eventually, Jami's maternity leave was up and she had to return to work at Microsoft.

Steve was out of work, a fairly common situation, and he said he would look after Chris. Vaguely worried, Jami agreed—until she came home one day and found the floor covered with broken glass. Steve had deliberately smashed all their framed wedding pictures in one of his fits of rage. Chris could have crawled in the glass and cut himself badly; at the very least, he must have been witness to his father's tantrum.

The next day, Jami placed Chris in day care. If she had to be gone on a weekend, Jami could usually count on her mother to look after Chris. One weekend, Jami called Judy to ask her to baby-sit because Steve wanted to go someplace and Jami had a commitment. But Judy couldn't get off work early enough to suit Steve. "Jerry will be home at four o'clock," she said. "He'll be glad to take Chris then."

But Steve wouldn't wait. He didn't leave eighteen-month-old Chris home alone; he took the baby with him, wherever he was headed. Jami and her mother were worried sick and called each other all evening to see if Steve had left Chris with one or the other of them. Finally, just before eleven that night, Steve and Chris showed up. He had taken the toddler to the racetrack, stayed until the last race, and arrived home long after Chris was exhausted and hungry.

Judy edged along a tightrope, trying to help Jami but afraid to appear to be a meddler in her daughter's marriage. Steve constantly made it clear that he didn't want her involved and told Judy so often. "I was told [by Steve]: 'Leave us alone. If you don't stay out of our business, I'm going to take Chris and Jami and move. We're going to move to California.' So I knew I just couldn't show up when I wasn't supposed to," Judy said.

Judy feared that if Steve moved her daughter and grandson back to California, she would never see them again. "I don't know if Jami would have moved, but I wasn't going to push him on that."

In a sense, Steve now had control not only over Jami but also over her mother and the rest of her family. Occasionally, he would grudgingly allow Judy to come over and work in the yard with them, but he didn't want her doing anything to help Jami fix up the interior of their house. Judy was a slender and pretty blond woman who looked much younger than her age. She had a job at an auto dealership, and she was never the kind of mother-in-law who hovered, but she had reason to be worried about Jami and Chris.

June Young, Jami's longtime friend, who hadn't seen her since the wedding, came to visit Jami when Chris was less than a year old. "I'm not sure of the date," June recalled, "but Chris was sitting up, so he was probably about eight months old."

When June called to arrange the visit, she heard tears in Jami's voice. She regretted that they hadn't been as close as they once were, but she suspected it was because she had warned Jami not to marry Steve. "He didn't treat her well," June recalled, with massive understatement.

This time, Jami urged her to come over for a visit. When June arrived at Jami's house in Bothell, Washington, she quickly learned why Jami was crying. Jami confessed that Steve had hit her and pulled her down the hall by her hair. And it wasn't the first time.

"You're going to pack your things and come with me," June said firmly. "Nobody deserves to be treated like this."

For a moment, June thought Jami was going to come with her. Then Steve came home. When he saw June there, he glared at her and grabbed Jami's arm, pulling her into the bedroom, slamming the door behind them.

"Steve came out yelling and swearing," June said, "And then Jami came out, and she was crying. She told me that I should go, that she could take care of it."

Saddened, June had no choice but to leave, but she was troubled for a long time, remembering how diminished Jami was; her dear friend had lost all of her exuberance and her zest for life and there was nothing June could do to change it. She wondered if she would ever see Jami again.

Apparently, Jami was able to appease Steve after the incident with June—but not for long. Like almost all domestic abusers, Steve's assaults on Jami only escalated. Now he not only put her down verbally but he was also increasingly physically abusive when she annoyed him.

And Jami seemed to annoy Steve frequently; it was almost impossible to please him. He was given to large and sudden shifts of mood, alternately depressed, euphoric, and angry. It was hard for Jami to tell if this was a result of the drugs or his natural unstable personality. Jami continued to withhold a portion of his cocaine, but it was like mending a huge, oozing wound with a Band-Aid.

Most distressing of all to the few who knew about it, Jami herself sometimes used cocaine. Steve had finally coaxed her into trying the drug. Timarie couldn't fathom how anyone could truly enjoy getting higher and higher all night long—only to land with a crash when the supply of cocaine inevitably ran out. When Timarie asked Jami why she used cocaine, Jami answered, "Because the more I do, the less [Steve] will—and the less I will have to put up with. We won't have so much fighting. . . . I do it just to keep the peace."

Steve had pulled Jami down with him in his endless pursuit of newer and grander sensations. As impossible as it seemed for the little girl who had loved to climb trees, ride horses and play softball, Jami had long been caught up in Steve's shadowy world of chasing drugs. Not only that but what most people would consider "normal" sex didn't turn him on much anymore either, and Steve talked constantly to Jami about his increasingly bizarre sexual fantasies. She hated it, but she didn't know how to escape.

On November 5, 1989, King County Police Officer Paul Guerraro was dispatched to check on a domestic dispute at a house in Bothell. He found a near-hysterical Jami Sherer holding her toddler son. The right side of her face was bright red and there was a bloody spot on her scalp.

"Her hair was pulled out," Guerraro remembered. "I remember it well because that's the only time I had actually seen scalp fragments attached to hair."

In her statement, Jami said that Steve had been out most of the night, coming home at 4:00 A.M. She suspected that he'd been with another woman, and they had an argument about it. Jami said she had Chris in her arms and was preparing to leave: "I was at the door, turning the knob when my husband grabbed me by my hair and pulled me six feet across the floor."

She dropped Chris in the struggle and the baby got up and ran over in a pitiful attempt to help her. But when Steve saw her holding Chris, he was further enraged. He balled his hand into a fist. "He said he'd kill me if I didn't let go of Chris," Jami told Officer Guerraro. "He pulled the phone cord out of the wall when I tried to call 911. I finally got the plug back in."

Shortly thereafter in the foggy November morning, the Hagels' phone rang. Judy answered and it was Jami. She was crying and asking her mother to come and get her. "She said Steve had been out drinking and she reproached him and he was pulling her around the floor with Chris hanging on to her legs," Judy said. "So Jerry and I jumped in the car, and the police were there when we got there. [Steve] was gone. I took Chris from Jami and on the table was this long [lock] of hair—her scalp and hair lying on the table."

Guerraro gathered up the clumps of Jami's hair and scalp and bagged them into evidence.

Judy and Jerry took Jami and the baby home with them, hoping that this would be the last time—that even Jami would now see through this man she was married to. But she didn't.

"Within a day or two," Judy said, "Steve kept calling and calling. We got up the next day and there were flowers on her car. . . . He got her to come back and talk to him, and she moved back."

Steve had printed on a giant sign on the lawn, "I love my wife!"

It was inevitable that when Steve's court date came, Jami didn't show up to testify against him. He had sweet-talked her and promised never to hurt her again, urging her to think of Chris's need for both a father and a mother and begging her to save their marriage. As in so many other cases involving domestic abuse, the charges against Steve Sherer were dismissed. The piece of Jami's scalp and her long beautiful hair were tossed out of the evidence room; the case was closed, and there was no reason to keep the evidence.

Jami had more support than a lot of women caught in marriages where they became punching bags and objects of derision. She had a good job and a family who wanted to help her. But she seemed to have long since passed the point where she could distinguish between being loved and being owned. Judy could barely count the times she'd rushed over to get Jami and the baby and move them to the safety of her house, only to listen helplessly as Steve began his incessant phone calls.

"He would never give up. It would keep ringing and

ringing and ringing," Judy said. "Every ten, fifteen minutes. He'd insist on talking to her. And at night we had to take the phone off the hook and cover it with a blanket."

Jami still had her one link to safety. During the times she and Steve were reconciled, Jami insisted on visiting her parents. If he was at the racetrack, as he often was, Steve didn't object so much to her taking the baby to the Hagels' house. She liked to eat Monday dinner with them; that was chicken and rice night, Jami's favorite. She usually managed to sneak away from Steve and attend family birthday dinners and holiday get-togethers. Her image is there in most of the family pictures, with Jami most often sitting next to her father. Anyone looking at the Hagels' photo album would have seen a smiling, pretty young woman.

Jami Sherer was living in two worlds, trying in vain to balance them.

As the eighties drew to a close, Jami Sherer became desperate to hold a lid down on a relationship that was constantly threatening to explode. In her job at Microsoft, she was calm, friendly, and efficient. Someone who didn't know her well would have supposed that she didn't have a problem in the world.

Jami was bringing home a good salary, and, perhaps more important, she was eligible for stock options at Microsoft. The company's stock was doubling and redoubling constantly. Not only was Bill Gates a multibillionaire, but a large number of his employees were also instant millionaires. The dress code at Microsoft was casual but the work ethic was intense and well rewarded. Jami interviewed job applicants and helped choose those she knew would fit in.

Steve's job offered less of a future. He was working

as a sales rep for an air freight company. He and Jami had decided to buy a house, but their credit wasn't good and they didn't have a down payment. Steve's mother, Sherri, agreed to loan them enough to get them into a house. Jami may have held on to the slight hope that Steve would change if they gave up the transitory feel of living in a series of apartments and had their own place with a yard for Chris.

Sherri Sherer Schielke wanted her son's marriage to last, and it wasn't really a financial risk for her because Jami put up her Microsoft stock as collateral. Steve added a bit more collateral with his small portfolio of Nordstrom and Longview Fiber stocks, an inheritance from his father.

Steve and Jami started looking for a house. Jami knew she would have to put some sweat equity into it, because the area's burgeoning real estate market put most homes on the east side out of their range.

A house represented safety, respectability, and a chance to live like other young families. Maybe Steve would settle down and they could work toward a future that would be good for Chris—and for themselves, too.

5

The Hagels had no idea how much their daughter was hiding from them. Jami might have been using cocaine only to escape momentarily from the ugliness of her life or, as she said, to be sure Steve wouldn't use it all, but she *was* using. She had not been using enough for her friends at work to notice or enough to compromise her life, but the small amount she consumed made her more amenable to Steve's suggestions or, rather, less able to fight him.

By 1990, Jami was no longer fooling herself; she knew that her marriage was a horrible mistake, but how would she ever get free of Steve? She agreed to buy a house, but she told friends that she probably wouldn't stay with Steve after they moved. She had finally come to understand that another move or a new job for Steve or a baby would never change him. Now that she was a mother, she felt such love and concern for Chris that she dared not continue to risk exposing him to Steve's chaotic rages. Motherhood had made her more vulnerable because she had so much more to lose, but it had also made her stronger. She would fight for Chris.

Sara Smith,* who was dating one of Steve's high school friends—Eric Linde—met Jami and Steve in the summer of 1989. They went skiing and bowling together a few times and Eric and Steve went to Reno that winter. Sara liked Jami better than Steve and spent time with her. One evening the two women watched television and ate pizza while the men were out. Sara had already noted that Jami never said much when Steve was there. She was a little surprised when Jami opened up to her that night as the two of them ate pizza. "She wasn't happy," Sara recalled. "She planned to divorce Steve after they moved into their new house."

That seemed a little odd to Sara. She wondered why Jami didn't just leave—but then she realized that leaving Steve wouldn't be easy.

As alien as it might sound to women who were not involved in an abusive relationship, Jami had believed for a long time that Steve's violence erupted, in her words, because "he just loves me so much." But Jami had finally concluded that Steve really didn't love her and that her value to him was as a possession, not as an equal partner.

Nevertheless, in May 1990, Jami went along with buying a split-level house on Education Hill in Redmond. As agreed, with Jami's Microsoft stock as collateral, Sherri loaned them the down payment and the closing costs on the house: $27,186.53. Since Steve's employment was sporadic, Jami's salary would be used for the monthly payments on the house. Two months later they moved in.

"It was in awful shape," Sherri recalled of the house they bought. "It was a fixer." The previous owners had kept animals in the basement rec room, and they had urinated and defecated on the floor until the linoleum had practically melted and stuck to the floor. Jami and Steve bought a product called *Kilz,* applied it, and finally got rid of the odor. They found a carpenter who partitioned the basement into separate rooms, and Jami worked to fix up the rest of the house. It began to look better. It was a standard split-level plan, built in the seventies, but it was theirs.

Steve made a few halfhearted attempts at landscaping the backyard, which adjoined a thick woods. There was a single tree in the yard, and Steve had a load of sand dumped near it for Chris to play in, although he never actually made a sandbox. The rest of the backyard was only gravel and some never-planted flower areas edged with untreated wood. Steve had no interest in gardening.

Indeed, all of Steve Sherer's interests lay in things that could bring him an instant high or instant excitement. The new house made no difference at all in his behavior—except that Steve could now throw private parties without having to worry about people in an apartment next door overhearing. Despite the new house, all the vacation homes he had access to, his powerboat, and his little boy who was not yet two years old, Steve Sherer was bored, still looking for new thrills, and still spending a lot of time gambling in card rooms and at the racetrack. He set up his own weekly gambling pool with friends who bet on NFL games and draft choices, but even that kept his interest for only a little while. Steve was an empty vessel that needed to be filled constantly.

No longer satisfied by his sexual relations with Jami, Steve continually urged her to join him in "swinging." He took out an ad in a swingers' magazine without her knowledge. It was written from Jami's point of view, as if she was the one who was seeking sexual excitement by adding another man to her life. Steve received several replies, with photographs of naked males enclosed, at the post office box address he listed. They wrote that they were anxious to join Jami in her fantasies. It was, of course, Steve who was interested in threesomes; for a long time, he had talked about watching Jami have sex with another man. She was disgusted by his constant nagging at her to acquiesce to his sick scenarios about inviting people into bed with them. He was often impotent, which was not surprising considering the quantity of drugs he ingested, and he needed something to spice up his jaded sex life.

Whether Jami actually participated in threesomes with Steve is questionable—at least at that point. But something happened during that time that hurt Jami so badly that she wanted to go far away from him.

Nothing in his marriage was sacred to Steve. At one of his jobs, he regaled fellow employees with intimate—and exaggerated—details of his sex life with Jami. A young woman recalled working in a warehouse where Steve was her foreman. "He told everyone around about his sex life, where he made love with his wife, all about her physical characteristics. He said all the guys at his wedding were excited over Jami because of her breasts. He was bragging about it. He liked to talk about what they did in hotel rooms—wherever. He put it all out there whether we wanted to hear it or not."

Steve regaled the warehouse workers with stories about, in his words, "people who shall be nameless" who came to orgies at his house. He would then describe what happened in lascivious detail. "He hinted to me that I should come over some night," the woman said, embarrassed.

Through sheer coincidence, one of Jami's good friends since junior high school met Steve in the air freight building where she worked. She knew him only as a sales rep with a smooth pitch and a slightly skewed attitude. "He was giving away wine coolers once," she recalled, "because he said he became a very 'bad and evil person' when he drank—so he had to give it away."

She noted that Steve talked a great deal about his sex life, and was surprised to find out that he was married to her old friend, Jami Hagel. But she was revolted to hear the way he talked about Jami.

A number of women who worked with Steve soon learned that he slyly turned most conversations into sexual revelations. He often invited them to bring their boyfriends and come to parties at the Sherers' house in

Redmond. Most said no at once, but a few were trapped into accepting when they ran out of excuses. Steve never threw any real parties, however. He invariably gathered the men into the den, where he showed them pornographic videos. Jami, while polite, always seemed embarrassed and uneasy when they entertained like this.

There was no question that Steve had the toys to attract people to his home or his mother's vacation homes. He was able to persuade a few couples to go for boat rides on Lake Washington. Once he and Jami threw a Murder Mystery Game at their house in Redmond. But Steve most often turned people off by the way he treated his wife. All his joviality and energy were nullified by his cruelty toward Jami.

"He had a controlling personality," one of Jami's Microsoft co-workers said. "He didn't smile or talk nice to her. She was open and friendly at work, but around him she was full of apprehension, anxiety and fear."

Through it all, Jami stayed close to her mother and father. It was probably that connection that helped her survive emotionally. The things that mattered most to her were her son, Chris, her job, and the family she grew up with before Steve came along. By 1990, Jami realized that she couldn't stay in her marriage much longer. She still had too much self-esteem, however deeply buried, to allow Steve to destroy her. The old problem loomed, of course: walking away from Steve might be impossible. He never let go of anything or anyone until he was done with them, and he would use a dozen or so manipulative devices to hold on to Jami.

Another friend was Brenda Yamamoto, who had worked at Microsoft for eleven years. She and Jami had offices in the same building. There were other friends that Jami felt close enough to to confide her despair. Janet Gilman had been hired at Microsoft the same day Jami was, and Janet remembered all too well the disintegration of Jami's marriage and the fear that gripped her.

By mid-1990, Steve was apparently aware that Jami was inching away from him; he was jealous and suspicious. If it is possible to stalk one's own wife while still living with her, that was what Steve did. He called Jami continually at Microsoft, and she sometimes hid out in Janet's office to avoid his phone calls. They could hear the phone shrilling endlessly in Jami's office.

On occasion, Janet was in Jami's office when Steve called, and he sounded like a rage-aholic, always furious about something. Even standing a few feet away, Janet could hear him yelling at Jami, who held the phone away from her ear and rolled her eyes at Janet.

From those frequent calls, Steve progressed to dropping by Jami's office. Other employees' spouses came to their building only on special occasions. But not Steve. Most of Jami's co-workers at Microsoft knew Steve only by sight, but he grew more and more familiar as he appeared in Jami's office two or three times a day to check on her, just to be sure she was there. He called her even more often than before. It was difficult for her to get any work accomplished, and his calls and drop-ins interrupted her interviews with job applicants.

Although Microsoft maintains a low-key atmosphere, this behavior wasn't acceptable for long at any business complex. Jami was mortified by Steve's constant visits, and the more he clung to her and spied on her, the more she pulled away.

Sensing her withdrawal, Steve again began sending her flowers. One afternoon, Michael Sandberg, a mail clerk at Microsoft, delivered a long white box to Jami. She opened it, and he saw two dozen red roses nestled in the green tissue paper. "I said, 'Hey, you've got flowers,'" Sandberg said, "and she said, 'Yeah, they're from my husband.' She couldn't have cared less."

Jami's two worlds had collided. She sometimes came to work with dark circles and bags under her eyes, and the women she worked with noticed bruises on her arms. She seemed haunted. It was getting crazier. Jami had never sneaked around on Steve, and they all knew it. She went from home to work, then to day care to pick up Chris, and then home again. But Steve seemed obsessed with the idea that she was cheating on him. Her women friends asked each other, "When would she have the time?"

Occasionally, Steve stood out on the green campus at Microsoft and Jami—as well as everyone in her unit—could see him watching her windows. It was to them the sickest kind of voyeurism. Steve and Jami still lived together; they were still married. Why was he so obsessed?

Once, Jami had to call Security to have Steve escorted from her office when he shouted so loud that his voice carried to nearby cubicles. Jami was terribly embarrassed, but nothing seemed to embarrass Steve; he felt entirely within his rights as he shadowed Jami. In his mind, she still belonged, totally, to him. The words he had once written to her in a sentimental card, words that had thrilled her at the time, came back to haunt her: "I can't stand not having you within my sight."

Janet Gilman and Jami still had lunch together, most often at the Taco Time at the Bear Creek Shopping Center in Redmond. "Steve started to phone me," Janet said. "He wanted to verify that Jami had gone to lunch with me—where we went, what we had to eat, even what we talked about. After a few times, I just told him I wasn't going to do this anymore. He was spying on her."

Steve had good reason to worry; Jami was planning her escape with utmost secrecy. The wife he had controlled for a half-dozen years was straining at the bars of her cage. With Janet and with other women friends, she was now talking about how she could get Steve to move out of the house. She was making the payments, and it was her Microsoft stock that secured the loan from his mother. She said that she wouldn't be stealing anything from Steve because he had put virtually nothing into the house. It seemed only fair to her that she and Chris should have a home.

Sometimes Jami seemed strong and confident that she could have a life after Steve. She actually thought she could remain in her new house. She asked people about changing the locks, wondering if that would be enough to keep him out.

At other times, though, Jami was more realistic, and willing to find another place to live where Steve wouldn't know her address. She could never leave the Seattle area—she was too close to her parents and brothers. Most of all, she would never leave Chris; she knew Steve would fight her for custody, just to make her life hell. She also knew that she and Chris belonged together. "She wanted to get away," Sherri Gruber, another friend, said, "but she was afraid—afraid for her life, and she wanted to take Chris with her. She was looking for anywhere she could hide from Steve."

Sometimes Jami was pessimistic and stoic: "I'll never get away from Steve," she said flatly to Janet Gilman. "It doesn't matter where I go—he'll find me."

6

In 1990, Jami Sherer was twenty-six years old, and she had made some terrible choices in her life. She was not perfect, but she was a loyal daughter and sister, a wonderful mother and a dependable and intelligent employee. Then something happened that gave her hope that she could divorce Steve and leave all the bad memories behind. Ironically, it was Steve himself who introduced her to the man who would be the catalyst for her leaving. Lew Adams* was no prize; like Steve, he was addicted to cocaine. Technically, he was married, but he was separated from his wife. He was certainly not a man a woman should base her hopes on, but to Jami he looked like a lifeline. She came to know Lew because he was one of the sources of Steve's cocaine supply. Steve often suggested that Lew come home with him to make up a sexual threesome. He sometimes insisted that Lew spend the night on their living room couch. Steve even boasted to Lew that he enjoyed the idea of watching Jami with another man, but added that he would kill her if she ever cheated on him.

When Lew met Jami Sherer, his heart melted. She was a dainty little thing with huge dark eyes and a tremulous smile. Although Steve treated her badly, she never fought back. Lew soon learned that Steve had a way of making people do what he wanted. He wanted to see Jami again, but not with Steve anywhere around. Lew certainly wasn't in a position to offer her anything but a shoulder to cry on and an understanding ear, but he called Jami at Microsoft, and she was touched that he had. He felt sorry for Jami. He listened to her and told her she didn't deserve Steve's abuse.

Lew was a few years older than Steve, five feet ten, and a slender 160 pounds. He was handsome enough, but in a dissipated, tight-wired way that reflected his addiction. Lew had graduated from high school in 1978, but his recall of the eighties was only a drugged blur. He took a job with Costco, the huge warehouse-store chain based in Washington State. Later he transferred to a new branch that opened in California as the company boomed. But when the company cut back its work force, Lew was one of the first to go.

He later admitted that his cocaine use was out of control. He dealt from an ounce to five or six ounces at a time in order to supply his own needs. He snorted enough, however, to damage his nasal membranes. Concerned, he had gone to a doctor who told him, "I can't help you. You have to help yourself."

Lew did himself little good; all he did was switch to freebasing crack cocaine. His dealing was a penny-ante operation: He took buyers' money, bought some crack, kept a little, and gave the rest to his buyers. During those years, he married a pretty young woman, Dru Adams,* who worked for the warehouse stores, and they had two children. "I stole to support my habit," he admitted, "and to support my family. I didn't get caught every time I stole."

By 1990, Lew Adams was separated from his wife and living with his parents in the north end of Seattle. He had a job with a local Chevrolet dealer where he repaired used cars that were turned in for new models. He continued to sell cocaine, and Steve Sherer was one of his customers. There were parallels certainly between Steve Sherer and Lew Adams, but there were just as many areas where they differed: Lew had a conscience, no matter how deep he tried to bury it. Lew also respected women, and he did not believe in mistreating them.

His fledgling relationship with Jami was no storybook romance. How could it be? Steve was orchestrating the whole thing. Steve even urged Lew to make the first call to Jami at work, although she didn't know it. Steve had decided that Lew would be part of their first threesome.

Jami was drowning, starving, and struggling to be free of Steve. In her desperation, she perceived a great deal more in Lew Adams than he was able to provide. He was as embarrassed by Steve's sexual scenarios as Jami was.

Meanwhile, by September 1990, Jami's friends at Microsoft saw a change in her. For the first time in a long time, she seemed optimistic as she told them she'd met a man who really seemed to care about her. She was like a schoolgirl when she talked about Lew, and even though they could see trouble ahead, her friends were so glad to see Jami smile again that they didn't have the heart to tell her to slow down. Surely she didn't have to be reminded that there would be trouble if Steve found out. They had no inkling that Steve had set it all up.

Lew and Jami spoke on the phone a few times during the final days of the month. They met on Thursday, September 27, and Jami confided to several friends that she was going to see him alone on the weekend. On Friday, Jami told Brenda Yamamoto that she was so happy—she was going to meet Lew on Saturday.

Kay Eck, who always felt like a kind of mother figure to Jami at Microsoft, recalled talking with her that week. "She put on a good front," Kay said, "[but] she felt like someone was stalking her for a few weeks. . . . She had hang-up phone calls. But she was so happy on Friday [September 28]—like a weight was lifted from her shoulders."

That bright and sunny final week of September 1990 stood out in many people's minds. Lisa Cryder recalled it well. She and Jami had been friends since they were little girls playing in front of their houses in Bellevue, and they'd ridden horses together. "Then in the middle of the eighth grade," Lisa said, "my mother got remarried. Jami was an eastside kid and we moved across Lake Washington to Seattle, but we stayed friends."

Lisa and Jami became really close again as adults when they gave birth to their babies only nine months apart. They got together to do fun things with their infants. At first, Lisa was surprised at Jami's changed physical appearance, but she soon realized that she was the same Jami underneath. Lisa's reaction to Steve, however, was similar to that of Jami's other friends; she was outraged by the way he treated Jami. On the last Saturday of September, Jami confided to Lisa, "I've met someone who listens to me—who's comforting me."

Lisa was glad for Jami. "I told her to leave Steven," Lisa said, "that she should divorce him."

Lisa offered Jami a place to run to. Her own marriage wasn't working well, and she and her husband were about to embark on a ninety-day trial separation. There was room in her Rose Hill home for Jami and

Chris. This time, Jami said yes. She was enthusiastic about moving in with Lisa.

Jami was finally ready to leave Steve. She knew he would be furious, but she felt strong enough to face him. If it meant leaving her house too, that was the price she would have to pay.

Jami Sherer was playing a dangerous game, though. In order to spend Saturday, September 29, with Lew Adams, she told several untruths: She told her mother that Lisa had an advertising promotion event in Tacoma on Saturday, and she was going with her. She told Steve the same thing. She was lying to both of them, something that she had never done until she met Steve. Other things about her personality had changed; they were ways of surviving. Jami learned to be devious from a master, doing what she had to do to avoid violent fights, but she was ill equipped for deceit. She didn't feel strong enough to face life alone, so she lied about her date with Lew. Steve had undermined her self-confidence to a point where she couldn't leave him until she had another man to leap to.

The old Jami would never have considered Lew Adams a safe jumping-off spot, but she no longer felt pretty or smart or interesting or lovable. Steve had chipped away at her self-esteem with his constant derogatory comments. If she had ever really been his "little rose," he'd long since forgotten about that and all the promises he'd made to her.

On Friday night, Jami visited her parents and left Chris with her mother. On Saturday, she spent the day with Lew Adams. Remarkably for her, when Jami found out that her mother had to work on Saturday morning until almost noon, Jami had agreed to leave Chris with Steve for a few hours. But Steve called Judy

Hagel in a short time and said he had decided to go out himself and he was going to bring Chris to her.

It was a fairly ordinary Saturday for the Hagels; they often had Chris on weekends. Steve picked him up at about five-thirty that evening, and Judy assumed Jami would be home at the Redmond house within half an hour. But Jami called her mother about seven and said that she would be a little bit late.

"I told her to call and tell Steve that," Judy remembered. "So she did and Steve brought Chris back over to our house and left him with us and went out."

Jami's twin brothers, Rich and Rob, went out with Steve. They would remember later how angry he seemed and that he spoke again of what he would do to Jami if he ever caught her being unfaithful.

At 2:00 A.M., Judy Hagel answered her phone and it was Steve asking if Jami was at her house. She could tell he was on something, but didn't comment on it. "I said, 'No, Jami isn't here,'" she recalled, "and then I didn't hear from him again until he called one more time and asked for her."

Judy was concerned. She had never known Jami to stay out so late, but Jami knew that Chris was safe with Judy, so maybe she had gone to Lisa's to sleep. Judy tried to tell herself that.

Steve called Judy Hagel again at seven-thirty in the morning to tell her that Jami had come home and was on her way to the Hagels'.

That was a relief for Judy, who felt that her worries of the night before had been silly. "I gave Jami a big hug, and she walked in and Jerry was sitting at the table. She crawled up on Jerry's lap and she said, 'Daddy, I want to come home.' So we said, '*Okay!* Gladly!'"

Judy could tell that Jami had something on her mind, so she asked her husband to take Chris downstairs so they could talk. "I asked her what was going on. I said, 'Where were you last night?' "

"I was with Lew—he's a friend of Steve's. We went out for a pizza."

"Why?"

"Because he's somebody to talk to. He understands what's going on."

"Jami," Judy sighed, "you're not improving yourself any here. Where does he work?"

Jami had mentioned "Costco, in Lynnwood," but Judy wasn't sure if Jami had said that Lew or his wife, Dru, worked there or if she'd said that both of them worked there. All in all, it didn't sound good to her. Why on earth would Jami go out for a pizza and stay out all night with some friend of Steve's? Why hadn't Jami talked to Dru about her worries? If anyone understood how awful Jami's marriage was, Judy thought it would be Dru.

Jami never got a chance to explain the situation to her mother because the phone began to ring. "It was him [Steve] calling for her, and I said, 'Give us time to talk,' and I hung up. We didn't even get to sit down at the table before he was on the phone again, and she kept saying 'I don't want to talk to him—I don't want to talk to him,' and it just kept on ringing. I finally said, 'Jami, you've got to talk to him, just for a minute.' "

Judy was surprised to finally hear Jami say, "Steve, it's over. I don't love you anymore. I want a divorce. It's over."

But as flatly insistent as Jami was, Judy could tell that Steve was wearing her down, begging for a meeting.

"Finally," Judy remembered, "she says, 'Okay. I'll meet you down the hill at the Samena Club.' I asked her not to go, and she went to get Chris, but Chris was still in his jammies, so she left him with me. I said, 'Well, Jami, I don't want you to go.' She walked out the door, and she said, 'All he can do is kill me, Mom.' "

Judy ran after Jami, calling, "I'm going to give you twenty minutes, and then I'm going to be down there."

The house was quiet, as the clock ticked way past twenty minutes. Frantic, Judy called Jerry and asked him to go down to the Samena Club. "Please go over there!"

And then it was all right again. At 8:40, before Jerry could even run to their car, the phone rang, and it was Jami. She told her mother she was at home. She was a little upset because when she drove up to meet Steve, he jumped into her car, grabbed her purse, and ran off with it. Jami said she knew he'd taken it to their house, so she drove there to get it back and to pack a few clothes for herself and Chris.

"Jami," Judy said with frustration, "You can't keep going back to him. If you're going to leave him, you're going to leave him. You can't say you're going to do it and keep going back."

"Mom," Jami said firmly, "this time I mean it."

"And I knew she did," Judy said later. "I knew she meant it. She went and got clothes for Chris. I asked her to please hurry and come home. She said, 'I'm just going to jump in the shower and change clothes and I'll be there.' "

It was a morning suspended in time, where every event would be frozen in Judy Hagel's mind. She was frightened, but she kept telling herself there was no need to be. At last Jami was coming back to them. Judy stayed close to the phone all morning, holding her breath as she waited for Jami to call.

"I didn't hear from her again until a quarter to twelve," Judy said. "She called me and said, 'Hi Mom! I'm on my way; I'm going to be stopping at Taco Time,' because she always used to stop by Taco Time and bring the food to the house and eat it there. . . . She said, 'I'll be there.'

"And she never came."

Jami should have been in and out of Taco Time within a few minutes, and the drive from her house in Redmond to her parents' home in Bellevue shouldn't have taken more than twenty minutes. Judy told herself that Jami must have run some other errand on the way. She looked after Chris and armed herself for a typical barrage of phone calls from Steve. Sure enough, he called at 12:15 and asked for Jami. Told she wasn't there yet, he hung up, only to call again at 12:30. Jami still wasn't there, and Judy told him so.

She expected him to follow his usual pattern and call every fifteen minutes until Jami got there, but he didn't. Steve didn't call the Hagels again until 6:30 that evening. Judy's heart sank; that surely meant that he had found Jami and the two of them were together, with Steve begging Jami to forget all the nonsense about leaving him. He was so good at talking circles around Jami.

Or maybe Jami was with Lisa Cryder, working out the details of their plan to move in together, or with someone else. Judy just didn't know.

Steve had said he was coming to get Chris, but when he got there, Judy smelled alcohol on his breath. He wasn't supposed to be drinking. She didn't want him driving like that with Chris in the car, so she invited Steve to stay the night. He refused, took his two-year-old son and left.

Judy still hadn't heard from Jami and she was beginning to feel very anxious. "About nine or nine-thirty,"

Judy recalled, "the phone rang and it was Steve. He said, 'I can't stay here. Can I come back?' I said, 'Yes. Bring Chris.' "

By ten o'clock her grandson was asleep at her house, and Judy turned to Steve, determined to get some answers. She asked him what he'd done that afternoon and he told her he'd stayed at home until two o'clock and then gone over to his mother's house and fallen asleep. He hadn't heard from Jami all day. Steve explained that his mother and stepfather were away on vacation in Cancún, Mexico, and he'd promised to stay there part of the time, check on the mail, and generally keep an eye on their home to give them a break. She thought that was peculiar; Judy knew that Sherri Schielke invariably turned to her daughters, Laura and Saundra, to look after things while she was away. As far as Judy knew, Steve didn't even have a key to Sherri and her third husband Wally's home in Mill Creek. But Steve was insistent that this time he had been asked to stop by.

The next morning, Steve was up at six and announced that he was going over to his mother's house again to see if Jami had shown up there. Judy stared at him. Why in the world would Jami go to Sherri's house? Even if she had gone there, she would have seen Steve's car in the driveway and left to avoid a confrontation. If she was going anywhere, she would have come home to her family, or she would have gone to Lisa's or some other girlfriend's.

Steve called a little while later from his mother's home and said Jami wasn't there.

"I started calling Microsoft about seven-thirty A.M.," Judy Hagel said. "I started calling her office and then started getting scared. Up until then, I wasn't as scared.

73

I was calling Microsoft and she never answered the phone."

By then Judy was beginning to panic, and she did something that was out of character for her. She hadn't heard from Jami since she said she was on her way home with tacos for everyone. That had been *twenty hours ago.* "I thought about [Lew Adams and his wife] and Costco. So I called Costco and asked for Lew's wife. I didn't quite know what I was going to say to her, but I had to know what was going on. The first time she answered the phone, I told her I was Steve's mother, because I knew she didn't know me. She said, 'I have nothing to say to you.' "

That struck Judy as odd. Why would Lew's wife be angry with Steve or with his mother?

"Then I called back," Judy said. "I'm sorry, but this is who I am. I'm Jami Sherer's mother. Your husband was with my daughter last night, and I need to know if they're still together."

Dru Adams said she knew that Lew had come home early in the morning and had gone to work. He was just getting off his shift.

"Where is she? Where is my daughter?" Judy asked desperately.

"I know nothing about this," Dru Adams said and hung up.

Moments later Judy's phone rang. It was Lew Adams, and he sounded distraught. "What do you mean, Jami's not there?"

"She's not here," Judy said, "and she's not home either."

"I told her not to go home," he said. "She was so scared to go home, and I told her, 'Don't go home.' I kept telling her not to go home."

Judy didn't know what to think, but she had a feeling that something terrible had happened to Jami. She kept hearing Jami's voice saying, "I'm on my way. I'll be there." And underneath that, although Judy tried not to remember, she kept hearing Jami say, "All he can do is kill me."

7

On Monday, October 1, 1990, Judy Hagel could wait no longer. She called the Redmond Police Department and reported Jami as a missing person. It really should have been Steve's place to do that, but he hadn't mentioned doing it. When Steve came back from his mother's house, he agreed to go with Judy to the police station to make a formal complaint. The two rode in his car, a 1987 Blazer. The rig was in terrible shape, with both doors smashed from wrecks. Its dents and holes were patched with Bondo and the interior was awash with junk and crumpled wrappers. It was filthy and muddy. But that day, Judy Hagel didn't notice anything different about Steve's vehicle. It was always like that.

Patrol Officer Brian Steinbus took the first missing persons report on Jami Sherer. After Steve and Judy had filled out forms at the police station, an officer accompanied them to the Sherers' house on Education Hill in Redmond. The policeman walked through the house, opening up doors and poking his head in to check each room. Everything seemed normal, but Judy noted a large suitcase sitting on the bed in the master bedroom. Jami had been packing to leave Steve; why hadn't she taken the suitcase with her?

"Then we went into the kitchen," Judy recalled, "and right by the fridge, there was a little [dried] red spot on the floor. The policeman was standing there and could see, so I reached down and picked it up, and I said, 'What is this?' . . . And Steve took a towel and grabbed it and said, 'Oh, that's just juice of Chris's,' and threw it in the garbage."

The police explained that they couldn't mount a full-scale search for Jami until there was more evidence that she was the victim of foul play. She was an adult, and their experience told them that the vast majority of husbands and wives who disappear during an argument come home of their own accord. If they mobilized to look for every missing adult, they could do nothing else.

Jami Sherer had said she was leaving Steve; her car— the 1980 Mazda RX7 she was so proud of—was missing; and she knew that Chris was safe with her mother. In the investigators' minds, there was every reason to believe she was probably giving herself an opportunity to think things out—or perhaps she was with another man.

Judy Hagel knew better, and so did Jami's friends and her co-workers at Microsoft. Jami would never worry her family this way, and most of all, she would never have left Chris for a whole day without explaining to him why Mommy was going away and promising to be back very soon.

Friends began to gather at the Hagels' house. They mapped out the area around Jami and Steve's house on Education Hill, Sherri Schielke's house, the Bear Creek

Taco Time, and Judy and Jerry's house. Then they broke up into search groups. Microsoft management immediately agreed to print up thousands of flyers with pictures of Jami on them. They also gave many employees paid leave to join the search.

Steve Sherer seemed reluctant to stay in his own home. He spent a lot of time at the Hagels' house, even though they suggested that he stay at his own house in case Jami called. The search for Jami was in high gear, but Steve didn't join in, nor did he pick up any flyers from the stack on the hall table. If he was looking for her at all, he kept it to himself. He seemed upset; he slept uneasily and said he couldn't understand why this had happened to *him*.

"Steve felt very sorry for himself," one of Jami's friends recalled. "It was 'Poor me, poor me,' instead of 'Poor Jami.' "

Steve was behaving oddly, to say the least. When he walked into Judy's kitchen, she and Sheila, her son's girlfriend, saw that he had some kind of lacy material twisted around one of his biceps, like a sleeve garter.

"What's that?" Rich Hagel asked.

"Jami's panties," Steve answered. "I'm wearing them because it makes me feel closer to her."

The Hagels stared at each other in shock. That was crazy.

Steve wore the panty-garter into a bar he often frequented, and told patrons there the same thing. He also started wearing a necklace he'd given Jami for Valentine's Day; it was a diamond heart, definitely a woman's necklace. Steve explained that wearing her things kept him connected to Jami.

How odd that he never joined one of the search parties that had fanned out all around Redmond and Bellevue as scores of volunteers searched for Jami or her car. There were so many places to look; someone as tiny as Jami could be in the woods, in Lake Sammamish, or even in Lake Washington and no one would ever know. No one understood why Steve wasn't helping them look for her. If she was in trouble, the more people out there the better. If she was dead, at least her family would know the truth. As it was, they were in agony.

Judy Hagel tried not to think that Jami could be dead. She questioned Steve again and again, trying to get him to remember what had happened after Jami vanished on Sunday at noon. He shook his head, saying that he'd been gone when she left, on his way to check his mother's home in Mill Creek and repeated that he'd fallen asleep there. "No way," Judy said flatly. "No way you were sleeping, Steve. You would have been on the phone every fifteen minutes if Jami was gone. You always are."

She kept counting the hours between Steve's phone calls that Sunday. It had been five or six hours! He called after Jami said she was on her way to Taco Time—he called twice, fifteen minutes apart, as he always did. And then he didn't call again until six-thirty. That behavior was so unlike him that Judy felt cold dread. She had to be careful about questioning him; if he became annoyed, he would take Chris and leave— and she couldn't let Chris go with him. So she tried to space out her questions.

During the first or second day he stayed with the Hagels—Monday or Tuesday—Judy heard Steve making a phone call, evidently to an auto detailer. She knew cars and all the lingo because she worked at a dealership in Bellevue.

"I heard him call," she said. "He wanted a detail on his vehicle." Steve wanted all the trash inside cleaned up, and the interior vacuumed and shampooed, with a wash and wax on the outside. He'd never bothered to have his cars cleaned before; Steve's vehicles were always a mess. Why now? What did it matter if his Blazer was clean when his wife was lost somewhere?

Judy walked into the room where the phone was. "Steve," she said carefully, "why do you want a detail on your car?"

"Oh, well," he stuttered. "Ah, ahh, Rich spilled beer in it. I'm not supposed to be drinking beer, so I want to get it detailed so the smell won't bother me—tempt me, I guess."

Judy had ridden in Steve's Blazer the day before. There was no smell of beer in it. Nevertheless he was adamant that he was going to have it detailed. She wasn't sure if he ever accomplished that, but as he drove the Blazer, more and more mud and weeds dropped off. The Redmond investigators had not searched the Blazer, nor had they put it up on a hoist to look at the undercarriage. One of the best methods criminalists use to determine where a vehicle has been is to test the mud, dirt, and vegetation caught beneath it. It was too late for that now.

By October 4, 1990, there had been no word at all from Jami Hagel. Her smiling face beamed from telephone poles, store windows, and bulletin boards all over the eastside. Microsoft printed up a second flyer with a picture of Jami's car and a description of the charcoal-gray RX7 with a sunroof, and Washington plates: 541-AHX. The last time her parents had seen Jami, she had been wearing blue jeans, a white T-shirt, and new white tennis shoes.

The Redmond police no longer believed that she had

run away or taken a vacation from her life. They worked now to learn as much about her world as possible. It didn't take long for them to find out that Steven Sherer had a long rap sheet, mostly for traffic offenses and harassment, and that he was on record for having an incredibly violent temper. But then, Lew Adams, the man Jami had seen the night before she vanished, wasn't exactly an upstanding citizen either. Both Sherer and Adams were known cocaine users. The obvious conclusion was that one of them knew what had become of Jami, but there was always the slight chance that she had been abducted by a stranger who spotted the beautiful young mother somewhere between her home and her parents' home early Sunday afternoon.

Jami would have made a perfect victim. She was distraught and frightened about what would happen now that she was finally leaving Steve, and she told her mother during their last phone call that she was hurrying to get out of her house before Steve came home. She would have been a prime target for someone who wanted to grab her—too distracted and too tiny to put up much of a fight. The chances of a stranger abduction were slim, but it had to be considered.

If the investigators couldn't find Jami, they needed to find her car, which might contain evidence or, in the worst-case scenario, Jami's body. Meanwhile they set out to learn what motivation someone might have had to kill her.

On October 2, Sergeant L. M. "Butch" Watson got a page from Lew Adams shortly after 8:00 P.M. When he talked to Adams, Watson noted that the man was extremely emotional, and concerned that Steve Sherer had harmed Jami. Asked why he felt that way, Lew Adams said that Steve had "many things over Jami" and that Steve was a recovering alcoholic with a gambling addiction. Steve had apparently confided in Adams that he had committed a number of crimes, including robberies in California.

That was interesting, but not necessarily a motive for murder. Finally, Lew Adams admitted that he had been sexually involved with Jami on about five occasions. The first three had been Steve's idea. "He likes to watch," Adams said.

Steve had manipulated both Lew Adams and Jami into having sex. He woke Adams up as he slept one night, intoxicated, on the Sherers' couch and told him to come into the master bedroom. There he awakened Jami too and began to remove her nightclothes as if offering a prize to Adams.

Over the next few weeks, Lew Adams said, he had watched Steve badger Jami, drug her, and coax her until she finally capitulated and participated, albeit unwillingly, in the threesome that Steve wanted. Steve's impotence made him a voyeur rather than a participant.

On the third occasion, Lew Adams said that Steve had videotaped them. It had all been for Steve's pleasure, Adams said. He was positive that Jami had been mortified over the whole episode.

What Steve didn't count on was that Jami was so desperate for a helping hand and kind words that she began to visualize an actual relationship with Lew.

After being married to Steve for three years, her self-esteem was practically nonexistent, and Lew Adams was the first man in years who had roused her long-dormant belief that she could love a man again— or that any man would want her.

So Jami obediently dressed in the garish outfits Steve bought her: spike heels, diaphanous lingerie, miniskirts, and long black gloves. But that wasn't her; that was a woman acting out a part that her husband had written for her. Lew and Jami halfheartedly went through the motions, following Steve's directions for his homemade porno movie. Lew couldn't imagine that a man would use his own wife like that, and he was ashamed afterward.

In the resultant videotape, it was obvious that Jami was under the influence of some drug Steve had given her. It was also clear that she wasn't enjoying herself. Her eyes were hollow and vacant. She was acting—and clumsily—responding to the director, who was just out of camera range.

Lew Adams told Sergeant Watson that he had been with Jami the day before she disappeared, that they had gone to the Crest Motel on Aurora Avenue and stayed until early in the morning. Lew suspected that Steve knew what had happened because he learned from his estranged wife that Jami had called Dru's house the next morning. So had Judy Hagel, and of course Judy learned from Jami that Steve had run off with Jami's purse, in which he would have found Lew's business card and the motel receipt. Lew felt that Jami had been trying to get a message to him to warn him.

"Steve never called me on it," Adams said, "and that might be because he took out his anger on Jami."

Lew Adams feared that Steve had killed Jami or driven her so far away that she couldn't get home. He told Sergeant Watson that the videotape Steve took of them had been filmed on the night of September 21, and though Jami said that Steve promised to destroy it, Lew didn't know if he had done so.

Lew Adams was not eliminated as a suspect, but he had certainly raised some questions about Steve

Sherer. Lew had nothing to gain from Jami's death or disappearance, but Steve did: revenge, for one thing. Steve had told a number of people, including Jami's brothers, that she was as good as dead if she ever cheated on him.

Jami's Microsoft co-workers cooperated fully with the Redmond detectives. Two of her friends remarked that Jami had stopped wearing her diamond ring a few days before she disappeared. It was the same ring, of course, that Steve had already collected insurance on. Jami was reportedly afraid that Steve would pawn it, as he had done with several other items they owned. Steve was not drinking for the time being, but he had threatened to start again if Jami left him. He'd also told her he would commit suicide if she deserted him.

If Jami was dead, however, Steve would realize much more financial gain than he would from pawning her ring. Microsoft provided life insurance to its employees. In Jami's case, the payoff would be twice the amount of her salary. She was making $23,000 a year, so her beneficiary would collect $46,000. Steve Sherer was that beneficiary in May of 1987, designated as Jami's "fiancé." However, Jami had changed the beneficiary on July 21, 1988. Her son, Chris, would now collect her insurance. Whether Steve knew about the change in her beneficiary is questionable.

But Microsoft was an excellent company to work for, and there were other benefits that would probably go to Steve if Jami was dead, including the company stock she still owned, which was exploding exponentially.

On October 5, King County sheriff's deputy Roger Bleiler, who was Steven Sherer's maternal uncle, found

Jami Sherer's car. It was parked in a grassy area near the parking lot of the Unitarian church at 14724 First Avenue N.E., just to the north of the Seattle city limits. Several Redmond investigators joined King County detectives at the site. The address was in Bleiler's patrol sector, and he remarked that Steve had called him and asked him to be on the lookout for Jami's car in his patrol area. Coincidentally, the Mazda *was* found in his uncle's sector.

Actually, the caller who spotted the car first was someone from the church office. The Mazda had been there so long that they thought it might have been abandoned or stolen. Jami Sherer always kept her car clean and polished. It still was, but now it had water spots on it. That was easy to explain. A wild windstorm had hit Seattle in midweek. There were downed branches lying around the car, but the area beneath the car was clear and dry. The driver's door was unlocked, and they could see a black leather coat on the passenger seat and a duffel bag on the floor behind the driver's seat.

The hatchback portion of the Mazda was empty; if Jami had been in the car when it was driven to this spot, she was not here now. There was no other place in the small car to hide a body. East of the car was a large tract of undeveloped land, with trees, blackberry bushes, and weeds.

Before any human touched the car, the investigators put in a call for help from the Search and Rescue bloodhounds. Since there was clearly no one in the car now, they needed to know who might have driven it last, but no one except that person could tell them that. They needed a creature with a sense of smell beyond human capability to identify the last driver.

Richard Schurman III, responded with his dog, Maggie. According to Schurman, Maggie was the most dependable of all the search dogs he had worked with, and that was saying a lot. He'd been working with the bloodhounds since 1984. Although Schurman was a technologist in the aerospace industry, his avocation was Search and Rescue, and his heart was with his dogs. Maggie—formally known as Slo-Motion Magnolia Bark—had been on over two hundred missions, looking for lost children, runaways, disoriented Alzheimer's patients, and others who were so lost that humans couldn't find them.

"We teach [the dogs] obedience first," Schurman explained, "and then scent. They smell the scent article of the quarry [something that smells of the person pretending to be lost] and that person stands in plain sight and calls them. From there, the quarry only half-shows himself. And then a magical thing happens—the bloodhound drops his head to the ground and goes by scent alone."

Maggie and Schurman had worked together for twelve years, and though he had other dogs, he described her as "incomparable."

Schurman volunteered with Northwest law enforcement agencies, the FBI, the Washington State Patrol, and all the county and municipal agencies. He explained that a dog like Maggie, given enough time, could locate a single person in a crowd of many thousands at the Kingdome or Safeco Field, and she certainly could follow the trail of one person.

When Schurman arrived with Maggie, he found that the police had no scent article available. They had no way of knowing who the items in the Mazda belonged to. The next best thing—and maybe *the* best thing—in this instance was to have Maggie sniff the area around the headrest of the driver's seat. The upper back of a car seat and the headrest itself are areas where a driver's hair and the bare skin at the back of the neck touch most often. Scales of dried skin, hair follicles, and perspiration are all deposited there in infinitesimal amounts.

Maggie clambered into the car and sniffed avidly at the back and top of the Mazda's driver's seat. And then Schurman ordered, "Find!"

Maggie went from the car to an area behind the church and then to a thickly vegetated field. She continued on to fenced-in sections around the church until she found a path that seemed to fascinate her. And then she got down to business.

"You can read your dog," Schurman said. "Maggie raised her tail straight up and put her nose down. She reached a trail between a brushy line along I-5. She seemed to be working a valid scent trail. She tracked the I-5 trail southbound to an off-ramp that led to a bus stop. And then she stopped. She was no longer interested."

It appeared that the driver of the Mazda had left the car in the church lot and made his (or her) way to a narrow path along the freeway until that person reached a transit bus stop. Presumably, they had boarded a bus. At that point, even the best tracking dog in the world would have lost the trail.

The next morning, the detective team decided to do another dog search, this time with scent objects. Accompanied by an officer, Schurman went to the Sherer home at 10709 161st Avenue North in Redmond. Steve gave them permission to search—but only for Jami's clothing, just enough to obtain a scent object that the

Search and Rescue dogs could track. Schurman was able to find what he needed for his dogs.

Schurman had long forceps and sterile bags to be sure that the items he selected would not be contaminated by the odor of anyone but household members. "Our DNA constantly sheds in the skin cells and bacteria," he said later, explaining that stress scents were stronger. Anyone who is tense or afraid exudes more odor. Schurman gathered clothing in three bags. The first was from the floor of the master bedroom, and the next two from the closet and the laundry basket.

The first scent item was Jami's underwear from the bedroom floor. The search dogs circled the car and went nowhere. They couldn't get interested in a scent because, clearly, Jami had never been there in that church parking lot in that car. She was not, apparently, the last person to drive her car.

They had not had permission to take Steve Sherer's clothes, but his clothes and Jami's were mixed in the laundry basket. A pair of Steve's trousers had been entangled with Jami's clothes in the hamper. When those items of Jami's were given to the bloodhounds, they picked up the male scent—Steve's scent that had transferred there; the dogs had already shown a complete lack of interest in Jami's scent. It was the second scent they picked up on. From 9:39 on the morning of October 6, until 10:13, a fresh team of bloodhounds followed the male scent—Steve's scent—on exactly the same route to I-5 that Maggie had tracked the day before. They too stopped in bewilderment when they lost their trail at the bus stop.

If those dogs could have talked—and they almost could have, in their own way—they would have told the detectives that Steve Sherer had left Jami's Mazda

RX7 in the church parking lot and then made his way to the bus stop where he either boarded a bus or was picked up by someone.

8

Although Steve Sherer wasn't participating in the search for Jami, he did conduct a search of his own shortly after 10:00 A.M. on Sunday morning, September 30. He knew from the receipt in Jami's purse that she had been at the Crest Motel the night before. He went there and said he wanted to search the room she was in because she had lost her diamond ring. The clerk finally allowed him into the room Jami and Lew had used, but wrote down the time and his license number on the room ticket. No one knew whether he had really been looking for that same expensive ring or just snooping to find evidence that Jami had cheated on him.

Sergeant Watson, along with Detectives L. C. Conrad, Steve Hardwick, and Oscar Guttormsen, processed Jami's Mazda RX7 at 7:30 A.M. on October 6. They dusted it for latent prints on the outside and the interior door windows, and bagged the fur seat covers, floor mats, and front and rear carpeting for further examination. They located a set of keys to the Mazda in the pocket of the woman's leather coat.

The Mazda's seat was pushed back to accommodate a driver at least five inches taller than Jami. Judy Hagel had told the investigators that Jami had such short legs that she could drive her car only if the seat was pushed all the way forward, and even then she had to have a pillow behind her back. Judy also told them that Jami was a fanatic about never leaving her car unless the alarm was turned on. Detectives found that the alarm was off.

As they ran their hands along the console, they found what Steve had been looking for in the Crest Motel. There, in a small manila envelope that someone had stuffed under the driver's side of the console, were Jami's ring and her diamond-studded wristwatch. For her own reasons, perhaps, she had hidden them there. If Jami had run away of her own accord, why would she have left jewelry worth thousands of dollars behind? For that matter, why would she have left her car behind? She loved her car, and she had just put a new CD stereo system in it. Her mother had given her the sunroof as a present.

And who would she have run away with? She was a very open woman, who shared her intimate thoughts with several girlfriends and with her mother. She was involved with a man other than her husband, just on the verge of a full-blown affair, but that man wasn't missing. The detectives knew right where Lew Adams was, and all of her friends swore she had never cheated on Steve before.

No one who knew her could even imagine that Jami Sherer was devious enough to pretend she was excited about being with Lew just to hide a *real* affair with a man she planned to run away with.

The bag behind the driver's seat held clothes, all right, but it was an odd assortment for a woman to have packed as she prepared to leave her husband for good. Although it contained items like shampoo, curlers, and a hairbrush, the clothes made no sense. There were only sports clothes—sweatshirts and T-shirts. There were no clothes that Jami could wear to her job at Microsoft, no nightclothes, no diapers for Chris. There was no underwear at all; it looked as if someone had grabbed things mindlessly and stuffed them into the duffel bag.

Had Jami been truly frightened that Steve would hurt her, she might have done that. But all reports indicated that she wasn't afraid that last Sunday morning. She had even felt safe enough to take a shower in her own house. And she had evidently already packed when she called her mother to say she was on her way to Taco Time and then to the Hagels'. Moreover, Jami was too well organized to have packed such a jumble of things in such a haphazard manner. More likely, she had packed carefully, and someone, enraged, had grabbed the duffel bag and dumped her things out. Perhaps, Judy Hagel thought, the suitcase she had seen on the bed in the master bedroom had been Jami's bag.

Forensic testing of the items taken from Jami Sherer's car revealed no blood or fingerprints that might have helped build a case against a suspect. It was unlikely that Jami, injured or dead, had been transported in the Mazda RX7. The car appeared to have been left there by someone who wanted to make it look as if she had driven away from her home and then deliberately abandoned the Mazda.

Steve insisted there had been only one key to the Mazda, and that Jami had it. He identified the key found in her leather coat pocket as that key. Redmond detectives again asked permission to walk through Steve Sherer's house. He agreed.

"We did a general walk-through," Butch Watson wrote in his follow-up report. "The upper level consisted of a living room, dining room, kitchen, bathroom, and three bedrooms. The lower level consisted of a family room, bathroom, washroom, and garage. A general inspection of the residence revealed no obvious signs of a struggle although it should be noted that the residence was very unkempt and disorderly, with clothing stacked everywhere . . . We checked some carpet stains with hemo-test tablets and found no obvious signs of blood."

Hemo-test tablets could detect the presence of blood and give criminalists reasons to test it further for origin and type, but that was all they could do. The tablets themselves could not differentiate between human blood, deer blood, and rabbit blood, for that matter. Steve's explanation for the stain in his living room was that it was Kool-Aid, and it might very well have been. It was not blood.

Lew Adams had told the detectives that Steve was interested in swinging, and indeed they did find magazines called *Swing and Sway* and *Let Us Entertain You,* which catered to couples and singles who wanted to mix and match with strangers. They located one smashed videotape and an intact tape, which they took for viewing to see if it had any bearing on Jami Sherer's disappearance. The other tapes in the Sherers' bedroom were all commercially made movies.

The intact tape was clearly the one Lew Adams had described. It showed Lew and Jami, obviously drugged, with Steve Sherer playing director and producer. The Redmond detectives had seen it all, but they were disgusted by the flickering images, the sickening desecration of a man's marital vows to cherish his wife.

Days went by, but the search parties didn't let up, despite the sometimes fierce rain and windstorms that buffeted the north end. It was terrible to think of Jami out there in the icy cold, alone, and it was inconceivable that she would not have called to see if Chris was okay. "Chris was her life," her friends said often. "He was the most important thing in the world to her."

Jami had no car, and she hadn't cashed her last paycheck for just over $500. Her normal habit was to deposit her check in Key Bank on the day she got it. This time, she had not. Nor did they find any other bank accounts that she might have maintained secretly to have running-away money.

Meanwhile, Lew Adams was rapidly becoming a basket case. He felt tremendous guilt because he had been unable to talk Jami out of going back to Steve's house. He regretted that he hadn't been more forceful in convincing her that she was in danger.

Of course Lew had a second worry. He had been with Jami at the Crest Motel the night before she disappeared. He knew he had to be a prime suspect in whatever had happened to her, and he had his own secrets. He was a grown man, still married but living with his parents, and he was involved in the drug world. When Lew was interviewed again on October 8, he said he had known Steve for ten years and been a cocaine source for him in the early 1980s, before Steve moved to Palm Desert. "I met Steve through his cousin," Lew said. "I ran into the cousin again about eight months ago, and he put me back in touch with Steve."

Lew described the last day he had spent with Jami—Saturday, September 29, 1990. They had met at noon at Alley Chevrolet, where Lew worked. Jami parked her car down the street on Lake City Way and joined him in his classic 1959 Volkswagen Bug, which he had painted neon pink. That car was his most prized possession. He and Jami went to the Omnidome to see a movie about the eruption of Mount St. Helens, but the special effects made Jami dizzy.

They went next to a restaurant for a late lunch and sat at an outdoor table, drinking beer and talking. Lew, sensing that Jami was eager for someone to listen to her, just sat quietly and listened. She was such a sad woman, and so trapped in her marriage, but he could see a little sparkle in her. He wondered what she had been like before she met Steve, and he was sorry that she ever had. There was really nothing Lew could do to help her, except listen to her and warn her to be careful.

It was a good Saturday, with the first sense of true autumn in the air, and they watched the sun go down over Elliott Bay. Jami called her mother to check on Chris, and then called her friend Lisa to cover herself with an alibi, in case Steve started looking for her. Then she and Lew went to a pizza place for dinner, where they drank more beer.

They had, Lew admitted, decided to spend the night together at the Crest Motel. He was adamant that they used no drugs at all. This time they didn't have Steve with a video camera aimed at them, calling directions and suggestions.

They parted company at about seven the next morning, after stopping for apple juice. Lew liked Jami and felt sorry for her. He said again how fearful he had been for her when he dropped her off at her car, advising her to go to her mother's house and not to her own. Then he headed home to his parents' house.

"That was the last time I ever saw or heard from her."

Jami had promised Lew that she would go to her mother's house and stay there. She would call an attorney about a divorce or separation on Monday morning.

Interviewed again the next night in the Redmond

police station, Lew said he felt personally responsible for Jami's absence. "If I hadn't become involved with her, she wouldn't be missing."

"Do you have any idea where she is now?" one of the investigators asked.

"In heaven," he said, with a sigh. "I don't know."

Was that a confession? Or was it only an utterance from a man who felt tremendous guilt for contributing to the death of a woman simply by being out all night with her? Lew Adams seemed to be genuinely remorseful, but then, a lot of killers appear the same way.

He went through Sunday with the detectives questioning him. "After I left Jami at her car," he said, "I went to my parents' house, and my mom let me in. I went to bed until about eleven, and then I went to Al's Car Quest and bought some glass tint. . . . I washed and waxed my car."

His mother had been selling something in a booth at a church bazaar at Saint Thomas's in Lynnwood, and Lew said he dropped in there sometime in midday. After that, he went back to his parents' place and tried to tint the windows of his pink Volkswagen. His estranged wife came by about three so they could show a prospective buyer a car they were trying to sell.

"I didn't see Jami at all on Sunday," Lew Adams insisted. He readily agreed to give saliva and hair samples and to take a polygraph, if needed.

Dru Adams, Lew's wife, verified that he no longer lived with her and their children. Asked about any phone calls she received on Sunday, September 30, she remembered that Steve had called early, looking for Lew. That wasn't unusual; Steve called often and repeatedly, "every half hour," until he found Lew.

Dru said she was aware that Lew and Steve were using drugs, but she didn't question Lew. She just wanted to live her own life. She had seen Steve Sherer in person only two or three times, and she had never seen either man doing drugs in her home.

It was something of a surprise for her when Jami Sherer called about ten or ten-thirty, asking for either Lew or Steve. Dru had met Jami only once—six months earlier, in a restaurant. "I told her neither of them were here and that Lew didn't live here anymore."

Jami had probably been trying to find Lew to warn him that Steve knew she'd been with him the night before, but she could not very well have left that message with Dru Adams.

While hardly the ideal husband and father, Lew Adams had been willing to talk to the Redmond investigators whenever they asked, and the only questions that made him sweat were about drugs. He got tears in his eyes at questions about Jami, but the tears seemed real, as if he was grieving for her.

Steve Sherer was not at all anxious to talk in depth with the police. He told them he had no idea where Jami was. The last time he saw her, he said, she was packing a bag to leave him. It had been a quiet end to their sometimes explosive marriage, and he was coming down from a night of cocaine use and exhausted. But he had gone about keeping his promise to check his mother's house while she was in Cancún. He fell asleep on the Schielkes' couch and awakened an hour or two later to call the Hagels to talk to Jami.

There was a cockiness about Steve Sherer, strange in a man whose wife had stepped through some hidden door and completely vanished. Steve continued to wear Jami's panties around his biceps, drawing either sympathy or incredulous stares from those who frequented the same bars and card rooms he did.

9

Steve Sherer's reaction to Jami's infidelity was ambivalence. Initially, he had been a man on fire with jealousy, but once she disappeared, he seemed more like a bystander than the one person who should be most concerned.

Although he did not sign a formal statement, Steve did agree to talk with Steve Hardwick, a Redmond police detective whom he knew slightly. To Hardwick, Steve gave his recollection of that bizarre last weekend in September. Lew Adams had been willing, actually eager, to talk about Jami's disappearance—even with a polygrapher—but nervous about any discussion of his drug use. Steve Sherer was the opposite; he was voluble when he spoke of his cocaine addiction, but he didn't see much point in talking about Jami, and was definitely leery about taking a polygraph.

Steve told Hardwick he'd been with Jami's brothers late on Saturday night, September 29. The beginning of his evening had been spent in a search for cocaine. After he scored, he said, he drove back to the eastside and attended a party near the Hagels' house. When he returned to his home in Redmond in the wee hours of Sunday morning, Jami wasn't there. Steve said that he and her brother Rich had looked for her.

At that point, Steve said he was very worried about Jami and called everyone he could think of in his attempt to find her. He admitted he was jealous, too. He called Lisa Cryder, the friend Jami was supposed to be with. Lisa said that Jami should have been home by then.

Steve told Detective Steve Hardwick that Jami finally came home around seven-thirty on Sunday morning. She had lied to him about staying at Lisa's; he already knew she wasn't there. Jami left then and went to her parents' house.

Steve admitted he was strung out that morning. He'd snorted some more cocaine and then gone back to bed. Hardwick didn't comment on the obvious: cocaine was hardly a sleep aid. Steve contradicted himself when he followed that by saying he had called the Hagels at eight, shortly after Jami left.

His story was disjointed, and the Redmond detective noted that Steve's time sequence changed often. Steve remembered that he called Lew's house looking for more cocaine, but couldn't find him. He had spoken with Lew's wife. And then, he said, he called the Hagels again, and asked Jami to meet him at the Samena Club, a block away from her parents', so they could talk. She finally agreed to meet him.

Steve said he had seen an overnight bag behind her seat and her brown leather coat in the car. Still angry and suspicious, he'd taken her purse and run to his truck, locking it. Searching through her handbag for some clue to where she had been, he found the receipt from the Crest Motel from the night before. Steve said he didn't put two and two together "until I found Lew's business card. I still didn't know about their affair."

Steve explained that the card itself wasn't as damning as the fact that Lew had written his parents' address and phone number on the back of it.

Steve continued pawing through Jami's purse, finding her credit cards, bills, makeup bag, and birth control pills. "I threw [the pills] away," Steve said, smugly.

Jami had driven off by then. Determined to find out everything he could, Steve said he stopped at a pay phone and called the Crest Motel. He had headed there and convinced the desk clerk that he had to search the room listed on the receipt. "I told them that my girlfriend had left her jewelry there."

He did not find the diamond ring he sought, but he said the room had been used, and he insisted he had seen cocaine residue on the headboard of the bed.

Jami was at their house, Steve said, when he got home. At this point, his attitude changed markedly. He said that he was no longer jealous or furious with Jami. "We agreed to go our separate ways—until we both straightened out," Steve said quietly.

According to Steve, Jami went to his truck, gathered up her belongings and put them back in her purse. She stayed in their house only long enough to make a few phone calls, and then she walked out the door. He let her go without any objections. It was, he said, a quiet ending. "She didn't say good-bye," he said mournfully.

Steve reiterated the many errands he had to do for his mother. He had their mortgage check and some packages to mail. So he hadn't called Judy Hagel until about suppertime to see if Jami was back. He recalled that he had also talked to a friend, Jeff Caston, earlier in the day and might have called his sister Saundra. Then he had spent the night at the Hagels'.

"I got real concerned when Jami didn't show up for

work on Monday morning," Steve said. "She didn't say good-bye, but she didn't leave pissed off."

While Judy Hagel was frantic about Jami's disappearance and had mobilized a huge group of friends who were working day and night to look for her, Steve's mother was not as concerned, but as soon as she heard from Steve, she cut short her vacation and flew home from Cancún four days after Jami vanished. On October 8, Sherri and her daughter Saundra cleaned the Sherers' messy house, after obtaining police permission. "I guess I'm kind of a neat freak," Sherri explained. "I assumed Jami would be back, and I wanted it to be nice." She explained that she didn't want Jami to come home to a dirty house. The place was very clean when she finished. She had the carpets shampooed, and the house looked great.

For Steve's family, his involvement in a police investigation was almost business as usual. This time, the circumstances were more ominous than a disappearing—and reappearing—diamond ring or broken windows in a mobile home, but most of Steve's relatives felt that Jami would soon come home. Steve didn't have a lawyer, and no one blamed Sherri Schielke for being reluctant to hire still another attorney for her son. He had been putting her through the mill ever since he entered puberty, running up so many bills with lawyers, rehabs, fines, crashed cars, bad debts, gambling.

Sherri didn't think about hiring a criminal defense attorney at this point.

Shortly before 2:00 P.M. on October 10, the 911 operator received an emergency call to send help to Education Hill in Redmond. An aid unit had already responded to the Sherers' address, and the Redmond in-

vestigators arrived in time to see them carrying Steve
Sherer from his garage.

He had apparently tried to kill himself with carbon
monoxide. When the first units arrived, they found him
in his garage in his Blazer, with the windows down, and
the engine running. He appeared to be semiconscious
and had trouble speaking or moving.

Detective Steve Hardwick leaned over him and said,
"Hang in there, Steve. You'll be all right."

His condition appeared critical, so the paramedics
called for an airlift to the ER at Harborview Hospital in
Seattle for treatment of carbon monoxide poisoning. As
the helicopter disappeared to the west, the Redmond
detectives looked into the front seat of Steve's truck. A
picture of Jami in her wedding dress rested there and,
beside it, a cordless phone. Steve himself had used it to
call for help.

He had also taken the time to leave a long good-bye:

> I am sorry Everyone
> BUT
> Jami is my life. She made me a better person
> and kept me under control. But I kept hurting her
> with games I would play.
> I can't live without her. I really need her and I
> have lost her one way or another. Maybe now, she
> won't be afraid to come home. I have been a real
> bad person in the past and she has changed me.
> But I had ruined what we had!
> Jami Honey. Just remember I really do love you
> and Chris, and Chris when you can read and un-
> derstand this, Please understand that I need your
> Mom real bad and if she won't come back, I won't
> be able to handle that, much less your life. Please

give everything to Chris and/or Jami. They are the
ones I've made suffer.

I didn't mean too! [Sic]
Love You ALL
Steven Sherer
My dad's ring goes to Chris when he is married.

Was it a sincere plea for forgiveness from a man
who had lost the center post of his life, or was it a carefully contrived letter meant to make him look innocent?
Steve Sherer had seen the devastation and the guilt that
suicide could bring to a family when his father took his
own life. The detectives wondered how he could do that
to his own son. Chris had no mother, and now it looked
as though he would have no father, either.

Sherri Schielke and Steve's younger sister Laura
rushed to Harborview Hospital and sat anxiously in the
waiting room while doctors treated him in the emergency room. Detective Steve Hardwick waited with
them there. He couldn't talk to Steve Sherer because he
was on a respirator, but the doctors told him that he was
not in critical condition, nor had he ever been. He had
called 911 in plenty of time to be rescued.

Hardwick waited for hours to speak with Sherer; it
was almost midnight when he was allowed to go in.
Steve's mother and sister hovered nearby, and Hardwick had only ten minutes to talk to Sherer alone.

"I told him no matter what he had done, it was not
worth taking his life," Hardwick recalled. "I reminded
him that he had to think about his son. He was reflec-
tive, somewhat remorseful. He continually made comments such as 'I've made bad mistakes,' and 'It's all
my fault.' He also mentioned that 'I'm going to miss
Jami.' "

This struck the detective as somewhat strange since no one was convinced yet that Jami was gone forever. But Steve apparently was: he had begun to speak of Jami in the past tense.

The next morning, Detectives Hardwick and Conrad returned to Harborview, hoping to interview Steve about the reasons for his attempted suicide. They learned to their surprise that he had already been discharged and taken across the street to the mental health center. No sooner had they located him and asked how he was feeling than Steve's new attorney arrived. He was Peter Mair, a former assistant U.S. attorney and now one of Seattle's better-known criminal defense attorneys.

Mair, hired by Steve's mother, directed the detectives to stop questioning him immediately and asked them to leave.

When Hardwick asked about Steve Sherer's taking the polygraph exam, Mair looked at him and said, "I'll get back to you on that."

It would be weeks before Steve Sherer was released from the hospital, ultimately frustrating weeks for the Redmond investigators. They were working on an impossible case, if indeed it was a case at all.

A missing person? A runaway wife? A murder?

If Jami had been murdered, the police had two excellent suspects. However, they had no body, no crime scene, no witnesses, and no physical evidence, and the circumstantial evidence was confusing. They had some bizarre stories from self-styled clairvoyants and a few reports from people in bars and minimarts who thought they had seen Jami.

If Jami Sue Hagel Sherer was dead, no one knew or no one was telling where she waited for someone to find her.

The most baffling case in a decade had just begun. For Jami's mother and father, her little boy, her brothers, and the friends and co-workers who loved her, this was a terrible ordeal of hope and disappointment, anxiety, fear, and nightmares.

Somehow, Jami had stepped through a gap in the here and now and disappeared completely.

It was a stormy autumn, and the winter rains of the Northwest moved in to take the last of the golden leaves off the deciduous trees. Hunters fanned out in Washington State, hiking off-trail and through woods. Every year, men looking for deer and elk stumbled across a body or two, and 1990 was no different. But none of the weathered skulls turned out to be Jami Sherer's.

She hadn't used her credit cards or her checkbook, nor had she applied for new cards. She made no phone calls to her home. Weeks became months, and it was a new year.

For a time in January 1991, Redmond police officers and detectives put a round-the-clock surveillance on Steve Sherer, following him as he went to work, to card rooms, to bowling alleys, and home again.

Steve continued to attract police attention long after they stopped tailing him.

In June 1991 he got into a fight outside a bar in Bellevue with a man who pulled out a pistol and shot him in the forearm. He wasn't badly hurt. In 1992 he spent a short time in jail for violating his probation by using cocaine and failing to meet with his probation officer.

If Steve knew where Jami rested, he didn't visit her.

Her family had somehow gotten through the first Christmas without her. They could never have imagined how many more there would be before they would know what happened to her.

10

It would be virtually impossible to list all of the investigators and prosecutors who spent thousands of hours looking for Jami Sherer. She was precious to her family, but her life and her fate would soon become, in a different way, as valuable to the professionals who took over her case. Jami had once been the four-year-old who helped her mother raise her twin baby brothers, the bubbly little girl who was an indispensable member of the Hagel family, the popular teenager who seemed to have a wonderful future, and the responsible employee at Microsoft who was on her way up—but she had now become the photo image smiling from thousands of flyers in windows and tacked on telephone poles. She was a young wife and mother who had completely disappeared, and though her face was now familiar to thousands, her fate remained completely mysterious. The task of finding Jami Sherer was an awesome challenge. Several of the investigators who worked on her case in 1990 and 1991 finally announced that it was impossible to find Jami—that the case was, in the words of one detective, a "loser" that would never be solved. The years passed, and Jami's case file was pushed to the back as new cases demanded attention.

Unless someone offered new information or confessed to harming Jami Sherer, the search for her was over. A new team of detectives would have to pick up the gauntlet flung down by those who termed the case hopeless. A relatively small police department like Redmond's might not have the resources to find a team like that.

Judy and Jerry Hagel, however, refused to give up. They tried another route: They hired a private investigator who came highly recommended. "He told me it was a cut-and-dried case," Judy recalled. "He promised that he would find Jami within six months. He said, 'No problem.' "

The P.I. traced Steve Sherer's battered Blazer to the Deep South, where he arranged to have a private lab test the rig for blood. There were positive reactions, which meant only that someone had shed blood in Steve's Blazer. After so long, it was impossible to determine whose blood it was or even whether it was animal or human blood. The sample wasn't large enough, and it had been years since Jami vanished.

For all anyone knew, Jami Hagel might never have bled at all. She was so delicate that it wouldn't have taken much to strangle her or break her neck.

"That first P.I. took our money," Judy said, "but he didn't find Jami—didn't come close. He found out it wasn't as cut-and-dried as he thought."

Stung once but desperate to have some closure to their pain, the Hagels hired another private investigator. Allegedly, this man was a retired FBI agent. That seemed to them to qualify him as a superior investigator. "We paid him, too," Judy recalled, "and nothing happened. I told him that I felt sure there were friends and family connected to Steve who knew more than they were admitting and asked him to interview them. That day, I'd even taken a thousand dollars in cash with me to pay him because he said what I wanted would cost more than we'd already given him. But that wasn't enough either. The next day, I went back and gave him two thousand dollars. I waited a few days before I called to see if he'd learned anything. His phone was disconnected! He took our money and left us hanging."

Judy and Jerry Hagel never accepted that whoever had killed Jami—and they finally had to believe that she was dead—would escape punishment. The Hagels were awarded custody of Chris and raised him as they had raised their own four children. But Judy and her family had lost a good deal of faith in the system.

Judy Hagel, attractive, slender, and blond, was worn down from years of waiting and dashed hopes, and she was quietly angry that her daughter could disappear and apparently no one cared enough to try to find her.

By February 1997, Judy was out of patience. How could the world simply go on without Jami—or at least some acknowledgment that her daughter was important enough to merit a continuous investigation until her killer was arrested?

Three months later, Dr. Donald Reay, the King County Medical Examiner, officially declared Jami Hagel Sherer dead. He wasn't uncaring—not at all—but it had been almost seven years, and there were no indications at all that Jami still lived.

Judy Hagel marched down to the Redmond Police Department with fire in her eyes. "I've *had* it! Why doesn't *someone* try to find my daughter?" she demanded.

* * *

The City of Redmond had grown tremendously between 1990 and 2000, and there was a new city hall and police station. Most of the original detectives who had searched for Jami Sherer had retired or moved on to other departments or other professions. Sergeant Butch Watson had become a massage therapist. Detective Steve Hardwick was an investigator for an insurance company. They had given the investigation into Jami's disappearance their best efforts and anything more seemed futile.

In January 1997, Lieutenant James Taylor was appointed to head the major crimes unit of the Redmond Police Department. J.W.B. Taylor isn't easy to describe. More Irish than the Kennedy family, Taylor's unit is almost booby-trapped with Irish paraphernalia that would intimidate the stoutest Scandinavian—of which there are many in Seattle. Taylor marches with the Greater Seattle Pipe Band in kilt and full regalia, equally adept at bagpipes and drums. In August 2000 the Seattle group joined 10,000 other pipers and drummers in the Millennium March Past the Castle in Edinburgh, Scotland, to raise funds for the Marie Curie Cancer Nursing Service. Taylor's mother and father had marched the same royal mile fifty-eight years earlier with the Canadian and British forces, and his grandfather had marched one hundred years ago with the Gordon Highlanders.

In addition to being a police lieutenant, Taylor is a special agent with the Coast Guard Investigative Services, a board member of the American Association of Chiefs of Police, and a member of a task force that specializes in investigating Asian gang crime. As an investigator, he is also as stubborn as they come. He listened to Judy Hagel's harangue with interest—and sympathy. Like everyone else in his department he knew of the disappearance of Jami Sherer, although he had been head of a traffic unit at the time she vanished. Now he pulled out the file on Jami Sherer and committed it to memory. The fact that it had been deemed an impossible case was probably what challenged him the most.

"I went down to where Judy Hagel worked," Taylor said, remembering his first visit to the car dealership where Judy manned the front desk. "I introduced myself and told her I'd been reviewing the case for a few months and that I thought it was solvable."

"She didn't trust me," he recalled. "She looked at me as if she had heard too many promises before and she didn't believe anything. I told her I'd prove her wrong."

He didn't say *when* he'd prove her wrong because he had no idea how long it was going to take. And he didn't say *how* because he didn't know yet exactly how he was going to do it, but Taylor knew he *would* do it. "Judy Hagel was angry and upset at the whole Redmond Police Department, and she vented some at me. I didn't blame her. She said, 'I supplied you people with information. I told you what happened, and you never did anything with it. I even walked through the house with you and pointed out clues, and the officer with me just overlooked them.' "

Judy told Taylor that the first year Jami was gone, she cried out loud every night for her lost daughter. "After that, over the next years, when I went to bed, I cried in my heart."

She looked directly into Taylor's eyes. "Do you know what happened to my daughter?"

"Yes, I do," Taylor answered.

"What?"

"Your daughter is dead."

"Yes," Judy said quietly. "I know."

"But," Taylor promised her, "I will do my very, very best to determine how it happened, who did it, and—if we can—hold them responsible."

In the hour that Judy spent telling Taylor of her frustrations, he heard several aspects of the case and bits of information that were new to him. Perhaps they were buried somewhere in the thick file on Jami Sherer and he had missed them. Perhaps not. "What you need to do," he said to Judy, "is to sit down like you're writing a college thesis and, once again, tell me *everything,* everything at all that you told the police department that you feel perhaps we overlooked."

A few weeks later, Jim Taylor received a package in the mail: a written record of Judy Hagel's seven years of suspicion, frustration, and unending loss.

Winning alliances are often composed of disparate components. Hundreds of people had looked for Jami and her killer. Now seven would join forces to avenge her:

Three cops.

Three prosecutors.

And one bloodhound.

Jim Taylor had two young detectives in mind, men he had known since the days when he had commanded them in the traffic division and on patrol: Greg Mains, age forty-seven, and Mike Faddis, thirty-two. Mains was deceptively quiet and looked nothing at all like a homicide detective. Neither did Mike Faddis, a tall, gregarious man with the shoulders of a fullback. Taylor asked them what they remembered about Jami Sherer, and Faddis said quietly, "I was there when they found her car. It's been a long time."

Jim Taylor recruited Greg Mains and Mike Faddis

for a three-year investigation that would take them all around America and even outside the country. If they couldn't find Jami herself, he wanted them to bring him enough evidence to convict her killer.

He asked them to begin with the file that existed on Jami Sherer. "Now," he said, tapping it with his finger, "I don't care if this is true or this is true. I want you to take me to the file and prove that what's in it is fact—or it's not true. I want you to read Judy Hagel's summary and tell me if what she says is true or not. And that's how we're going to start."

Greg Mains and Mike Faddis went through the 1990–1991 file and began to flesh out information that had come in just after Jami Sherer vanished.

"I wanted to be able to give Judy Hagel some hope by our next visit . . . to tell her we were aggressively pursuing it, but there would be no guarantees," Taylor said. "Even if we were able to arrest someone, it wouldn't be a given that they would be convicted."

For the first time in a very long time, Judy trusted the people investigating her daughter's case. As Greg Mains and Mike Faddis began dropping by to check in with her every other day or so, Judy began to believe that somehow, some way, Jami would finally have justice.

Taylor meant it when he said he wanted Faddis and Mains to pursue every avenue. "I don't care how much money you spend," he told them, "or how long you have to work on it. If I come to work on a Monday and hear you got a tip Friday night that was important to this case, and that tip was in Boston or Paris, you had better have been to Boston or Paris and back by the time I see you—or you're fired."

The two detectives took him at his word and got tips from as far away as Bogotá, Colombia. They never got to Paris, but they did follow leads in California, Arizona, North Carolina, Hawaii, Wisconsin, British Columbia, Germany, and all over the Northwest.

Taylor's part-time assignment as a special agent with the Coast Guard requires him to do background checks on individuals. He has learned a dozen ways to work back through people's lives and find out who they really are. He decided to send out Greg Mains and Mike Faddis—and whoever else he could pull off other cases, if only temporarily—to find out everything they could about the last man Jami was with: her husband, Steven Sherer.

"We are going to do an autopsy on Steve Sherer's life," Taylor told them, "and we're going to find out everything we can about every phase of his life, starting with the day he was born. I've found out you can see patterns early: if you find a reasonably good kid in junior high and high school, he's probably going to be a good man. If you start to find negative behavior patterns and negative attitudes about truth and the law in high school, you often find an adult criminal later."

One of the other six members on the fresh team investigating Jami Hagel's disappearance was King County Assistant Prosecuting Attorney Marilyn Brenneman. When she first encountered the Sherer case, Brenneman had already successfully prosecuted more than her share of criminally manipulative males. It was Brenneman who prosecuted Randy Roth, the serial wife killer I wrote about in *A Rose for Her Grave*. Another of her successful cases trapped a con man who made millions of dollars by stripping Washington beaches of one of their prime resources: the mammoth geoduck clams. Brenneman also closed down the

Monastery, a nightclub that lured children and young teens into drugs, prostitution—and worse. When she was pregnant with her son Adam, her co-prosecutor was her husband Phil Brenneman. "It had to be the 'Love Beds Scam' case," she said, laughing. That was the name the prosecutor's office gave to a chain of phony water-bed stores set up to get around a statute that closed down prostitution masquerading as massage parlors. Instead of "masseuses" in the windows; the water-bed stores had scantily dressed women offering "demonstrations" of how the water beds worked.

"There I sat," Marilyn Brenneman recalled, "very visibly pregnant. To keep the jurors from giggling at a husband-wife prosecuting team in a case like that, Phil did the legwork while I did the courtroom work."

After prosecuting so many woman-killers and bunco artists, nobody would have blamed Brenneman for distrusting all men, but nothing could be further from the truth. She and Phil are happily married, and he now heads the Civil Enforcement Unit for the city of Seattle, while she's mother to a blended brood of four sons—hers, his, and theirs. Although she came to the law in an era when the profession was far more fraternity than sorority, Marilyn Brenneman rolled up her sleeves and plunged into cases that involved stakeouts, death threats, and endless days working beside both female and male detectives. Still, even today she occasionally encounters the good-old-boy syndrome, where male attorneys pontificate that "little ladies" shouldn't worry themselves about bloody homicide.

Such comments roll off her back, and she just laughs when defense attorneys patronizingly call her Marilyn rather than Ms. Brenneman. She knows the jurors aren't fooled by this ploy.

She was raised on St. Simons Island off the coast of Georgia, but she went to school on the mainland in Brunswick. Her dad was an auto mechanic who repaired police cars. He built himself a Ford with the biggest engine around, and often tested its police intercept engine on the straight flat roads of the Georgia coast, sending up a plume of red clay dust as he revved up to 150 miles an hour.

"I was a teenager bent on growing up fast," Marilyn said. "When I was about sixteen, I took my dad's car out and I was hitting over 150 miles an hour too. I was busted when the local cops told my dad they'd seen him out driving—and he knew he hadn't been that day, that it must have been me. He traded in the car he loved for a 1965 powder-blue Mustang with a six-cylinder engine. It wouldn't go very fast, but it looked great. That was the car my mother and I shared. I probably drove my parents crazy."

Like most teenagers, Marilyn Brenneman believed in her own immortality. "Today I can connect with my victims," she says, "because I understand that a woman can get into a relationship without any idea of the consequences. They are sure that nothing bad can happen to them. They can't believe that someone they've been intimate with could kill them. I made my share of bad decisions too," Brenneman admitted, "but I had an angel on my shoulder, and my victims didn't."

For the past two decades, Marilyn Brenneman has worked in the Special Operations Unit of the King County prosecutor's office. It says "Fraud Division" on the door, but the three deputy prosecutors there—Hank Corscadden, Susan Story, and Marilyn Brenneman—work everything from bunco to murder. They also advise police departments who need another opinion, and they often actually prosecute the cases.

In 1990, Marilyn Brenneman read about Jami Sherer's disappearance as did most people of western Washington. But the Special Operations Unit of the King County prosecutor's office doesn't go out looking for business; they are available to police agencies for consultations and for advice, *if* they are asked. "If we could," Marilyn said, "we wanted to be in on a case from the beginning—to brainstorm and form game plans with the investigators. I know I'm always asking the detectives for more—and more again, even when they've brought me piles of statements and evidence. And they do."

Brenneman met once or twice with some of the Redmond investigators who were working on the Sherer case in 1991, but they didn't ask for further help. In truth, as the months passed and they deemed it an unsolvable case, they saw no point in brainstorming with the prosecutor's office. Without a body, the case died of inertia. Entries in the case file became fewer and fewer and further apart.

There were plenty of cases for the Special Unit to work on. Marilyn Brenneman never forgot about Jami Sherer, but her disappearance was filed somewhere in the back of the prosecutor's mind while she went on to more active cases.

In 1997, Jim Taylor contacted Marilyn Brenneman and asked for her assistance. "I knew it was going to be almost impossible," Brenneman said, "to try and find Jami Sherer and her killer—because I always believed she was dead—but it was something I couldn't turn away from. Sometimes you have to do something simply because it's the right thing to do."

The Jami Sherer case was probably the most daunting case Marilyn Brenneman ever took on. Few prosecutors relish homicide cases without bodies. Most people think corpus delicti refers to the corpse of the victim, but, in truth, it means the body of the *case,* which is made up of all the circumstantial and physical evidence gathered by the investigators, the witnesses, the profiles of the principal characters, and the motivation behind the crime. Physical evidence can be seen, touched, smelled, by a jury. Circumstantial evidence, however, can be just as strong if there are enough factors present to lead a reasonable person to believe there is far more than coincidence involved when a number of circumstances combine to point to a suspect as guilty.

The detectives who had worked the Jami Sherer disappearance seven years earlier had done a yeomanlike job as far as they went, but Jim Taylor and Marilyn Brenneman believed that much remained hidden. As Mains and Faddis brought in the first fragments of new information, they all began to weave a spiderweb of information and evidence, with each new contact a strand that linked with other strands until, they all hoped, they would catch a suspect firmly in the center.

One of the first things Taylor, Faddis, and Mains did was to list the names of Jami's high school classmates. They then added Judy Hagel's list of everyone Jami had known in her life. "We sent letters to every one of them," Taylor said, "asking 'Have you heard from Jami since the end of September 1990?' and even though no one had seen her, we got leads out of the answers to our letters."

They conferred with a prosecutor in Marion County, Oregon—Diane Middle—and Alan Scharn, a lead detective who had successfully prosecuted a double murder case with no bodies found. "We got tips from them and expanded on them," Mike Faddis said.

The Redmond detectives didn't want to make the mistake that the Boulder Police Department had when they refused assistance from other agencies as they investigated the JonBenét Ramsey murder. Boulder hadn't investigated a homicide for two decades before the Ramsey case, and by the time they acknowledged that they needed expert advice, their crime scene was contaminated, and it was too late.

Of course, there *was* no crime scene in the Sherer case. No one knew where—or if—Jami had died. But everyone was heartened when Mains and Faddis uncovered one detail that had been overlooked by the original investigators. Steve Sherer had replaced some carpeting in the lower level of his house—in an area where the rug was almost brand new. There was no rational reason for him to have patched the carpet there. They set out to find the workman who had installed it.

It was a start. And if they had one new direction to go, they knew there would be others.

Legally, Jami was dead. But how could they prove that to a jury? It wasn't going to be as simple as saying she met the legal time limit for a missing person to be construed as deceased.

A forensic anthropologist told them that their chances of finding any identifiable part of Jami Sherer's body were slim to none. In Washington State, where the rocky clay soil challenges gardeners who attempt to dig down more than 12 to 18 inches, all graves are shallow graves. Unless the weather is freezing cold, the detectives learned that a body buried a foot or slightly more beneath the surface or left *on* the surface in some isolated wilderness could completely disintegrate within twenty-eight days! When the soft tissue is gone, little animals carry away small bones and large animals take the femurs and humeri and skull.

The trail was seven years cold, but to these detectives, that didn't matter. They would make up the seven years. Among them, Jim Taylor, Greg Mains, and Mike Faddis had nearly seventy years of experience in law enforcement, with Faddis, the "rookie," having only a decade on the Redmond Police Force. Taylor had thirty-one years in police work, and Mains twenty-seven. "All of us had tremendous curiosity," Taylor said. "And my detectives were totally focused; Greg Mains was like a bulldog who got his teeth into something, and he was never going to let go."

One of the best things they had going for them was the fact that Mike Faddis was currently assigned to the Puget Sound Violent Crimes Task Force. This was an innovative way to let Seattle area law enforcement agencies pool their resources—and their officers—to wage war on crime. It allowed the agencies instant access to each other's personnel and special knowledge. There were six FBI special agents, four Seattle Police detectives, two King County sheriff's detectives, and representatives from the Secret Service; Alcohol, Tobacco, and Firearms; the Drug Enforcement Administration; and a number of small-town police departments in the area.

Mike Faddis had been tapped to represent Redmond on the Violent Crimes Task Force. The task force goals were to cut down on the bank robberies that put Seattle at the top of the list in America for such crimes and to bring closure to a number of unsolved homicides in the Puget Sound area—including the case of Jami Sherer. Having Faddis in the task force opened up information opportunities that the Redmond Police Department had

ANN RULE

never before had. The computer age had opened up a whole new world of information, and Mike Faddis was now able to utilize it in the search for Jami.

Jim Taylor's network of police contacts was prodigious, and it was almost uncanny the way he could pick up a phone and find an old friend willing to assist in tracking Steve Sherer. When he needed a surveillance on Steve in Scottsdale, Arizona, Taylor called Norm Beasley, who was a colonel in the Arizona State Police and a fellow member of the board of the International Association of Chiefs of Police. Beasley told Taylor, "Just tell me what you need."

Beasley had Steve under watchful eyes by the next morning, in a sporadic surveillance operation that continued for fourteen months. Whenever Steve moved, Greg Mains was blocking his path, although Steve didn't always know that. When Mains found an important witness in Southern Pines, North Carolina, Taylor realized that yet another member of the IACP board was the chief of police in Southern Pines: Gerald Galloway. "He told me he had been to a breakfast with the woman [the witness] that morning," Taylor marveled. "She had been in Jami's wedding party, and all Jerry had to do was run down to the bank where she worked!"

It was as if Mains and Faddis and Taylor were meant to solve this case. And of course the contacts Taylor had maintained for three decades were vitally important. If they needed surveillance of Steve Sherer's travels outside Washington, they had it. If they needed to find women he had been in touch with since Jami disappeared, Jim Taylor could usually come up with an associate who could get the information within hours. He got help from Two Rivers, Wisconsin, and Palm Springs, California, and many spots in between. Of the ten people who attended IACP committee meetings with Taylor, three had access to exactly what the Redmond investigators needed.

Greg Mains and Mike Faddis had no idea how many people they would eventually talk to: not dozens but hundreds. Starting with the original case file, school yearbooks, old neighborhoods, Microsoft co-workers, friends, friends of friends, old tips, and new tips, Taylor wanted them to follow up every single lead with the full expectation that they would find more. "Even if you get nothing from a contact but the name of another person to talk to," he told them, "you've got another place to go, and another and another . . . or at the very least, you know you've checked that lead and proved that it ended nowhere."

In the end, Greg Mains and Mike Faddis would talk to more than three hundred people in their search for Jami Sherer.

The Redmond investigators knew they had to find enough information to convince Marilyn Brenneman that she had a case solid enough to take before an inquiry judge—the Washington State counterpart of a grand jury. Just as in a grand jury session, witnesses would be called, many of whom had devoutly hoped that the search for Jami was over and that suspicion was no longer focused on Steve.

But that wasn't going to happen.

Finding Jami Sherer's killer began as Greg Mains and Mike Faddis's occupation, but it would become their avocation, and then their obsession. Steve Sherer was in the crosshairs of their microscope of Jami's life, but they were also looking for Lew Adams. He had moved away from Seattle. They eventually found him in Idaho, and as before, his involvement with drugs made him anxious. He still felt guilt over Jami, but he was willing to testify against Steve Sherer if it came to that.

What Mike Faddis and Greg Mains eventually uncovered was amazing. Much of it came about because of hard work and some of it by luck.

But perhaps some of it came through angels.

11

In order to establish that Jami had not simply run away and begun a new life somewhere, the Redmond detectives contacted every state to see if, after September 30, 1990, Jami Sherer or Jami Hagel had applied for a driver's license or for unemployment benefits or welfare. She had not. She hadn't filed an income tax return, used her credit cards, or tried to get new credit cards. She had not attempted to get a passport. She had never touched her bank accounts. In the past seven years, no one had ever done a credit check on her. She had never been arrested. There were no death certificates in her name in any state.

All human beings—who are still alive—leave paper trails. But Jami Sherer left no trail at all.

Taylor, Faddis, and Mains called police departments all over the Northwest to see if they had found any unidentified bodies. "It was interesting," Taylor said. "Often the police departments told us they had no bodies that were unaccounted for, but when we called the coroners' offices, they often said, 'Yeah, we do,' so we checked a lot of those out. Maybe a dog had brought in bones, or someone had found a skeleton we could compare to what we knew about Jami."

They had Jami's dental records, medical records from knee surgery she once had, and the information from her breast augmentation surgery. They had blood samples from Judy and Jerry Hagel and from Chris Sherer for mitochondrial DNA testing. "We also had some of Jami's hair," Taylor said. "Judy had asked for years to have Jami's things. Finally Steve gave her a box of things, all taped shut. It sat in Judy's garage until Greg Mains and Mike Faddis opened it to inventory it, and Jami's hairbrush was in there—with strands of her hair caught in it."

But none of the bodies or bones they checked matched the information they had on Jami Hagel Sherer.

As the two Redmond detectives expanded their investigation, they found more and more incidents between Steve and the police. They contacted every police department in western Washington to see if their officers had ever stopped Steve Sherer or someone using one of his three aliases. Even when they weren't on duty, Mains and Faddis dropped in at police stations all across the state. "Greg got so he wouldn't take a vacation," Jim Taylor said, "without stopping to check at every little department on his route to see if they recognized Steve."

And they found more arrests, mostly for drunken or reckless driving. Again and again they heard, "When Steve drinks, he's a crazy man with a terrible temper. He's out of control."

One of the problems with potential witnesses to Jami's fate initially was that they were afraid of Sherer.

But years had passed and people who had stories to tell about Steve had grown up. "Many witnesses with key information—through the process of becoming more mature—became responsible," Faddis said, "and came forward. Some were just too afraid to say anything. For others, the more they thought about their interaction with Sherer, the more their memories started to click."

They noted that Bettina Rauschberg's name appeared frequently in Steve's rap sheet. She was the girlfriend just before Jami. When Greg Mains talked to her, he realized she was still terribly afraid of Steve. But Bettina finally opened up and told Mains how often she had feared Steve was going to kill her. She gave Mains the name of the woman who had befriended her in Balboa Beach years before.

Interestingly, when Mains located Marj Tuttle* and said he was calling about Bettina Rauschberg, Marj gasped. She told him, "When I heard you were calling about Bettina, and that you were a detective, I knew it was an almost absolute certainty that the reason you were calling me was to let me know she had been killed. . . . I was wondering if she had died back then [1984] or recently and he had dumped her body."

It had been five years since Marj had seen Bettina, but she remembered a grotesque encounter with Steve Sherer very clearly. From her description of Bettina, she might have been describing Jami. "She was a very pretty girl, very thin . . . real young," Marj recalled of the girl she met at the accounting firm where they both worked. "I believe she was nineteen years old then, with blond, very curly, long hair. She took very good care of herself. She was a really nice, sweet—a very innocent— young girl."

Marj, who was twenty-six at the time she met Bettina, told Mains that Bettina had come to work with a black eye. "She said her boyfriend had hit her."

Marj said she'd met Bettina's boyfriend only once and described Steve Sherer as "blond-haired and very good-looking. Back in those days we called 'em surfer dudes."

After she'd been beaten and left with a black eye, Bettina had accepted an offer to move in with Marj and her husband. "She drove her own car and followed me to get her things. I remember we walked into her apartment and there were small stuffed animals and dolls lying there with their heads cut off. There was a butcher knife there on the floor."

It was a huge butcher knife, Marj told Mains, bigger than any she had ever seen, and she was sure it was sharp enough to cut off someone's head.

Marj thought there must have been forty little toy animals and about a dozen dolls scattered around, their little heads rolling. Most of all, she remembered the note: "It said, 'If you ever leave me, that's what I'm going to do to you—cut your head off the same way.' "

Marj said that Bettina hadn't been intimidated into staying—not at that point. She had followed Marj and her husband and daughter to their house and stayed with them for a few weeks. But then Bettina's mother had become concerned because Marj was a Jehovah's Witness.

"I don't think her mom really understood the situation," Marj said. "I was a complete stranger to her and she evidently knew Steve. She encouraged Bettina to go back to her boyfriend and move back to Washington. She left within a day or two and went home. And I never heard from her again after that. I was always afraid of what might have happened to her."

Marj was sad for Jami, a woman she never knew, but she was relieved that it was not Bettina who was dead. Marj reiterated, "I remember making the statement to my husband, 'She'll probably wind up dead if she goes back to him.' "

Bettina was still alive, but Greg Mains could see she dreaded coming face-to-face with Steve again. In one of his interviews with her, Bettina told Mains how cruel Steve had been to Jami in the mid-eighties when he was going back and forth between Jami and her. If she had ever been jealous of Jami, Bettina said she got over that quickly and was simply grateful to be free— and alive. "One time we were all in my spare bedroom," Bettina recalled, "and he said he wanted to come back to me. Jami was upset and crying. He just picked up a vase or something and hit Jami on the head with it."

After Jami disappeared, Bettina said she had seen Steve twice. "Once I ran into him in a video store and he came up to me and grabbed my arm. He said he really needed to talk to me. He started talking about Chris, and saying, 'He's a nice boy, he'd like you.' I told him, 'Get away from me!' "

Bettina saw Steve again at the Flamingos in the Alderwood Mall in Lynnwood, and he was obviously very drunk. "He was crying," she remembered, "and saying that Jami hated me. I don't think she did. He was talking about her disappearance and he said, 'A drug dealer probably got her.' "

Bettina ran from the club, but before she could get her car started, Steve jumped in. "I had a charcoal Mazda RX7, like Jami's, and Steve said, 'You stole Jami's car.' Then he kept saying, 'I never meant to hurt you. . . . I never meant to hurt Jami. . . . I never meant to hurt you.'

"He told me what he'd said before—that he believed a drug dealer probably got her."

The Redmond investigators also talked to Sara Smith, the wife of Steve's old friend, the woman who had eaten pizza with Jami the year before she died. Jami had opened up to Sara, telling her how miserable she was with Steve.

"Jami and Steve came to our wedding in August 1990," Sara told Greg Mains and Mike Faddis. "And I talked to Steve two weeks after Jami disappeared. He called me between 1:00 and 2:00 A.M. and said he was lonely and how much he loved Jami. He told me he thought Jami might have been kidnapped. And then he said, 'We probably wouldn't have anything in common to have an affair.' I was taken aback! He said that he and Jami had a good sex life, and he missed the sex."

Sara had only been married for two months, and Steve was slyly suggesting she have an affair with him. When Sara turned him down, he asked for her sister's phone number.

As one source passed them on to another, Mains and Faddis realized that Steve Sherer probably tried to pick up almost every attractive woman he encountered. The two detectives reported to Lieutenant Jim Taylor that their investigation was turning up more and more women whom Steve had approached for dates. Most men would have been out searching for their missing wives, but not Steve Sherer. Within two weeks of "losing" his wife, Steve had begun to date other women. He had evidently approached women from his past, his friends' wives, and their girlfriends first.

One woman contacted the Redmond police with a rather bizarre story. "I went on one date with him—that Steve Sherer," she said.

"When?"

"In 1990—in November, I believe."

The woman, Margaret Ryan,* had an amazingly precise memory. She recalled that she had taken her car, a red Corvette, to be washed on a Wednesday. She knew it was a Wednesday because it was two days after that when she had her one and only date with Steve Sherer. He had been driving an S-10 Blazer two-tone, blue-and-white. Margaret knew cars, and her own car was a classic. Paradoxically, she was a woman who looked more like a spinster librarian than a car buff. Nevertheless, Steve smiled at her as she stood at the car wash desk waiting for her key.

"It was pretty busy, and he just came up and started talking to me—said hi and introduced himself. And we talked—you know, small talk," she said. "But he asked me if I wanted to go on a date sometime, and he seemed nice. So I said yes."

They exchanged phone numbers, and although they had spoken for only ten or fifteen minutes, Steve called Margaret that very evening. She could not remember the spot, but she arranged to met him someplace on Friday night. She got in his Blazer and he headed toward a residential neighborhood in Redmond. He was taking her to his house. As they drove, he told her that he was a recent widower and that he had lost his wife in a car accident.

Steve's voice faltered, and she supposed that the death of his wife was a very emotional subject so she didn't pursue it.

He pulled into a driveway of a home, but it was very dark outside, so she didn't think she could identify the house again.

"It was a split-level," she said. "I don't remember what color it was, and it had a driveway that was sort of elevated. The living room was on the left and then the dining room right after that and then the kitchen was like right in front." Margaret closed her eyes to remember. "And then we went left. There was a bedroom on the right side that was full of kids' stuff. It was very clean."

She had the floor plan right; that fit the house Steve and Jami had lived in.

She recalled that Steve showed her around, pointing things out, and then led her into the master bedroom. "We just sat on the bed and we were talking."

Steve explained that his child or children—she wasn't sure how many—were at their grandmother's house. He soon began to talk about his wife. "I was wearing a pearl necklace at the time, and he told me that it wasn't real, after he rubbed a pearl on his tooth. And he said he would show me a real pearl necklace. So he went into a closet. He pulled out a pearl necklace and told me that was real and he had bought that for his wife."

At that point, she said, Steve teared up and began to sob. "He was talking about his ex-wife or dead wife or whatever," Margaret said. "And then he brought up the subject of a heart, a diamond heart necklace that he had bought her and went to the closet and took it out and showed it to me, and he got very emotional."

It wasn't the best first date Margaret Ryan had ever had. Steve seemed to her to be not only grief-stricken but somehow guilty. That was the only way she could explain it.

After he showed her the diamond pendant and stopped sobbing, Steve surprised Margaret by lunging at her as she sat on the bed. He pushed her backward and kissed her hard on the lips. "I got bad vibes," she said, "because of the forcefulness of it. I decided that this was not a comfortable situation for me."

When she stood up from the bed and said, "Let's go," Steve stopped trying to force himself on her. They left his house and went out to eat at Azteca, a Mexican restaurant.

Steve never called her for another date, which was fine with Margaret. She didn't think about him again for years, until she saw his face on television in connection with the reopening of the investigation into his wife's disappearance.

Since he had told her several times that his wife had died in a car crash, she was surprised that he was being investigated for the possibility that he had murdered his wife. She was also troubled, of course. Margaret Ryan suffered from agoraphobia, from the Greek for "fear of the marketplace" or, in modern terms, fear of leaving home. Margaret had taken a chance by accepting a date with Steve Sherer, and that had done nothing at all to alleviate her panic attacks.

Over the years since Jamie was gone, Steve became so consumed with meeting women that he almost seemed to suffer from satyriasis, an obsessive and often uncontrollable sexual desire in men, similar to nymphomania in women. Greg Mains and Mike Faddis learned that Steve was a member of several singles clubs on the east side. He also spent a lot of time on his computer making contacts with women all over the world.

He had leaped upon Margaret Ryan only moments after he sobbed at the sight of Jami's diamond heart pendant. Apparently he used any line that he thought would work to add to his roster of women. Was he really grieving for Jami? Or was he posing as a bereaved widower just to soften women up?

Grieving widowers are lonely, but most of them wait

a respectful length of time before they seek out female companionship. Steve Sherer had never shown grief, sadness, or loneliness about losing Jami. The only mourning anyone had noted was for Steve himself, as he asked why such a tragedy should have happened to *him*. Never once had he voiced sorrow or concern for Jami, or for Chris over the loss of his mother. Jami's friend Lisa Cryder had seen Steve out partying with a girl only weeks after Jami's disappearance.

It was abundantly clear that Steve had used the disappearance of his wife in an attempt to turn himself into a "babe magnet," the forlorn widower who needed love. He attracted women all right, but in doing so, he had made some significant mistakes.

12

There was another aspect of the Sherer case that the Redmond investigators found disturbing. Within a month of Jami's disappearance, Steve, who was unemployed, as he often was, applied for Jami's last paychecks, her accumulated vacation pay and her sick pay at Microsoft. He received a check for the full amount. One of the perks at Microsoft was the stock offered to its employees. Jami had taken advantage of that and had begun buying company stock on December 12, 1987. Records showed she had bought more whenever she could: June 16, 1988; December 7, 1988; December 12, 1989; and June 30, 1990. Up through

1989 it had been possible to change ownership or add payees by e-mail. At one time Jami had asked to have Steve's name removed from the stock certificates, but she later put him back on.

So Steve was able to cash in a number of Microsoft stock certificates within a month or so of Jami's disappearance.

In November 1990, Sherri Schielke moved Jami's Microsoft stock—the collateral Jami had put up for their house loan the previous spring—into her own stock account. At that point, Microsoft was trading stock at under three dollars a share, and Jami had many, many shares. Sherri explained that Steve was out of work and that she had been making the mortgage payments on his house, since Jami was no longer around to pay them. Steve retained some of Jami's Microsoft stock.

Without the wife who had supported him for four years, Steve was having financial trouble. In early December he asked Judy Hagel if she would loan him $15,000 to "clear up Jami's credit." It was an outrageous request. Judy knew that Jami always kept current on her bills and that she also saved receipts, bills, and all manner of documents that would validate her yearly IRS forms. Judy had co-signed with Jami so she could buy her Mazda RX7 because Steve's credit was worth nothing. There was simply no way Judy would lend Steve $15,000.

Evidently, he went to his mother too. Sherri suggested that he rent out part of the house to help him make the mortgage payments. He rented one bedroom to a man who soon moved out. Next, a couple named Troy and Pam moved in. They told the Redmond detectives that they remembered a tanning bed in the garage, and also several boxes stored there. Troy never went through the boxes, but Pam was curious. She found they were full of women's clothing and other feminine items. Steve told her she could take anything she wanted. She took a few pieces of clothing, but most of them were far too small for her. The couple didn't stay in Steve's house for long.

Seven months after Jami vanished, Sherri Schielke retained an attorney so that she could be named trustee and manage Jami's estate. The Hagels were looking after Chris, and spending as much as they could afford to pay to the private investigators who were, shockingly, taking cruel advantage of them. They assumed that whatever Jami had owned would come to her son, to pay for his education and for the things he needed as he grew up. Still, they hoped that Jami was alive somewhere, and that was what mattered the most to them. They were unsophisticated about financial matters.

Sherri Schielke published an announcement in several small newspapers that she intended to take over Jami's assets as her trustee. The probate matter was filed in King County Superior Court, which noted that "the Court being fully advised in these premises: the Court finding that notice having been published and the whereabouts of the absentee remain unknown and cannot be ascertained."

Responding to Sherri's attorney's motion, "In the matter of the estate of Jami Sue Sherer, Absentee," Sherri's request was granted: "(1) It is hereby ordered that Sharon Schielke be appointed trustee of the Absentee Estate of Jami Sue Sherer; (2) That trustee shall file an oath for faithful performance of duties and shall prepare an inventory of the estate and file such within sixty days of the date of this order."

The date was May 17, 1991.

Both Steve and Sherri were anxious to retrieve the diamond ring and watch that had been found taped on the console in Jami's car. The police had had the ring appraised and knew that it was now worth $13,500. The watch, worth $1,700, and Jami's Mazda were being held in evidence by the Redmond Police Department, which galled Steve and his mother.

On June 10, Sherri wrote to inform the Redmond Police Department that she was now the trustee of Jami's estate. "It is my understanding that you are still holding her wedding ring and also her car, which is a Mazda RX7. In order to have these appraised, I will need to have them released. Could you get back to me as soon as possible regarding this matter? Thanks for your cooperation."

To Steve's chagrin, the police were not very cooperative and the items of value were not returned to him or his mother. Nor was the Department of Social and Human Services eager to decide on permanent placement of Chris Sherer. Legally, Chris's mother was not dead. He was being well cared for by his maternal grandparents. It was far too soon to grant custody of Chris to anyone.

By 1992, Sherri decided that she and Steve should sell the Education Hill house, and it was purchased by Russian immigrants. Part of the proceeds of the sale went to Sherri, to pay off the mortgage and Steve's bills. When he never paid his mother back for her loss on the house, she sued him in civil court for $32,000. It was a business matter. Sherri had a good head for business, and Steve apparently took no offense at the suit.

When Jim Taylor, Mike Faddis, and Greg Mains came aboard the Sherer case, one of the things that bothered them the most was how soon Jami had been virtually swept under the rug. Her assets were under her mother-in-law's supervision, Steve was giving her clothing away to anyone who wanted it, and her child's permanent placement was under contention long before it was time. For Steve and some members of his family, it was like "Jami's gone, let's get on with our lives with as little fuss as possible."

Sherri had apparently always had a very tight mother-child bond with her oldest child. Whatever Steve did, she backed him up, although she didn't count on him to take care of her house in Mill Creek. Despite his protestations that he had been there on September 30, 1990, to mail packages, leave a mortgage check and generally oversee things, Faddis and Mains learned that it was invariably her daughters, Saundra and Laura, who were given keys to their mother's house in Mill Creek.

There had apparently been two incidents where Steve got inside the Schielkes' home when they were out of town, but it hadn't been with a key. The front door of the Mill Creek house was flanked by narrow panels of glass. Once Sherri came home to find shards and sprinkles of glass in the foyer, although the window itself had been repaired. The detectives learned there had also been a second broken window, one that was repaired so neatly that even Sherri never realized it.

Mains and Faddis discovered that on the Sunday Jami disappeared, Steve did not have a key to Sherri and Wally's house in Mill Creek. The only way he could have gotten in was to shatter the glass panels again. The Redmond detectives didn't hear this from Sherri; she was very defensive about Steve.

Lieutenant Jim Taylor suggested that Mike Faddis and Greg Mains look into David Sherer's alleged suicide in Palm Desert. At first, the Riverside County Sheriff's Office couldn't locate any records of the incident. Officially, it might never have happened; there was no file on it in the sheriff's office. Finally, they found a death certificate and a two-page report from a Riverside County coroner's deputy. It said, of course, that the elder Sherer had been alone and depressed on that Thanksgiving Day, and that Sherri Sherer had flown down there and discovered her estranged husband's body.

Judy Hagel told the two detectives that she had always wondered about David Sherer's death, although it had happened a few years before Jami met Steve. She said that Steve had explained it to Jami, who in turn told Judy: "She said Steve told her he was living down there with his dad—to help cheer him up," Judy recalled. "The night David Sherer died, Steve said he told his father he was going out for the evening. And when he came home, he was the one who found the body. The only reason I know that is because Steve confided in Jami. I don't believe he ever thought she would tell me."

When Jami told her mother about this entirely different version of the elder Sherer's death, Judy wondered why on earth Steve would have been down there living with David. She knew from a number of sources that Steve had never gotten along with his father, and Steve had never been the type to rush to anyone's rescue to cheer them up.

Indeed, the detectives learned that Steve told as many versions of how his father had committed suicide as he did about Jami's disappearance. Maybe he was simply a pathological liar; maybe he had other reasons for clouding the details of both incidents.

Mains and Faddis learned that Sherri Sherer had remarried in 1984, less than a year after her first husband died. Her second marriage—to Jack Johnson—lasted only until 1985, but they remained good friends. Greg Mains found that Johnson still lived in Mill Creek, not far from Sherri. Johnson told Mains that David Sherer had been a difficult man to live with—"with a very bad temper, a drunk." He said flatly that Steve and his father had never gotten along. "Steve had a bad temper just like his dad, David, did," Johnson said. "David Sherer was an animal when he was drunk, and Steve is just like him."

Johnson characterized his ex-wife, Sherri, as a "very moral and upstanding person," and told Mains he was friendly with her third husband, Wally Schielke. The men even occasionally golfed together.

Johnson was well acquainted with Jami Sherer, and he was adamant that he knew of no reason why she would disappear.

"Would she ever abandon her son or quit her job and leave without a trace?" Mains asked.

"Jamie would never leave Chris."

"Would she have committed suicide?"

"No way!"

"Why do you think Jami Sherer disappeared?"

"Oh, I believe Steve killed her," Johnson said, almost casually, as if it was a foregone conclusion. He said he suspected that Wally Schielke felt the same way.

Anyone who had seen an example of Steve's temper had come to suspect him in Jami's disappearance.

Although Steve took various jobs from time to time, he seemed to expect a fortune to drop into his lap one day, if not from his gambling then from one of his scams. "He was always on the phone or the computer,"

Judy Hagel commented. "He always had some big deal going."

But in the early nineties, none of Steve's scams seemed to net him much. He sold posters from a sports company he worked for—but he kept the money. One co-worker said, "He was basically scamming under the books. And there was something with snowboards. He was just a scamming kind of a person. Mostly scamming in, like, money and drugs and stuff, because I'd do my share of drugs with him. He did his share of drugs with me. And at the same time, what he was doing was trying to get me involved in it so he didn't have to pay for all of it. You know what I mean?"

After the house on Education Hill was sold, Steve lived in a number of places. He still traveled between Seattle, California, and Arizona, almost always staying in property that his mother owned. Sherri Schielke had sold the country club house where her first husband had died and had bought a more secluded ranch near Palm Springs.

She also had a luxurious condominium in Scottsdale, Arizona, where Steve lived much of the time. Neighbors there didn't see much of Steve, but some of them told Mains and Faddis how chagrined they were when their morning papers began to disappear. Getting up early to play detective, one woman discovered that Steve was tiptoeing out each morning to steal a morning paper before his neighbor could pick it up. She laughed as she told them that the paper thief was always careful to vary his pattern, so that he didn't steal the same condo's paper too many times in a week.

Steve's basic personality hadn't changed. He took what he wanted. He was in his mid-thirties when the investigation into Jami's disappearance began again in earnest, but he acted more like a juvenile delinquent.

Only a small portion of the money realized from the house or from Jami's Microsoft stock went directly to Chris, who was living with the Hagels. Had Jami lived, and kept the Microsoft stock that she gave to Sherri Schielke as collateral, in a decade it would have been worth more than any of Steve's deals. If Jami had simply held on to that $27,000 worth of stock, she would have been one of the company's scores of millionaires. By 2000, Jami's Microsoft stock would have soared and split again and again until its value would have been $928,524! And Steve still retained other shares.

For Chris's sake, Judy maintained a friendly relationship with his other grandmother, and Chris visited Sherri's home occasionally. Sherri and Wally had him over for birthday parties and at Christmastime, and sometimes Chris went on trips to Lake Chelan with his aunts and Sherri and Wally. Less often, he spent time with his father, although it was agreed by everyone that it would be best if he didn't travel alone to visit Steve in Arizona. His grandmother Sherri escorted him on his visits to the Southwest.

He saw Chris infrequently, however. Mains and Faddis learned there was good reason not to leave Chris alone with his father for long. One day, when Chris was about eight, Steve told him that he had business to take care of. They drove out into what was essentially desert. There, Steve left Chris in the car in the hot sun for almost an hour. The boy survived, but apparently Steve hadn't the slightest concern for his son's safety.

Steve lived in Scottsdale most of the time from the mid- to late nineties. He seemed to sense that Jim Taylor, Mike Faddis, and Greg Mains were circling closer and closer. He usually worked as a cabdriver, and he somehow fashioned an I.D. that didn't draw dozens of hits for traffic violations when he applied for an Arizona cabdriver's license. His boss, Joseph Volpe, told the Redmond detectives that a clean driving record was mandatory for their drivers. Volpe said that Steve lived in his mother's home in the Spanish Oaks section of Scottsdale. "One day he told me his son was coming out to visit," Volpe recalled. "He said his mother was bringing him, and then he said, 'My wife was killed in a car crash.' "

Steve's year with the cab company ended abruptly. "One day he called," Volpe said. "He said he'd met some girls and was partying and still drunk. I went to get our car and the pager at his mother's house."

Steve's drinking and drugging continued, making him emotionally chaotic. One night while he was living in Arizona, he called his sister and threatened to kill himself, but the family managed to talk him out of it— if, indeed, he had really intended to take his own life.

There was something peculiar about Steve's travels: He always carried a heavy suitcase with him. It was an old suitcase, made of light blue simulated leather, with wide straps that buckled over the zipper so that the contents were secure. Even during the times when he was without funds and had to ride the bus, Steve lugged that blue suitcase with him.

The only constant they were discovering in Steve Sherer's life was that there *were* no constants. Over the eight years since Jami disappeared, Steve had continued to tell different stories to different people about what had become of his wife. He embroidered the story as the years passed, sometimes showing new acquaintances creased and yellowed newspaper stories about

Jami. He usually varied his accounts of her disappear-ance by sticking to three basic scenarios: Jami had been kidnapped, Jami had been killed in a car accident, or Jami had divorced him. He had a more chilling version, however: he told one friend that Jami was the "last vic-tim of a serial killer."

A Phoenix, Arizona, man told Greg Mains that he knew Steve from playing poker with him at the Casino Arizona in 1998.

"Did he ever talk about his wife?" Mains asked.

"Steve told me that his wife was murdered five or six years ago," the man recalled. "He said the person who did it was in prison."

One woman told Mike Faddis and Greg Mains that she had been romantically involved with Steve's friend Ron Coates in 1990. She and Ron had spent a night at Steve's house during the autumn after Jami disappeared.

"I met Steve at a café. There was another woman there. We went out on Steve's boat." This informant—Victoria—said she and the other woman, Steve's date, later went to buy more beer. During the time they were gone, Ron and Steve evidently did a good deal of talk-ing. Ron was curious after Steve explained that his wife was missing. "He [Ron] was somewhat alarmed about what Steve had told him," Victoria recalled. "Ron told me later, 'I think he did it!' "

Ron Coates went to the top of their list to interview. Mains and Faddis only needed to locate him.

On February 26, 1998, Greg Mains met with a man on the other side of the Cascade Mountains in Yakima, Washington. Alan Aboli* had worked with Steve at a sports merchandise company in Seattle, and they had become friends. "He's a pretty nice person when you meet him. He has a bit of charm, a bit of personality.

He doesn't have any problems getting along with people pretty well. As I got to know him, my vision of him decreased—we'll put it that way. It got worse and worse," Aboli said. "I noticed more and more things he was into: the scamming, the drugs, the women. I basically lost respect for him."

Aboli said Steve usually looked fairly clean-cut and that he bleached his hair blond. He had been the warehouse manager, Aboli's boss.

"Was Steve Sherer married?" Mains asked.

"Yes," Aboli replied, "he was previously married." Then Aboli told Mains that Steve had said, "My wife was the last victim of the Green River Killer."

The Green River Killer was believed to have struck in the Seattle area for the last time in April 1984. Jami, of course, disappeared on September 30, 1990, so that story sounded suspect to both Aboli and Mains.

At the time Aboli visited Steve in his West Seattle apartment, it would have been late 1992. "He said he loved his wife and he missed her," Aboli recalled, "that his son really needed her, and he worried about how his son was gonna be without her."

Aboli also recalled that he and Steve had often socialized outside of work, and especially after Alan took a job in a bar down in Puyallup, Washington. "Steve had dated a lot. I remember one girl named Lisa and one named Monique. He dated both at the same time."

The biggest problem with Steve, Aboli said, was that he was a mean drunk who "made a fool of himself" in bars, insistently trying to pick up women. If a woman turned him down, he got angry. "The drunker he got," Aboli said, "the more of an asshole he became." Aboli said he had been embarrassed to be associated with Steve, especially when he came into the bar where Aboli worked. "When he's drunk, he's a completely different person."

When women did accept Steve's offer to buy them a drink, he characterized himself sometimes as a widower and sometimes as a divorcé. Whatever he told women, he was dating often, meeting women in diverse spots. It didn't seem to matter to him, Aboli said, if they were nice girls or prostitutes, eventually Steve treated them all badly.

Alan Aboli remembered a woman who was a cocktail waitress in a card room at a bowling alley in West Seattle. "They got together a few times and they were apparently getting along pretty well. The third time they got together, they were going to California for a weekend. But she called me up on the phone at work, and said he had left her there. I ended up getting hold of him, and he basically told me he left her there because she was being a bitch. She called me, trying to get back home."

Aboli wired her some money to get home, since she'd been left in the middle of a street, completely without funds, in a strange city.

"Do you have any opinions," Greg Mains asked, "as to what happened to Steven Sherer's wife, Jami Sherer?"

"My personal opinion," Aboli began, and then paused. "My opinion is that it's between him and God."

"Okay."

"And that's all I can say about that," Aboli said, but he continued to talk. "He *is* capable. He is capable of doing it, though. He's more than capable. . . . He blacks out. I've had to go into the deepest part of Seattle and bail him out of the ghettos—high, drunk, whatever it is, and walking out with his jacket on upside down and backwards. . . . You know, 'cause he was drunk and couldn't remember where he was. Lost his pickup a few times."

"So what do you think about what happened to Jami?" Mains asked again.

Aboli shook his head, repeating only that it was "between him and God."

So far, Steve Sherer had played the system and won.

But in the fall of 1998 he returned to Washington and said he wanted to surrender on his numerous drunk-driving warrants. He was sentenced to eight months in the King County jail, his longest jail time ever. Before then, he had deftly managed to creep out of areas where he was wanted without being arrested. If he was arrested, he'd been sentenced to probation or threatened with house arrest. He always seemed to call the shots and live the life he wanted. But this time he'd guessed wrong.

It would be the summer of 1999 before Steve walked out of jail.

As he sat in the crowded jail pods and considered what had been done to him, Steve Sherer grew more and more angry. And when Steve got angry, he acted out. But he'd never been angry in jail before and acting out was frowned upon by the guards. He could only seethe inside and consider what he would do when he was free again.

When Steve turned himself in for those DUI warrants, Jami had been gone for eight years. During most of those years, Steve had lived an entirely self-indulgent life, most of it far away from the house on Education Hill where she was last known to be alive. His little boy, Chris, was thriving in Judy and Jerry Hagel's care, and the world was going on. But for Judy and Jerry, a life without answers was bleak.

Marilyn Brenneman was impressed with the growing pile of reports and interviews the Redmond detectives were bringing her. True to form, she sent the men back to find more. And true to *their* form, they grinned and went back out to see what else they could find out about Steven Sherer.

They all knew it was going to take a mountain of circumstantial evidence to bring this case before an inquiry judge and convince him that a crime had been committed.

So the "autopsy" on Steve Sherer's life continued, but it wasn't easy. For every person who opened up and gave the Redmond detectives a solid opinion or an anecdote that helped, there seemed to be three who were still afraid of Sherer. Taylor, Mains and Faddis listened to everyone, even psychics, believing that there was someone out there who could fill in the pieces of their baffling puzzle. They were getting a much more comprehensive understanding of Steve Sherer, but there were still too many empty spots where there were no pieces at all to fit in.

Most significant, they now understood how Steve was able to keep so many people under his thumb. He choreographed his illegal and illicit activities so they involved his friends, while he kept his own hands clean. That allowed him to control the balance of power; he always threatened to turn his friends in if they talked too much. It wasn't that he didn't partake of the fruits of his con games and drug schemes. He always did, but he managed to put other people in a position where *they* would be hung out to dry if he chose to snitch on them.

But the longer Steve remained in jail, the more willing those people were to come forward. They could see now that he wasn't nearly as much in control as he wanted them to believe.

13

Finally, even Jami's brother Rob decided to tell the police what he had not wanted to acknowledge as anything more than his brother-in-law's usual rantings on the Saturday night before Jami vanished. Steve had been blindly furious when Jami didn't come home that night. He and her twin brothers and their girlfriends had looked for her in vain.

Rich and the girls had finally gone home, and Rob was alone with Steve when he muttered, "If I find out she's cheating on me, I'll kill her."

But Steve was always threatening to kill people, or making grandiose—and violent—statements. It was difficult for a brother to accept that he hadn't paid enough attention to the man who probably had actually destroyed the sister he loved. As the years passed, and Jami didn't come home, Rob agonized about what might have been if only he had done something. Finally, he told the Redmond police about Steve Sherer's threat against Jami.

On October 6, 1998, Marilyn Brenneman and Hank Corscadden felt they had enough evidence to begin calling witnesses before Inquiry Judge Robert Lasnik. IJ hearings are secret, just as grand jury proceedings are. The testimony is secret to protect the target of an investigation. If the inquiry judge should decide that there is not reasonable suspicion to believe that a crime had been committed, the suspect's name would never have been broadcast throughout the media. If the judge agreed with the prosecutors and a trial lay ahead, the media would have plenty of opportunities from testimony in open court for headline stories.

"What I try to do," Marilyn Brenneman says, "is think like a defense attorney. What would *I* do in this instance?"

It was important to have the potential witnesses in an actual trial testify before the inquiry judge, not only to give information and build a case, but also so that transcripts of what they said could later be used either to help them or to haunt them.

To Brenneman's relief, Lew Adams said he would be glad to testify. She phoned Lew in Idaho and tried to reassure him that any drug charges against him in the state of Washington took second place to the tremendous help he could offer to the Sherer investigation. He told her he wanted to straighten things out, but he was nervous. She assured him that he wasn't going to be arrested the moment he crossed into Washington State. Lew needed to come to Seattle and tell what he knew about what were, quite probably, the last two days of Jami Sherer's life.

On the first day before Judge Lasnik, Carolyn Willoughby* testified. She was one of Sherri's closest friends, and she and Sherri had often speculated about what might have happened to Jami. Despite the front that Sherri kept up to protect Steve, Carolyn sensed that even his own mother sometimes had doubts about his innocence.

Carolyn Willoughby was disturbed by that, but she

was more disturbed by something she had found when she was helping Sherri clean the Sherers' house after Jami vanished. She knew Steve had told the detectives that there was only one key to Jami's Mazda RX7. That was the key found in the pocket of Jami's leather coat on the seat of her car when it finally turned up in the church parking lot.

If that was truly the only key, then it seemed likely that Jami herself had driven the car there. But to Carolyn's horror, she found another key to Jami's Mazda in the laundry area of Steve and Jami's house. That meant that Steve had lied to the detectives. Carolyn didn't want to know why he had lied, but she had a pretty good idea. Her first concern was for her best friend, Sherri, and so Carolyn kept the secret of the key to herself. It took a toll on her, however. When she was subpoenaed to the inquiry court, she was apprehensive.

At a certain point in her testimony, her words came out in a rush. She admitted she had found the second key—a key that Steve must have had all-along. She was convinced that her information would do great damage to her best friend's son and cause pain to Sherri. It certainly was valuable information, but it was only one small detail. Carolyn Willoughby need not have felt like such a traitor.

Judge Lasnik listened to a number of witnesses over three days. New names surfaced and new information spilled out. If there was not an organized effort to protect Steve Sherer from the detectives who trailed too close behind him, there certainly appeared to have been a tacit agreement among the social circles Sherri Schielke moved in to avoid saying anything more than was absolutely necessary.

146

The picture emerging was that of a sadistic hedonist. Steve Sherer's rap sheet showed he had been flouting the law since he was eighteen, and people who had gone to school with him before that remembered him as a mean, enraged child and teenager.

The first session with the inquiry judge ended, but there would be another. The investigation continued even as the inquiry process had begun. In the meantime, Steve himself languished in jail.

Many people around Steve were worried. Greg Mains had heard rumors about Steve's stealing a gun. In October 1998 he and Detective Lon Shultz traveled to the little eastern Washington town of Chelan to follow up on a report that Steve had stolen a .357—from one of Wally Schielke's houses. "We were concerned about officer safety," Mains explained. "We needed to know if Steve was armed."

Because a number of new names had come up, Greg Mains and Lon Shultz wanted to talk to some longtime friends of the Sherer-Schielkes who lived in Chelan. Sherri had owned a summer place there for many years and Steve had spent a great deal of time partying in it when his mother was not present.

One report came to Greg Mains from someone on the Chelan Police Department who said his parents lived next door to the Schielkes' place.

Mains and Shultz met first with a couple who owned one of the largest resorts on Lake Chelan and learned nothing that would help their investigation. They did, however, learn the names of other Chelan friends of the Sherers.

John Walcker, who owned the Caravel Resort, offered Mains the cell phone number of another friend of the late David Sherer and his widow, Sherri. Mains called Grant Logan,* another friend, who agreed to drive to the resort and speak with the two detectives.

Logan picked up his wife, Nyssa,* on the way, and the two showed up at the resort within fifteen minutes. They seemed friendly enough—until Greg Mains said he and Shultz were investigating Jami Sherer's disappearance. "The case is still open, you know," he explained. "We're investigating any new leads we can find."

Grant Logan said he and his wife had been friends of Sherri Schielke's for over twenty-five years. They had known her and David Sherer since the early days of construction in Mill Creek. The Logans, along with Wally Schielke and the Sherers, often wintered in Palm Desert. The men played golf together in the California sun while Chelan was covered with drifting snow.

"What was Steve like when he was growing up?" Mains asked.

"We only saw him once in a while—during the summer when he vacationed over here with Sherri."

"Was he a problem kid?"

"Never violent or aggressive," Logan said quickly. "Just the usual preteen, pubescent temper tantrums."

When Mains said he understood that Logan and Wally Schielke sometimes played golf together, and that they had a conversation about the theft of a gun from Wally's house, Logan tensed. "Can you recall the details of that conversation?" Mains asked.

Logan said that Wally *had* told him a gun was stolen, and that it was "inferred" that Steve took it because he was the only one in the house when the theft occurred.

"About David Sherer's suicide . . ." Mains began.

"What does that have to do with Jami being missing?" Logan asked.

"Part of our investigation always looks at family violence and the long-term effect it has, sometimes for generations," Mains answered.

Grant Logan said he had no idea why David Sherer had killed himself. He knew he was an alcoholic and he and Sherri had been fighting. He could only surmise that David had probably been drunk and alone. Beyond that, he had no answers.

"Who found David Sherer?" Mains asked.

"Sherri—and she called me and John Walcker."

Mains was never an overtly tough interrogator; his forte was his dogged pursuit of what he wanted. He was deliberately mild as he asked the Logans to give him a written statement about the conversation Grant had with Wally over his stolen gun. Mains looked up from his paperwork and saw the Logans exchange a glance.

"I don't think I should do that," Logan said. "I don't think I should write anything down, until I get the opportunity to talk to my attorney."

At that point, the interview was abruptly over. When they again contacted the Logans' son and asked him to give a statement about the gun theft, he stonewalled them too. His parents insisted that they wanted nothing to do with a reopening of the suicide investigation into the death of David Sherer. As far as Jami Sherer's disappearance was concerned, they had nothing to offer the detectives.

In the meantime Steve Sherer must have been getting some information from his jail visitors. Even though he had always skated away before, he must have felt a chill in the wind.

Mains and Faddis traveled a lot in 1998, and it probably wasn't good for Steve Sherer's peace of mind to hear that they had been in Chelan and Scottsdale and Palm Desert and Mill Creek and Redmond and Puyallup and a dozen other places he frequented. Nor would he have been serene if he'd known how many people who knew him or who had once known him had spoken to the detective partners.

Sometimes the cops got really lucky. More often, it took them months, even years, to locate witnesses. One of the dead ends that Greg Mains and Mike Faddis kept running into was an empty space in their chronology of Jami and Steve's relationship: the time they lived in Palm Desert in 1986. Judy Hagel tried to help, but she wasn't sure exactly what had gone on during the months Jami lived with Steve in the mobile home.

She knew that they had shared the rent with a young woman for a while, and she knew her name: Sally Kirwin. Judy even knew that there had been some kind of an incident with a knife and that Steve had been so out of control that Jami had called home, crying.

"But the next day, she said everything was all right," Judy said. "Jami told me not to come."

"We'd been looking for Sally Kirwin for almost *nine years*," Greg Mains said, "and we couldn't find her. And then I did—back in Wisconsin!" He phoned her and found she was still extremely upset by her memories of Steve Sherer.

Mains wanted to ask Sally about the alleged burglary of the mobile home and hoped that it might have occurred while she was living with Steve and Jami. Since the diamond ring Steve claimed was stolen that night in 1986 had turned up taped to Jami's car, it would really help their case against him to have a witness to an insurance ruse.

Sally Kirwin said she remembered the burglary very

well. "I thought it was phony the whole time," she said. "I know that Steve did that."

"That's what I understand," Greg Mains said.

"But that one other night," Sally went on, *"that* was awful! I'll never forget it the rest of my life. It was so scary."

"What other night are you talking about?" Mains asked.

"That night Steve was chasing Jami around and going to kill her with that butcher knife—it was horrible," Sally said, her voice hushed with remembered terror. "She had to get behind a table to protect herself! I thought we were both going to die that night."

Mains had gone looking for verification of something they already knew. They got that and more. He hit the mother lode. They had heard only vague rumors that Steve had stabbed himself once when Jami decided not to marry him, but they didn't know when or where or if it had ever really happened. Jami had told her mother bits and pieces of what really happened during that terrible Christmas season. Since his Christmas Eve arrest occurred a week later in the Hagels' home in Bellevue, Jami probably hadn't wanted to go into detail about the stabbing incident.

"That's when it all happened," Mains said. "But we were on our way to trial and we still weren't sure—not until we found Sally." Sally Kirwin described Steve's rage as he broke up the mobile home and ended up stabbing himself. "And, finally," Mains said, "we had a witness to the whole thing."

Steve Sherer was in jail, but planning to be free soon. Quite possibly he was unaware of how numbered his days really were. He had come back to turn himself in to Washington State authorities, bringing his oddly bulging blue suitcase with him on the bus. Sherri Schielke said he could store his things in her home and garage, but she didn't pay too much attention to the bags and boxes he left there.

Steve Sherer had used and discarded many people in his past. One of his closest associates at the time Jami vanished was a man named Jeffrey Caston. The new investigators wanted to talk to him, and in 1999 Taylor assigned Mike Faddis to find him.

Caston was still in the area. Faddis noted that Caston was about fifteen years older than Steve and that he had served in Vietnam in the mid- to late sixties. He had been remodeling houses in early 1990, finding customers by putting "work wanted" ads in the newspaper, when Steve and Jami called in response to his ad. They told him they were looking at a house they wanted to buy, but it would need considerable work. Caston went to the Redmond house to give them a bid. He recalled that Jami had come home on her lunch break from Microsoft to meet him.

Steve hired Jeff Caston as their remodeler, and the two had soon become "very good friends." Caston was frank in admitting to Mike Faddis that he had been addicted to heroin off and on throughout his life, beginning at the age of fourteen. He had managed to stay clear of the drug for many years, however, while he was raising his daughter, and he was clean when he first met Steve Sherer. Not surprisingly, Caston also had some convictions for theft during the heroin periods. He wouldn't make a very credible witness for any prosecutor, but as he spoke, it was clear he knew things that no one else did.

Becoming best friends with Steve Sherer wasn't the best thing that ever happened to Caston. For a man with an addictive personality, it was akin to putting the honey jar in front of Winnie-the-Pooh. Caston told Faddis he had joined Steve in a number of activities: "Card rooms, the racetracks, car races, Mariner games, various things . . ."

During the two months that Caston worked on the Redmond house, he saw Steve every day. "I finished the remodel in July—August, maybe. It was in the summertime in 1990."

Even though the job was finished, Caston and Sherer continued to be friends, with Caston far more dependent on Steve Sherer than the other way around. Caston said that Steve was cunning. Both Mike Faddis and Greg Mains had heard that before.

"He has a criminal mind smarter than any I've ever met in prison. But as a normal human being, he wasn't that smart," Jeff said. "But put him in a criminal situation where he needs to figure out a device to cheat anyone out of money, he was brilliant. He knew how to do it and keep himself distanced from it. He was the mastermind. He would get someone else to do it."

Caston recalled a time when he was broke and Steve phoned him from Arizona. "He asked me, 'Are you hungry?'

"I told him, 'Yeah, I haven't eaten.' He asks me what I want and we hung up. And then Steve calls me back and says, 'Go over to the McDonald's next to where you are. And pick up what's waiting for you.' Steve had called the McDonald's and said, 'Hey, I ordered a bunch of stuff and the order is all wrong. I'd like to pick up the stuff I paid for.' "

Caston shook his head, remembering. Steve's scam had worked and he had done it all from Arizona. "I walked in and they gave me a big bag of hamburgers and fries, milk shake, all free."

While they were in Redmond, Caston said Steve sold him a computer and the two, along with some other friends, put together a gambling pool on the computers. "We had a pool and whoever won the most games at the end of the season was supposed to get the pool," Caston said. "It was depending on which players you had drafted to your team."

Caston wasn't adept at working with computers, so Steve helped him. He said he and Steve worked on their strategy for winning every weekend. They were either together or on the phone for most of the morning on both Saturday and Sunday and quite often in the evening as well.

Caston was an early riser; he was wide awake by 5:30 or 6:00 A.M. "I would watch the clock so I could find a decent hour to call. Usually I would get Jami first, and she would be upset because I was calling so early, and I'd say I would call back. I would usually wind up getting hold of them maybe by nine or ten."

When Mike Faddis asked him about a particular weekend—September 29 and 30, 1990, Caston said that he hadn't been able to reach either Jamie or Steve on that Saturday. "So I started calling earlier on Sunday." He finally got an answer to his calls.

"Who did you first talk to?" Faddis asked.

"Jami."

It was somewhere between 10:00 and 11:00 A.M. by then, and Jami was in a hurry. "She eventually told me," Caston recalled, "that they had been gone all weekend and that they had an argument. And she was trying to pack some stuff and get out of there and go over to her mom's."

Caston thought she sounded apprehensive and upset. "She seemed a little scared."

He estimated that he talked with her for ten or fifteen minutes. She told him that Steve would probably be back soon, and if he ever needed to talk to her again, he would have to call her at her mother's house.

Caston said he waited for twenty minutes and then started calling Steve. Within a few calls, Steve answered. "He was upset," Jeff Caston said. "I didn't let on that I had already talked to her. I didn't want to take sides. Steve told me pretty much what Jami told me, about their having a fight and her going to her mother's house."

One rather odd thing happened as they talked. "Steve said, 'Did you hear that?' and I said, 'Hear what? Is she still there?' He said, 'I'll call you back,' and he hung up."

It was about half an hour before Steve called Caston back, asking him if he had heard Jami yelling in the background.

"I never heard her at all," Caston said, "but he told me she had come back for her purse or money or something and that they spoke for a couple of minutes, and then she'd left. He was pretty upset. He didn't sound like normal."

Jeff Caston said he'd offered to go over and talk with Steve, but Steve declined, which in itself was unusual. Steve always liked to have someone who would listen to his troubles when he was upset. When Steve called Caston next, it was about one o'clock in the afternoon. "Steve told me Jami had disappeared. He was *really* upset then."

Steve told Caston that Jami had never arrived at her parents' home, and Caston had tried to calm him down, saying that she probably stopped on the way or that maybe her mother was just telling him that. "I told him to get some sleep—they both should get some sleep—and something to eat and talk about it later."

Later that afternoon, when Caston called back, there was no answer at Steve's house. Sometime in early evening, Steve had called him, saying he was at his mother's house to sleep because he just wasn't "comfortable" at his house.

"Did you ever talk to Jami again?" Faddis asked.

"Never."

Jeff Caston described Jami as a wonderful mother and said he was sure she would never have left Chris voluntarily, "never in a million years," he said.

Over the next few days, Caston recalled that Steve continued to be agitated and upset. He picked up Jeff Caston to ride with him while he drove around, looking for Jami's car. Indeed, Steve ultimately called him to tell him that the car had been found, and Caston said they drove to the place where it was parked, by the church.

"Were the police there?" Faddis asked, intrigued. He had been there himself soon after the car was located, but he hadn't seen Steve there.

"No." Caston said. "The car was just sitting there, and there wasn't any yellow police tape on it and there was no one around."

Is it possible that Steve actually drove Jeff Caston to Jami's car *before* the police found it? Is it possible that he had known where it was all along?

A few days after Jami vanished, Caston said, Steve asked him to go with him to his mother's house. "He had forgotten his key to his mother's house, and he said he had to break a window to get in," Caston said. "He asked me to repair it."

Caston agreed to that, and Steve drove him to Sherri

and Wally Schielke's house in Mill Creek so he could take measurements to get glass cut. He was surprised at that time to see a shovel in the back of Steve's Blazer. Caston had never known him to carry tools because he just wasn't handy. Steve told Caston that he had borrowed the shovel from his mother and had to return it.

Steve wanted the long, narrow window beside the front door of his mother's house repaired as quickly as possible, as she was on her way home from Cancún after hearing about Jami's disappearance. Faddis knew that Sherri Schielke had come back from Mexico on Wednesday, October 3, three days after Jami vanished. That pinned down the time of the window repair.

When Mike Faddis reported his interview with Jeff Caston, it sounded to Jim Taylor as if Steve never had a key to his mother's house—but that something had distressed him so much on that last day when anyone talked to Jami that he couldn't bear to stay in his own house. His own house scared him, and so he ran to his mother's even though she wasn't there, and he broke a window to get in.

"Mike," Taylor said, "go find Jeff Caston. Take him up to the Schielke house, but don't tell him how to get there. He's going to tell you—and be sure that *he's* the one who determines the route. I don't care where he takes you. He can take you to Mount Vernon, for all I care. You drive and just follow his directions."

As hopeless as such a search might seem, they were still looking for Jami's body. They worked within the framework of the five hours when Steve was incommunicado on the afternoon of September 30. The very fact that he had missed his every-fifteen-minute call that afternoon made his activities highly suspect. No one they had talked to—*no one*—had heard from Steve between

1:00 P.M. and 6:00 P.M. If Steve had killed Jami in their own home, he would have had to dispose of her body, probably bury it somewhere, and get back to his house in time to call her mother again. The Redmond investigators figured he had a period of an hour and a half to actually get Jami's body out of the house, dispose of it, and be back at his mother's house.

With Jeff Caston picking the route, Mike Faddis felt his heart leap when his passenger did *not* take the 405 freeway, but rather directed him to a two-lane back road that led north, winding its way to Mill Creek from Redmond. It was October and the Cascade Mountains off to their right were already dusted with snow. The date and the weather were almost exactly right; Jeff Caston had driven this route with Steve Sherer eight years earlier, and the mountains would have looked the same. They were twenty-five or thirty miles away, but they looked close enough to reach out and touch.

It was Jim Taylor's contention all along that someone with guilty knowledge of Jami Sherer's fate would have a compulsion to confess. As Faddis and Caston drew closer to a short road that cut over to the Schielke house in Mill Creek, Jeff Caston gestured toward a desolate area to the east and said, "You know, when we went by here, Steve kind of waved his arm and said, 'You could get rid of a body out there, and no one would ever find it.'"

Greg Mains and Mike Faddis would spend days driving up and down those back roads, especially along 35th S.E., the area where Jeff Caston had quoted Steve's telling remark. They found three locations that appeared to be reasonable places to look for Jami's remains. One was the property of a company called Pacific Topsoil on the east side of 35th S.E.

Fortunately for the detectives, if not for the owner,

Pacific Topsoil was under constant surveillance by environmental agencies, that wanted to be sure the topsoil operation didn't interfere with waterways or forests. So every so often, the owner had arranged for aerial photographs to be taken of the area. He showed the detectives the photos from 1987, 1989, 1990, and 1993.

In essence, the land was a massive peat bog, and from time to time over that period, it was covered with water. "There were a couple hundred acres there," Taylor said, "where someone could dispose of a body."

The other two sites they thought likely were close by. They knew that Steve needed to dispose of his wife's body rapidly so he could check in with her mother by early evening. First, the investigators had a chemical analysis done to determine the makeup of the soil and the peat bogs in the area. Depending on the acidity and the alkalinity of the substance tested, bodies left in a site will either decompose rapidly or will last forever: the outer layers will turn to a soap-like substance known as adipocere while the internal organs remain relatively unchanged. Test results indicated that if Jami was in the peat bog or in the other two locations, she would be frozen in time, and if her body should ever be found, she could be identified.

Cadaver dogs were brought in to search those areas. Necro-search dogs, or cadaver dogs, are trained much like bloodhounds, with rewards and praise when they find what they are supposed to. But different dogs are suited to different search items. Some dogs like to look for living things; cadaver dogs home in on dead tissue, bones, and teeth. Many of them are used in flooded areas, where they can actually sniff down a chimney to see if anyone is alive in houses below water. The best cadaver dogs can smell a body 20 feet below the surface of a body of water. They are incredible creatures, and not in the least macabre. When they're not working, they are as friendly and cheerful as any pet. And like most search-and-rescue dogs, they travel in their own plane seats and are never relegated to the baggage areas deep in the bowels of the plane.

Andy Rebmann, retired from the Connecticut State Police, is known worldwide for his work with cadaver dogs. He agreed to bring his dogs in to search for Jami.

Every Saturday the Redmond detectives were on the 35th S.E. site, watching the dogs work and looking for Jami. Although they had never met her, she was very real to them. They wanted very much to bring her home.

"We were probing and looking," Jim Taylor recalls, "but we didn't find her. What we were able to determine was that on the east side of 35th S.E. there had been an office and a security system at the time of Jami's disappearance, but farther up, on the other side of the road, there was no gate at that time [1990], and people would go in to dump garbage, or lovers would go there to park. Given that knowledge and the proximity to Steve's mother's house—which was a mile, mile and a half at the very most—and what Caston had said, we knew we had to be in the area where he left Jami, or relatively close."

Although they had never given much credence to psychics, one of the seers had sent word that Jami Sherer would be found near a "block building" with a big tower with "arms." About half a mile south of the area the Redmond investigators finally focused on, there was a Seattle City Light building, now fully fenced. When Greg Mains contacted them, one supervisor remembered that there had been a cinder-block building there at one time. It had since been dismantled.

Taylor, Mains, and Faddis believed they were close to Jami. They went back again and again to wooded areas in South Snohomish County and in the northeastern part of King County. Twice they used police divers and sonar equipment to search the murky bottom of Lake Stevens. There was no way to search Lake Washington where Steve often took his power boat. The vast lake is so cold and so deep that it rarely gives up its secrets.

And then the winter storms roared in and made any further searches impossible until the spring came again.

It was Christmas 1998. The Hagels had spent nine Christmases without Jami and without closure.

14

Judge Robert Lasnik was appointed to the Washington State Supreme Court, and Superior Court Judge Bill Downing took over as the inquiry judge in the matter of Steve Sherer. Steve was fully aware now that the IJ was hearing witnesses for the second time. He scoffed to friends, "I don't know why they keep looking for Jami—there's nothing to find."

Steve finished his eight-month jail sentence on May 24, 1999. He knew who his enemies were, and his rage erupted within a short time. Incensed by Lieutenant Jim Taylor and Marilyn Brenneman's unrelenting investigation of his life, Sherer made three incredibly stupid phone calls. Taylor had given Steve his business card eighteen months before, and for some reason, he'd kept it in his wallet ever since.

His first call was to Taylor: "Hey, Lieutenant Dick-head," Steve snarled. "Now that I'm out, why don't you come fuck with me now, you piece of shit," and he hung up.

He called back: "I want you to stop messing with me. If you don't have [the investigators] back off, I'm going to go out and cut someone's fucking throat."

Taylor signaled frantically to Greg Mains to come to his desk and gestured for him to write down what he was saying. He had no recording device on his phone, so Taylor deliberately repeated everything Steve was saying to him. "What you're telling me, Mr. Sherer," Taylor said calmly, "is that if I don't have my detectives back off, you're going to go out and cut somebody's fucking throat? Is that right?" Greg Mains wrote down the whole call, just as Taylor was repeating it. There was a click and the line went dead.

Marilyn Brenneman wasn't in her office when Steve called her, so he left a message on her answering machine: "This is Steve Sherer. I'm out now and I want to talk to you. You better call me back. I want what's mine. I want my wife's car back. I want her ring back. I want it *all* back. I'm not gonna go away. You better not fuck with me. It's my turn to fuck with you. You'd *better* call me back." There was a short pause and then he said, "Have a good life."

When she listened to the message, Brenneman doubted that he meant the last part of his message, but she believed the first part absolutely.

Sherer had just committed a felony: Threatening a public official with bodily harm is against the law. He had been more explicit with Jim Taylor, however. Steve had been out of jail less than a month, and he was about to go back in. On June 23, 1999, he was arrested by King County sheriff's deputies. Seattle District Court Judge Eileen Kato set his bail at $30,000, cash only.

Steve told the judge he had no money for bail. He asked to be released so he could make a court appearance in Wenatchee, Washington, where he had posted $6,100 bail for traffic violations. His protestations were to no avail.

The court record was sealed. The public knew only that Steve had been arrested for allegedly threatening a Redmond police officer and a King County senior deputy prosecutor whose names were not given.

Eventually, Steve's family came up with his bail and he was free again. He moved into his mother's Mill Creek home.

Jim Taylor and Marilyn Brenneman had bigger fish to fry than the threat charges. The inquiry judge had finally decided that there was indeed enough evidence to make the reasonable assumption that a crime had been committed: the murder of Jami Sherer. They had a massive amount of circumstantial evidence, dozens of witnesses, and the "autopsy" of Steve Sherer that Jim Taylor had sent Greg Mains and Mike Faddis out to create.

Beginning in early January 2000, Redmond detectives and the FBI worked a round-the-clock stakeout of Sherri Schielke's Mill Creek home and Steve's usual haunts. Steve must have felt the net ready to drop over him. Armed with an arrest warrant, Greg Mains and Mike Faddis waited on Friday morning, January 7, at the office of Steve's probation officer in Lynnwood, but Steve did not show up for his appointment. For the next twenty-four hours, the Redmond investigators searched the area around the Schielkes' Mill Creek home without spotting Steve. All local police agencies were asked to have their personnel watch for him.

On Saturday FBI agents, watching for any activity around Steve's mother's home, spotted one of Steve's friends knocking on the door. The agents slid through the tall evergreens in the yard and were standing behind the friend when Steve opened the door. Before he could protest, they grabbed him.

Nine years and three months after Jami Sherer vanished into some never-never land where no one could find her, the man who was the main suspect in her disappearance was at last in police custody. At 1:00 P.M. on January 8, Steven Sherer was arrested on a charge of first-degree murder. His bail was set at a million dollars.

The Redmond detectives and Marilyn Brenneman did not release much information: "We have unearthed every bit of information possible on this case," Jim Taylor said. "Now it will be judged by a jury of his peers."

"I'm not going to deny this is a circumstantial case," Marilyn Brenneman said. "But we believe the charging documents show a very strong case, and we're prepared to go to trial. We are just convinced a jury should hear the evidence, and when they do, they will do the right thing."

Sherri Schielke hired Peter Mair and his associate, Peter Camiel, to defend Steve on the first-degree charges. Marilyn Brenneman would lead the prosecuting team, which included co-counsels Hank Corscadden and Senior Deputy King County Prosecutor Kristin Richardson. Trial was set for May.

On the evening of April 14, Greg Mains and Detective Anne Malins prepared to execute a warrant on the Schielke residence. The warrant specified that they would search the entire house and the vehicles parked

there for Steve Sherer's personal papers and the suitcase he reportedly carried with him from state to state.
According to their information, Chris Sherer should
have left after visiting Sherri Schielke by the time they
served the search warrant. Mains and Malins rang the
doorbell at the front door of the large Heatherstone residence. There was no response and no noise from inside the house. But a car belonging to Steve's sister
Laura was parked in the driveway, along with a pickup
truck and another car. They knocked on the door and
this time Laura came to the door. The whole family
seemed to be there: Laura, Saundra, Chris, and Sherri
Schielke.

Mains and Malins saw that a birthday party planned
for Chris Sherer that Friday evening was still going on,
and they were sorry to interrupt. The last thing they
wanted to do was to hurt twelve-year-old Chris any
more than he had already been hurt. His mother was
dead and his father was in jail awaiting trial for first-
degree murder. Sherri asked them to wait an hour before they began to search. But of course they could not
do that. Had they known, they would have arrived later,
but once they were there, they could not leave for fear
that vital evidence might be moved or disposed of.
They had no choice but to proceed with the search.

Sherri led them to the guest room and pointed out a
suitcase with a Greyhound tag on it. There was nothing
in it. They didn't find the blue suitcase that he carried
with him always. It wasn't anywhere in the large two-
story home.

A few days after the Redmond detectives left, carrying away the items they had found that were listed on
the search warrant, Sherri happened to be in her garage.
There she saw the blue suitcase that Steve took with

him whenever he moved. "I thought he had left it in Arizona," she commented later. "The last time he came home, he was on a bus."

Sherri told Steve's attorney, Pete Mair, that she had found the blue suitcase and that she didn't want to give it to the detectives. He explained to her that he had no choice; as an officer of the court he could not withhold evidence from the police. He called them on April 20 to say that the blue suitcase was in his office.

At last, the battered pale blue suitcase was turned over to Taylor, Mains, and Faddis. With some trepidation about what they might find, they undid the buckles and straps. Jami Sherer had been tiny, and although they didn't say it out loud, they all had the same thought: Could Jami's remains be inside?

In a sense, they were. Steve Sherer had kept things in this heavy suitcase that represented Jami to him. There were numerous pieces of clothing in sizes so small they would have fit a child, but they were not childlike: a sheer black negligee, a black bra, a black slip, the black leather skirt he had asked other women to try on, and elbow-length black gloves. There were eight pairs of transparent bikini and thong panties in various colors, a bikini bathing suit, and a black silk dress with a peplum and a pattern of pink, white, and purple tropical flowers. In contrast, he had also packed Jami's long-sleeved cotton nightshirts and her T-shirts that said "Super Mom" and "Moms Are Wonderful People!" The suitcase also contained their bowling shirts and a key to a Mazda.

Jami's clothes were as light as gossamer, but their wedding album and yearbooks were heavier. There were framed pictures, and for some reason, Steve had carried Jami's accordion file with all her paperwork everywhere he went: IRS receipts, credit card bills, and anything Steve could find with Jami's distinctive rounded script. The file also held the contract for her car loan. She had put $3,000 down on the $11,429.26 cost of her Mazda and carefully taken out insurance to cover the loan if she was disabled or deceased; Judy Hagel had co-signed for the car loan.

The way she kept such careful track of her bills and records helped the investigators to know Jami; she had been Steve's opposite. He honored no contracts or bills, while Jami had been meticulous and dependable. The clothes Steve kept were mostly her Barbie clothes, but a few of them must have brought back an image of Jami in the kitchen, fixing breakfast or feeding Chris.

How bizarre that a man who began dating two weeks after his wife disappeared should have carried the essence of her with him for almost a decade. "He had it all," Marilyn Brenneman commented. "A beautiful wife who loved him, a wonderful little boy, and they would have been rich by now. And he destroyed it."

15

Steve Sherer's trial for the murder of his wife was set for April 17, 2000. The trial was held in King County Superior Court Judge Anthony Wartnik's courtroom, but it took until May 3 before a jury was selected: half women and half men, who looked to be from their early thirties to their early seventies.

The courthouse had once been majestic, but it now

faced demolition. Seismologists had declared its marble halls unsafe in case of a major earthquake. The wooden gallery benches seemed to turn to stone after a few hours, but Judge Wartnik's courtroom was as modern as any, with paintings gracing the wall, and plants drooping in the windowless room.

Brenneman, Corscadden, and Richardson sat on the left side of the courtroom. Flanked by defense attorneys Peter Camiel and Pete Mair, Steve Sherer sat at a table facing Judge Wartnik. The twelve jurors and four alternates sat in padded chairs that were the envy of the spectators. Both the Hagels and the Sherer-Schielkes were represented each day by a dozen or more family members and friends. Since he knew it would be a long trial, Judge Wartnik decreed the two families would alternate sitting in rows two and three on a weekly basis.

Despite his effect on the women in his life, Steve Sherer was not a prepossessing man. He was short with very small hands and feet. His California blond hair had grown out to its natural faded brown, and it looked as if it had been cut by an amateur. The jury never saw the long, wavy hair and goatee he usually affected. He wore slacks and a jacket that didn't match, an open-necked shirt without a tie, and white socks with black shoes. To those who knew nothing of his background, he appeared to be a weak, almost pathetic-looking man down on his luck. That may well have been the image the defense wanted. He never looked at the gallery except when he stood up to be handcuffed during breaks in the trial. And then his icy eyes swept the reporters who sat on the front bench.

The rage was still there, but it was suppressed.

Marilyn Brenneman made the opening statement for the prosecution. Brenneman, tall and attractive with thick, blunt-cut hair that tumbled over her forehead when she concentrated intensely, looked from one juror to another and told them that Jami Sherer had never been found and possibly never would be: "Jami was a devoted mother who never would have absented herself from her young son's life. And [Sherer] has a long history of control and domestic violence against Jami."

She described a chaotic, abusive four-year marriage that ended when the defendant "hit [Jami] in the face, and she bled. Ten years ago there was a vicious punch to the face, a rush of blood, and a fall." Brenneman promised to present a witness who would recall Steve Sherer's description of Jami's fall down a flight of stairs and her death.

There was a suitcase and the jury would see "items in the suitcase that are all that is left of the life of Jami Sherer."

Sherer, Brenneman pointed out, didn't participate in the search for his missing wife, began dating other women two weeks after she vanished, cashed in her stock options, and spent her vacation and sick-leave pay.

"Jami Sherer vanished without a trace," Brenneman said. "She left behind a loving family. She left behind her friends. She left behind all her worldly possessions. And she left behind her most precious possession of all, her two-year-old son, Chris."

Steve Sherer rested his head on his hand, and shook his head from time to time as Brenneman spoke. Other than that, he showed no emotion at all.

Pete Mair, a onetime football star, rose to give the defense's opening statement, favoring knees damaged by his gridiron days. His attitude was deprecating, and he stopped just short of being amused that the state would bring such a "flimsy" case into court.

Mair didn't deny that his client's marriage had been stormy and that he had once pulled out a clump of Jami Sherer's hair during an argument. "You may not like him," Mair told the jurors, "but proving a first-degree murder case is a big jump. At the end of this case, we'll be where we were in 1990—with an unsolved mystery, as unpleasant as it is."

Mair said there was not even conclusive evidence that Jami was dead, although he allowed that she probably was. "Proof," he reminded the jurors, "has to be beyond a reasonable doubt."

Mair characterized Steve Sherer as an innocent widower being falsely accused, even badgered, by detectives whose investigation was based on the recent memories of a cast of shady characters, one of whom might even be the real killer.

And it was certainly true enough that the prosecution's roster of witnesses contained characters whose own histories were not stellar. Brenneman, Corscadden, and Richardson knew that. But Steve Sherer was a man whose life revolved around drugs and sex, and he interacted with people with similar interests.

The previous Halloween, Steve had sent his son Chris a card from jail, perhaps the most honest communication he ever had with his son: "You have my bad blood in you. Don't do drugs and alcohol. They've ruined my life. . . . But you have your mother's blood, too. I'll be watching you."

Lew Adams took the stand on May 11. He was one of the witnesses the gallery was most curious about, the man who had spent the last night of Jami Sherer's life with her on that Saturday, September 29, 1990, at the Crest Motel. He was thin and tightly wired, wearing a long-sleeved silk shirt with a bright pattern. He had dark circles under his eyes.

As Marilyn Brenneman questioned him, Adams almost vibrated with tension.

"When did you learn that Jami Sherer was missing?"

"Early on Monday morning. I was sleeping, and my mother woke me up and said Jami was missing, and then she said, 'What's going on? Who is this Jami?' "

Lew Adams admitted that he had spent Saturday, September 29, with Jami. "I had no intentions toward her. She was beautiful—a special lady. We both had problems in our marriages."

Tears streamed down Adams's face and choked his voice as he berated himself, still, for letting Jami go home to an angry husband.

Mair grilled Adams hard, but the witness insisted he would never hurt a woman. Yes, he'd fought once with his wife, and they'd thrown food at each other. Yes, he had dealt drugs and used drugs.

Lew Adams's ex-wife took the stand. She recalled that fight. It was in September 1997. Lew *had* kicked at her and pushed her down, even smeared his lunch in her face, but she had spit in it, she admitted.

The defense maintained that Dru Adams had told police that Lew told her during that fight, "I've killed before. I can kill again." Dru, who had known Lew longer than anybody, said that "he wouldn't have the guts to hurt anyone. If he did have the guts to hurt anyone, he would have hurt me—and I'm still here."

It was obvious that Dru Adams no longer cared for Lew, but just as obvious that she hadn't left him because he was violent or abusive. She was embarrassed to have been dragged into the trial, and she left the courtroom hurriedly.

The prosecution called a number of tiny, attractive young blondes who had been involved with Steve and had left the relationships after being abused. Bettina Rauschberg hadn't seen Steve in years, but her fear of him was palpable as she entered the courtroom and took the stand, a position that forced her to face him. She described in detail her hospitalizations and the injuries she had suffered at Steve Sherer's hands.

One witness came as a complete surprise to the prosecution and the Redmond investigators. Her name was Connie Duncan.* In May 2000 she was twenty-five years old, but when she met Steve in 1991, she had been sixteen. She had called Marilyn Brenneman when Steve Sherer's trial was well under way.

"I happened to be home that day," Connie said. "My daughter was sick, so I had to stay home with her. The news was on and I wasn't even paying that close attention. And then I saw the courtroom, and I saw Steve. I didn't get to hear exactly what was going on because my daughter wouldn't stop talking to me. [But] I knew he was on trial for murder."

Connie worked for the state of Washington as a financial service specialist. She coached small children in gymnastics and soccer in her spare time.

Connie Duncan explained to Marilyn Brenneman that she had once dated Steve Sherer and remembered a long-ago nightmare trip to California with him. As she listened, Brenneman realized that *this* was the witness who would fill in a very important chink in the prosecution's case.

It was May 15 when Connie Duncan walked forward to be sworn in. It must have been a shock for Steve to see her again, but he maintained his composure as he had done for most of the trial, his usual expression half-bland and half-glowering. Only rarely had jurors seen the icy threat in his eyes as he stared hard at a prosecution witness.

Connie Duncan fit the pattern; she was slender and softly pretty with dark blond hair. She looked remarkably like the huge Missing poster of Jami Sherer that had been propped up against the court clerk's desk during the prosecution's case.

Brenneman stood far back from her witness, near the alternate jurors' box, as she often did. She was not a prosecutor who got in witnesses' faces. "Could you tell us when you first met Mr. Sherer?" Marilyn Brenneman asked.

"I met him at Lake Chelan in August of 1991."

"How old were you?"

"Sixteen, seventeen years old."

The witness explained that she and her girlfriend had met Steve at a hamburger stand in the small town. He would have been thirty at that time, and he had charmed the teenagers. "We ended up staying at his mother's cabin. . . . We had planned on camping."

"How long do you think you stayed at the house with Mr. Sherer and his friends?" Brenneman asked.

"A couple of days."

"What was your relationship with Mr. Sherer in that couple of days?"

"It was an intimate relationship." Connie explained that she had dated Steve Sherer for a few months after that.

"Do you recall meeting Mr. Sherer in Seattle during those few months?"

"I went up to his house in Redmond that he had bought with Jami."

"When did you first hear about Jami Sherer?"

"It was after some time. It could have been a few weeks. At first I heard a different story than what I heard later."

"Tell me what you first heard."

"He was telling me about a situation where Jami was having sex with another guy, and he was watching. And he told me that a bigger, more powerful man had taken Jami away from him."

Connie explained that she had been spending the weekend with Steve at the time.

"Did he provide alcohol for you?"

"He always did."

"How about drugs?"

"Not at that point. I think that came later."

Connie testified that she had opened Steve's glove compartment and found a stack of flyers with a picture of Jami and her son on it. "One thing I remember is that he made the comment that it was a dumb picture because people thought that his son was missing also."

"Did you have further conversation?"

"He did fill me in a little bit on the disappearance. He said she went to Taco Bell or Taco Time and she disappeared, no trace after that. He stated they found her car later, abandoned."

Connie said that Steve drove past the Taco Time and showed it to her.

"In your conversations with the defendant about his ex-wife, did he ever show you any items of hers?" Brenneman asked.

"He had me try on a black skirt. At the time, I was very small. Obviously, after having a child, I am not anymore. But I remember it was snug."

"What size were you wearing then?"

"Between a three and a five. I would bounce back and forth between a hundred pounds to a hundred and five."

"And how tall are you?"

"Five-four."

Marilyn Brenneman showed Connie Jami's tiny black leather miniskirt, which they had found in the blue suitcase. "Do you recognize this?"

"Yes, I do. He actually bought me one that was very similar. Mine was suede." Connie Duncan testified that Steve kept the blue suitcase under his bed and that he pulled it out to get the skirt.

"Were there any other items in there?"

"I remember a dress that he said Jami had worn on some special occasion. I thought he also had me try on a jean shirt."

Connie recalled also that he had put a necklace around her neck. "He pulled it out of his closet. He had a safe in the closet."

"What was your response to putting these items on?"

"At first, I didn't think much about it. I was sixteen. I thought I was invincible. I did have a friend with me. She was sitting in the living room and I remember her remarks were something along the line of 'That's gross that you have got her clothes on.' I went and took them off."

"Did you have any further conversations with the defendant in the house about things that happened between him and Jami?"

"There is a spot by the stairs at the very top of the stairs where the kitchen is. There is a wall right here"— Connie pointed to the floor plan of the house on Education Hill—"and then a little wall right there, and the walkway. He told me he had gotten into an argument, fight, with Jami. And I don't know how he did it, but he had given her a bloody nose. I don't know if he

punched her or if he was trying to restrain her or el-
bowed her. He said he didn't mean to do it, but that he
was sorry he did it, but that it had happened."

From her testimony, it was clear that Steve had confided many things to Connie Duncan, a thirty-year-old
man telling secrets to a high school junior. He told her
about the insurance scam in California and how he had
taken things from his house and pretended they were
stolen.

"I think he did it while [Jami] was at work. But anyway, one of the things he said was that with the [insur-
ance] money he got her a boob job."

"Did you ever go on a trip with the defendant?"
Marilyn Brenneman asked.

"There was one to Canada, and then there was one
to California where he drove his truck down. . . . We
stayed at a motel.

"He asked if he could go out with some of his friends
because I wasn't twenty-one at the time. And I said,
'Sure.' And he was supposed to be back that night. And
he never showed up. He never showed up. He finally
showed up late the next afternoon, and he had been up
the whole night. He was higher than a kite. He was very
agitated, yelling at me. He wanted to go to sleep.

"When his mom came in, his attitude changed. He
was totally nice, cordial. And we went to Disneyland
with his mother and his son. And as we were getting on
the little trolly train to go to Disneyland, Chris called
me Mommy."

Marilyn Brennaman had asked Connie Duncan to
bring a photograph of herself as she looked in 1991.
Brenneman offered it as evidence that Connie had been
a dead ringer for Jami. Little Chris Sherer had been
confused. He continued to call Connie Mommy

throughout their Disneyland trip. Steve didn't correct him, but Sherri Schielke was upset. "Steve's mom jumped in right away," Connie testified, "to say, 'No, she is just a nice young lady.' "

By the end of the day, Steve had finally said, "No, Chris, she is not your mom."

Connie told the jurors that Steve had suggested some bizarre sexual arrangements. "He asked if one of my fantasies was to have two guys. He said that he had a friend that could fulfill it. I shot that down. I was sixteen, seventeen—that was inconceivable to me. And then he suggested about having sex with another woman while he watched. And I shot that one down too."

The trip to California only got worse. Steve was so "agitated," Connie testified, that she had to drive his truck home.

"When you got back, what was your state of mind as far as being with the defendant any longer?"

"I never wanted to see the man ever again. This is probably the first time I have seen him since."

Pete Mair cross-examined Connie. She admitted that she could have been off on the year of the California trip. It could have happened in 1993 rather than 1992. She also admitted that she drank alcohol before she met Steve; he hadn't introduced her to drinking.

But Connie Duncan was positive about her memory of Steve's telling her that Jami got a bloody nose at the top of the stairs in the Redmond house while she was fighting with Steve. The prosecution team and the Redmond detectives had believed all along that Jami Sherer died in her own home as she attempted to leave Steve for good. Connie Duncan wasn't the only witness who had heard that version of an injury to Jami.

"When did that statement occur?" Mair asked. "What year?"

"Well, it must have been 1991."

"What month?"

"I had on shorts. It must have been August—September, perhaps."

Steve had joined a number of dating services. A representative of Great Expectations explained that their company simply allowed "members to date more successfully." Jana Cheney testified that people came into their offices for a free consultation. If they could prove they were single and ready to date, they paid a fee.

"Steve Sherer was one of our lifetime members," she explained. When he joined in July 1991, he filled out the standard application form and put his marital status down as "separated." In January 1995 he changed that to "widowed" and wrote "widowed" again in August of the same year. Steve had no paucity of women. His trouble appeared to be holding on to them.

Ron Coates met Steve Sherer in a Bellevue nightclub in 1991, less than a year after Jami vanished. They drank together and seemed to hit it off, Coates testified. Coates and his girlfriend, Victoria, ended the evening by following Steve and his date to his home after the bar closed. Steve showed Ron his photo album, and Coates commented how attractive Jami was. Steve told him she had simply disappeared the year before.

"Do you miss her?" Coates asked.

"No, she was going to leave me anyway," Steve answered.

As the liquor flowed, the group settled in for the night at Steve's house. His tongue loosened as he talked with Ron Coates. As Victoria had told police, Coates began to suspect that Steve had something to do with his wife's disappearance. Staring into his glass, Steve talked on and on.

"He told me that he flew off the handle just before his wife disappeared," Coates testified. "He told me they'd gotten into an argument and that things got out of hand. He said he was sorry and that he shouldn't have done that. She lashed out at him, and he gave her a bloody nose."

Standing to demonstrate for the jury, Coates drew back his fist and feigned a blow to within an inch of Marilyn Brenneman's face. "He went 'Boom' and caused her nose to be hit, and it proceeded to bleed.

"It was kind of like a weight lifted off his shoulders, like he wanted me to know," Coates testified. "He indicated he was the prime suspect."

But Steve Sherer also said that the Redmond police were "dumb. He said they could never prove anything, basically."

To the prosecution's frustration, Ron Coates had not asked for many details. "I really didn't want to know much more than that, to tell you the truth."

Despite what was tantamount to a confession to the murder of his wife, Steve was apparently such good company that he and Coates had kept a friendship going. They went water-skiing on Lake Washington in Steve's boat the next day. Steve's mind had still been on dark subjects. He remarked to Coates that if anyone drowned in Lake Sammamish, "they would never find her body because the water was too murky."

And then Steve had crumpled his beer can and tossed it into the lake and said, " 'That's a good place for your trash,' " Coates testified.

The jurors looked interested in Coates; his story of a

bloody fight between Jami and Steve was remarkably like the testimony given by Connie Duncan.

Peter Camiel asked Coates on cross-examination why he had waited five years to tell the Redmond police about his conversations with Steve. He said he had left messages, but no one called him back. He admitted he hadn't given anywhere near the details he had just testified about. Camiel suggested that Coates had called the police again within ten minutes of reading that there was a $20,000 reward for information about Jami Sherer's whereabouts.

Ron Coates maintained the reward didn't matter to him. What mattered was his fear of Steve Sherer. He had written down statements for the police before, he said, but he always held some things back. It was far easier for him to reveal everything that Steve told him *after* Steve was arrested for Jami's murder. "So I wouldn't be like a sitting duck out there."

Dozens of witnesses took the stand. It had been ten years since Jami's disappearance, and many lives had changed. Two women who had seen someone with long hair riding in a car that looked like Jami's Mazda on that Sunday in 1990 tried to recall what they had seen. One of them had suffered brain damage during the intervening decade and couldn't even recognize her own signature. As a witness, she was worse than useless. The other woman wasn't sure any longer who she had seen.

Lew Adams's mother remembered Sunday afternoon; she had been selling "duster gloves" at the church bazaar—"canvas gloves with fingernails and rings on them, and yarn on the bottom," she explained. Yes, she said, Lew had come to see her. "He looked normal."

Lew drove his bubble-gum pink Volkswagen Beetle in those days, and treated it like a baby, washing it again and again. It was not a car that anyone would forget. And it was not a car that could have maneuvered off-road to dump a body, low-centered as it was.

Sara, who had married one of Steve's good friends and once heard Jami's regrets about her own marriage, testified that Steve propositioned her within weeks of Jami's disappearance. He glared at her as she stepped down from the stand.

That night, Sara received a phone call from the King County Jail. Steve Sherer was calling. She didn't accept his collect call, the only way the inmates could make phone calls. Frightened, Sara reported his attempt to talk to her, and detectives warned him that there would be big trouble if he tried again to intimidate a witness.

There were witnesses who said that Steve had rented a steam cleaner for his carpet a few times after Jami vanished. The first carpet cleaner said he had cleaned the carpet at 10709 161st Avenue N.E. in Redmond on October 9, 1990. He knew the police had searched the Sherer house the day before. His records a decade later showed that he had marked a large spot to be pretreated. "It was six inches by eighteen inches," he said. He could not recall if he had cleaned the lower level of the home. One of the spots had been in the living room, a pinkish spot near the coffee table. The police had already tested it for blood and found it negative. Steve's sister thought it was Kool-Aid. His mother told Carolyn Willougby it was grape juice.

There was sealant under the carpet in the basement near the door to the garage. The carpet and pad had been cut out, because someone had evacuated there, leaving a urine and fecal stain. Steve blamed it on their dog. After so much steam cleaning, no criminalist

ANN RULE

could say what species had lost body fluids there. Someone had treated the floor with *Kilz*.

Records showed that the original carpet purchased for the basement in the spring of 1990 measured 11.8 square yards. That made sense because Jami and Steve were refurbishing their home at that time, getting ready to move in. However, Steve had purchased more carpet in January 1991, and some of it was used to patch the 3- by 5-foot area near the garage.

All of the pieces of the giant puzzle that Jim Taylor, Mike Faddis, and Greg Mains had set out to solve were now being set in place. Separately, many of the witnesses would have had little impact. Together, however, they formed a picture that was cruel and grotesque.

It was May 18 and the prosecution case was winding down. Throughout the trial, Judy Hagel had listened to horrific testimony and managed to maintain her composure. In the next row, Sherri Schielke appeared concerned but unruffled.

However, when Dr. Katherine Taylor, a medical investigator and forensic anthropologist for the King County medical examiner's office took the witness stand to discuss what happened to a human body disposed of in the wild, Judy Hagel tensed. Taylor spoke in the matter-of-fact way of a professional. She had tramped through forests and desert and examined numerous human remains. She was not a grief counselor, but a scientist.

Jami's image smiled from the Missing poster facing the gallery—and the defense table—as Taylor began. "A body above the ground is affected by the environment: temperature, sunlight, rainfall, insects, carnivores, how close it is to water," she told the court. "Human bodies are a valuable food source. Underground, it depends on whether the body is clothed or unclothed, the biomass [size of the body]—larger bodies take longer, how deep they are buried."

Taylor quoted a study done in 1989 that concluded the fastest a body would be reduced to a skeleton in Washington State was twenty-eight days. After that, all manner of natural phenomena—running water, rockslides, high winds—separate the bones left behind. "Coyotes, dogs, bears, squirrels, rats, mice, take hair for their nests." Small and large bones are dispersed "one half mile to a mile away. The cranium is the easiest to mark as human." Dr. Taylor explained that body recovery around Seattle would be difficult.

"What's left after a year?" Brenneman asked.

"There's good body dispersal, but heavily altered. The body would be unrecognizable after two years, even more so if small animals had chewed on the bones. Trauma attracts carnivores. They smell blood."

Marilyn Brenneman had warned Judy Hagel that this part of the trial would be very difficult for her, but she had opted to stay in the courtroom. Even with her back to the gallery, however, Marilyn could sense Judy's despair. Every mother in the courtroom could.

"Wrapped bodies last longer," Dr. Taylor continued.

"What about the areas where they are left?"

"Anywhere from neighborhood parks to open areas to forests. Sometimes, no one finds the bodies or they don't recognize them as human. Hidden bodies have usually died of unnatural causes."

"After nine years?" Brenneman asked.

"[Around] an ungraved body or one in a shallow grave there would be excessive vegetation growth. When you dig a grave, you aerate the soil. Two feet down, you hit rock or clay around here," Taylor said.

"You wouldn't have to have a rectangular grave. A small biomass only requires a small hole in the ground."

After all these weeks, Judy Hagel had come to a point where she could not bear to hear such details. She let out a wail of grief and stumbled past eight members of her family as she fled into the corridor, sobbing.

The testimony was awful to hear, but Taylor soldiered on. She explained that the most they could hope to find of Jami would be a skull and some small bones.

And if she was in the water?

"Adipocere is common," Taylor said, "but Lake Washington has a very uneven, muddy bottom. You'd have to be looking for her and have a pretty good idea where she was."

On cross-examination, Dr. Taylor said the human teeth don't decompose.

"Do silicon implants decompose?" Mair asked.

"My assumption would be no."

Mair pointed out that cadaver dogs had failed to find Jami and ground-penetrating radar had also found nothing. She could be in blackberry thickets or in the roots of trees.

"Yes," Taylor answered. "It's difficult to say."

"How time-consuming would it be," Brenneman asked, "to find a place to leave a body on the surface in this area?"

"Not hard at all. Cadaver dogs need an area in which to search, though."

And that was true. There were endless miles where Jami could have lain, undetected, for almost a decade. The snow, the rain, the sun, had come every year. Leaves had brightened and died and fallen to cover her, perhaps, in nature's blanket. Many bodies in the Green

River murders had proved to be "self-buried"—that is, left on the surface of the ground but covered by so many seasons of decomposing leaves that they appeared to be buried.

It was, in the end, academic. Jami could be anywhere within an hour or two of the house she had decorated so lovingly.

But no one in Judge Wartnik's courtroom believed that Jami was alive, living another life far from her son, her mother and father, and her brothers.

The prosecution called their last witness on June 23.

Judge Wartnik denied two motions from the defense—the first to dismiss the case for lack of evidence and the second to dismiss the charge of first-degree murder because the prosecution had failed to establish premeditation.

The trial would proceed.

16

It was the defense's turn to call witnesses. Would Steve Sherer testify in his own defense, a decision that is usually dangerous for a defendant? If he took the stand, he would open himself up to cross-examination by the prosecution. No one had yet heard his voice. Did he have some explanation for what had happened to Jami?

If he chose not to testify, the defense would have to resort to only a handful of witnesses. Sherer was not a man laden with friends. His sisters had both been witnesses for the state, however reluctantly. Laura, the younger of Steve's two sisters, had testified that Steve had told her that he and Jami had an argument and "she just left."

As far as Laura knew, Steve had not had a key to his mother's house. Usually she or her sister took care of their mother's home when she was away.

Saundra, who was next to Steve in birth order, admitted in the state's case that she had a nonexistent relationship with Steve. "I love him," she said, "but I don't like him."

Steve had spent at least half of the 1990s in Arizona. Saundra remembered he had called her from Phoenix in the fall of 1995, and that he'd been very upset and sounded as if he'd been drinking. He told her that he had done "bad things" that would upset people if he told them. Saundra remembered that call vividly because Steve was extremely distraught and thought he should sit down and talk with a priest. Saundra had asked if it had something to do with Jami's disappearance, but Steve didn't answer. Saundra had been concerned enough to call Laura and ask her to call their uncle who worked at the Seattle crisis clinic. Steve was sounding suicidal again. But he hadn't killed himself or staged an attempt, as before.

On the Sunday Jami vanished, Saundra recalled that Steve had phoned her in the evening while she was watching a *Star Trek* rerun. "That would have been between six and seven P.M." She wasn't sure if he had called an hour or so later, too.

Now, with the defense case beginning, Saundra was about to testify for the other side.

There was a legal scuffle as Marilyn Brenneman and Pete Mair both claimed the same witness. In the end,

Judge Wartnik allowed Brenneman to cross-examine Saundra, who was now Mair and Camiel's witness.

"Do you think that Steve felt guilty because he had something to do with Jami's disappearance?" Brenneman asked.

Saundra hesitated, and then answered, "That crossed my mind."

"Did you try to help Steve get custody of Chris at your mother's behest? Would you say that was a family obligation?"

"That would be fair."

"When you saw the spot on the rug [on October 8], was it because you thought it could be blood?"

"Yes."

Mair recalled Laura, to establish how worried the whole family had been that Steve was suicidal.

Then the defense called Christopher Moon, age forty-one. He was positive he had seen Jami Sherer hanging out in a card room three days after she was supposed to have vanished. He remembered her "because she looked like this girl I used to know in Arkansas. She was small, wearing a plaid top and she had light brownish blond hair. She was there forty-five minutes to an hour. She appeared to be killing time, waiting for someone."

It seemed impossible. Jami had been headed for her parents' house, and she hated card rooms.

Mair questioned a Redmond businessman who said he had met Steve in September or October 1990, when Steve came into his framing shop. "He was representing an artist who was selling a limited edition of Ken Griffey Jr. baseball prints. He was looking for seed money," the witness said. "Six months later, Sherer came back in. This time he had a handful of posters about his missing wife and asked if he could put one in the window.

"I had the impression he was in mourning a year later," the witness said. "He wasn't seeing anyone."

But on cross-examination, the man admitted that he had actually met Steve well before Jami vanished. The defense was antsy: they were afraid that deputy prosecutor Kristin Richardson was going to bring out the information that the witness once gave Steve a reference as a good employee when, in fact, Steve had never worked for him at all.

Pete Mair began reading from an earlier transcript, and Judge Wartnik stopped him. "You can't read transcripts; you have to ask questions."

"Why did you believe that Steve was not seeing anyone at that time?" Mair asked the framer.

"I answered that in 1991 or 1992," the witness said. "Steve seemed to be in mourning."

"Seeing anyone?"

"I don't know."

"Steve Sherer slept with ten women within three months of Jami's death," Kristin Richardson said. "Does that change your opinion?"

"No. He was upset and concerned."

The defense now attempted to enter into evidence the videotape of Jami having sex with both Lew Adams and Steve Sherer. Moreover, they wanted to show it to the jury. Their client had been painted with a black brush by witness after witness. Now they wanted to erase Jami's image as a good mother and a loving daughter and show her as a wanton woman.

But it seemed like such a vicious thing to do. How would the jury react to such a move, and how would Jami's mother and father cope with it? For days, the rumor that the tape was going to be allowed circulated through the courtroom. A number of court watchers vowed to leave the courtroom if the video was shown. At that, it might be a horrendous tactical error on the part of Mair and Camiel; the video reportedly showed their client directing sex play between his drugged wife and another man. That might not endear him to the jury.

In the end, Judge Wartnik refused to allow it, and there were sighs of relief.

Pete Mair read Steve Sherer's suicide note, the note he had beside him in his car when he attempted suicide shortly after Jami vanished. The prosecution argued that the suicide was staged, and that Sherer had never intended to die. If he had, why did he have his cell phone so conveniently beside him?

One of the defense's prize witnesses backfired badly on them. Perhaps Mair and Camiel didn't fully grasp the techniques used in bloodhound searches. They had interviewed Richard Schurman, Maggie's handler, and knew she and other dogs had followed a track from Jami's abandoned Mazda to the bus stop on I-5. Perhaps Peter Camiel's intention was to show that a stranger had dumped her car near the church and then caught a bus.

By the time Schurman finished explaining how the scent objects obtained from the Sherers' laundry hamper led the dogs to the last spot where their quarry stood, however, the defense had clearly experienced a disaster.

It was clear that the skin flakes and odor on the back of the driver's seat were not from Jami. Add to that the fact that the seat had been pushed too far back for Jami to reach the accelerator and brake, and any reasonable person would infer that Jami didn't drive her car to the church lot.

But the dogs *had* picked up on a scent, and that scent was from Steve Sherer's clothing, which had touched Jami's in the hamper. That was the scent they got off the headrest of the driver's seat *and* from the hamper. Both Maggie and the second team of bloodhounds had proven that it was Steve Sherer who parked his missing wife's car sometime on Sunday afternoon, September 30, and then walked or jogged to the bus stop.

It was impossible now for Camiel to deconstruct his own witness; he had spent a long time proving that Schurman was an expert in his field when he brought him to the stand.

"The dogs pursued the male scent," Schurman explained once more, "because the female scent had been eliminated the first day."

The male scent was that of Steven Sherer.

Sharon Ann "Sherri" Schielke took the stand. She was very attractive, with soft dark hair worn in a pageboy with feathered bangs. She had perfect features, and, like her missing daughter-in-law, she was very petite.

Sherri explained how she had helped Jami and Steve buy their home on May 31, 1990. She said she had never seen the shattered window beside her front door, so she had no personal knowledge that it had been broken on Sunday, September 30. "I saw fresh putty around the glass around New Year's 1990."

"Did you get some Missing posters of Jami?"

"Yes, Carolyn Willoughby gave them to me, and then Steve had some."

"How many?" Mair asked.

"A stack about that high." She held her hands about a foot apart. "I have about twenty left. Carolyn and I and my daughters left them along the Bothell Highway and in Lynnwood."

Sherri admitted that she had never seen Steve take

any to distribute. She had heard that Jami was missing when she was in Cancún on Sunday morning.

Mair asked Sherri to explain the arrangement she had with Steve to be in her house that Sunday.

"Well, I paid the mortgage, and they paid me back on the first of the month. On the twenty-ninth Steve was going to bring me a check—"

"Objection," Hank Corscadden interrupted. "Hearsay."

Corscadden's style was very different from Brenneman's and Richardson's. Almost military in his bearing, he fired off objections and questions in a staccato fashion that left witnesses stuttering. He knew his law and he caught every slip away from proper questions and answers. He shot out "Hearsay" again and again.

Sherri Schielke picked up the thread of her testimony at Mair's urging. "I asked him to mail packages for me whenever he could," she said. "He was coming the next day anyway. I asked him to drop off the check for the mortgage and put it in the bank. I left a deposit slip. We had a hidden key. Wally had two kids; I had three. Laura had lived at home, and she still had her key."

Sherri explained how she had cut her trip short and arrived home on Wednesday. "I went to the Hagels'. Steve was extremely upset."

She was the first witness who had noticed that, and they had been in trial for weeks. Steve's mother told the jury that she thought it would be a nice thing for her and Saundra to clean Jami's house October 8 so it would be clean when she got home. Sherri intimated that she was sure Jami was coming home.

Steve's mother cried as she read his suicide note, especially when it said, "I've lost Jami one way or the other." Once more, she detailed the financial arrangements about the house and why eventually they had to rent it and then sell it: Jami was no longer there to make the mortgage payments.

Hank Corscadden cross-examined Sherri. He peppered her with questions about the Microsoft stock, the house sale, the broken window, the replacement carpet next to the garage door and why she had chosen to clean Jami's house this time when she had never done it before.

"The other times when he assaulted Jami, you didn't clean the house?"

"I picked her up after one assault."

"How long have you been in court?"

"Four weeks." Sherri had heard seventy witnesses testify.

"You talked with Mr. Mair?"

"I spoke with him every day about the witnesses' impact."

Sherri's brother had been a police officer and was now a private investigator. She agreed that she had signed a note for a loan to set up his business with no collateral.

"You knew that any information your brother uncovered would incriminate your son?"

"No!"

"You confided to Carolyn Willoughby that there was a good chance that Steve was involved?"

"No—I said that *anyone* could be involved."

Corscadden prodded her with questions until Sherri Schielke answered, "There is always that possibility, but I hoped it wouldn't be true."

"You knew of your son's assaultive behavior."

"I only knew about that one time with Jami."

"Actually two," Corscadden reminded her. "There was another time where Steve was arrested for pulling Jami's hair out."

That was a coup for the prosecution; the memory of earlier testimony brought back ugly images of a piece of Jami's scalp lying on the floor. Sherri was clearly downplaying Steve's propensity for physical violence. Bettina had called her for help from California once and Sherri had ignored her plight, too.

"Do you believe your son is involved in Jami's disappearance?" Corscadden asked rapidly.

"I don't know."

Sherri said there was no way for her to know if her front windows had been broken. "I usually don't inspect my house for damage or broken windows. If it was well done, I wouldn't have noticed."

"Your son took your car [a Bronco] at New Year's? You would not have entrusted your son with a key—but he drove your car?"

"I didn't know."

"There is no doubt in your mind that Jami is dead?"

"No."

As Corscadden pelted her with facts and with the many times Steve had taken advantage of her, Sherri's answers grew foggier and less precise.

"After the case was filed," Corscadden said, "you gave the *Seattle Times* an interview over the phone?"

"I spoke to someone. I don't recall."

"You said, 'Ten years later, this is a little bit much.' If your daughter was murdered, would you feel the same way?"

Mair roared out an objection, and Hank Corscadden moved on to other aspects of the case.

"Did you think the police meant to interrupt Chris's birthday party?" he asked Sherri, who had complained bitterly that the Redmond police had deliberately ruined Chris Sherer's birthday.

"I think they knew Chris was there."

"You've heard all the police who have worked to solve this case and traveled all over," Corscadden said. "Would they actually go to your house and further harm Chris?"

"Of course I don't think that."

Sherri seemed relieved to be talking about the Redmond investigators' annoying invasion of her family's life. But before she could comment further, Corscadden brought her back abruptly to the real issues at stake. "You believed Jami was dead somewhere along the line?"

"Yes."

"Do you know where . . . when . . . how she died?"

"No. No. *No.*"

Mair and Corscadden argued. The defense attorney could sense that his witness was faltering.

Sherri Schielke had done her best to support Steve's story. Did the jury believe that he had free access to her house and her cars? Her Bronco would have traversed the wilderness off-road far more easily than Steve's Blazer, but would she really have allowed Steve to drive her vehicles when he had so many traffic violations on his record? She had a Mercedes and the new Bronco; any damage to them when Steve was driving would probably not have been covered by her insurance. She was too good a businesswoman to have allowed that.

Sherri Schielke seemed to be trying valiantly in her testimony to show that Steve had as much access to her home and her vehicles as his sisters did. She had gone to the wall so many times for her firstborn, figuratively walking behind him and cleaning up the messes and catastrophes he left in his wake. As he entered his thirties, Sherri had tried to make Steve more responsible for his own life, but he hadn't really changed. Now he stood accused of first-degree murder, and she reverted to her protective stance, trying to save him from a life behind bars.

As Sherri stepped down from the witness chair, obviously relieved, Pete Mair recalled Richard Schurman, the bloodhound handler, in an attempt to erase his earlier devastating testimony. This time Mair asked the witness about a dog named Major, who had also participated in the search for the last driver of Jami Sherer's Mazda in October 1990. Police records noted that Major had gone off in an entirely different direction from Maggie and the other search dogs, showing "intense interest" in another area and ending up two blocks from the car and nowhere near the freeway or the bus stop.

"It's apparent you don't understand dogs," Schurman said to Pete Mair. "That dog has never made a find in its life."

He explained that Major had been a dog in training. "His handler retired after Major proved unreliable," Schurman said. "That dog would show 'intense interest' in a Milk-Bone dog biscuit."

Marilyn Brenneman could not resist one question on cross. "Is that where the expression 'That dog won't hunt' comes from?"

Schurman nodded. "That dog was not a good search dog."

If Steve Sherer was going to testify in his own defense, the time would be now. But he sat, as always, at the defense table, somehow detached from the whole legal process. The defense rested without the jury's ever hearing from Steve himself.

That was probably a good move on the part of

Camiel and Mair. If Steve had testified, he would have
been subject to cross-examination, and those who knew
him also knew he was given to bursts of fury. There
would undoubtedly have been questions that he didn't
want to answer. Still, for the gallery—and the jury,
too—one question remained unanswered: Who was
Steven Sherer?

17

Neither the prosecution nor the defense
denied that somehow, some way, Jami Sherer had died.
There was simply great disagreement about whether
Steve Sherer had caused her death.

On May 24, 2000, Peter Camiel asked that Judge
Wartnik dismiss all charges against Steven Sherer for
lack of evidence and, barring that, to dismiss the charge
of first-degree murder because the prosecution had
failed to establish premeditation. "Because we don't
know the manner and means of death," Camiel argued,
"all we can do is speculate about premeditation."

Judge Wartnik denied both motions after the prosecution team cited a Kansas case where appellate judges
had ruled that premeditation can be proved by circumstantial evidence and what a jury may infer from prior
events. Steve Sherer had made threats against Jami before she disappeared, they contended, and that showed
he planned to destroy her.

The two charges against Steve Sherer were still in

place: premeditated murder in the first degree and second-degree murder that occurred as the killer was in the process of committing a felony. In this case the felony was assault in the second-degree.

Kristin Richardson rose to present the final argument to the jury. Dark-haired, with a calm manner, Richardson had been impressive throughout the State's case. Now she could not keep the scorn from her voice as she spoke of Steve Sherer's "squalid, voyeuristic life."

She began by stressing that fear was Steve Sherer's weapon. "He had tight control over other people: his mother, his in-laws. He threatened that he would take Jami and Chris away from them. And finally, Jami."

Kristin Richardson told the jury that sometimes a prosecution team cannot offer them a situation where there is no doubt about the guilt of the defendant. "We can't always have an eyewitness or a videotape or a diary. But you don't have to have a body to convict," she stressed. "If you're smart enough about where to put a dead person—the bottom of a lake, the base of a tree, a hole somewhere in the wilderness, you *can* get away with murder. We will probably never know the last minutes of Jami's life. We may never know why she stayed with him or how he got rid of her body.

"But the body is *not* the case. [The case is] the final picture of the little pieces of a puzzle—the forest made up of the single trees."

Richardson explained the elements of a murder case: Did this murder take place in the state of Washington? Yes. Was there an intent to kill Jami Hagel Sherer? Yes. Premeditation, she explained, means that intent was present for more than a moment in time, even a minute or two before the murder itself. Was there premeditation? Yes.

"Look at Steve's treatment of Jami: control," she said. "The first time they met, he picked her up in a bar and talked her into leaving her friends and coming with him. He sent her a dozen roses. He was forceful. He gave Jami a full-court press. He was quickly in control of her. Jami's biggest mistake? Moving to California with him. He threatened suicide with a knife. And Jami said, 'It wouldn't have happened if he didn't love me so much.' He put a sign in their yard, 'I love my wife!' He sent her roses to Microsoft. He gave her diamonds.

"And then"—Kristin Richardson's voice rose—"he embarrassed her. He called her stupid, worthless. He put her down in the Balderdash game. That was the way it was going to be. He missed her labor by two hours. All she wanted to be was a mommy, but he discussed the most private moments of their sex life. He was happy to talk about his sex life to anyone who would listen. He kept sex photos of her, her underwear.

"He made her have a boob job with the money from insurance fraud. At their wedding, he bragged that 'all the guys had hard-ons.' Jami was the proverbial inflatable doll to him."

Richardson made no effort to deny that Jami had indeed engaged in three-way sex with Steve and Lew Adams, but she pointed out that it was at Steve's coercion. "Lew said that Steve called him into the bedroom, saying, 'I need help here.' Steve was undressing Jami, who was just roused from sleep. Steve was taking her bra off. Steve couldn't maintain an erection. Jami told Lew later that she was humiliated.

"Steve wasn't working. He spent his time obsessing over whether her job was lessening his control over Jami. He had no concern at all for Jami. Jami would do *anything* to avoid a fight, but she was unable to break the cycle, although everyone pulled out the stops to get her free of him."

Kristin pointed out what Steve had said the night before Jami vanished: "If I ever catch her cheating, I'm gonna kill her."

And Jami had finally cheated on him, going out with Lew Adams because, in Jami's words, "Lew listened to me and gave me the courage to leave."

"She asked her dad, 'Daddy, can I come home?' She took the ring," Kristin submitted. "It was a metaphor—the final payment to her, a symbol of her value to him. She taped it under her car seat."

Kristin Richardson gave a timetable for September 30, 1990, the last day she believed Jami was alive:

7:30 A.M.: Steve calls Judy Hagel and says, "Jami's home."

Before 8:00 A.M.: Jami is at Judy's. Steve calls, calls, calls. Judy prevails upon her to speak to him. Jami agrees to meet Steve at the Samena Club. Steve grabs her purse.

8:40 A.M.: Jami calls Judy. She's just getting clothes together for Chris. "Then I'll be leaving."

10:00 or 11:00 A.M.: Jeff Caston calls. Jami's anxious to leave before Steve gets home. He has found the receipt from the Crest Motel in her purse. He's starting to lose it. He goes to the motel, looks for the ring, checking the bed in the room. No one has slept in the bed.

11:45 A.M.: Jami's on her way to her folks' house. She plans to stop by the Bear Creek Taco Time. She tells Judy, "I'll bring food when I come." It's a fifteen-minute drive to Judy's from the Sherer home.

12:15 P.M.: Steve Sherer calls Judy, asking for Jami. He talks to Jeff Caston and says Jami has disappeared.

12:30 P.M.: Steve calls Judy.

"At that point," Richardson said quietly, "Jami was dead. Somehow he knew she'd disappeared at 12:15."

Kristin Richardson told the jurors that Steve had changed his usual behavior. Instead of calling the Hagels' house every fifteen minutes, on this Sunday they heard nothing at all from him from 1:00 to 5:00. "Utter silence. He had four hours, and they heard not one word.

"He called his sister, Saundra, during *Star Trek*, and said, 'Jami's disappeared.' *How did he know so soon?*

"He threw out Jami's birth control pills."

To Richardson, the most obvious lie Steve Sherer told all day was when he said to Jeff Caston, "We decided to go our separate ways until this can be straightened out."

"Inconceivable!" Richardson said vehemently.

And during that afternoon when no one heard from Steve Sherer, he had been busy. Kristin Richardson asked rhetorically, "Who had the best car to hide a body? The *Bronco*." His mother's Bronco.

"His actions after Jami disappeared form a picture—all incidents of a cover-up." She itemized the elements of that picture:

"He broke the window to Sherri Schielke's house. *To sleep? Why?* He wasn't looking for Jami at all.

"He sleeps in another house for a week. Why not be there at their home to take Jami's call if it came? He was 'uncomfortable' there. Because he committed murder there?

"He signed a cleaning order for the carpet in his house. It was only four months old. His mother cleaned the house. She had never cleaned it before when Jami left.

"He tells his uncle Roger to look for Jami's car in his patrol sector in north Seattle. How did he know the car would be there?

"He knew about Jami's duffel bag.

"He stages a suicide attempt. He never intended to die. He's got the picture of Jami in her wedding dress. A picture of Chris. A note and a cell phone. It was a cry for help—to get out of being interviewed by the detectives.

"He puts Jami's panties around his biceps. He has sexual control of her *even after death*. Her most intimate thing tied around his muscle."

Kristin Richardson's voice was a metronome, ticking off the actions that simply didn't compute with what a normal, innocent man might be expected to do after his wife had vanished.

Steve never helped in the search for Jami. "He took a pile of flyers to look good, but he left them in his glove compartment. He started dating twenty-five to thirty other women within two weeks. He 'missed sex.' He told a girl in a bar 'The bitch is gone,' but he told Bettina, 'I'm sorry I hurt you or her.'

"He never asked the police for an update on the investigation; he never asked Jami's friends."

Kristin Richardson spoke of how the car seat of the Mazda was pushed too far back for Jami to reach the pedals. The alarm wasn't on, she reminded the jury, and the duffel bag was hastily packed with things Jami would not have chosen. "He had a key to her car, but he said he didn't. Carolyn Willoughby found it." Nor, Richardson suggested, had Sherri Schielke ever left a key to her house for Steve.

"There was *Kilz* sealant under the carpet in the base-ment near the garage. [Steve] said 'The dog did it,' but something had evacuated there," Richardson said. "He bought more carpet for that house in January 1991 . . . a piece five by three feet in the hall.

"He liquidated Jami's assets. Sherri wanted her money back two months later. They both knew that Jami wasn't coming back."

Steve's Achilles' heel, Richardson suggested, was his drinking. "When he drank, he leaked out things. [To his uncle]: 'They can't prove murder without a body.' To Ron Coates: 'I'm the prime suspect—she was going to leave me anyway,' and 'I've done something bad. I'm going to miss her.'

"And then there was silence until he was arrested," Kristin Richardson said. "And then he said, 'So you found the body?' "

She asked the jury to remember Steve Sherer's Hal-loween card to Chris in which he urged his son never to drink or do drugs because they had ruined his life.

"Remember, [most of] the witnesses don't know each other, but their stories dovetail. Nuns or priests make bet-ter witnesses, but these are the people who want to spend time with this man, people on his level. Remember his history, his actions, his reactions and his statements.

"Just because we don't know how she died doesn't mean Jami isn't dead. We heard of shallow graves and animals.

"He took Jami's purse so she'd have to come home to get it. He *lured* her," Richardson said, winding down her final arguments. "She told her parents on the phone on Sunday morning, 'Steve's here but it's okay—I'm getting ready to leave.'

"He called Judy Hagel as if Jami wasn't already

dead. And now Steve Sherer is in a place where his desire for control has no power whatsoever. He has lost control at last."

Pete Mair, in his final argument, of course, attacked the state's case. "It's way too long on theories. It's very long on speculation. But it's very short on what I consider to be evidence. They have no evidence of when, where, how, the victim died," he said with a shadow of contempt in his voice. "They haven't proved their case beyond a reasonable doubt. What they do is decide he did it, and then they work backwards. At some point they just assumed that Steve must have done it. Then they dredged and they dredged until they found people to support their theory."

The jury watched Mair alertly, their mouths looking oddly pinched. "Don't let the state put it on *you!*" he warned them.

Mair offered his own timetable:

2:21 A.M. Sunday: Steve calls for information to
   Lisa Cryder.
8:45 A.M.: He tries to call Lew Adams.
9:43 A.M.: Jami calls Lew Adams.
9:51 A.M.: Lew's at work.
10:00: Jeff Caston speaks to Jami.
10:30: Jeff calls Steve.

Mair suggested that Steve did everything he could to find Jami and that he grieved for her intensely. "He was in the hospital for three weeks after his suicide attempt."

At least three jurors had a look on their faces that seemed to say they had shut Mair's arguments out.

"At 7:00 P.M. that night, Steve took Chris to their

home in Redmond. At 8:00, he called his sister. He tried to call Lew. He went back to the Hagels'."

Steve, Mair said, had called Microsoft looking for Jami and gone to the Redmond Police Department to report her missing. He had met a uniformed officer at his house, given an interview at the police station the next day, Wednesday. "He was interviewed again on Thursday by the police. He gave a consent to search his car. On Friday, he gave them scent items."

According to Mair, Steve had been the epitome of the helpful spouse, whose suicide attempt was very real. "He hooked up a hose to bring carbon monoxide into his car. He had to be put in a hyperbaric chamber. . . . From his house to the church [where the Mazda was] was 17.4 miles, or a forty-six-minute trip. It was 14.7 miles to his mother's house, or thirty minutes. It was fifteen minutes back to the Hagels'. [Getting rid of a body] would be an awesome task to accomplish in three to five hours."

Pete Mair suggested that the real killer was probably Lew Adams. "He had eighteen hours without observation. . . . No one searched Lew's place . . . while Steve is frustrated after looking under every rock for evidence [of Jami]."

Mair disparaged the number of witnesses who hadn't come forward for years: Ron Coates who, he suggested, talked to police only after a reward was offered; Rich Hagel, who spent most of Saturday night with Steve and never told the police or his own family that Steve had said, "She's cheating on me. I've gotta kill her," until after Steve's arrest.

"No neighbors heard or saw anything on Sunday afternoon." Again, Mair emphasized that the prosecution was trying to force the jury to make an impossible decision, to bring in a verdict on a case that could never be proved.

Marilyn Brenneman was the last to speak in this very long trial. Over the past seven weeks, the plants in the courtroom had grown dustier and droopier; everyone had memorized the paintings on the wall.

The rail in front of the judge's bench was decorated with photos and written mementos of a tragic marriage: wedding photos of Steve and Jami, Jami and little Chris on the Missing posters, stacks of greeting cards, the blue suitcase, paper bags full of Jami Sherer's panties and filmy black negligees, contracts she had signed long ago. In essence, the pieces of her life, and perhaps her death, were all scattered over the varnished wood. Jami's likeness still smiled toward Steve from a huge poster—a grown woman, yes, but one who looked like a high school girl, happy and unafraid.

Marilyn Brenneman told the jury that Steven Sherer's threats against her gave her "no personal ax to grind. I've been threatened before and I will be again," she said.

She described the defendant as a very angry man. "He told me, 'I want what's mine!' And he owned Jami, too. He had plenty of time Sunday morning to lie in wait for her. They had a fight. She went to her mother's, and he wanted control again."

But finally, she said, Jami wanted a divorce. Brenneman suggested that Steve's searches of the motel, Jami's purse, and her Microsoft office were not about Jami at all. He was looking for the diamond ring.

Of course, the neighbors heard no noises that Sunday almost a decade earlier. "She was taken off guard. He didn't need to make a sound to strangle her. He didn't need to shed her blood or fire a shot," Brenneman said. "Strangulation causes voiding or evacuation [of the bowel]," she explained. "He objectified Jami and he broke her, and we should all *feel sorry for him?*" Marilyn Brenneman asked incredulously. "Chris needed a mother who was alive, not a seventeen-year-old who looked like her.

"Justice grinds slow but exceedingly fine. It's taken ten years, yes. But it bleeds out. Steve told Ron Coates little bits and pieces: 'She bled from the nose.' It's a little bit of a confession—but not all true. Steve has to be a tough guy.

"Silence is a form of affirmation. When Saundra asked about his 'bad thing. Is this anything to do with Jami?' There was only silence.

"It bleeds out a little bit more in the [Halloween] letter to Chris and the suicide note, and what he said to Ron Coates and to Bettina. Steve Sherer made a promise to his victim of what would happen if she did certain things."

Brenneman pointed out that Steve knew all the back roads between his house and his mother's house. "He had the time, the motive, the opportunity, the knowledge, and the vehicle.

"Justice delayed is justice denied," Marilyn Brenneman quoted. "But that's not always true." She pointed out that Pete Mair had tried to suggest that Jami was not the person they thought she was. "But she had dreams. She had everyday events in her life, as we all do. She went to work and to day care. She bought groceries and went home to cook supper—only she often got beaten up.

"The justice system must protect the least of us to protect all of us," Brenneman said, as she acknowledged that Jami Sherer might have done some things that others would not. "She made some bad life choices."

But Jami Sherer did not deserve to die at the age of twenty-six, just when she was finally escaping the man who controlled her, just when she saw a future for herself and her little boy, just when she once again longed for the safe place that waited for them in her parents' home.

Late on Thursday, June 1, 2000, the jurors drew lots to pick the dozen who would remain to deliberate whether Steven Sherer was innocent or guilty. Eight women and four men remained. Their job now would be far from the easiest case a jury had ever received. Their first task would be to elect a foreperson, and then the actual deliberation would begin. They chose a retired teacher as their foreperson.

Jurors—all jurors—are inscrutable and no one in the gallery or at the prosecution or defense tables, for that matter, knew what they were thinking for the seven weeks they listened to testimony.

"The first thing we did," one juror said later, "was to decide how we would deliberate. We decided to go back through all the evidence from the beginning. Many of the jurors had filled their notebooks, and some of us seemed to feel more of a sense of the truth by watching the defendant and the attorneys."

There had been a great deal of evidence and testimony. The sessions were "intense," as the jurors deliberated from nine to four each day. "We kept from getting claustrophobia," a juror commented, "because we had a window in the jury room and Judge Wartnik let us take occasional breaks outside the jury room."

A jury is always made up of diverse personalities with different backgrounds, professions, education, and yet somehow they usually meld into a solid entity. They acknowledged that Jami was dead from the beginning.

Most of them were in agreement on a verdict within the first two days on the murder charge, but of course no one waiting anxiously outside the closed door knew that.

Again and again, the twelve of them went over the points that seemed the most important: Jami would never have willingly left Chris; Steve apparently had uncontrollable fits of anger; he was physically and mentally capable of killing; the odd collection of items in Jami's duffel bag; the suicide attempt that seemed orchestrated; the extra key; and—very important—the trail the search dogs followed.

A few jurors had seen Steve Sherer mouth what seemed to be threats to certain witnesses, especially Rich Hagel and Bettina Rauschberg, even though his usual expression had been cold and stony.

It was much harder for one juror, in particular, to grasp the concept of premeditation. Within her frame of reference, the thought that *anyone* would deliberately plan to kill another human being was incomprehensible. Humans just didn't do that.

The frustration level in the room mounted, although no one actually got angry. Finally the juror who couldn't comprehend premeditated murder said suddenly, "He thinks differently than the way the rest of us do! I've just realized that I've been basing my decisions on how *I* think. Murder on purpose? I couldn't even imagine it."

And still the days crept by without any signal from the jurors that they had reached a verdict. Someone had suggested they go through all the salient points one more time, just to be sure.

The usual rule of thumb is that the more rapidly a jury returns, the more likely they are to find the defendant guilty. As the days passed, both the prosecution and the defense waited with one ear tuned to the phone.

For the Schielkes and the Hagels, the hours stretched out interminably, and the Redmond detectives wondered if they should have gotten just a few more interviews or looked for Jami's remains in a wider circle.

Six days passed. The defense began to be cautiously optimistic. It was quite possible that Steven Sherer was going to walk out of the King County Jail a free man. Steve himself believed he would. Marilyn Brenneman, who admits to eating chocolate at times of stress, admitted to friends that she was going to have to double her workout time in the gym and in her garden to burn off the extra calories. In their offices high up in one of the tallest buildings in Seattle, even the view of Elliott Bay and the ferryboats crisscrossing the water failed to ease the prosecution team's apprehension. Other prosecutors assured Marilyn Brenneman, Kristin Richardson, and Hank Corscadden that they had all had cases under deliberation far longer than this one. They cited juries in some of their cases who had deliberated for two weeks or more and had still come back with guilty verdicts. They may have exaggerated, but they were trying to ease the tension.

It was 2:00 P.M. on Thursday, June 8, before the jury foreperson signaled Judge Wartnik that they had a verdict. They worried that it might be too late in the day to assemble all the principals in the courtroom. But it was quickly jam-packed with families and friends, and attorneys interested to see if anyone could get a conviction of murder when there was no body.

Judge Wartnik glanced at the paperwork, and shook his head slightly. The jurors had failed to write in their verdict on both of the charges. He sent them back to the jury room and cleared the courtroom. "We'd made up our minds on both counts," a juror recalled, "but we

ANN RULE

forgot to sign Count Two. It only took us five minutes, but it took a lot longer to reassemble Mr. Sherer, the lawyers, and all the spectators."

"Mr. Sherer looked as if he expected to go home that night," another juror said. "He seemed very sure that we were going to acquit him. I read later that he actually told people that."

But Steve Sherer wasn't going home.

The foreperson handed the verdicts to the bailiff who passed them to the judge. Judge Wartnik then handed them to the court reporter to read aloud. Some of the jurors avoided looking at the defendant, but several stared directly at him as the verdicts were read aloud.

Steven Sherer was found guilty on both counts: guilty of first-degree premeditated murder and guilty of second-degree felony murder. He seemed shocked initially, but he turned toward the jurors and shouted across the courtroom, "How do you go to prison for something you didn't do? When Jami comes back, you can all rot in hell!"

The jurors were quickly escorted from the courtroom and down the back stairs where no one could approach them. "It had been so long," one recalled. "And it was over so shockingly. One of the men told me that he went to the transit station across the street and just caught the first bus going north. He didn't even care if it was the right bus. He wanted to get out of there."

The jurors didn't know about Steve's next outburst until they read it in the newspaper. As he was being led out of the courtroom by corrections officers, Steve turned toward Judy Hagel, his face contorted with rage. "Fuck you, Judy!" he roared.

If the jury had any doubt that they had done the right

thing, their first look at the anger Steve Sherer was capable of erased that doubt. They had now seen the man that tiny Jami Sherer knew all too well, seen the rage she had encountered perhaps in the last moments of her life. One of the jurors—who had been the single holdout—was almost relieved at the sight of Steve's ferocious temper. "Now, I know," he said, "that my decision was the right one."

Another said, "It would have been almost criminal if we had *not* come back with a first-degree verdict of guilty."

On July 22, Steve appeared for sentencing. Mair and Camiel had sent Judge Wartnik a defense-sentencing memo that somehow made domestic violence seem prosaic. In part, it read, "Inasmuch as domestic violence is a pervasive societal illness and is common in the United States (one need only look to the amount of men and women in our local jails currently on charges associated with domestic violence), it is not a crime of the unfettered exercise of free will and choice."

Reading this excerpt carefully, one can deduce that the defense now maintained that their client wasn't *really* responsible for the actions that resulted in Jami's death because almost everyone was committing domestic violence. Pete Mair insisted there was nothing exceptional about Sherer's alleged crimes that would call for a sentence higher than the standard range of up to thirty years for a murder that occurs during spousal abuse.

In the bright-red jail coveralls worn by King County's most dangerous felons, Steve Sherer pleaded with the judge, "Your Honor, I stand here before you found guilty of a crime I did not commit. I've made a lot of mistakes in my life, but I'm not a murderer. I did not murder my wife. I had nothing to do with it."

Wartnik was not impressed, apparently, with this argument. Anthony Wartnik looked directly at Steve Sherer as he prepared to hand down the sentence. He said he was concerned about the lasting scars that Chris Sherer, now twelve, would suffer throughout his life because of the loss of his mother and the knowledge that his father had killed her.

Moreover, in the judge's opinion, it had taken methodical planning for Sherer to murder his wife and to pull off the "cruel hoax" that had only served to prolong her family's suffering, as they spent a decade without knowing where Jami was or how she had died. "A crime that would be a perfect crime doesn't happen by luck or chance," he said to Sherer. "It requires cunning planning and calculation.

"I have great fear not only for the women who may get involved with Mr. Sherer in the future . . . but for the safety of Jami's friends and relatives and the other witnesses in this case," Judge Wartnik added, referring to Steve's reputation for exacting vengeance.

One of the most convincing witnesses who appeared before the jurors was Karil Klingbeil, director of social work at Harborview Medical Center and an expert on domestic violence. Although the jury didn't know it, Klingbeil had lost her own sister to homicide at the hands of Mitchell Rupe, a bank robber who shot two female tellers in an Olympia, Washington, bank many years ago. A dynamic and brilliant woman, Klingbeil strives to protect women caught in relationships where they are denigrated and abused.

Klingbeil had found Steve Sherer a "classic abuser," who demonstrated nearly all the characteristics of a chronic wife-beater. "On a scale of one to ten," she testified, "his danger level is an eleven." His alcohol and drug use, and his controlling and manipulative relationships with Jami and with his previous girlfriends, made him the quintessential abuser. "The batterer carries his behavior on to different relationships," Klingbeil said. "That appears to be the case in most of Mr. Sherer's relationships."

Klingbeil was adamantly against the defense's stance that killing a wife or husband when a spouse loses control is such a common thing that "everybody's doing it," and not a crime as reprehensible as stranger-to-stranger murder.

The time had come. Judge Wartnik sentenced Steve Sherer to *sixty years* in prison, twice what the standard sentence is and many more years than either Jami's family or the prosecution team had hoped for. If he lives that long, Steve will be almost 100 years old when he walks out of prison.

As he was led in handcuffs from the courtroom, Steve turned once more toward Judy Hagel, his former mother-in-law and the woman who had fought for so long to find some justice for her daughter. He didn't swear at her this time. He blew her an insolent kiss.

Judy realized there was little chance that he would ever tell her where Jami's body lay. She wanted so much to have a grave for Jami, someplace she could take flowers from her garden, someplace just to sit and talk to her lost daughter.

"I definitely do not think he's guilty," Sherri Schielke told reporters. "We will be appealing, and it will all come out then. This was an injustice."

Afterword

Judy Hagel believes she knows what happened in her daughter's Redmond house ten years ago. She can close her eyes and visualize it, even though Steve Sherer will probably never admit his crime.

"I *know* that Jami was finally going to leave Steve that day," Judy says firmly. "She had made up her mind that nothing he could do would stop her. She told me she was on her way, and I believe she was. Steve would have pulled out that videotape and threatened to show it to me. He'd probably done that many times, but this time, I think Jami told him, 'I don't care anymore. Go ahead and show it to my mother. I'm still leaving you.'

"That [videotape] was the one thing he could hold over her head to keep her in line. When he realized that Jami was really going and that he had no power left over her, the only way he had to stop her was to kill her. I think he choked her at the top of the stairs and she fell down them."

Judy's voice choked a little as she spoke of that. "I wouldn't have liked to see that awful videotape, but it would not have changed how I felt about my daughter one bit. I would still have loved her. Nothing would have changed my love for her. She would have been welcome with us, and safe with us. I wish she could have understood that sooner. When I think of how my daughter must have suffered during those four years she was married to Steve, I can hardly bear it.

"I never knew just how bad it really was."

An updated epilogue to this case appears on page 525.

Bitter Lake

Children are often involved in the tangled lives their parents choose. They are the complete innocents, and their stories the ones that make you cry. The little boy in the following story had no choices in his life. Nor, in the end, did his mother.

The old man tossed and turned, caught in that drifting place between wakefulness and deep sleep. He wished for the thousandth time for the vigor of his youth when nothing had kept him awake at the end of a hard day's work. Roused from the edge of a nightmare, the elderly resident of the cozy house on the shore of Bitter Lake snapped awake, startled by angry shouting outside. When he bought this place, the Bitter Lake shoreline had been buffered by thick stands of evergreen. It was isolated and peaceful then, but the neighborhood had changed; the building boom around Seattle had crept out even to this serene little lake with its deceptive name. Where there had once been trees and marshes full of wild geese, there were now condos and apartment houses with every beehive unit populated by young people who seemed to come and go at all hours of the day and night.

This was a Saturday night during the last weekend of March. Though it was the threshold of spring, the weather was cold and windy. But the stormy night didn't seem to stop any of his new neighbors. They were partying, as they always did. Didn't they know that some folks needed their sleep? It was no use going to bed early. Cars were backfiring, tires screeching, and somebody was still shouting. He rolled over and looked at the clock beside his bed. It was nearly 2:00 A.M. The taverns would be closing in a few minutes. It was Sunday morning now.

Sitting on the side of his bed with his bare feet on the cold floor, the old man realized that a car had pulled up just below his window. He could hear someone talking loudly, and he figured it was some teenagers whooping it up when they should have been sleeping. But then something caught his attention and he listened more closely as the shouts outside grew sharper. There was a frightening hostility in the voice that carried up through his open window, an anger that seemed to swell and then recede. Holding his breath instinctively, he got out of bed and walked across his dark bedroom to a window that looked out on Bitter Place North.

Below, he could see a shiny reddish sports car. A very tall man stood next to the car, shouting at someone inside. The old man could tell that the occupant of the car was a female by the sound of her voice, although he couldn't see her. Her voice was loud too, high-pitched and full of stress, or maybe fear; the pair seemed to be engaged in a violent argument. Unaware that he was being observed, the man walked around to the driver's side of the car and grabbed the door handle. But the woman had apparently triggered the locks and the door didn't budge. Suddenly the big man's foot rose and crashed against the door with a crunching sound. He kicked the window until it smashed.

Later, it would be hard for the old man to remember if what he was watching had happened rapidly or if it was really being played out as it seemed—in slow motion. The driver's door was flung open and the woman emerged, running almost gracefully at first as she crossed the street, heading away from the lake shore. Then she scrambled up a terraced slope. The silent witness observed this from his bedroom window, shocked to see that the woman was half naked; she wore only a bra and a light skirt, or maybe a half-slip. The man was dressed, and as he whirled beneath the streetlight, the old man saw that he had a thick head of hair and a beard.

The woman had apparently surprised him by running away, and she labored up the grassy bank, through a dark patch of ivy and was almost to the giant fir trees at the edge of a lawn when she began to scream. "Help! Help me!" she cried, although she surely couldn't see the old man standing there in the window.

He realized now that what he was witnessing was more than a quarrel. This woman was in trouble. "This isn't the usual little thing," he told himself. "I'd better call the police." But before he could move to the phone, the man reached out an improbably long and muscular arm and grabbed the fleeing woman around the waist. He dragged her back down the embankment as if she was weightless. She was very slender and small. Next to her, the man looked huge.

There was no phone in his bedroom, so the old man had to leave the window to get to the phone in the kitchen to call the police. That was probably just as well. If only he were younger, he berated himself, he could go out to help the woman, but he knew that at his age, he would be no match for the bearded man. Where were all the rowdy young guys now, when they were needed? The street was deserted, save for the frightened woman and the man who had caught her in her flight.

The old man's call for help was recorded at Central Communications on the 911 line just before 2:00 A.M. The Seattle Police Department dispatcher immediately alerted Officers J. R. Sleeth and R. T. Mochizuki in patrol car 3N12. At this time of night, most calls were about drunks weaving along the roadways between the taverns and their homes.

"We've got an assault that's taking place now in the 13300 block of Bitter Place North, the dispatcher announced." Sleeth and Mochizuki weren't far away; they reached the address in minutes. Nothing could have prepared them for what they found.

The cries for help had stopped, the street was deserted, and the red car was gone. All that was left was a pitiful and tragic sight. After one look, Sleeth picked up his radio mike and said tightly, "We've got an assault here. Bad one. Better start us an aid car. Have the aid car enter off Greenwood."

"Received. What type of injuries?"

"Checking right now." The dispatcher waited until Sleeth replied, "You'd better send Medic One. I hope they make it. We've got a lady with a serious head injury. And we've got a little child here that's also been injured."

With their flashlights and the paler glow of the streetlight, the uniformed officers saw that the woman lay face down in a pool of blood that was rapidly seeping into the damp grass. Her face was a horror of bruises and cruel cuts; one of her eyes had actually been kicked or beaten out of its socket.

A little boy lay beside her. He appeared to be two or three years old. He was dressed in yellow clown pajamas and a tiny Seattle Seahawks jacket. His face, too, had been so brutally beaten that the patrol officers could hardly bear to look at him.

As they knelt over him, they held their breath, but they could detect no sign that he was breathing. Sleeth and Mochizuki performed CPR, breathing into the toddler's mouth, and pressing carefully on his tiny chest so they wouldn't break a rib or do more damage. They continued to work on him, stopping to listen for some sign that he was drawing in air on his own.

The woman moaned and tossed. She was breathing, but she was unconscious. As the Medic One rig's siren came closer and closer, Sleeth picked up the radio mike again. "You'd better notify homicide," he said tightly. "And get them out here right away."

The Seattle Fire Department paramedics looked at the little boy and shook their heads. They were too late to save him. They worked frantically over the woman, knowing that it would be a miracle if she lived.

More officers arrived on the scene. They questioned the elderly witness who had watched the struggle from his home. He was able to give them a remarkably detailed description of the man he'd seen chasing the woman. "He wore a brown jacket, maybe leather. He was big, husky," the man said carefully. "Not a teenager but not old either. Maybe in his twenties or early thirties. He looked like that basketball player from Portland, that Bill Walton. He had a beard like him. I could see him driving away in the red car after I came back from calling you."

It hadn't been that long. Maybe ten minutes at the most. The dispatcher alerted all police units in the area to be on the lookout for the suspect in the shiny red sports car.

The area was soon alive with police vehicles and Medic One units. What had happened had occurred with deadly speed, and neither the stunned policemen nor the paramedics could do much to help the victims, but they might have a chance to trap the attacker within the net of patrol cars that were blocking exits from the Bitter Lake neighborhood.

It was 2:05 A.M. on March 30 when the phone rang

in Homicide Detective Sergeant Don Cameron's home. Cameron's crew was on call for the weekend. When the regular shift of detectives left the homicide offices in the Public Safety Building at 11:45 P.M., the calls automatically went to the standby crew. "Patrol units are on the scene of a very brutal assault," the dispatcher said tersely. "They're requesting Homicide."

Cameron threw on his clothes as he talked. He called two of his detectives, Mike Tando and John Boatman, at home and asked them to swing by Homicide to pick up the cameras and investigative kits and bring them to Bitter Lake. "I'll head there now and meet you," he told them.

It was 2:30 A.M. when Cameron arrived at the scene. Patrol officers told him the Seattle Fire Department rig had just left with the injured woman. "She's not expected to live, according to the medics," Sleeth said. "The baby's still here. He's over there."

Cameron walked to the second Medic One rig. The child lay inside. The huge detective sergeant whom everyone called Mr. Homicide took a deep breath and peered into the brightly lit ambulance. He could see that the little boy had suffered numerous blunt-impact-type injuries to his head, and Cameron forced himself into the objective mode of a detective. If he didn't, he wouldn't be able to do this. He saw a strange pattern emblazoned in the middle of the toddler's forehead; he had been hit with something that left a circular indentation with several distinct impressions in the center of the circle. Not a hammer. A hammer would have left a solid circle. What then? A ring? Maybe.

There would be no rush to the hospital for the baby. It was too late. The woman, who was drawing in air with great difficulty, was alive when the ambulance reached Harborview Hospital on the highest hill overlooking downtown Seattle. If anyone could save her, it would be the physicians in Harborview's trauma center, where they were accustomed to treating terrible damage inflicted by car crashes, industrial accidents, and the extremes of human rage.

The obvious question remained unspoken. How could anyone do this to a fragile woman? To a helpless child? What could they possibly have done to send someone into such a violent rage?

Don Cameron called the medical examiner's office, and when John Boatman and Mike Tando arrived, he assigned them to measure the area where the attacks had occurred and to pick up any evidence the killer might have dropped. It had to be done, of course, and he wanted to keep them away from the paramedics' rig. "Don't look at the baby," he told them. They had toddlers, too; the sight of the dead child had been rough enough for Cameron, whose children were older.

Homicide detectives do what they have to do, but all of them will admit that the murder of a child always affects them deeply. This little blond boy in his clown pajamas was one of the most shocking victims any of them had ever encountered. It didn't matter how much tragedy they had seen or how impervious they seemed in the face of death; the murder of a child could make tough cops cry.

Dr. John Eisele, the King County assistant medical examiner, arrived and examined the child. He gave official verification that the youngster had succumbed to severe trauma to the head within the preceding hour: "Massive head trauma with a large laceration and skull fracture at the rear of the head. It happened just a short time ago."

The baby's body was moved to the medical examiner's vehicle and transported to the morgue to await autopsy.

Mike Tando and John Boatman walked up the bank to the spot where the attack had occurred. The uniformed officers cordoned off the entire grassy slope with yellow crime scene tape.

In addition to the old man, another witness told them he had seen the tall, bearded suspect beating and kicking both the victims. He too said it had happened very quickly and he could only watch the huge man as he sped away in a small red car.

"Anybody know who they are?" Tando asked the officers who had been first on the scene. "Did they live in one of the apartment houses?"

"No," Mochizuki said. "Nobody here knows them."

But the officers who had seen the woman speculated that the victims had probably been a mother and child. They both had the same blond hair. The police found no identification—the woman's purse was gone. It was clear they had been in the car with the killer. The prime witness was certain he'd seen the woman emerge from the vehicle and run away.

The grassy slope where the woman and baby were attacked was across the street from the homes fronting Bitter Lake. There was no moon, and the area was only dimly lit by streetlights at 3:00 A.M. But the detectives' auxiliary lighting revealed three distinct blood splotches on the grass: the place where the woman had been found was still marked by a blood pool 13 inches by 11 inches, and the baby had lain in a puddle of blood 7 inches by 6 inches. The third pool of blood marked where the child's head rested as responding officers tried to save him. The detectives photographed the blood and took samples for typing.

It was ten minutes to four in the morning when the investigators cleared the scene and returned to homicide headquarters downtown. They had retrieved very little in the way of physical evidence, and there was nothing more they could do until morning light made it possible to search the scene further.

Tando and Boatman drove up the hill to Harborview Hospital to check on the condition of the woman victim. The head resident in the ER told the two detectives that she was in "very critical" condition. She was still in surgery, where doctors were attempting to reduce the swelling in her brain, which had been so traumatized that it was now being crushed by her skull. "There's very little chance that she will survive," the doctor said. "But we're trying. Do you know who she is?"

Tando shook his head. "No idea at all."

The night's work was far from over for Cameron and his crew, but they didn't mind working through the night; a suspect in the brutal attack had surfaced. He had been caught in the police net they had dropped over the Bitter Lake neighborhood. And based on first reports, he certainly sounded like the huge bearded man their prime witness had described.

At 1:58 A.M. on that Sunday in March, Officer Mary Brick was working third watch in Unit 3U6. She had heard Sleeth and Mochizuki calling frantically for assistance from the paramedics. Then, as she turned toward Greenwood Avenue from the I-5 freeway, she listened to the information broadcast about a possible suspect on the loose in the vicinity. She made a mental note to watch for a bearded man driving a small red car, but she hadn't had long to look because the next call was directed to her unit: "Go to 345 North 133rd. Possible suspect vehicle located at that location. Washington license DBV-624." Brick's patrol unit rounded the corner near that address, and she saw fellow officers Steve Knectel and Andy DePola running toward a maroon Toyota Corolla a block ahead. A tall white male was just getting into the driver's seat. She maneuvered her unit close to the suspect vehicle and heard Knectel and DePola shout at the man, "Get out!"

The man didn't move.

"I said get out!" DePola snapped.

The man finally emerged, unfolding himself from a car that seemed too small to hold him until he stood towering over it. Knectel handcuffed him and walked him back to Mary Brick's vehicle. DePola followed, and the three officers and their suspect crowded into the patrol car. They then advised the suspect of his Miranda rights.

Knectel and DePola had been on the scene as the paramedics worked over the two victims. They had followed the killer's trail, after noting that the elderly witness mentioned "screeching tires." The two officers walked southbound down Bitter Place and saw fresh tire marks leading away from the crime scene. The tire tracks turned onto 133rd Street.

The burned rubber was fading, but at that hour of the morning, they found only one set of recent tire tracks on the rain-slick cement of North 133rd. Knectel and DePola moved forward on foot like Indian trail-cutters until they spotted a red foreign car parked up ahead. It was unoccupied, but when Knectel felt the hood, it was still warm. That was when he radioed for Mary Brick to "sit on" the car while he and DePola went to the nearby houses.

A house-to-house check proved unnecessary. Even

before Mary Brick pulled up, Knectel and DePola observed a large man with a fiery red beard walk toward the suspect vehicle and get in. They were beside him before he realized they were there. Glancing through the driver's window, Knectel and DePola saw crimson stains on the large man's hands and ordered him to get out of the car.

Oddly, the man seemed scarcely disturbed at being arrested. He gave his name as Patrick David Lehn, and his birthdate as March 9, 1952. He was a huge man, well over 6 feet, 3 inches tall, and he looked to weigh about 230 pounds. He had a thatch of curly brown hair and a bright red beard and mustache. He did indeed resemble Portland Trailblazers star Bill Walton.

Mary Brick studied the prisoner. He sat in a relaxed position in the backseat of her patrol car, but sweat continually beaded up on his forehead and rolled down his cheeks into his beard and mustache.

"Do you know who those people are?" Brick asked, gesturing toward the scene of the attack, which wasn't that far away. She didn't say "victims" or "the woman and the boy," but he seemed to know who she was talking about.

Lehn replied quite calmly: "Kathi and Kris ... Kathi Jones and Kris Haugen."

"You know them?" she persisted.

"I dated her once," he said. "She worked at a French restaurant in Seattle."

But when Brick and DePola questioned him further, Lehn was adamant that he hadn't seen Kathi Jones the previous evening. He couldn't have seen her, he said, because he didn't know where she lived. "I talked with her on the phone last night, though." Lehn said he'd gone to dinner alone at a steak house in Seattle and then had headed toward his north end home on I-5. He said he'd left the freeway at the Northgate Mall and gone to a 7-Eleven to purchase a bottle of champagne and a bottle of chablis.

"How did you get those stains on your hands?" De-Pola asked. "You cut yourself?"

Lehn stared at his hand as if he was surprised to see the cracking red marks, but then he explained that he had gotten into a fight with some "middle-aged guy" outside a Chinese restaurant.

Not surprisingly, the records department listed a number of Katherine, Kathy, and Cathy Joneses in the Seattle area. One of them was a Kathi Jones, who lived in an apartment at 322 North 134th Street—half a block from the attack site. It was also close to where they'd arrested Patrick Lehn.

Despite what Lehn was saying, he had to have seen Kathi Jones the night before. There was little question that he was the man she had been frantic to get away from, but he stonewalled, insisting that he had only spoken to her on the phone.

In a sense, the case seemed to be over; in another sense, the investigators knew nothing at all about the relationship and the emotions that had provoked the savage beatings on the grassy slope. What were Patrick and Kathi to each other? Was the dead child theirs? Like so many homicide investigations, this one started at the end and they would have to work backward until they discovered some sort of semirational explanation for what seemed to be complete chaos.

Pat Lehn was taken first to the Wallingford Precinct in the north end of Seattle. At DePola's instruction, he removed his clothing and it was bagged into evidence. His hands were swabbed with sterile water and the traces of blood obtained would be tested for type. He didn't seem to be wounded. He was given a blanket to cover himself, videotaped to show his demeanor at the time of his arrest, and then driven to the fifth-floor offices of Homicide in the Public Safety Building for further questioning by detectives.

It was 4:55 A.M. when Mike Tando and John Boatman introduced themselves to the hulking suspect. Tando was a wiry man with a quick grin and bushy blond curls; Boatman had a round, pleasant face and ruddy cheeks. Neither looked like a homicide detective, which proved to be an advantage in a number of cases. The man before them had massive shoulders that protruded from the blanket he clutched around him. He would have been a formidable opponent for anyone. The detectives were tremendously curious to know about what could have made him angry enough to beat a woman and a child. But of course they couldn't let him know how anxious they were to understand his motivation. They began slowly, asking him blandly general questions about his background.

Pat Lehn said he was currently living in Lynnwood, a small town about fifteen miles north of Seattle. Before that, he had lived in Seattle for most of his twenty-eight years. He had graduated from Shoreline High School and had attended one year of junior college. He worked as a field supervisor for a construction company building a skyscraper in downtown Seattle. That was a good job, a high-paying job that carried with it a good deal of responsibility. Lehn explained that he had no criminal record, except for a few minor charges. He read the Miranda rights form thoroughly and signed it, but he didn't seem eager to share any details about the previous evening with them.

"Do you want an attorney?" John Boatman asked.

Lehn seemed to debate this in his mind. "I don't know," he said, slowly. "I've watched a lot of television and I know an attorney would be mad at me if I told you guys the whole story."

The detectives waited. At length, Lehn decided he didn't want an attorney, and he did seem to be under some inner pressure. He clearly wanted to talk; he even said he wanted to discuss not only his arrest but what he knew about the victims. "But I don't want to get into it any deeper than that," he said.

The two detectives agreed to take this tack. At this point, they would have been grateful for anything that might shed light on the deadly attack on Bitter Place.

Lehn gave them Kathi's name again, and spelled it. He spelled Kris's name, and said he thought Kris was about three. He said that Kathi and her son lived just around the corner from where the "incident" happened.

This spontaneous statement was interesting, since none of the police or the investigators had yet told Pat Lehn where "the incident" had happened—or even what "the incident" was. It was he who was offering the information, apparently unaware that he was implicating himself.

And yet there was much that Lehn did not want to discuss; he claimed that it was "such a long story" and would take a long time to explain his relationship with Kathi Jones.

Boatman and Tando assured him they were not trying to trick him or trap him—he could stop talking at any time, and he was under no pressure to discuss anything that he didn't wish to. "But I have to remind you," Boatman said, "that if you make any oral statements, they can be used against you in court."

"Was it jealousy?" Tando ventured. "Did it all start because you were jealous—or was she jealous of you?"

Lehn nodded his head slightly. He spoke generally of the treachery of women. As far as he was concerned, none of them could be trusted. When the detectives didn't disagree with him, he took this to mean that they went along with his theories.

"You were jealous of her?" Tando asked. "She betrayed you in some way?"

If the suspect admitted to that much, at least they would have some kind of motive for what he had done. Lehn agreed that there had been jealousy in his relationship with the woman who was now fighting for her life.

"Were you lovers?"

Lehn said that he had been intimate with Kathi Jones in the recent past—but then he drew back into himself again. "I don't want to discuss that anymore."

The detectives waited. The silence in the cramped interview room with its faded green walls grew almost louder than words.

"Her father didn't like me much," Lehn finally offered.

"Why was that?"

Lehn made a dismissive gesture with his hand, but then he said cryptically, "You have to understand there have been things in the past that have continued to be a problem."

Quite sure that this was a massive understatement, the two detectives waited to see what the suspect would say next. His conversational style had fallen into a pattern of denial, followed by bursts of information.

Lehn told them he had recently spent a night with Kathi at her condominium. He said he thought everything was going fine, but then he left for a while.

When he came back, Kathi was angry with him. "Everything changed," he said. "She discovered that somebody had vandalized her Mazda RX7. I came into the condo parking lot and she immediately accused me of doing the damage. I kept telling her that I hadn't touched her car, that I wouldn't have had time to do that much damage, but she didn't believe me. She always thought that I trashed her car." He said Kathi prized her car highly. He couldn't come up with any reason someone else would have set out to destroy it.

Boatman and Tando had their own ideas about who had damaged the Mazda, but talking to Pat Lehn was like trying to drive parallel to another car that kept veering off the road. He picked certain incidents out of the air, but they were remote in time and had nothing to do with the terrible attack that had happened just four or five hours before the interview. He hadn't seen the victims the night before; he hadn't hurt them, he insisted. He took the stance of an innocent man who was being blamed for things he didn't do.

Lehn was vague when Boatman and Tando asked him the hardest questions. He said he hadn't been with Kathi in the early part of Saturday evening because she was working. "She was a hostess at L'Tastevin."

They knew the restaurant. It was a very popular, very upscale bistro on Lower Queen Anne Hill.

"You didn't go there to eat?"

"No," Lehn said. "I ate at El Gaucho."

El Gaucho was another top restaurant in Seattle, a place that had mink-lined booths, thick steaks, and the best martinis in town. Lehn had been drinking on Saturday night. He told them again about buying champagne and white wine at the 7-Eleven. He must have been saving the wine for later because he also said he went to a Chinese restaurant for a few drinks after dinner.

"You said you talked to Kathi early last night on the phone?"

Lehn nodded. He said he was supposed to meet Kathi after she got off work. It would have been usual for her to pick up Kris from his baby-sitter on her way home.

"You went to her place to meet her?"

He shook his head. No, he hadn't met her at her condo. Rather, he said he had encountered Kathi and her little boy near her home as their cars both approached Bitter Place North, "where it happened," Lehn said, again unconsciously referring to the attack. "I just bumped into them." He was giving his version of their meeting, but it was so obvious that this was his agenda. "We just happened to meet there, and we stopped our cars about three feet apart, and rolled down our windows . . . and then she just started to jump all over me."

He said Kathi brought up the trashing of her Mazda. Lehn said she had accused him once again of messing with her car. "She said somebody had taken all the lug nuts off of her front wheels. I got out of my car, and sure enough, there were lug nuts missing, one from each front wheel."

"You didn't do that?"

Lehn looked mystified. He denied being anywhere near her car on Saturday night. "She started to scream at me. She said she was going to file a police report about it and have the cops watch her condo so I couldn't come near her anymore."

The big man before them insisted that he hadn't been staking out Kathi Jones's condo, stalking her, waiting for her to get home. He did admit that he was getting angrier and angrier as she screamed at him and accused him of following her, tampering with her car. She kept telling him to leave her alone.

It was a tragically familiar story to the detectives—a man who wouldn't take no for an answer, a suitor who wouldn't go away. Nevertheless, Lehn maintained the stance of an innocent man, a man falsely accused.

"I finally just gave up fighting with her at one point and tried to reach inside and kiss her on the cheek, but she was so angry at me. That's when things started." Lehn said he had no memory of getting into Kathi's car. He could not remember how her clothes had come off, but he thought they might have come off inside her car. He claimed no recall of how their argument had ended.

"Where was Kathi—and Kris—when you left?" Boatman asked.

"I don't remember."

"Do you remember if you hit Kris?"

"I don't—but he could have gotten in the way."

Lehn said he left the scene after "everything just sort of happened," and he drove his car around the corner. Then he went back and drove Kathi's car to a supermarket parking lot a few blocks away. He left it there and returned on foot to retrieve his own car. It was at that point that the officers had arrested him.

Tando took Polaroid pictures of Pat Lehn, including close-up shots of his hands. They could see that his huge hands were swollen and red around the knuckles, and that he had long fresh scratches on both forearms. Lehn wore a round ring studded with small diamonds. He also told them his right foot hurt.

"How did that happen?"

"I might have kicked them, I guess—but I think it's from an injury on the job."

The county jail was across Cherry Street from the

Public Safety Building, but it was accessible through a tunnel. Tando and Boatman walked their prisoner over to the jail through the tunnel. The sun had yet to come up on that Sunday morning before Pat Lehn was booked without bail on suspicion of homicide.

At 6:50 A.M., Tando and Boatman returned to Harborview to collect the clothing that Kathi Jones had worn. She was still alive but in very critical condition, still in the operating room. The detectives were now into a new day, a day where sleep would be forgotten. They checked Pat Lehn's bloodstained clothing and noted that his right shoe was dented at the toe. That spot on the shoe was covered with dried blood which had blond hairs caught in it.

Thus far, Sergeant Don Cameron's team had one homicide victim—the three-year-old son of Pat Lehn's estranged lover—and they had been told that if Kathi Jones lived, it would be a miracle. They believed they had good solid physical evidence in Lehn's clothing, not to mention the bruises and scratches on Lehn himself, and they had his vague statement about "the incident." Now they needed to find out more about the suspect himself. He was a handsome man who had a good job, a nice apartment, and a new car. But something about his emotional affect was skewed; his responses to their questions had been strangely flat and deceptively mild, given the violent nature of the attack they were discussing.

Homicide detectives Gary Fowler and Danny Melton took over part of the investigation at 7:30 A.M. when they reported for duty on the day shift. They located Kathi Jones's red Mazda just where Pat Lehn said it would be—in the parking lot of a supermarket some blocks away from the scene of the beating. There were bloodstains on the right front wheel. A great deal of blood had splashed onto the hubcaps and then it had dissipated over the metal in droplets when the wheel turned as it was driven away. They could see blood inside the car too, on the gearshift lever, on the seat, and on a woman's white sweater that lay on the seat. From all appearances, the evening before had begun in a totally normal fashion for the victims. Kris Haugen's tiny tennis shoes and a bag of groceries were still inside the sports car.

Fowler and Melton canvassed the building where the victims lived to see if perhaps the argument had begun in Kathi's apartment, but no one had seen or heard anything the night before. So that much of Lehn's story was probably true: He had encountered his former girlfriend outside her condo as she drove up after picking Kris up from his baby-sitter and shopping for groceries. She must have been upset because the lug nuts on her wheels were loosened and she was probably anxious to get home safely.

A call came in to Homicide from a man who lived in the north end of the county. He said he had been dating Kathi Jones sporadically for several years, and when he learned about the attack on her and Kris, he became afraid for his own safety. He said that Kathi had broken up with Pat Lehn two or three months earlier, but Lehn wasn't letting go gracefully.

"She still saw him occasionally because he had some diamonds that belonged to her," the caller explained. "She thought she had a better chance of getting them back if she kept in touch with him. Pat had those stones set into a ring for himself, but she still hoped to get them back."

The caller said that he had told Kathi all the diamonds in the world weren't worth it. He warned her to avoid Lehn completely, but she believed she could handle him.

Kathi Jones survived surgery, but her condition deteriorated throughout the day until it was listed as "very grave." Her life was being maintained only by artificial means, with machines breathing for her; the damage to her brain was profound. Brain scans showed that she had suffered such massive trauma that she was clinically brain dead. So with her family's permission, her respirator was disconnected. She breathed on her own for a very short time and then died.

Patrick Lehn was now charged with a double homicide.

A check of records in Lynnwood, Washington, showed that Lehn's rage toward women was not something new. He was already on probation following a series of threats and instances of malicious mischief against another woman in that city. Lehn reportedly had been living with the woman in Lynnwood at the time of those charges and was physically abusive with her. She left him after he beat her, but then he encountered her in a local club and became enraged to see her sitting with two men.

When she went to the parking lot later, Lehn's ex-girlfriend found that three tires on her car had been flattened. Someone had methodically gone through her car, disabling it. The spark plug cables had been cut, and so had the fan belt, the alternator wires, and the pressure gauge wires. An attempt had been made to cut the fuel line, the brake line, and the transmission vacuum line. She told the Lynnwood police that she was sure the vandal was her former lover, Pat Lehn.

Two weeks later the woman was terrorized with

anonymous phone calls, where either no one spoke at all or the voice was clearly disguised. Fed up, she'd finally screamed into the phone, "I know it's you, Pat!" She told police he'd admitted it was him. He had also admitted to vandalizing her car and promised to pay to have it fixed if she would move back in with him. She refused.

Lehn had been right when he told Tando and Boatman that Kathi Jones's father didn't like him. The older man, actually Kathi's stepfather, confirmed this. Kathi had started a relationship with the suspect the previous fall, and things seemed fine at the beginning. It wasn't easy for a single mother who worked long hours, but Kathi was happy—at least for a while—when the tall, good-looking construction foreman came along. He gave her a diamond ring to show his good intentions. "It wasn't long before she told me that she felt stifled," her stepfather recalled. "The guy was extremely possessive."

Lehn started to haunt the French restaurant where Kathi worked, watching to see if any men came on to her. The man who at first seemed so perfect had become a nightmare to deal with. Kathi was afraid she would lose her job because of Pat's lurking around the restaurant. He would stare at her and listen to any conversation she might have with a stranger. It was part of her job to make diners feel welcome, but Pat was primed to discourage any men who approached her.

Lehn had given Kathi some "diamonds," but she and her stepfather had begun to wonder how he could afford expensive gems on his salary. She had the stones appraised, and both turned out to be fakes. In fact, everything about him was either threatening or phony. Kathi was miserable in the suffocating affair, and she tried to break it off only to find out, too late, that it was almost impossible to get free of Lehn.

Her stepfather verified that she was sure it was Lehn who damaged her Mazda, especially since Kathi knew he had almost destroyed his former girlfriend's car when she had attempted to break up with him. "I thought she'd broken off with him completely," Kathi's stepfather said. "But I saw Pat at Kathi's condo about two weeks ago." And Kathi assured her stepfather that she wasn't afraid of Pat Lehn; she was positive she could defuse his anger. She said he had some of her things and she had worked too hard to just let him walk away with her possessions.

Don Cameron studied the results of the postmortem examinations on the two homicide victims. Three-year-old Kris Haugen had succumbed to massive head injuries that were consistent with his having been kicked in the head. The homicide sergeant sighed when he read that there had been six separate identifiable blows to the youngster's head and neck. The imprint on his forehead had probably been made by a ring with a distinctive pattern.

Kathi Jones had sustained fatal brain-stem injuries and facial fractures. Like her son's, her neck appeared to have been stomped on as well as kicked. She had been hit or kicked so many times about the head and neck that it was impossible to count the blows; Dr. Eisele was able to isolate only eight to ten areas of trauma.

Neither Kathi nor her small son had a chance of survival once their attacker had started to pummel and kick them. The child must have run after his mother when she fled her car. She was probably trying to lead Lehn away from her little boy, even if it meant losing her own life.

Now that the detectives knew they were dealing with the aftermath of the jealousy and rage exhibited by the classic stalking ex-lover, they set about reconstructing the last evening of the lives of Kathi and Kris. It wouldn't change the ending, but the full scenario might help a judge or a jury to decide the fate of a heartless killer.

They talked with the owner of L'Tastevin, the restaurant where Kathi worked on the last night of her life. Her employer recalled that her shift as a hostess at the front desk ended at 12:30 A.M. She had received a phone call around 7:00 P.M., and the co-owner of L'Tastevin had overheard her side of the conversation. He recalled that Kathi seemed quite upset, but he wasn't sure why. She couldn't hide her distress, but she hadn't confided the details of the call to the owner.

"Did she talk to anyone here—any of the other employees?" John Boatman asked.

"No, she wasn't close enough to anyone here to share really personal things," the co-owner said. He also said that Kathi parked her car in the restaurant lot, but to his knowledge, no employees or diners had witnessed the removal of the lug nuts from her wheels while she was at work inside. At least, nobody reported it.

Kathi's sister told the detectives that she always took care of Kris while Kathi worked. On March 29, Kathi took her little boy to her sister's home a little before 4:00 P.M. She returned to pick him up at 1:10 A.M. "She said she was late because the lug nuts had been taken off her wheels and she had to get help to put them back on," the victim's sister said. "Kathi said she hoped Pat wasn't up to his stuff again."

"Did she say anything about receiving a phone call

at work that upset her?" Detective Boatman asked. "Did she mention Pat again?"

"No. Nothing about a call. Nothing more about Pat. She just stayed to visit for a while, and then they left to go home."

Apparently Kathi Jones had been angry over the missing lug nuts, but she was not overly frightened. She had bundled up her little boy in clown pajamas, packed him and his overnight bag into the car, and driven to a convenience store to get milk and eggs for Sunday breakfast, a breakfast she would never cook.

Another former boyfriend of the striking blonde told detectives: "I was at Kathi's about four months ago, and someone threw a rock through Kris's window. About fifteen minutes later, some guy named Pat called, and he was very irate. Later that night somebody vandalized her car, and she said there was $4,000 damage done to it."

Kathi Jones didn't want to be tied down to any man until she found one who would treat Kris as his own. She never talked about Kris's biological father, and friends knew he was out of her life and Kris's. Until she found someone who would be a good father, she wanted to date casually, but ever since she'd met Patrick Lehn the previous autumn, she had found herself boxed in by his possessive jealousy. No matter what she did, she couldn't escape. She was a strong woman, however, and for a long time she was unaware of Pat Lehn's jealous tenacity. At first, she was more annoyed with him than afraid; she thought she could handle him, play along with him until she got her things back. She had told friends that she planned to break up with him for good, but she hadn't been able to do it yet. She had no idea what a dangerous game she was playing.

Lehn himself admitted to running into Kathi and Kris on the dark side of Bitter Place North late that night, but he said that when he left them, they were "outside the car." There were witnesses who had seen the couple during their screaming argument and who had seen the bloody bodies of the victims afterward, lying on the grassy slope as a large man bent over them, still beating them. They saw a tall man who "looked like Bill Walton" driving away in the little red sports car that Kathi Jones had prized so much.

Why did Lehn think he could get away with murder? Maybe because he had barely gotten his hands slapped after destroying his last girlfriend's car. Maybe because his constant harassment of any woman who dared to break up with him had caused the woman far more trouble than it had ever caused him. Perhaps he thought he could walk away from a double murder too. But the ring on his hand matched the mark on his smallest victim's forehead perfectly, a brutal piece of physical evidence that inexorably tied Pat Lehn to the scene of the crimes.

On April 4, 1980, Patrick David Lehn was charged with two counts of murder in the first degree, and his bail was set at half a million dollars. On September 24, he was sentenced to serve a minimum of fifty-four years and two months for the murder of Kris Haugen and a minimum of ten years for the murder of Kathi Jones. Lehn is now housed in the Washington State Reformatory in Monroe. His earliest possible release date is November 19, 2016.

Young Love

Unrequited love can be as painful as an abscessed tooth. The pain is throbbing, searing, and anyone who has suffered from it remembers the wakeful nights when sleep would not come. But there is nothing more agonizing than the loss of first love. Those of us who survive that initial heartbreak learn that love can—and will—come again, but try to tell that to a teenager who has lost that first, flawless love. Young people believe that there will be no tomorrow, and all you will get is an incredulous look if you try to tell them otherwise. When you are eighteen, you can visualize only endless years of aching loss. Most of us do get over it, and live to enjoy mature relationships. Some of us do not.

A lifetime relationship was never going to happen for eighteen-year-old John Stickney and Leigh Hayden,* but John refused to accept reality. He stubbornly believed that he and Leigh belonged together forever, and he was determined to do whatever he had to do to see that they would never part.

Mercer Island, Washington, is to Seattle what Grosse Point is to Detroit, what River Oaks is to Houston, and what Beverly Hills is to Los Angeles. Located near the south end of Lake Washington, Mercer Island is among the more expensive and desirable suburbs for those who can afford the good life. The lushly vegetated island was once almost inaccessible, but the construction of the first floating bridge across Lake Washington sixty years ago made Mercer Island ripe for a building boom. The first homes, naturally, were built along the waterfront and have their own docks to moor sleek cabin cruisers or high-masted sailboats. Many of the homes here have swimming pools and tennis courts. Even as construction moved farther inland, a sense of forest remains. Row houses have no place on Mercer Island. Homes here are built to accommodate the trees and native vegetation and are painted in earth tones. There are bicycle paths and jogging trails, and the residents, many of them doctors, lawyers, computer entrepreneurs, and CEOs, use the floating bridge to escape the city to this suburban paradise in only fifteen minutes.

Most Mercer Island kids grow up in affluent families. High school parking lots are filled with late-model cars belonging to students. There are the usual police problems caused by teenagers who are bored because they don't have to work after school, kids who sample drugs, kids who get drunk and drive too fast. But if one could choose a place to raise children, Mercer Island would be it. No ghettos. No high crime neighborhoods. Only parks and discreet shopping areas.

John Stickney grew up in a rural region on the southern end of Mercer Island. At eighteen, he was 6 feet 1, a handsome blond boy who excelled in athletics. The neighbors liked him; his friends liked him. He and his family were solid members of the Mercer Island Covenant Church, a Fundamentalist church that promoted the tenets outlined in the Old Testament and whose members eschewed alcohol and tobacco.

John seemed to be the kind of boyfriend that all parents would want for their daughter. But it was pretty Leigh Hayden he fell in love with. The attraction was mutual, and people smiled to see them together. They started going steady when they were fourteen years old; indeed, neither had ever known another love. Had it been another time, another place—perhaps back in the days of the pioneer settlers who homesteaded in Washington—they might have married when they were only sixteen and grown old together. But it wasn't 1850; it was 1979. John wanted to marry Leigh. He had no plans for college. In fact, he had dropped out of high school. But Leigh had plans and was nowhere near ready to get married. She was a good student and had been accepted at Washington State University in Pullman. "Wazzu," as Washington State was called, was 300 miles east of Mercer Island and a world away from John.

He couldn't bear the idea of Leigh going away. They had been attached at the hip for four years. Sure, they had broken up for short periods, but he'd always been able to persuade Leigh to come back. He couldn't really believe that she would actually pack up and move clear across the state from him. And he was afraid she would meet someone else or that she would change and they would no longer have anything in common.

John was a bright young man, but he suffered from learning disabilities. His schoolwork had never mirrored what he really knew, what his IQ really was. He was one of thousands of kids hampered by dyslexia and therefore unable to read well; words appeared backward or upside down or jumbled to him. As a result, there was no question of John's going to college with Leigh. The experience would have been frustrating for him. He thought about getting a job in Pullman so he could be close to her, but he sensed that might be even more painful. He would be on the fringe of her life, and he already had a good job at home, which he didn't want to risk leaving. His family cared deeply for John, as did his church congregation. They tried to help him, prayed for him, hoped that his life would straighten out, and that he would fulfill the promise he had shown.

John's job was with the Industrial Rock Products Company, a firm that specialized in rock blasting. Freeways were being widened, and it was necessary to literally blast away sections of mountain rock to accommodate them. There would be ongoing demand for skills in this area, so John's community felt that his future was off to a good start.

Blasting with explosives is precise and terribly dangerous work, but John proved adept at it, even when he was in his mid-teens. Many of the men he worked with in this hazardous occupation had known him since he was only twelve years old. They liked the kid who was always cheerful, who never seemed to lose his temper, no matter how difficult a task. By December 1979,

Stickney had worked in the rock quarry for a few years, and his boss considered him "one of the old-timers."

But John Stickney's fascination with explosives continued after he left his eight hours on the job. A friend who attended school with John recalled, "He liked to blow things up. He was always blowing something up—a tree, or whatever. He'd blow things up just for the hell of it."

The fall of 1979 was bitterly lonely for John Stickney. Leigh was so far away, caught up in the excitement of college life, going to football games, participating in dorm activities. She had told him that she planned on dating other men. That was the most agonizing part for him to accept. John was handsome, and he had a job that paid well; plenty of Mercer Island girls would gladly have dated him. But he wasn't interested. He wanted only Leigh. Every night he was on the phone calling her, trying to persuade her to come back to him. His constant calls only made her pull away more. What he had feared most was coming true: Leigh was interested in another man.

John's calls continued. Finally, Leigh's roommate complained to the dorm adviser that she couldn't use the phone because John called so much. The phone rang constantly whether Leigh was in her dorm room or not. When John did catch her in, he dragged out the conversations as if he could bind her to him with a telephone cord.

Several times during the fall, John drove to the Washington State campus, deliberately arriving unexpectedly. Each time, he convinced himself that everything would be all right again. And sometimes Leigh seemed glad to see him. But there were also times when she tried to tell him that it was really over between them and that he had to stop coming to Pullman.

It was a twelve-hour drive round-trip, which gave him time to obsess about what he had lost.

John was on an emotional yo-yo. Of course the more he tried to hold on to Leigh, the more she pulled away. She felt suffocated. One can only imagine his thoughts as he made the grueling trip—up over Snoqualmie Pass, where the blizzards piled up drifts of snow from November to May, and then across the endless rolling wheat fields of the Palouse country. There weren't many towns along the way to take John's mind off his mission.

As Christmas neared, John began to realize that Leigh really *was* leaving him. He had tried pleading and cajoling. Worse, he'd even tried physically forcing her into his car when he saw her walking on campus. Her reaction was to pull even further away from him. Any love she'd had for him was now gone. Leigh was only eighteen; she wanted to be free. At first, she thought John would give up peaceably. She was as deluded as every other woman who realizes too late that she has become the focal point of a man's obsessive love.

Leigh Hayden began to be frightened. She no longer wanted to see John at all. Leigh tried to focus on her new world. She told Janet McKay, a senior who served as a resident adviser in her dorm, that John had been bothering her. She wanted to make it official that he was not a welcome visitor. If he came around to surprise her, she didn't want to have to talk to him.

Lovesick boyfriends aren't that unusual in college dorms. Leigh's friends and counselors realized that John always seemed to be shadowing her, but they all assumed he'd give up sooner or later. Leigh and her roommate lived on the fifth floor of the Streit-Perham Dormitory in the middle of the Wazzu campus, near the Performing Arts Coliseum. The dormitory, which was built in 1962, consisted of two six-story towers connected by a common lounge and dining room. Approximately 550 students were housed in the towers, and 46 of them lived on the fifth floor of Perham Hall where Leigh Hayden lived. It was a coeducational dorm, a circumstance which would have horrified the parents of college students two decades earlier, and John Stickney hated the arrangement.

It was the week before Christmas 1979. Residents of the Streit-Perham towers were preparing to pack up and go home for the holidays. Washington State was on a semester system, so Christmas festivities were not marred by the tension of final exams. Those would come later, at the end of January. This was a time for fun and celebration, and many groups of students crossed the state line into Moscow, Idaho, less than fifteen miles away, where the legal drinking age was eighteen. The county and state cops kept a permanent watch on the roads between Pullman and Moscow, trying to keep accidents and DUI tickets among the student drivers to a minimum.

The towers of Streit-Perham were decorated for the holidays, and most of the residents had adorned their rooms with holly, fir boughs, and miniature Christmas trees. Winter snow was the rule rather than the exception in Pullman, and the frigid winds that swept across the hilltop campus did nothing to dampen the spirit of the season.

Leigh Hayden knew that she would have to talk with John when she got home; there was no way he would not try to see her when they were both on Mercer Island. They had shared wonderful Christmases together, but those were in the past, and she would have to let him know that. He had to follow the same rules at home that he did when he came to the campus. They were not going steady anymore. As far as she was concerned, they were no longer even dating.

For the time being, during this last week before the Christmas holidays began, Leigh decided not to worry about it. She didn't think John would attempt to make the drive over the snow-clogged mountain passes, especially when he knew she'd be home on December 22.

On Monday, December 17, John Stickney put in a full eight hours on his job, blasting rock out of a quarry with dynamite. His foreman and his co-workers didn't notice that he behaved any differently than he always did. He didn't seem upset or angry. He was just the same open-faced dependable kid they'd always known.

When John left the job that night, it was already dark. He shouted that he'd see his co-workers the next morning. But John didn't go home that night. He didn't call Leigh either. Instead, he got in his car and headed east. Up through Issaquah and North Bend, then up over the summit of Snoqualmie Pass. It was icy at the top, with snow drifting across the road as he neared the summit. Even the skiers had given up for the night, and the lighted slopes were deserted.

John Stickney had 300 miles to go. He had confided to a friend that he was going to talk to Leigh one more time and that this time it would be decided "one way or another."

His words were so cryptic and so unlike him that his friend was concerned. Just to be on the safe side, John's friend called the head resident adviser in the dorm where Leigh lived. "John Stickney is on his way over there again. He said he's going to see Leigh."

Later, there were rumors that the phone call included the warning that John had a gun. Except for the few times he had grabbed Leigh in frustration and pulled her into his car, he had never been a violent man. The warning that John Stickney was headed toward the Washington State campus was taken seriously, probably because the dorm adviser wanted to spare Leigh any embarrassment that John might cause her. Nobody was really worried that he would be violent. John's demeanor with the staff at Perham Hall had always been courteous and quiet. When he showed up there, he only asked to see Leigh; he had never caused a scene.

Leigh and her roommate were quietly moved to a room on the sixth floor of the dorm. If and when John actually showed up, he wouldn't be able to find her.

The night wore on. At 10:00 P.M., the outer doors to the dorm were locked. Leigh and her roommate tried to fall asleep in the temporary room on the sixth floor. If John was really headed for Pullman, which was still only a rumor, he would probably check into a motel and call Leigh's room from there.

John Stickney *was* on his way. A little before 11:30 his car reached the top of the hill approaching Pullman. He could see the campus lights across the valley, twinkling on the next hill. He knew Leigh was there, snug and warm inside one of the red-brick buildings. He was sure that this time she wouldn't be expecting him. She would really be surprised to see him this late on a weeknight. It was desperately important to him that this visit be a happy surprise.

The campus police had been alerted that John might show up at Perham Hall. Officers on the night shift patrol were asked to keep an eye out for him. Somehow—and no one knows how—John Stickney managed to get into the locked dormitory at 11:30 P.M. Without hesitating, he headed for Leigh's room on the fifth floor. He knocked. There was no answer. He knocked again and waited. He couldn't hear a radio or television or the girls' voices. He opened the unlocked door, and found the room unoccupied.

Where was she? She should have been there.

John turned swiftly and walked down to Adviser Janet McKay's room. She gasped when she opened her door. She wondered how he had managed to get into the Perham tower. Still, he was as polite and cordial as ever. He wore blue jeans and a parka, and he looked tired, but he didn't appear manic or dangerous.

"Where's Leigh?" he asked. "She's not in her room."

"I haven't seen her all evening," Janet answered. "You really shouldn't be here now. It's after lockup time."

For the first time, John showed irritation. He said he had no intention of leaving until he saw Leigh. Janet McKay managed to call the campus police, and they persuaded him to leave. He was not combative and he left quietly. The police kept an eye on him, but all he did was drive aimlessly around the campus during the early morning hours. He made no attempt to get back into Perham Hall.

It was Tuesday afternoon before John finally got Leigh on the phone. He said he needed to talk to her face-to-face, and he insisted that he would not go back to Mercer Island until she agreed to talk to him. That was all he was asking. It was finally arranged that the ex-sweethearts would meet on neutral ground—in Adviser McKay's room.

The meeting lasted only ten minutes. Exactly what Leigh told John was never made public, but it was clear that she was adamant this time. Finally and forever it was all over between them. There would be no more pleading, no more promises, nothing would change her mind.

John Stickney left. The romance seemed to be over, and everyone heaved a sigh of relief.

Less than fifteen minutes later, however, Head Adviser Mary Beth Johnson entered an elevator on the ground floor and was startled to find John Stickney inside. She recognized him and introduced herself. She told him that she was aware of his problem, and he replied that he had to see Leigh just one more time. There was an odd urgency about him that alarmed Mary Beth Johnson.

John Stickney had taken nothing to the meeting in Janet McKay's office, but Ms. Johnson didn't know that. Now she noted that he had a book bag over his arm and that it appeared to be quite heavy.

"I understand that you want to see Leigh," she said carefully, "but I'd like to talk with her for a few minutes first. Would you agree to that?"

Stickney nodded. But when the elevator arrived on the fifth floor he got off right behind her and she could hear his footsteps keeping pace with hers down the long hallway. Thinking fast, she reached Leigh's room, stepped inside, and quickly locked the door behind her. Now Leigh Hayden, her roommate, Janet McKay, and Mary Beth Johnson were inside a small dorm room with nothing but a thin door between them and John Stickney.

Before Ms. Johnson had a chance to say anything, there was a crashing, splintering sound at the door. John was trying to kick it in. Again and again, he slammed his boot into the door. It shuddered and held. The women huddled together, frightened. There was nowhere to hide, and they were five floors up, so they couldn't escape out the window. John's voice was very calm, but he gave orders in a forceful way. "Open the door," he said stubbornly. "I want you to open the door." While they huddled against the opposite wall, he kicked it again, and bric-a-brac fell off a shelf and shattered.

Mary Beth Johnson grabbed the phone and alerted the campus police that John Stickney was back, that there was trouble, and that they needed help.

Suddenly the crashing against the door stopped. There was dead silence for a moment or so. And then John began speaking again in a flat voice with no emotion. Leigh had never heard him speak in this matter-of-fact way and it was far more frightening than when he raised his voice.

"I have a bomb," he said in that same awful voice. "Someone's going to get hurt if you don't let me in."

He wasn't shouting; he didn't even sound angry, but Leigh knew that he meant what he said. She knew that he was an expert in explosive devices. He could have walked away from his job with everything he needed to make a bomb. He worked with dynamite, and he knew how to set a charge and detonate a device with enough power to blow away half of a rocky hill. It had been his craft for several years, and he was good at it. She knew he was capable of blowing the whole dorm to kingdom come. "He probably does have a bomb," she said. "He means it. He knows how to make one."

The women looked at one another and silently agreed to make a run for it. They had nothing to lose, and if they didn't try, they might all die—and so would the other residents in rooms along the fifth-floor hall. Mary Beth Johnson flung open the door, and the four women took John Stickney by surprise as they tumbled out of the room and ran screaming down the hall. "Run! Run!" they cried out to the other three dozen residents on the floor. "He has a bomb!"

It was chaos as frightened coeds raced down the hall, most of them so intent on getting away that they didn't even see the tall blond man in the parka. The fifth floor was soon deserted. The only person left was John Stickney. He hadn't tried to stop the fleeing women. He had watched them run, his face as calm as if everything was completely normal. He hadn't tried to follow them. Oddly, he didn't even reach out for his beloved Leigh one last time.

Anyone who thinks a campus cop has an easy job might consider the task facing the Washington State campus officers who raced to the fifth floor of Perham Hall, as the coeds fled. Lieutenant Mike Kenny, age thirty-five, and Officer David Trimble, twenty-six, reached the floor first, followed by Officer Roger Irwin.

They stopped when they saw John Stickney, standing almost motionless in the hallway. He had a bomb all right; he must have carried it in the innocuous-looking book bag. Now they could see that it was a metallic cylinder three or four inches in diameter and a foot long—just the right size to hold sticks of dynamite. He held two wires that led to a battery. If it was like most simple bombs, that battery would detonate blasting caps and dynamite. Kenny and Trimble held their hands in the air as John ordered; they were desperately fighting for time, and they didn't want to irritate the tall blond youth. They knew that other officers were frantically trying to clear the dormitory of the hundreds of students who occupied all the other floors. The crisis could have been worse; it was two in the afternoon by now and many of the residents were in class. But this was bad enough.

All working police officers take a class in dealing with bombs, and all of them fervently hope they will never come in contact with one. Compared to seeing a bomb in the hands of a deranged subject, facing a .357 Magnum is a picnic.

The two officers moved toward Stickney, talking quietly, fighting to keep the tremor from their voices. "Come on, John . . . we can talk," Mike Kenny said. "This isn't the answer. Think about what you're doing. Let's put the bomb down. Let's talk about it. Things aren't as bad as you think."

Stickney shook his head.

"Put it down, John. Put it down. You don't really want to hurt anyone. You're mixed up." Moving so slowly that the inches they covered were almost imperceptible, the two officers advanced down the hall toward John, their hands still high over their heads. From the end of the hall, Officer Roger Irwin watched, barely breathing.

"We'll help you work it out," Officer Trimble said. "You can talk to Leigh. She'll understand. What are you? Eighteen? Nineteen? Hell, there's a whole life ahead of you. Put [the bomb] down, and we'll see that you get some help. You don't want to hurt anybody. We don't want you to get hurt." Trimble was close enough to touch Stickney now. The bomb was within arm's reach. It looked deadly. It looked as if it could level the whole dorm. Trimble no longer thought about himself; he prayed that all the students had made it safely outside. "Come on, John. Give it to me . . . gently," Trimble said in as calm a voice as he could manage. "Just hand it over, and you won't be sorry. I promise you, you won't be sorry."

Trimble and Kenny felt as if they were moving through quicksand. The whole scene had a psychedelic quality. They were caught in a slow-motion horror film, red and green and silver Christmas decorations sliding past them in their peripheral vision.

One step.

Two steps.

Trimble reached out. And suddenly he had the bomb in his two hands. He concentrated on standing upright and maintaining minimum movement. But then suddenly John Stickney fought back. He and Trimble fell to the floor, wrestling, the bomb between them. A few steps down the hall, Roger Irwin held his breath. Surely it was going to blow now and take all of them with it.

But no. Stickney and Trimble were back on their feet, but now John Stickney was holding the bomb again. Suddenly, he turned away from the two officers and moved down the hallway, the bomb held tight against his stomach. David Trimble and Mike Kenny could see only his back.

And then there was a roar the likes of which Irwin had never heard in his life. Smoke and dust obscured his vision when he peered down the hall. He had a sense that the whole tower was coming apart at the seams. For the moment there was a floor beneath him, but surely it was going to crumble. Plaster and glass showered the whole area. Every window on the fifth floor was blown outward by the force of the blast. Four or five of the rooms closest to where John Stickney had stood forty-five seconds ago were simply gone.

Down below, shivering in the frigid winter afternoon, the evacuated students heard the explosion and saw the tower vibrate. They began to scream and sob.

Fighting his way through the debris, Roger Irwin fully expected to find his fellow officers dead. They could not have survived. They had been within ten feet of the blast. He braced himself for what he would find.

Young Love

John Stickney was dead. No one would ever know if he blew himself up deliberately or by accident. He would no longer suffer the anguish of unrequited love.

At first glance, Irwin thought Mike Kenny and David Trimble were dead, too. They lay still, their uniforms ripped into strips and tatters, their skin blackened. Irwin shouted into his radio, asking for paramedics and an ambulance, although he had precious little hope that anyone could help his colleagues.

As Irwin drew closer, he saw Kenny stir and heard Trimble moan. Miraculously, they were alive. John Stickney's body had taken the full force of the blast, and that alone had saved them. Had he been facing toward them when the dynamite detonated, the cops would surely have died too.

David Trimble, only twenty-six, was in critical condition. He had sustained puncture wounds in his chest, abdomen, and hands, and he had first- and second-degree burns all over his body. Both of his eardrums were ruptured. Mike Kenny had been a little farther away from the center of the blast, but his eardrums had been ruptured, too.

An ambulance rushed Trimble to Sacred Heart Hospital in Spokane where he underwent hours of surgery. Doctors stated cautiously that he would live but that his hearing would be permanently damaged. Lieutenant Kenny was treated at Pullman Memorial Hospital where physicians held out hope that his hearing would be only minimally affected. They were police officers and keen hearing is essential to their profession.

The two officers had come very close to sacrificing their lives for the students of Perham Hall. It could have been so much worse. Only three students were injured, and their injuries were only minor cuts and shock.

Leigh Hayden's new boyfriend hadn't been too concerned when he received threats from John Stickney, but now police checked his car carefully to be sure there wasn't a bomb hidden there. They found nothing. Nor was there a bomb in John Stickney's car. He had carried only the one bomb with him. Perhaps he had hoped that Leigh would agree to go for a ride with him. If she said she still loved him, the bomb would have stayed in the book bag. If she truly said it was the end for them, then he could have set off the bomb and they would have died together.

But in the end, nothing had worked for John and he had died alone.

Campus cops are often derided by students who delight in calling them pigs, but the students of Washington State University realized that Mike Kenny, Roger Irwin, and David Trimble had risked their lives to save them.

To show their appreciation, the residents of Streit-Perham immediately established a fund to help the families of Lieutenant Kenny and Officer Trimble. They started the fund by donating the money they had allocated for their social functions for the school year, and then solicited funds from other students and Pullman townspeople. It would be a bleak Christmas for the injured policemen, but the students were determined to do what they could to help.

In the meantime, sororities, fraternities, and the citizens of Pullman rushed to help the forty-six students who had lost all their clothing, books, and possessions when the fifth floor was leveled. University insurance eventually reimbursed them for some of their losses. As

Steven Sherer and Jami Hagel Sherer. Steve wanted a thin, blond wife with large breasts, and Jami tried to be everything he wanted. *(Judy Hagel Collection)*

MISSING

Jami Sherer

LAST SEEN ON 9/30/90 IN THE REDMOND EDUCATION HILL AREA. SHE WAS HEADING FOR REDMOND/BEAR CREEK TACO TIME.

HAIR: BROWN
EYES: BROWN
AGE: 26
HEIGHT: 5'1"
WEIGHT: 95 LBS
LAST SEEN WEARING WHITE T-SHIRT, BLUE JEANS AND WHITE TENNIS SHOES

10,000 REWARD

A REWARD OF UP TO $10,000 IS OFFERED FOR ANY INFORMATION WHICH LEADS TO THE SOLUTION OF THE DISAPPEARANCE OF JAMI SHERER

IF YOU HAVE ANY INFORMATION, PLEASE CONTACT: THE REDMOND POLICE DEPARTMENT, DETECTIVE SERGEANT WATSON, 882-6463 OR 882-6405.
CASE # 90-5612; OR FRIENDS & FAMILY OF MISSING PEOPLE 1-800-346-7555

ADVERTISEMENT

Jami and her son, Chris, in the poster that Microsoft printed by the thousands in the hope that Jami could be found alive and well. The $10,000 reward was offered by Microsoft and Jami's family and friends.

Seattle Police Department
Identification Information Card

01-17-1994

SHERER, STEVEN FRANK

AKA   SHERER, STEVEN JEFFREY
       MICHAELS, STEVEN CHRISTOPHE

Sex	MALE		
Race	WHITE	DOB	11-01-1961
Height	5'9"	Weight	180
Eye	BLUE	Corr/Vis	NO
Hair	BROWN	Length	SHORT

SMT

Charge   94 - Traffic

Seattle Police Department
Identification Information Card

05-20-1999

SHERER, STEVEN FRANK

AKA   SHERER, STEVEN JEFFREY
       MICHAELS, STEVEN CHRISTOPHE

Sex	MALE		
Race	WHITE	DOB	11-01-1961
Height	5'9"	Weight	180
Eye	BLUE	Corr/Vis	NO
Hair	BROWN	Length	

SMT

Charge

Seattle Police Department
Identification Information Card

06-23-1999

SHERER, STEVEN FRANK

AKA   SHERER, STEVEN JEFFREY
       MICHAELS, STEVEN CHRISTOPHE

Sex	MALE		
Race	WHITE	DOB	11-01-1961
Height	5'9"	Weight	180
Eye	BLUE	Corr/Vis	NO
Hair	BROWN	Length	MEDIUM

SMT

Charge

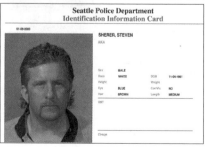

Seattle Police Department
Identification Information Card

01-09-2000

SHERER, STEVEN

AKA

Sex	MALE		
Race	WHITE	DOB	11-06-1961
Height		Weight	
Eye	BLUE	Corr/Vis	NO
Hair	BROWN	Length	MEDIUM

SMT

Charge

Steve often found himself in a police lineup. These four Seattle Police Identification Information Cards show how often his appearance changed. Note the different names and birth dates.

Yearbooks and wedding photos that Steve took with him in his constant travels after Jami vanished. *(Police photo)*

Steve and Jami's his-and-hers bowling shirts. Steve won trophies and money prizes at bowling. Jami hated bowling because he treated her so badly at the alleys. *(Police photo)*

The blue suitcase Steve carried with him after Jami's disappearance, although it was heavy and unwieldy. It was filled with secret things. *(Police photo)*

Steve had a fetish for certain clothing, and he made Jami dress to please him. Later, he often asked new girlfriends to wear these items. *(Police photo)*

Jami's size-1 black-leather miniskirt. Steve had his new girlfriends model it for him after Jami disappeared. *(Police photo)*

Steve also kept most of Jami's thong and bikini panties for years after she disappeared. *(Police photo)*

Steve liked Jami to wear these long black-satin gloves. *(Police photo)*

Jami's "Mom" T-shirts. Oddly, Steve remembered that aspect of Jami, too. In a certain way, he kept her with him. *(Police photo)*

One of Jami's favorite dresses, also size 1. Redmond detectives found it after a very long search. *(Police photo)*

Jami's prized Mazda was found in the
Shoreline Unitarian Church parking lot.
(Police photo)

The extra key to Jami's Mazda. Steve
claimed he had no key. *(Police photo)*

Investigators confer as Jami's car is
hoisted by a tow truck. Mike Faddis,
third from left, had no idea that seven
years later, his life would revolve around
the Sherer investigation. In 1990, when
this photograph was taken, he was a
traffic officer. *(Police photo)*

The transit station on the I-5 Freeway near the church where Jami's Mazda was found. Maggie the bloodhound and other dogs tracked the killer's scent to this spot. *(Police photo)*

Steve's mother's home in Mill Creek. On September 30, 1990, Steve broke the panes of glass beside the front door to get into her house. He undoubtedly needed her Bronco that day. A decade later, police and FBI agents arrested him here.

Lieutenant James Taylor, Redmond Police Department. Seven years after Jami vanished, he promised Jami's mother he would find out what happened to her.

Redmond Detective Mike Faddis, with Jami's brothers in the background, smiling after the prosecution won a crucial point in the Sherer trial. *(Leslie Rule)*

The prosecution team: Senior King County Deputy Prosecutors Hank Corscadden, Kristin Richardson and Marilyn Brenneman. *(Leslie Rule)*

Ann Rule talking to Redmond Detective Greg Mains during a break when the State's case was going well toward the end of the trial. *(Leslie Rule)*

The stairs to the front door of Steve and Jami's house on Education Hill. Redmond investigators suspect that Steve hit Jami at the top of these stairs, and she plunged down. *(Police photo)*

Steve Sherer hears the jury's verdict on the afternoon of June 8, 2000. After the jury was excused, Steve turned toward Judy Hagel, Jami's mother, his face contorted with rage, and roared a four-letter obscenity at her. Corrections officers escorted him out of the courtroom. *(Leslie Rule)*

BITTER LAKE

Police had questions for Patrick Lehn when they learned that Kathi Jones had been trying to break off a relationship with him. *(Police photo)*

Seattle Detective Mike Tando checks for further evidence at the attack scene. *(Police photo)*

Seattle Detective John Boatman supervises the processing of the victim's sports car at the police garage. *(Police photo)*

LOVE AND INSURANCE

Lorraine Lacey hurried to the spot on Hippie Hill where she'd seen the gun flash and found a man on the ground, his body pelted by

rain, bleeding profusely from the nose and mouth. She found a broken black umbrella and propped it over his face to keep the rain off him until police came. *(Police photo)*

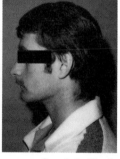

Gareth Leifbach was convicted of the murder of Larry Duerksen and is currently asking for parole. *(Police photo)*

Detective Mike Tando worked the baffling case. *(Ann Rule)*

Sergeant Don Cameron headed the probe into Larry Duerksen's murder. *(Ann Rule)*

THE GENTLER SEX

Carol Hargis being led from the court by an unidentified court officer. Carol plotted ineptly with her girlfriend Teri Depew to kill her husband, David.

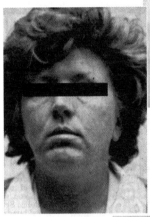

Sandra Treadway enjoyed a successful "open" marriage with her husband—until he asked for a divorce. *(Police photo)*

Detectives Walt Stout and Terry Murphy teamed up to obtain incriminating statements from the key witness. *(Police photo)*

THE CONJUGAL VISIT

Carl Cletus Bowles with an unidentified FBI agent. He already had a long string of felonies on his record and was in prison when he was allowed a conjugal visit at a Motel 6. He managed to dupe his guard and escape. His murderous path of destruction had only begun.

Lane County Deputy Carlton E. Smith lies alongside the road where he was ruthlessly shot dead after he stopped a car for a routine traffic check.

KILLERS ON THE ROAD

Pretty, trusting Deanna Buse vanished after work and was found days later on a lonely road that ended in a thick forest.

In the foreground of these photos, Thomas Braun (left) and Leonard Maine (right) proved key suspects. *(Police photo)*

The braided, tasseled rope that Arnold Brown described as the murder weapon. Police found the hemp rope lying against the fence on the east side of the backyard of a quiet family home. The medical examiner said it fit exactly into the indentations on Jannie's neck. *(Police photo)*

Arnold Brown was doted on by his family, and they always protected him from punishment. His sexual aberrations were deadly and bizarre and in the end, he alone decreed what his punishment would be. *(Police photo)*

Seattle Police Sergeant Don Cameron, "Mr. Homicide" of the Seattle Police Department, directed the probe into the bizarre death of little Jannie Reilly in her own home. *(Ann Rule)*

Detective John Nordlund looked at Arnold and said quietly, "I think you are a sick person, and that you killed Jannie. You probably belong in a mental hospital." The suspect replied, "I probably do." *(Ann Rule)*

Pretty Carole Adele often took a shortcut through a weedy lot coming home from the library. One night, she took her customary path and was viciously assaulted and stabbed to death.

Joann Zulauf's sweet smile lingers only in this photo. Like Carol Adele, she was attacked on a lonely path so sheltered by trees that no one could help her.

Court deputy John DeMattea (left) and defense attorney C.N. "Nick" Marshall (center) escort Gary Gene Grant from the King County courtroom. He was found guilty of murder in the first degree on four counts. Gary Grant seemed harmless and somewhat shy to those who thought they knew him.

THE STOCKHOLM SYNDROME

Investigators found the body of the victim where it had rolled down an embankment with a helping push from the man who had shot him. *(Police photo)*

Reporting the "accident," the suspect told probers that he shot Rusty, the victim's collie, when the dog tried to attack him. *(Police photo)*

The prosecution's tightly prepared case was ably assisted by Oregon Assistant Attorneys General Bob Hamilton, shown holding up the bullet from the antique gun used in the slaying, and Stephen Keutzer (right). *(Ann Rule)*

Jim Byrnes, the attorney general's investigator, found a way for the brainwashed victim to tell her story. He is a sensitive and intelligent detective, and Robin came to trust him. *(Ann Rule)*

for the dormitory itself, a policy was in place that covered explosions. It had a $10,000 deductible but that was a bargain, considering the awesome damage John Stickney's bomb had done.

Back on Mercer Island, John Stickney's boss and his fellow workers were "absolutely flabbergasted" when they learned of the tragedy. "We're almost speechless here," his boss said. "There was no indication he was having any kind of problems. There are people in our organization who have known him since he was twelve years old. He was a pretty popular guy and everybody seemed to like him. We never even knew he had a temper."

If John Stickney had been able to show a temper, if he had not kept his pain and frustration bottled up inside, his story might have had a happier ending. But no one knew he needed help.

Perhaps someone should have paid attention when John Stickney blew up things "for the hell of it." When his world crashed around him, he turned to the one method he had of showing anger.

In the wake of the Washington State bombing, the Bellevue Police Department reopened its investigation into a mysterious explosion that had occurred near the Mercer Island Slough two months before the fatal bombing in Pullman. In the predawn hours of a Sunday morning, someone had tried to blow up a section of the I-90 freeway. One of the concrete piers under the freeway structure that runs over the slough was damaged by a blast of tremendous proportions. It may have been only a coincidence that this bridge pier—within a few miles of John Stickney's home—was bombed. Or it might have been a test run to see how much dynamite it might take to blast through concrete and iron rebars.

Ironically, when it was far too late for John Stickney, a UPI feature story appeared in newspapers all across America: "Love Affairs on Campus Can Produce Signs of Stress." The text of the article noted that the top stressors, in order of importance, were "ending the hometown relationship," "staying free," and "breaking up."

Love and Insurance

I was amazed at this case when I first encountered it, and with a second look, I am still astonished that a man who had so many options for a successful future should choose the path he did. He promised his lover a great deal, while all the time he was coldly planning one of the cruelest crimes I've ever written about. There were so many other choices; why did he choose murder?

Larry **Dwayne Duerksen** and Gareth Stuart Leifbach* had a lot in common. They were both in
their twenties, both products of the Midwest. Larry grew
up in Nebraska, while Gareth was from Michigan. Each
of them had spent time in the armed forces, although
they had not met each other there. They were homosexual men who had kept their sexual orientation secret in
an era long before "don't ask, don't tell." The bizarre circumstance of their meeting was equaled, even excelled,
by the shocking manner in which they parted forever.

As he neared his twenty-ninth birthday, Larry
Duerksen's life underwent a tremendous upheaval.
Larry was handsome, with clean-cut aquiline features
and a neatly trimmed beard. He was very intelligent,
though he had never quite managed to finish all the requirements to get his B.A. degree. Maybe that was because he was always traveling, seeking some kind of
geographical resolution to the war between his up-
bringing and his desires. He had long since strayed
from the old-fashioned morality of small-town Nebraska where being gay was neither understood nor
condoned. Hiding and running away had become a way
of life for him. He had hidden his sexual preference
from his parents, his sister, and his many aunts and un-
cles for a long time. He was far away from Nebraska,

working as a nurse's aide in the Santa Barbara Cottage Hospital when he decided to come out of the closet. He made a trip back home to explain to his family the real reason he had never wanted to marry any of the nice girls they had introduced to him.

Larry Duerksen's revelation shocked his parents, but they tried to deal with it. His family still loved him, they said, even though they couldn't understand his choice. Sometimes they tried to tell each other that this was just one of Larry's "exaggerations."

And he did tend to exaggerate. The air force veteran's behavior had puzzled his family before. Larry tended to be overly dramatic, and he seemed to crave attention more than most, and he told wild stories that guaranteed he would get it. He once came home and announced that he was suffering from terminal cancer. His family and friends rallied around and were impressed by his bravery in the face of such an awful diagnosis. Hoping that there might yet be a cure for him, his parents insisted that he go through a series of tests. Surprisingly, the results of all the lab work indicated that Larry wasn't sick at all, much less suffering from a fatal malignancy. Faced with the facts, he admitted that he'd made it all up.

Larry had always had great difficulty managing his money. That spring of his twenty-ninth year, he was so deep in debt that he decided to declare bankruptcy. His life was in a shambles. That was why he had vowed to make an entirely new start. His first step had been to reveal his gay lifestyle to his family. Next, he decided to leave Santa Barbara and move to Seattle, Washington. He didn't have a job waiting for him in the Emerald City, but he had a friend and lover there. If their relationship was to move to the next step, he needed to head north and give it a chance. And so he left the sunny climate of Santa Barbara for the misty rain and bright green filigree of leaves that meant spring was coming to Seattle.

Larry soon found a job as a library assistant at the Suzzallo Library on the University of Washington campus. The money wasn't great, but the job meant security and he was popular with his co-workers. He found an apartment in one of the big old houses that lined the street across from the west end of the campus.

The move might have been a mistake; Larry and his former lover found they couldn't ignite the cool ashes of their relationship. And one or the other of them always seemed to be jealous about something. It was more a relief than a disappointment when Larry walked away for good.

He wasn't lonesome; he had many friends of both sexes, and he received a ton of mail from friends in Santa Barbara. He was working his way out of bankruptcy, managing on his small salary, taking the bus because he had no car, and, perhaps surprisingly, enjoying his Spartan lifestyle and the new ambience of Seattle.

Larry Duerksen was not into cruising, that danger-fraught practice of seeking rapid and anonymous sex in the shadows of the gay world. He wasn't looking for casual pickups or tawdry rest room encounters; he was hoping to find someone he could really love. In his tweed jackets with leather-patched elbows, Larry looked more like a young professor or a graduate student than a library assistant. He longed for someone he could look up to, someone strong and competent who could help him organize his life.

The decade of the eighties was fast approaching and there were oceanic changes in the mores and popular culture of America. In the summer of 1979, as Larry followed the media's coverage of events at Fort Lewis—the huge army base south of Tacoma—he was mightily impressed. For so many painful years, he had hidden his homosexuality, and when he felt close to exploding with guilt and depression, he shared it only with his immediate family. Now he read about twenty-one-year-old Gareth Stuart Leifbach, who was risking his whole army career by not only admitting he was gay but daring the army to do anything about it. Gareth Leifbach was making headlines all over America. His was the kind of controversial story that the media loved. He had been a perfect soldier during his two years of service, and no one had suspected that, like Larry Duerksen, he had a secret life. Larry could not imagine what might have happened to his air force career if he had ever let any of his barracks-mates know his secret. But here was Gareth Leifbach telling the whole world. Larry may have felt some envy of Leifbach's almost-celebrity status; he himself had always loved being in the limelight.

The *Seattle Post-Intelligencer* reported that Gareth Leifbach revealed his homosexuality when he learned that an old friend from Michigan was having trouble getting into the army because he was gay. Leifbach went to his commander and pointed out that his gayness hadn't interfered with his performance as a soldier. He felt it was grossly unfair that the military should bar men and women simply because of their sexual orientation.

Leifbach was handsome, a top-seeded player on the army tennis team, who had attained the rank of private first class. No one in his unit knew he was homosexual, and he had never seen any reason to mention it before. But now he had a cause and a friend who needed help.

Initially, Gareth Leifbach's revelations about his sex

life seemed to have backfired on him. Not only was his friend refused admittance to the army but Gareth himself faced discharge. The U.S. Army had decreed that homosexuality was entirely incompatible with military service. Although there were certainly thousands of gay soldiers, sailors, and marines, they all remained closeted. Only Gareth Leifbach had the courage and audacity to face an organization as rigid and conservative as the army.

Larry admired Gareth's bravery and his frankness. He was sorry for him when his military career ended on September 25, 1979. On that day, a three-man board of officers met to decide if he should stay in the army despite his avowed homosexuality. Several of Leifbach's superiors testified before the board that Gareth was an excellent soldier, but the final vote was two to one in favor of an honorable discharge. The decision was front-page news all across the country. Leifbach himself claimed a moral victory; at least one officer had voted in favor of keeping him in the army.

Although Gareth Leifbach's career in the service was over, he appeared to be elated over his new place at center stage. Indeed, he glowed with all the attention he was receiving and spoke volubly to any reporter who requested an interview. "I'm not wealthy, but I'm rich," he told them.

Gareth was confident of his future. He hinted that a millionaire in Tampa Bay, Florida, had offered to back him financially if he should decide to become a tennis pro. He said he had property in his hometown of Battle Creek, Michigan, which he could always sell for a profit. But Gareth Leifbach's ace in the hole was his plan to become the poster boy for gay liberation. He was prepared to sue the U.S. Army for $3 million to

$5 million because of its discrimination against homosexuals and because it had violated his constitutional rights. He said that he had friends in high places in the gay world. He was only twenty-one, but he was suddenly a man to be reckoned with and he clearly loved the spotlight. He was playing it for all it was worth.

Gareth Leifbach certainly made a compelling spokesman. He was tan and muscular and well spoken. One of his vast legion of admirers was Larry Duerksen. From his apartment in Seattle, Larry watched Gareth on television and read every word printed about him. He admired Gareth tremendously, and he had written to the embattled army private even before Gareth was banished from the service, even though he didn't really expect a response. Larry was thrilled when Gareth wrote back, and the men arranged to meet. They did meet and rapidly became close friends. The tall, almost languid library assistant and the tanned tennis player hit it off better than Larry had ever hoped. When Gareth left to go back to Michigan, Larry dared to believe that Gareth might return to Seattle and that he might even accept Larry's invitation to share his apartment. But that was probably ridiculous. Gareth said he had so many munificent and exciting offers to consider; he just wasn't sure yet about what he would do.

Larry didn't see one disadvantage in being with Gareth. He had always wanted to be the center of attention. By aligning himself with the poster boy for gay rights, he could bask in the reflected glow of Gareth's fame, and he could have a friend and lover whom he could admire and emulate. But, realistically, he had to admit that a millionaire in Florida had a lot more to offer Gareth than he did.

Once Gareth left Seattle, something dark and menacing entered Larry Duerksen's life. He began to tell friends and co-workers that someone was threatening his life. He repeated the details of disturbing phone calls that came late at night. He had no idea why anyone would single him out, but he was convinced that someone was out to get him.

Larry told a young woman who worked in the library that he had been horrified to find a stained sack lying outside his apartment door. When he peeked in, he gasped. Inside, there was a dead pigeon, its neck wrung. A few days later, he told her about a note slipped under his mat that warned him to be careful. In his letters to Nebraska, he told his relatives that he loved Seattle, but that his enthusiasm for the city was mitigated by the fact that someone was stalking him. He said he had just missed being run over by a car. "It was headed right for me. I was crossing the street on Capitol Hill—but don't worry," he wrote. "The police are checking it out and I've talked with detectives."

No one thought to verify Larry's stories, and he had never reported any incidents or threats to the Seattle Police.

Gradually his reports to his family and co-workers became more and more ominous—and fanciful. People began to suspect that this was all about getting attention. When they compared notes, they found contradictions in his stories. But he was such a likable guy that no one ever confronted him. If it made Larry feel important, they could overlook his outrageous fibbing.

Larry wrote to Gareth during the time Gareth was in Michigan and when he headed west for a short sojourn in San Francisco. No one ever saw those letters, but it would have been like him to tell Gareth about the threats. After all, he had thrown in his lot with Gareth and was prepared to stand beside him in his upcoming campaign to make the army pay for its injustices. Larry wanted to be important to Gareth. By telling him of the threats that he was receiving, Larry may have hoped to show Gareth that he was willing to face danger and even death, if need be, to prove his loyalty.

The holidays were fast approaching and Gareth Leifbach was still traveling. Larry didn't know if he would ever come back to Seattle.

In November 1979, Larry attended a party. True to form, he began a long, involved story about the perils of his life. People rolled their eyes. His anecdotes were just too weird to be believed. A psychologist whom Larry respected a great deal happened to be at this Thanksgiving party. He listened to Larry's tales, then drew him aside and bluntly asked if his story was true. "You know, you don't have to tell such stories, Larry," the man said gently. "People will like you anyway. They may even like you better if you stick to the truth."

Others at the party noticed that Larry became very quiet, and that was the end of his wild stories, at least for that evening. Chastened, he kept his mouth closed and for once just listened to other people talk.

In the first week of December, to Larry's relief and joy, Gareth Leifbach did come back to Seattle. And he did move in with Larry. For a man with such impressive contacts and grand plans for the future, Gareth had precious few possessions, only a few clothes and his shaving kit. It didn't matter. Larry was more than happy to share his furniture, stereo, and television with Gareth. Things would start to happen soon, and it would be exciting to be on the road with Gareth, to stand beside him as they toured the country on speaking engagements. Larry was sure they would be together for a long, long time.

December 14, 1979, was a blustery, rainy day. Final exams were approaching at the University of Washington and the campus was crowded that Friday night; some people were studying in the library, some had night classes, and many were attending Christmas musicals and plays.

A Christmas card rested on Larry Duerksen's mantel. It had been mailed on December 7 by a friend in Santa Barbara. Its sentiments were to prove prophetic, "Dear Larry, How are you? I hope all in one piece. Good Lord, you do attract strange ones! Be careful." It was probably a response to Larry's earlier letters describing the unseen enemies who were out to get him.

Larry was just one of the hundreds of people walking along the diagonal paths of the campus that evening. For once, he didn't tell everyone what his errand was. He confided in only one person.

Lorraine Lacey, a graduate student, got off a Metro bus at the intersection of 15th N.E. and N.E. 41st just before 7:00 P.M and headed for the campus. It had been dark for almost three hours by then. She was a little wary; the campus paths were like black tunnels between evergreens and rhododendrons, and she was alone. For that reason, she watched the two men who were walking toward her more closely than she would have if it were daylight.

The taller of the men held an umbrella over both their heads for protection against the driving rain. She would later recall to the police that she sensed they were no threat to her; they seemed to be very close friends, perhaps even lovers, focused only on each other. She continued down the dark path, her mind at ease.

Lorraine had just reached a circle of light beneath a lamppost when the night air was pierced by a series of loud noises. Firecrackers? No, this was louder. She whirled around and saw a man bent over in a crouch, his arm extended toward the ground. When she saw the flash of a gun, she shrank silently into the shrubbery, shocked and frightened.

It was all over in a matter of seconds. The man with the gun turned and ran away, headed north. Forgetting her own fear, now, Lorraine Lacey hurried to the spot where she'd seen the gun flash. She found a man on the ground, his body being pelted by the rain. He was bleeding profusely from the nose and mouth. He seemed to be comatose, and she looked for something that might at least keep the rain off him. She found a broken black umbrella, and managed to prop it over his face. Then she looked up to see two young women walking nearby, and she called out to them, "Run! Call the campus police!"

Within a few minutes, a half-dozen university police officers arrived. They were soon joined by a Medic One unit from the Seattle Fire Department. Oblivious to the fact that they were kneeling in an icy puddle, the paramedics began to work on the victim, a tall, bearded man who appeared to be in his late twenties. He had sustained gunshot wounds to his head and both arms. The medics inserted an airway to help him breathe, but his condition was very critical as he was rushed to the Harborview Hospital. Physicians there immediately monitored his vital signs. He appeared to have lost a great deal of blood and to have sustained terrible brain damage; there was only a slight chance that he would survive.

Back at the site of the shooting, the campus police officers rigged a tarp over the ground where the victim had fallen, suspending the cover from several chairs. The broken umbrella marked the spot where the violence had erupted. Attempted murder is not a crime that college police have much experience dealing with, and they called for help from the Seattle Police Department's homicide unit.

Detectives George Marberg and Rick Buckland were next up to catch a night call. Before Marberg left the downtown homicide headquarters, he checked with the Harborview emergency room and learned that the John Doe victim had died. He left for the scene. Seattle Police K-9 officers and their dogs milled around, as the animals tried to pick up the scent of the killer, but they went only so far and then came back to the umbrella, frustrated; the rain had washed away all traces of the man with the gun.

The scene of the shooting was known on campus as Hippie Hill. It was really only a grassy knoll near Parrington Hall, home to decades of classes for hopeful writers. Theodore Roethke, Dylan Thomas and Richard Eberhart had once taught there. Many writing students, including myself, went on to publish articles and books with skills learned in Parrington Hall.

On this moonless and stormy night, only faint light from the streetlamps filtered through the dense greenery of trees and shrubs as the detectives began their work. The ground beneath the tarp was still stained with blood and brain tissue and littered with paraphernalia left by the paramedics. Three expended cartridge casings—probably .32 caliber—glinted in the beams of the auxiliary lights the investigators had brought in. These and the broken pieces of umbrella were all they had to go on at the start of the investigation. A man had died—suddenly, violently—in the midst of a rainstorm on a black December night. They didn't yet know who he was or why he had died. They had one witness who'd seen a dark figure scurrying away. A quick solution didn't look at all likely. The scene was photographed, measured, and triangulated so that it would be recorded exactly, even though the wind and rain threatened to destroy it. The shell casings were bagged and retained. Held up in the light, Marberg could see that they were Remington-Peters .32 automatic cartridges.

The police left the bloodied knoll until it could be checked thoroughly in the daylight. University police would guard it through the night so that no one would contaminate the scene of the crime. Detectives Marberg and Buckland coordinated their investigation with Lieutenant William Dougherty and Sergeant George Vasil of the university police force. The college officers had obtained a name for the victim from his possessions: Larry Dwayne Duerksen. Duerksen's wallet contained forty dollars when it was checked at the hospital. Dougherty and Vasil went to the apartment house listed as Duerksen's residence. There they were met in the lobby by an apparently grief-stricken Gareth Leifbach, who said he was Larry Duerksen's roommate.

They could see that Leifbach had been crying. Since he was listed as Larry's next of kin in case of an accident, Leifbach said someone at Harborview Hospital had called to tell him about Larry's death. He requested that police come at once to talk with him. He had also called Tami Scott and Ruth Rudd, two young women who were Larry's close friends, and they had rushed to his apartment to help him deal with the shock.

Gareth Leifbach and the two women spoke to

Dougherty and Vasil in Larry's apartment, their voices hushed with shock. Unable to stop his tears, Gareth volunteered information that seemed way off the subject of their visit. Rather than talk about Larry, his recently deceased roommate, Gareth told them that he was gay, and that he'd been discharged from the army at Fort Lewis for that reason. Before they could comment, he rushed to open his briefcase and pull out a sheaf of clippings detailing his fight with the army. He seemed proud of his notoriety, and very anxious to let the police officers know exactly who they were dealing with. He was, after all, a kind of celebrity.

Dougherty and Vasil looked puzzled, but they knew that grief and shock could make people behave in unexpected ways. "How long have you known Larry Duerksen?" Dougherty asked Gareth.

"During the time I was contesting my discharge, Larry wrote to me. We met and became friends. I traveled around after my discharge, and then came up to Seattle about the third or fourth of this month. I moved in with Larry."

"Do you know of anyone who might want to harm Larry?"

"I got a phone call yesterday from a man who asked for Larry. I gave him Larry's number at work and his work hours. Before he hung up, he said 'You're Gareth Leifbach, aren't you?' The guy called today too. When I told him Larry wasn't here, he said, 'I hate faggots,' and then he hung up." Asked for a recap of his activities during the day, Leifbach said he had stayed in the apartment until 11:30 A.M., and then gone down to the "Ave"—the main drag of the University District, a block away—to have lunch at Pizza Haven.

"I did some window shopping," he said, "and got

back here about one-thirty, and Larry was here. They gave him the afternoon off from the library."

So far, Gareth Leifbach's and the victim's day sounded pretty normal, but Leifbach continued. "Around two o'clock, Larry called a cab and we both went to some bridge," Gareth said. "Larry took this gun from his jacket and handed it to me. He told me to throw it off the bridge, and so I did. Then we came back to the apartment."

When the two college policeman asked him to tell them more about the gun, Leifbach said, "Larry and I thought it was a good idea to have a pistol for protection." To make his roommate feel more secure, Leifbach explained that he had bought the pistol. On December 11 he'd paid $305 for it at a shop in downtown Seattle. He'd also bought a box of bullets. He hastened to tell the investigators that he knew nothing about guns. "Larry loaded it—it was a Beretta automatic—but we changed our minds. We agreed to dispose of it."

For a man with more than two years in the air force, it seemed peculiar that he claimed to know nothing at all about guns. And when one of the investigators deliberately referred to the Beretta as an automatic, Leifbach corrected him quickly, "No, it's a semiautomatic."

They asked him why they had thrown a $300 gun off a bridge. Why they didn't sell it, or take it back to the store, but Leifbach just shook his head. He had no answer for that. Instead, he moved through the rest of the day's events. He said that he had prepared dinner for the two of them—bacon and eggs—around five.

"Between 6:00 and 6:45 P.M. Larry told me he had some business to take care of at the University," Leifbach said. "He didn't tell me what it was, and he declined my offer to go with him."

"You've been here ever since then?" Vasil asked.

Leifbach nodded. The officers looked toward a jacket hanging in the closet, a jacket Leifbach said was his. It had a brown outer shell and a fleece lining. They noted that the cuffs of the sleeves and the bottom of the coat were soaking wet. That seemed odd. Leifbach insisted that he hadn't left the apartment since he and Larry had come back from "the bridge" at two-thirty.

Tami and Ruth spoke up, explaining that Larry had been threatened repeatedly by someone and that they thought the threats had been reported to the Seattle Police Department. Gareth Leifbach paced the floor. He seemed very agitated and he nodded as the women talked. He said Larry had told him about the threats, too. All three of the witnesses were emphatic that Larry Duerksen had been living in fear, but none of them knew if Larry had known who was after him—or why.

Asked if he would be willing to take a lie detector test, Leifbach agreed to do so without hesitation. "I'm thinking of doing my own investigation of Larry's death," he said. "Around the end of October, somebody tried to run over Larry in front of the Sexual Minorities Counseling Center on Capitol Hill. And then somebody left a dead pigeon in a brown paper bag outside the apartment here."

Gareth said he felt that the killer had been trying to get to him by hurting his roommate. "Larry was planning to make speeches on my behalf to assist in the $3.5 million lawsuit I'm bringing against the army," he said with tears streaming down his face. "I hate guns! If it hadn't been for that gun we had, Larry would still be alive."

Again, what an odd remark. He had just told them that he'd thrown the gun off a bridge hours before Larry Duerksen was shot. Leifbach signed permission for Lieutenant Dougherty and Sergeant Vasil to search the apartment. They did look around, but they found no bullets and no more wet clothing. The only thing dripping with rain was the fleece-lined jacket.

Detective George Marberg ran Duerksen's and Leifbach's names through the law enforcement computer network and didn't find any criminal record for either of them. He also checked for Duerksen's name at the records bureau of the police department. Although Larry Duerksen had told many people that he had reported the threats against him, his name wasn't in the police files as a complainant. It was becoming more and more difficult to separate truth from fantasy, and reality from the histrionic and attention-grabbing behavior of these two roommates—one dead and the other apparently immobilized with grief, yet not too stunned to trumpet his own fame to the detectives who questioned him.

Gareth Leifbach had been crying when the two University of Washington police officers talked to him; they couldn't mistake his red, swollen eyes. His ordeal wasn't over. He had gone from that interview to identify the body of his roommate-friend-lover, and he sobbed then too. It looked as though Larry Duerksen's complete devotion to Gareth's fight for gay liberation in the armed services had been the death of him.

The fatal shooting wasn't Larry Duerksen's first brush with death. In addition to Leifbach, both of his women friends, Tami and Ruth, verified that Larry had almost been hit by a speeding car shortly after he aligned himself with Leifbach. He had managed to leap to safety at the very last minute. It was perfectly understandable that Gareth Leifbach felt not only grief but guilt over Larry's death.

Early on the morning of December 15, Dr. Donald Reay, the King County medical examiner, performed the postmortem. He found that the fatal bullet had entered near the right side at the back of Larry Duerksen's head and then traveled through the brain before exiting above his left eye. There was also a through-and-through flesh wound in his right arm, a grazing wound across his chest, and another severe wound in his upper left arm. The humerus—the large bone in the arm—had been fractured by the impact of a bullet. From the angle of fire, Dr. Reay determined that the victim had been on his feet when the arm wounds were sustained, but was lying facedown when the fatal wound to the head was administered. It was a classic execution-style killing. Larry Duerksen had been knocked to the ground by the force of the bullet that broke his arm, and then had been shot in the head as he lay with his face pressed to the sodden turf of Hippie Hill.

When the day shift came on duty, the Duerksen murder case was assigned to Detectives Mike Tando and Duane Homan. They immediately began to receive calls from members of the victim's family. All the detectives could tell them at this point was that Larry had been shot to death and that there were no suspects yet.

Homan and Tando returned to the crime scene and viewed it in daylight. Although the scene had been well protected all night long, they found nothing that seemed to further the investigation. The detectives moved over the pale grass of winter with a metal detector, but there was no reaction that might suggest that a slug was lodged in the ground. They dug down six inches into the turf and still found nothing.

Gareth Leifbach had been open about where he'd bought the gun that Larry wanted "for protection." The detectives talked with the proprietor of a pawnshop near skid row where Leifbach said he'd bought the missing Beretta. They learned that he had also bought fifty rounds of .32 caliber Remington-Peters ammunition. "Mr. Leifbach picked a .32 caliber Beretta, Model 81, on December 14," the pawnshop owner said. That was just what Gareth had told the campus police. And the Remington-Peters casings matched those found at the shooting site. Interesting . . .

The detectives then verified Gareth's story further by checking the records of the Yellow Cab Company. Their trip records showed one call to Duerksen's apartment complex on December 14. "Our cab number 45 went out there in the morning at ten A.M. He took the fare on a round-trip to the Central Loan pawnshop," the cab manager reported. "The guy went in and came back a few minutes later. He was driven back to his home address. He tipped five dollars on a ten-dollar fare."

The physical description of the taxi passenger matched Gareth Leifbach. Leifbach had already admitted that he purchased the gun, but he hadn't mentioned that he picked it up only nine hours before Larry Duerksen was shot. He had told the University of Washington police that he and Larry had the gun for three days before they decided to get rid of it on the afternoon of December 14. It was a small variation on the truth. Was it significant? Minor inconsistencies in recollection don't matter much in ordinary life, but they can be crucial in a murder investigation.

Detectives Homan and Tando drove to the dead man's apartment and picked up Gareth Leifbach for a trip to Homicide for an interview. After reading and signing his rights admonishment, Gareth again launched into a strange monologue about his homosexuality, his fight with the army, and the huge lawsuit he had filed against the army.

His attitude seemed inappropriate. The only way to describe his attitude was grandiose; the grief he'd shown right after his roommate was shot was no longer evident, and the change was startling. "I'm into a heavy schedule of appearances and speeches for my cause," he said proudly. "I've had a lot of publicity. You've probably seen me on television."

Homan nodded noncommittally. He had heard the guy was pretty full of himself, but he had never seen him on television. The tall, easygoing detective asked Gareth about his life, and how he and Larry had met.

Gareth said he was born in Battle Creek, Michigan, on June 9, 1958, and joined the U.S. Army on August 7, 1977. He was honorably discharged on November 2, 1979. He had met Larry Duerksen for the first time the month before his discharge. "He wrote to me and I wrote back, and we began to talk on the phone," he said.

He told Homan that Larry proved to be a really loyal friend who readily threw in his lot with Gareth. He said they'd planned to tour for gay rights together. Gareth Leifbach was affable during the interview, bristling only once when Detective Mike Tando asked him to define his relationship with Larry. "That's too personal to discuss," he said imperiously.

If he expected the detectives to voice any opinion one way or the other about his lifestyle, he was disappointed; they didn't care. They wanted only to solve his roommate's murder, and in that sense, it might matter whether the men were lovers as well as friends.

Once more, Gareth repeated his version of the events of Friday, December 14. He was precise in his recall of the phone calls from the stranger—the man who had called Larry and him faggots on December 12 and again on December 14. And this time, he included in the day's events his trip to pick up the gun. Yes, now he recalled that he'd bought it the day Larry died.

Gareth told about his lunch at the pizza place and recalled that it was raining so hard, his jacket had been soaked through and didn't dry until the next day. It was almost as if he had noted the investigators' doubting expressions during his first interview. Now his version dovetailed smoothly with the facts as Homan and Tando knew them. "I showed the gun to Larry when he got home around one-thirty, and he loaded it," he said. "He stepped out to empty the trash, and when he came back he said 'Gareth, we shouldn't have gotten a gun. If someone wants to get us, they will anyway.' So Larry suggested we throw it off the bridge. I called a yellow cab and we took the gun, without the ammo, and threw it off the Aurora Bridge."

But they already knew that the cab company had no record of a second call to the victim's address on December 14. Gareth insisted that he and Larry had thrown the gun away. He even described the cabbie who'd driven them to the bridge: "A bald guy with a big mustache. Didn't say much."

Gareth insisted that he had no idea whom Larry planned to meet "to discuss business" with on the campus at six o'clock that evening. All he knew was that Larry had promised to return within an hour.

There is one axiom that detectives count on: If none of the facts match, be careful. But if a witness or suspect remembers details *too* precisely, be very, very careful. Gareth Leifbach remembered the day his friend (and probable lover) was murdered as if he had a photographic memory.

"After he left," Gareth continued. "I watched Walter Cronkite and then *All in the Family*. Tami Scott called about eight o'clock, and we discussed a party we were going to go to on Saturday. Right after that, the hospital called and said Larry had been shot and that he'd 'expired.' " Gareth said he was so distraught that he'd called Tami back at once and asked her to come over. Then the police from the University of Washington arrived to question him. The story Gareth was telling Homan and Tando made a weird kind of sense. The victim had talked of threats, even though his stories were so bizarre that his friends doubted them. Maybe Larry hadn't been crying wolf after all. He had walked away from the apartment to meet someone, still unidentified, and he had been shot to death. Maybe there was some wacko out there who hated "faggots" so much that he would actually murder a campaigner for gay rights. If that was true, then Gareth Leifbach was probably even more of a target than Larry Duerksen had been.

Something niggled at Tando and Homan: Leifbach's bravado, his love of publicity, and the fact that his story continued to change, however imperceptibly, troubled them.

"Was Larry nervous that night?" Tando asked, suddenly. "Did he act frightened about his meeting?"

"Yeah . . . yeah, he did seem kind of nervous," Gareth agreed.

Duane Homan and Mike Tando obtained a search warrant for Larry Duerksen's apartment. Although Gareth had given permission for a first, more casual, search, they now looked in every drawer, every corner.

When they were finished, they were convinced there was no gun there.

Gareth Leifbach showed the detectives his few belongings. And again, he couldn't resist bragging about his fame. He opened his attaché case and pulled out a handful of articles written about him.

The detectives swabbed Leifbach's left hand, telling him this was routine, that a neutron activation analysis test would show if he had fired a gun recently. At this point, it was a "psychological swabbing" rather than one that might detect gun debris. Leifbach had probably washed his hands dozens of times since Larry's death.

But Gareth appeared apprehensive about the test. "Maybe it would show positive," he offered, "because I handled the gun before I threw it away."

"No," they said. "Only if you fired it."

"Well, I haven't fired any gun, especially that Beretta."

His vehemence about this made the detectives hold their breath. They half-expected him to say more, but he didn't. The neutron test surprised him and, for the first time, seemed to throw him off stride. In moments, however, Gareth Leifbach was his old confident self.

Detective George Marberg, working the third watch, found himself in the Homicide offices at 3:40 A.M., taking a phone call from Larry Duerksen's father, who was calling from Nebraska. Still reeling from the shock of learning that his son was gay, he now had to deal with the fact that Larry had been murdered. He promised to help detectives in any way he could. "I talked to Gareth the night Larry died," the elder Duerksen said. "He said something about Larry having insurance policies and that Larry had made him the beneficiary of those policies."

Larry's father said the only policy he knew about

was one for $10,000 that was part of the benefits package provided by his employment at the University of Washington. He said he himself was listed as the beneficiary of that policy. He was surprised to hear that there had been other policies. It didn't make sense, not for a single man with no dependents. Marberg said he would check further on this new information.

"Larry told me he was homosexual about six months ago," the elder Duerksen said. "I don't know anything about his life in Seattle, though."

University of Washington investigators advised that they had talked with Larry Duerksen's supervisor at the library. "The witness reports she had lunch with Larry on the fourteenth," the follow-up read. "He told her that he and Gareth were supposed to meet with a man from the Dorian Society [a gay support group in Seattle] at the base of the George Washington statue that night to discuss publicity for Gareth Leifbach's case."

Homan and Tando shook their heads. Why on earth would they meet outside in the dark in a driving rainstorm when they could have met with the Dorian representative in their apartment? To back up their growing suspicions, the detectives checked with the Dorian Society to see if anyone there knew of such a meeting. Nobody did.

If he and Larry had planned to meet the activist, why hadn't Gareth mentioned it to Tando and Homan? He had repeatedly assured them that he didn't know where Larry was going that night. The investigators approached the problem from another angle, brainstorming possible scenarios. "Okay," Tando began. "The witness said she saw two men—who seemed to be very close companions—sharing an umbrella. Is it possible that Gareth led Larry out into the dark campus on the pretext of some secret meeting, which never existed?"

"Possible, sure—but why?" Homan asked. "What would Gareth Leifbach hope to gain if Larry died? He had a lot more to gain by keeping him as his strongest supporter if he wanted to continue to gain publicity. Larry apparently idolized him."

"Larry was afraid of something," Tando said, repeating what they already knew. "All those people he worked with at the library verify that. They're telling us he was obsessed with the idea that someone was going to kill him. He was really scared. This wasn't his usual tall tale."

The investigation became increasingly puzzling. Sergeant Don Cameron received a frantic phone call from Gareth Leifbach. "About thirty minutes ago," he said, his voice trembling, "I got another of those calls! The guy said, 'I got Larry and I'll get you if it takes a year!' "

"Why did you wait a half hour to report this?" Cameron asked.

"I don't know," Leifbach answered. "I think I'm just going to stay in my apartment. I'm very frightened."

No sooner had Cameron hung up—after promising to see about putting a tap on Leifbach's phone—than he received a phone call from the Seattle Police Department's communications center. "A guy just called—sounded young, probably Caucasian," the officer reported. "He said, 'Tell Sergeant Cameron I killed Larry Duerksen and I will kill Gareth Leifbach . . . or whatever his bastard name is.' "

The caller had, of course, refused to give his name. Either there was an assassin out there stalking gay activists, or someone wanted the homicide detectives to believe there was. Unfortunately, the anonymous call had come in on a business line and was not recorded, as a 911 call would have been.

Love and Insurance

Detective Darryl Stuver of the University of Washington police and the three Seattle detectives assigned to the case were working almost full time now, trying to ferret out the truth behind Larry Duerksen's murder. Larry had told almost everyone he knew that he'd been threatened, but no one had believed him. A check with the phone company elicited the information that Duerksen had gone so far as to call a representative on October 8 to report that he had received six threatening calls, but he hadn't requested a tap or any follow-up from Pacific Northwest Bell.

All of the investigators working on his murder had come to have doubts not only about Larry Duerksen's respect for the truth but also about Gareth Leifbach's. The two were so much alike—both given to braggadocio and elaborate exaggeration. Which one had lied? Or had both of them lied? Or neither?

Now Gareth was the only flesh-and-blood suspect they had. But they still had no motive. If it was he who shot Larry Duerksen, they didn't know why. No one who knew them recalled so much as a minor argument between them. They seemed to be genuinely fond of each other and united in their friendship.

Larry's father thought that his son had a $10,000 insurance policy that was connected to his job at the library, but the detectives couldn't find it. The only insurance policy they found was a $10,000 policy on Gareth Leifbach's life. He explained that he had taken that out because of the dangers inherent in activist work. After all, he reminded them, he was the figurehead of gay rights and he was taking on the U.S. Army.

There had to be other insurance policies, if only they could locate them. "Larry told me Gareth suggested that he take out a large policy too," one of his close

291

friends said, "with each of them—Larry and Gareth—being the beneficiary of the other's policy."

A reporter from the *Seattle Gay News* interviewed the investigators, telling them that he had already interviewed Gareth. "Leifbach told me about the threats Larry Duerksen got," the reporter said. "Leifbach thinks the killer is someone from the library."

"Why?" Duane Homan asked, amazed.

"Because Duerksen's phone number was unlisted," the reporter explained. "No one had his number beyond Leifbach and the people at the library."

The new controversy involving Leifbach was, of course, front-page news for the gay paper. The man was a magnet for trouble and intrigue and he made wonderful copy.

On December 19, Lieutenant Dougherty and Detective Darryl Stuver reported that their department had come upon some startling new information: An insurance policy had been taken out on Larry Duerksen's life. It was written by the Prudential Life Insurance Company, and their records revealed that the payoff on the policy was $500,000.

The beneficiary? Gareth Leifbach. The policy was brand new—in force for only one week at the time of Larry Duerksen's murder. He and Gareth had approached a company representative on December 7 and arranged to insure each other's lives. But Gareth's policy had been written for a fifth of Larry's—only $100,000. He told the Prudential salesman that he would seek an additional $400,000 from another company.

Policies that paid out over $100,000 required that each man take a physical examination, and they had readily agreed to do so. Although Gareth and Larry had physicals on December 12, the paperwork had not yet been completed at the time of Larry's murder two days later. Because of that, the death of his lover would allow Gareth to collect only 50 percent of the face value of the policy. He would get only a quarter of a million dollars.

And there, finally, was a very good motive for him to kill Larry. The investigators had seen people killed for a lot less than $250,000, but they suspected Leifbach might not have realized he'd jumped the gun, both literally and figuratively, on the night Larry died.

Insurance companies have their own investigators and compile intricate profiles of who buys insurance and why. A representative from Prudential explained to the detectives that it is quite unusual to have someone call to inquire about life insurance. Most calls that came from potential clients were about homeowners' policies or car insurance, she said. Usually, an agent had to approach someone and sell life insurance. People want to be protected in an automobile accident or if a tree fell on their house, but they were reluctant to contemplate their own death.

The whole transaction with Duerksen and Leifbach had been unusual. Red flags went up immediately when they requested such large policies. It is far out of the norm to insure a man with a modest income for half a million dollars. That was the reason the company required an immediate physical and the first year's premiums paid in advance.

"Who called your company first?" Homan asked.

"Mr. Leifbach," replied the insurance representative.

Leifbach had done most of the talking when he and Duerksen came to the office. He explained he was living off savings and contributions from supporters of his campaign. No mention was made of alleged threats against Duerksen, but Leifbach had admitted that their activist work might be dangerous, and that was why he and Larry wanted insurance. True to form, Leifbach had insisted on showing the agent all his newspaper clippings. "He struck me as being very egotistical."

There was some concern that Larry Duerksen might have been suffering from a fatal but hard-to-detect illness, so his physical exam was very thorough. And he turned out to be in great shape.

"See for yourself," the agent said to Homan, tapping a polished nail on a manila folder. "Larry Duerksen was in perfect health." This was an unusual situation, but the agent said that, in the end, it wasn't her job to refuse insurance just because the insured's best friend had an outsize ego. She went on to say that it was Gareth Leifbach who paid the initial premium of $1,400, and he paid in cash.

The policy was granted.

Now Leifbach was running scared. He made a steady stream of defensive phone calls to the homicide detectives. He sounded increasingly anxious, asking often if the results of the neutron test had shown any gunpowder on his hands. The investigators stalled, telling him that it was a very complicated test and they didn't have any results yet. In truth, it is not a particularly complicated test and results don't take long. Leifbach was concerned about his coat too and asked to have it returned. They told him it was in evidence, which, indeed, it was. Larry's relatives came to Seattle to settle his affairs. Larry Duerksen's father was surprised when the detectives told him about the very large insurance policy his son had recently purchased. That wasn't consistent with what Gareth had told him. "He said that Larry had taken out only a $5,000 policy—not a $500,000 policy!"

The insurance company was far from ready to pay off that new policy. Gareth Leifbach continued to live in Larry's apartment, although it was virtually empty after Larry's family had removed his belongings. With no furniture in them, the rooms echoed hollowly. For a man who had "millionaires" lined up to back him, it seemed strange that Leifbach was clinging to three bare rooms with only a few more weeks of paid-up rent remaining. Mike Tando and Duane Homan went next to the pawnshop where Leifbach had purchased the gun which, according to him, was now in the water beneath the Aurora Bridge. They obtained a gun identical to the missing Beretta. The ballistics section of the Western Washington Crime Lab test-fired the gun, and found that ejector and extractor marks left on the bullet casings by the duplicate Beretta were microscopically almost identical to those on the casings found beneath Larry Duerksen's body—almost, but not quite. Every gun, even of the same make and caliber, produces slightly different tool marks, but the casing comparison was so close that it seemed highly probable that it was indeed a .32 Beretta that was used to kill Duerksen. They knew that Leifbach had purchased a .32 Beretta from the pawnshop only hours before Duerksen was murdered. They wondered, however, if he had done so at the victim's suggestion.

Larry had been hit with .32 caliber Remington-Peters bullets, the same kind of ammo Leifbach had purchased.

Both circumstantial and direct physical evidence tied Liefbach to Larry's murder, and the case against him was growing.

Detectives visited Gareth Leifbach once more in an attempt to heat up their subtle war of nerves. They asked him if they could take some pictures of him "for elimination purposes." He agreed, but they could tell he was biting his tongue to keep from asking them what this was about. Once more he asked about the results of the gunpowder test and when his coat would be returned. "When will this be over?" he asked uneasily.

"We don't really know," Don Cameron replied calmly. "Oh, yeah—that reminds me, we've heard you're telling people that you're a suspect and will be arrested any day. Why is that?"

"Well, I was his roommate," Liefbach said. "It's only logical. Roommates are always the main suspect."

"No, that's not always the case."

"I got another threatening phone call," Liefbach offered. "I got mad and told the guy that his threats didn't scare me, called him an s.o.b. and said I'd take care of him myself. He hasn't called since."

Leifbach was protesting too much. The Seattle detectives felt certain he had invented his shadowy stalker.

Two investigators showed a collage of photographs to Lorraine Lacey, the only witness to the shooting. Gareth Leifbach's image was among the eight men pictured. She wrinkled her forehead and sighed. She could not say for sure—she could only narrow her identification down to two men. One of them was Leifbach.

The detectives were positive now that Leifbach was their man, but they needed something more to take to the prosecutor's office. They called the Yellow Cab office and asked that a renewed search of the company's records be made for the time between 5:00 and 8:00 P.M. on the evening Duerksen died.

"Maybe you missed something?" Tando asked.

A few hours later the dispatcher called back excitedly, "I found *two* trips to the Duerksen apartment on the fourteenth—one in the morning to the Central Loan and one at 7:17 P.M."

It was a very important discovery; by 7:17 on that night, Larry Duerksen was already dead, and Gareth Liefbach swore he had never left his apartment. The second driver called to the victim's apartment remembered his fare. The man who got in his cab had a mustache and was wearing a fleece-lined brown jacket. "I drove him to the south end of the University Bridge. I took the guy to the Red Robin Tavern just across the bridge from the U District," he said. "He was gonna meet a friend there. I let him off. Anyway, I let him off at the tavern. It's maybe a five- to seven-minute ride when there's no traffic. I turned around and just got to the north end of the bridge when I got the call to go *back* to the Red Robin. The guy told me his friend didn't show up and he wanted me to take him back to his place."

Asked if there was anything unusual about his fare, the driver nodded. "He was soaking wet when I picked him up at his apartment—a lot wetter than he would have gotten just running from the apartment to the cab."

"Anything else you might remember about him?" the detectives asked.

"Well, like I said, he was sopping wet when I picked him up at 7:17, and he was really excited and jumpy. He sure didn't wait long for his friend to show up."

It was one mile from Duerksen's apartment to the Red Robin Tavern. The popular spot backed up to the Lake Washington Ship Canal, a waterway that was very deep—deep enough to accommodate large ships that passed under the drawbridge a few hundred feet to the west. It took the investigators exactly four and a half minutes to retrace the route from Duerksen's apartment to the tavern.

They knew now what led up to the events of the night of December 14. Gareth Leifbach had led Larry Duerksen to believe they would be together forever, promising him a life of adventure and commitment, the things Larry had always longed for. Then, on December 7, Gareth persuaded Larry to have his life insured for half a million dollars. The policy became 50 percent effective on December 12.

On December 14, Larry told friends that he and Gareth were to have a secret meeting with someone from the Dorian Society on campus. Shortly before 7:00 P.M., Lorraine Lacey saw two men walking toward the George Washington statue. She heard gunfire and saw a flash as the shorter of the two—the man wearing a fleece-lined jacket—reached toward the other, who had fallen to the ground. Then she watched the shorter man run away.

The movements had been choreographed perfectly, down to the minute, if not the second. At 7:12, Gareth Leifbach called a cab. He took that cab to the University Bridge area at 7:17. At 7:22, he left the cab, walked behind the tavern, and in all likelihood, threw the Beretta into the ship canal. At 7:29 the cab picked him up again and brought him back to Larry's apartment by 7:34.

Gareth was there moments after 8:00, when the hospital called to tell him that his roommate had been shot and killed. Leifbach reacted with appropriate shock and began to sob. He then called Larry's women friends to come over to help him "cope with my sorrow."

When the campus police arrived to question Leifbach, they noted that his coat was still soaking wet, although he claimed to have been inside the apartment since 2:30 P.M.

Leifbach continued to perpetuate the myth of threats against Larry Duerksen. Was it possible that he'd listened to Larry's tall stories and decided his roommate's exaggerations provided the perfect setup? Perhaps, but more likely, someone had tortured Larry with scary phone calls and threats, and that someone was Gareth Leifbach. If everyone believed that Larry had been threatened, there would be a good reason to take out a huge insurance policy on him. More important, there would be a built-in suspect if something should happen to Larry.

Detectives now felt they had probable cause to arrest Gareth Leifbach for the murder of Larry Duerksen. After discussing it with Chief Criminal Deputy Prosecutor Phil Killien, an arrest warrant was issued. It was one week almost to the minute after the murder when Seattle police and University of Washington investigators knocked on the door of Larry's apartment. Leifbach answered the door and invited them in.

"Remember us?" a detective asked. Leifbach nodded apprehensively. "We're placing you under arrest for the murder of Larry Duerksen."

After listening to his Miranda rights, Leifbach stated only that he wanted his attorney. He was no longer bragging about his celebrity or giving his theories about "the real killer."

Police divers searched the Lake Washington Ship Canal for three days, but found nothing they could link to the murder case. The water was too murky and far too deep to locate one Beretta semiautomatic.

Gareth Leifbach spoke intensely to a reporter, his expansive charm regained. He said he had refused to take a polygraph test on the advice of his lawyer. "I hired one of the best lawyers in town because this is a serious offense," he said. "I told my lawyer that I know

I didn't do it, and if I end up going to jail for something I didn't do, then I want the gas chamber because I couldn't live in jail knowing I was there for something I didn't do. I've been framed. The evidence is against me. The government is framing me in an attempt to stop my lawsuit against the army. I'm mystified that there is no cab record showing when I went to the Aurora Bridge early in the afternoon of the fourteenth to throw the gun away. I only went to the Red Robin to buy a couple of cheeseburgers for Larry and me, but when I saw the long line, I decided not to wait. I'm not ashamed to say that Larry and I were just roommates and very good friends." If Gareth Leifbach hoped for a groundswell of support from the gay community, he was disappointed. Larry Duerksen had led a homosexual lifestyle, too, and the evidence against Leifbach was so strong that the community's sympathy went to Duerksen, not Leifbach.

On January 2, 1980, Gareth Leifbach pleaded not guilty to the charge of first-degree murder. In February, he was found guilty of first-degree murder in Judge James Dore's courtroom.

After serving twenty years in prison, Leifbach was due for his first parole hearing in the summer of 2000. He has served his time as a loner, with no family visiting or writing. His reputation faded away years ago, and few remember the man who claimed to have an honorable reason to challenge the army and who said over and over that he only wanted justice for himself and for others who wanted the right to be good soldiers, despite their sexual orientation. During his two decades in prison, his cause was taken up by others far more trustworthy than he.

Ironically, Larry Duerksen always wanted to be the

center of attention. And he wanted to find true love with a man he admired and cared for. It was the answer to Larry's fondest dream when Gareth Liefbach allowed him into his life. But it was all a setup. Duerksen was murdered by the man he loved and trusted the most. Larry Duerksen *did* make headlines, but in the most heartbreaking way.

The Gentler Sex

*"**Divortium** (Latin): separation, divorce, a fork in the road."* By its very definition, divorce is not a particularly amicable transaction, but it was never designed to be deadly. As they come to a fork in the road, the wife goes her way, the husband goes his way, and the community property gets split in a relatively equitable fashion down the middle. Alas, there are those husbands who provided for their wives in happier days by taking out large life insurance policies, and when these marriages break down, friendly divorce is not a part of some wives' plans. The thought of all that money just lying fallow is more than an embittered wife can bear. No one will ever know how many ex-husbands die accidentally, leaving distraught widows to collect on insurance policies that let them grieve in comfort.

Throughout the annals of crime, there have been women bright enough and devious enough not only to get away with murder but also to collect on double- and triple-indemnity policies. And then there are other widows who are so unbelievably klutzy in their attempts to commit murder for profit that they might as well have the word *"Murderess"* tattooed on their foreheads.

Of course it's not just wives who look to murder as a way to avoid divorce; there are faithless husbands who *are more interested in financial gain than in honey-mooning. We are more disturbed when women kill because we believe that the female is the kinder, softer, and gentler sex. And as far as statistics go, they are. According to the Diagnostic Statistical Manual—the bible of psychiatrists—three percent of all males are deemed to be antisocial and without conscience, while only one percent of females seem to lack compassion for others. But the icy manipulations of that one percent are utterly fascinating. No one can be crueler than a woman without a conscience. Very clever bad girls rarely get caught; only the dumber femme fatales make headlines. In the running for Klutzy Killers of the Millennium are two San Diego, California, women—Carole Hargis and Teri Depew.*

In the mid-seventies, the Vietnam War raged and disco fever prevailed at the nightspots that Carole Hargis frequented. Carole was very feminine-looking, with a delicate but well-proportioned figure and long, wavy golden hair. She looked much younger than her thirty-six years. She met Marine Corps Sergeant David Hargis in the mid-seventies. He was a handsome drill instructor at the Marine Corps Recruit Depot in San Diego. David was thirteen years younger than she was, but he assured Carole that age didn't matter—he loved her. He wanted to marry her and he accepted her two sons from a previous marriage as his own. The only problem the couple had was an accumulation of debt. David reenlisted in the marines because they needed the bonus that came with re-upping. He paid off their pressing bills and, with careful budgeting, was chipping away at the remaining debt.

Carole, David, and her sons lived on Laurel Street in a typical Spanish-style home with a terra-cotta tile roof. It was close to Balboa Park and their little house was high on the hilly street so they had a wonderful view of San Diego Bay.

The Hargis marriage might have succeeded—but for Carole's good friend, twenty-seven-year-old Teri Depew, who lived next door. Where Carole was blond

ANN RULE

and willowy, Teri was short and chunky and she
cropped her hair as short as a boy's. Her arms were
covered with tattoos, and she occasionally wore a buck
knife on her hip. A physical therapist who was temporarily out of work, Teri was proud of her physical
strength.

Teri had never married and didn't intend to; she preferred girls, and she especially preferred Carole. Carole
liked Teri, and they spent a lot of time together. Teri figured everything would have been perfect if it were not
for David, who had to be the most trusting, naïve man
ever to come out of marine boot camp. He was never
concerned about his wife's friendship with Teri; he
considered them best friends who spent time together
sipping coffee and exchanging girl talk.

Soon after he married Carole, David took out a
$20,000 double-indemnity insurance policy, naming
Carole and her two sons as beneficiaries. He was in a
very dangerous profession and he wanted to be sure
they were taken care of if he should be sent to Vietnam
and not make it back.

But David wasn't ordered overseas; he was so superior at training troops that he was much more valuable
Stateside. Marine Corps drill instructors are among the
toughest military men around. As they march recruits
through deserts and swamps and lead them over obsta-
cle courses, the DIs have to be in such good shape that
they can run rings around the rookies. David was muscular and perfectly coordinated, and he could run for
miles with his gear on his back. But he was softhearted
when it came to Carole, and he was grateful when orders kept him in San Diego.

Teri, Carole, and David got along as neighbors and
even got together for beers and board games on the

evenings when David was home. He liked Teri well enough, and she seemed to like him, although her opinion of men in general wasn't favorable. She didn't care much for the male sex.

As time went on, Carole and Teri grew closer. They waited impatiently for David to be sent overseas and became frustrated when that didn't happen. They were romantically involved and David was in the way. Carole had no skills or training and Teri was unemployed, and besides, they didn't want to get jobs.

Carole told Teri about the insurance policy David had purchased. It seemed the perfect answer for them; they wanted to enjoy a comfortable life without David, but even if he was sent overseas, there was no guarantee that he would be killed in battle.

The women have never agreed about which of them suggested the first plan designed to give them the easy life they envisioned. Later, each would blame the other for coming up with the idea of killing David for his insurance money.

Teri and Carole realized they would have to make his death look like an accident—both to fool the police and to qualify under the double-indemnity clause in his policy. Killing a big husky marine drill instructor wasn't going to be that easy. The only thing they had going for them was the fact that David was a home-loving, doting stepfather who never doubted his wife. He never asked why Teri was always around; he just figured Carole got lonesome while he was off training recruits.

The first plan to kill David came from a television program they watched—an episode of *Alfred Hitchcock Presents*. David always took a shower after a day's duty out in the scorching California sun. They decided Carole would leave her hair dryer plugged in and throw it into the shower while David was standing there naked and wet. They knew this would work better if David was in the habit of taking a bath, but the shower would have to do.

Carole did her part. She started to dry her hair and then pretended to stumble, and the hair dryer flew out of her hand and landed in the shower stall with David. Fortunately for him, there wasn't much water in the bottom of the stall and David was standing on a rubber mat. He didn't die. He didn't even get a shock. He did give Carole a stern lecture on home safety, reminding her that it could have been one of her children taking a shower.

The second plan to do away with David involved putting a hefty dose of LSD in David's French toast. Carole and Teri had plenty of time to find and buy the hallucinogen while David was away on a bivouac. When he returned, they beat the LSD in with the eggs and milk and dipped slices of French bread in the mixture before they fried them in butter. David ate two helpings with plenty of maple syrup. They watched him expectantly, but he seemed fine. When he got to work that morning, though, he became nauseated. The medic said he just had a case of twenty-four-hour stomach flu.

The general philosophy of their essential plan wasn't what was wrong. Teri always maintained that they had to work David's murder into his regular routine. They had to study things he did every day so that his death would seem, if not natural, a tragic accident. Up till that point, that's what they had done. But David was proving to be far more impervious to attack than they had reckoned him to be.

"Martinis!" Teri cried one night. "He drinks a martini every night of his life—sometimes two."

The two woman put household lye into David's

The Gentler Sex

gin bottle, hoping that his next martini would be his last. Carole thought he'd probably spit it out when he realized he wasn't drinking gin and vermouth, but Teri had an answer for that, too: "He'll surely ask for water, and then you can hand him a glass full of lye water and he'll swallow it. Then he'll die and we can pour some gin on him and tell the doctor that he was drunk and accidentally drank out of the wrong bottle."

Carole didn't think the plan would work. What if he didn't die? Surely, after this he would be suspicious. As good-natured as he was, he wasn't stupid—and once David lost his trust in her, their marriage would probably end. Then she would lose the insurance money even if he ever *did* die.

Teri grudgingly agreed that this was something to think about. Carole said she had a plan of her own, and it was far more subtle than putting lye in David's gin. She had owned a pet tarantula for some time, long enough that it was a familiar sight in its glass cage. (It was an apt pet for a woman with homicidal tendencies, given that many female spiders eat their mates after their union is consummated.) Carole said her spider still had an intact venom sac. She suggested they wait until David went to bed, and when he was asleep, they could slip the tarantula into bed with him. Sometime during the night, he was bound to roll over on the furry spider and be bitten. In light of his wife's plans for him, David Hargis might have been better off going to bed with the tarantula than with Carole.

Teri was enthusiastic about the tarantula plan, but she thought she could improve on it. She suggested they buy a blackberry pie and hide the venom sac from the spider in David's portion. "It will look just like the berries—unless he looks really close, and why would he do that?"

David ate his pie with relish—but when Carole cleared the table, she saw that he had pushed the venom sac to one side. He saw her staring at it and said, "I don't know what that is, but it doesn't look edible—it's probably a leaf or part of the blackberry vine."

If David had linked the recent odd events together, they would have seemed ominous, but hindsight is always 20-20. If he thought about the oddities in his life at all, he would have recalled: a clumsy slip in the bathroom, a day of stomach flu, and a leaf in his pie. He didn't know about the lye-in-the-gin idea because the women had never tried it.

Things weren't working out as neatly as they did on television, but Carole and Teri were only slightly daunted. They kept refining their scenarios for homicide. "If we could slip sleeping pills into his beer," Teri said, "he'd go to sleep in a hurry, and then we could inject an air bubble into his bloodstream. I've heard that a bubble goes straight to your heart and you die—and they can't tell a thing when they do the autopsy. It looks like you had a heart attack."

Twenty-three was a little young for a healthy marine to die of heart failure, but the women were confident the doctors would assume that David had some kind of congenital heart defect. They got him to sleep all right, with a mug of beer loaded with sleeping pills. But when Teri jabbed inexpertly at his arm, he jumped and the point of the hypodermic needle broke off in his arm. Now, they had to get the broken point out of his arm without waking him up. Luckily, he was sound asleep and the point of the needle wasn't deeply embedded in his flesh. They managed to retrieve it and immediately threw away the evidence.

David Hargis awoke in the morning with a very sore arm and assumed that some desert insect had bitten him during the night. He still didn't have a clue about the danger he was in.

Teri and Carole were becoming exasperated. All that lovely insurance money just beyond their grasp, and they couldn't seem to kill David. They considered grinding up poisonous insects and sprinkling them on his spaghetti, but they weren't sure they could convince him it was only oregano. And there was no guarantee that bugs in tiny fragments were toxic enough to do the job.

Carole and Teri were not the smartest women in San Diego. Their murder plots grew increasingly bizarre and ridiculous. They even thought they could put bullets into the carburetor of David's car, which would make the engine explode. But Teri nixed this idea because it seemed awfully complicated and they couldn't be sure that the bullets wouldn't be found in the wreckage. She wasn't sure how bullets could be traced, but she had heard that was possible.

While all this devious plotting was going on, David Hargis continued to go to work happily every day and sleep beside the woman he loved every night. Teri couldn't stand to think of her lover being in bed with David, and she decided they would have to take stronger action, even though it meant they would actually have to get their hands bloody. Their problem had been that they were too squeamish about actually confronting David. Carole, particularly, didn't want to look in his eyes if he ever realized that she wanted him dead.

"We'll put the rest of the sleeping pills in his beer," Teri said firmly. "You don't have to do anything. When he's asleep, I'll hit him with a heavy sash weight. Once we're sure he's finally dead, we can take him out somewhere and dump him."

"But somebody will find him," Carole said, horrified.

"If they do," Teri said, "we can say that he was missing—and how worried you were. Nobody is going to pick on you—you'll be the broken-hearted widow with two little boys to care for."

On July 20, 1977, David Hargis took his two stepsons to a Boy Scout meeting. While they were gone, Teri came over, ostensibly to play Scrabble. When David came home, he joined Carole and Teri and they continued to play—and drink beer—until nearly 10 P.M.

The ever-trusting David Hargis went to bed, this time for the last time. Teri looked at the man sleeping so peacefully as she held the sash weight in one hand. She was appalled at herself, and she suddenly felt guilty. She went out to the hall where Carole was waiting. "Carole, I just can't do it," she whispered. "I really do kind of like him—he's a nice fellow."

This time, it was Carole who took action. They had come too far to turn back. She threatened to leave Teri if she didn't go right back in there and kill David.

Fortified with more beer and some tranquilizers, Teri was finally ready to try again. She muttered to the sleeping victim, "I'm sorry but I gotta do this," and she swung the sash weight with all her might. There was a terrible crunching sound as David's skull shattered and a spray of blood made an arc on the pale wall. Tearfully, Teri went out to tell Carole that it was all over.

But it wasn't.

They could hear David's voice, very faint now, but they knew he was still alive. Carole shoved Teri back in to finish the job. "I hit him some more," Teri said, "until his head looked something awful and I knew he was dead."

Their final, icy plan had worked. Carole was now a widow. She and Teri worked frantically to clean up all signs that murder had been committed in the neat little house. Somehow, they hadn't expected it was going to be so messy. Working in the dark of night, they were like two women from the movie *Diabolique,* in a scene that was half horror and half comedy as they struggled to cover up their murderous handiwork.

Every time they got the blood washed from David's head, he would bleed again from the ears. Teri took some adhesive tape and taped his ears closed to stanch the blood flow.

Then they tried to carry David's body out of the house; they were shocked to find how heavy "dead weight" could be—they could barely lift him. Somehow they managed to get him down the outside stairway in the back of the Hargis home to the carport and finally into the bed of the Hargises' pickup truck. Teri drove off to dump him in some lonely spot. She found what she was looking for on a bridge along Black Canyon Road near the Mesa Grande Indian Reservation, east of the small town of Ramona, California.

Pulling and tugging, Teri managed to get David's body out of the truck bed on her own, and she rolled him to the edge of the bridge and pushed him off. It was too dark for her to see where he landed; all she heard was brush crackling and the sound of rocks displaced and tumbling somewhere beneath where she stood. Exhausted, Teri drove back to the house where Carole was waiting. It was 4:30 A.M. when she got back to Laurel Street.

While Teri was gone, Carole had washed all the

sheets and blankets, but she couldn't get the blood that had sprayed the walls and ceiling to disappear completely. Despite all her scrubbing, a faint shadow remained. They realized that they had to paint the room. Somehow, by the time Carole's sons woke up, everything looked clean and normal again.

The women agreed that they shouldn't stay together—so Teri left. They agreed that Carole would call and report David missing, but didn't work out the details. Whether unconsciously or deliberately, Carole put Teri in the spotlight in her first call to the San Diego County sheriff's office.

It was early morning on July 21, when a sobbing Carole Hargis called the San Diego Sheriff's Department. The dispatcher listened as Carole said her husband, a marine sergeant, had left the evening before with their next-door neighbor. "It was about 10:30," she said, "and they were going to go snake hunting somewhere in the east part of the county. I'm actually calling from Ramona," she said. "Our neighbor—Teri Depew—is back, but my husband isn't, and I'm so worried. She said some guys may have hurt him . . ."

Teri and Carole had what they considered to be a very convincing story to explain how David had "disappeared." It would be dicey for a while, but they were confident that things were going to be fine now.

By noon, a sheriff's helicopter headed for the rugged country in eastern San Diego County; if the missing man was injured or alone out there in baking July heat and they waited the usual twenty-four hours to look for him, all they could expect to find was a corpse.

Of course, the hapless David Hargis was already dead. As the helicopter pilot passed Ramona, he swept his eyes over the Santa Ysabel Creek below and spotted what looked like a body lying beneath a bridge. He radioed the location and San Diego County Homicide Detectives Joe Cellucci and Fred Balmer headed out from downtown San Diego for the mountainous, pine tree–dotted wilderness. It took them forty-five minutes.

David Hargis had been dead for over twelve hours. He was fully clothed and his wallet was in his pocket with his military ID and two one-dollar bills. Balmer and Cellucci stared at the body, perplexed. It was the first time in their experience that a killer had bothered to bandage the ears of his victim, and Hargis's head was swathed in gauze, tissue paper and bright yellow vinyl tape.

Joe Cellucci crouched down to look at the dead man. He lay on one side, his face twisted toward the sky. The detective couldn't begin to count the numerous crushing blows on Hargis's skull, or the bruises on his neck, shoulder, lower back and hip. His wrists had been bound with shoe laces that were threaded through his belt loops.

Hargis had lain in plain sight of the road. If anyone had happened to pause and look down into the dry creek, they would have seen him. Balmer and Cellucci had no idea of the movitation of the killer or killers; it was possible that it *was* a robbery and that the robber had left behind the two single bills and taken away a much larger amount.

The San Diego detectives climbed up to the road and studied the shoulder there. There was a partial tread mark from a tire and they photographed that, along with a shoe print a bit closer to the drop-off. The print indicated that the shoe had a waffle design on its sole. There were dried bloodstains on the bridge and they found a piece of the yellow vinyl tape that was identical to the "bandage" on the victim's head.

A quarter mile down the road, Fred Balmer located a bloodied sheet and a brown corduroy jacket. But the investigators found no appreciable bloodstains in the sandy soil or on the concrete bridge and its supports. David Hargis had clearly not been killed here; he had only been thrown away here.

After they had gathered what physical evidence they could find into neatly labeled plastic bags, Cellucci and Balmer faced a dreaded task. They had to inform the widow. Waiting at the sheriff's substation in Ramona, Carol Hargis had managed to control her emotions and was no longer sobbing. She was stoic as they informed her that her husband was dead—murdered.

She said she had expected that. Her dear friend—Teri Depew—was afraid that someone might have beaten and robbed David.

"Why?" Balmer asked. "What was he doing out here in the middle of the night?"

"He was hunting for snakes," Carole said, adding that she hadn't thought a thing about it when David decided to take advantage of the cool of night to hunt rattlesnakes. A lot of his friends did that, too, collecting the rattles and the skins. Skeletal snake heads, their fangs exposed, were in demand to hang from rearview mirrors. "The snakes hide under rocks in the daytime when it's so hot," Carole explained. "Teri wanted to go along with him last night, and that was fine with me. I stayed home with my little boys."

But Carole said Teri was very upset when she came home. "They were up at Black Canyon Road and they ran into a bunch of guys that were partying," Carole said. "Teri said David joined in while she went out to buy more beer—but when she got back he and the strangers were gone."

Carole had called the sheriff and then talked to another marine who lived in her neighborhood into taking her up to the campgrounds to look for David. "But I didn't find him," she said softly, "so I went back to your substation in Ramona."

Traditionally, the first place any good detective looks for a killer is among those near and dear to the deceased. They begin with the spouse and the family, and move on to the victim's circle of friends and co-workers. The San Diego detectives started their questioning with Carole. There was something "hinky" about this widow. Her affect was all wrong—too flat and empty of emotion—and she fumbled with her story. She contradicted herself and her eyes darted around nervously.

Next, Cellucci and Balmer obtained a search warrant for the Hargis residence. After the rest of the Laurel Street house yielded no clues, they concentrated on the bedroom. Catching a whiff of fresh paint, they stared at the walls and touched them—only to find the paint was still tacky. They knelt to run a fine, sharp tool along a crack in the baseboard, and along with balls of paint, they saw dark red. Women who thought tarantula venom sacs were deadly had no idea what secrets even small amounts of blood could reveal. David's blood had soaked into the wall and the baseboard, and there was enough left to match exemplars of his blood type that were readily available from Marine Corps records.

When the detectives told Carole that evidence indicated that her husband had expired in the bed they shared, she turned pale. They pointed out the spot they found on the wall, and explained about how the crime lab could match blood types.

Then Balmer and Cellucci worked their way down the back stairs to the driveway where a shiny pickup truck sat. Oddly, someone had recently washed the truck; the cement around it was still wet. They peered at the bench seat that was upholstered in gray with white stitching. At least the stitching on the driver's side was white. The stitching on the passenger side was pink—and damp. When they lifted up the floor mat on that side, they saw why. Blood had puddled on the steel floor.

Teri Depew had already admitted that *she* was the last person to see David Hargis. The detectives questioned her now. She initially told the same story Carole had—about the wild partyers she and David had met in Black Canyon. When they mentioned the blood they found in the truck, Teri shifted uneasily in her chair.

"I have no idea how it got there," she said.

During the questioning, Teri had volunteered that she was a lesbian and was disgusted when men made moves on her. Joe Cellucci was sympathetic. He commented that he would understand if she had been defending herself against David Hargis that night. "If he was drunk and made advances toward you, it would be understandable for you to fight back . . ."

Teri nodded, thinking hard.

"That would have been pretty upsetting for you, and you say you'd both had a lot of beer," Joe Cellucci pressed.

"That's what happened—" she said. Teri followed Cellucci's lead; it gave her a way to confess, and perhaps plead self-defense. The San Diego detective doubted that David Hargis would have been attracted to this masculine-appearing woman, but Cellucci listened with an expression on his face that *looked* as though he believed her.

Teri said that she and David had originally gone out

in the middle of the night to catch rattlers, but when they got to the wilderness area David suddenly became irrational and tried to rape her. "I panicked when he reached for me . . ."

Teri said she had fought him off and finally found something to hit him with.

"What was the weapon you used?" Cellucci asked.

"I don't know what the hell it was. There was this thing about twelve inches long."

"What was it? . . . What are we talking about—twelve inches?"

"Oh, I guess it was."

"Where did you find it"

"It was down on the rocks. I picked it up and started hitting him with it."

"How many times did you hit him?"

"I don't know."

"What happened after you hit him with it?"

"He yelled, 'Carole!' "

"Did he fall on the ground?"

"Yes."

"Then what did you do with him?"

"I picked him up and put him in the truck. I drove to the bridge and threw him over the bridge."

Teri admitted that she had tied David's hands to his belt loops. She said she took a roll of tape from her car and taped his head, so he wouldn't "bleed all over the place."

The detectives found it odd that Teri would have been so concerned about blood if she had killed David way out in the wilderness. And why had he called out "Carole!" who was allegedly in their house back in San Diego?

Teri was confabulating; she was telling part of the

ANN RULE

truth, but she had completely changed the location of the crime. They were already convinced that David Hargis had, indeed, died in his own bed on Laurel Street. They didn't know what part Carole Hargis had played in her husband's murder.

But they soon would. One of Teri Depew's friends visited her in jail and was outraged to learn that Teri was taking the fall all by herself. The woman walked to the sheriff's office and confronted Fred Balmer and Joe Cellucci. "Hey, you guys," she said. "You'd better take a look at *Mrs.* Hargis because she's not telling you the whole truth."

When her friend told Teri she was being a patsy, she began to talk to the detectives. The floodgates opened. She blamed Carole for having the idea in the first place. With the tape recorder turning, Teri regaled the amazed detectives with almost a dozen wild plots they had considered *together* to get rid of David, so Carole could collect $40,000 worth of insurance.

But when Carole Hargis was invited to sheriff's headquarters to give a statement to Balmer and Cellucci, she gave them a different version.

After listening to Teri's confession about all the murderous schemes they had tried, Carole burst into tears.

"I didn't do it," she sobbed, burying her face in her hands. "It was Teri's idea. She made me do it. I had to—or she would have killed my children!"

Carole insisted that she didn't even know Teri was planning to bash David's head in with the sash weight. She was horrified, she said, when she saw Teri emerge from the bedroom carrying the bloody sash weight and laughing. "She said, 'I just killed your goddam husband for you, you bitch.' "

Carole insisted she'd tried to call the police but that

she was too afraid of what Teri might do to her and her boys if she told the truth.

The crime lab specialists had turned up enough evidence in the Hargis house for three or four trials. There was a bloodstained nightie in the hamper, blood flecks on the ruffled bedroom curtains, and the mattress had been sprinkled with bleach to erase the blood there. They even found odd bleach marks on the cement *outside* the house. They determined the women had used toilet bowl cleaner to get David's blood out of the cement.

Two deputies searched the stretch of Highway 67 where Teri said she'd thrown the sash weight used to crush David's skull. *And they found it!* They waded through the thick weeds in the median and somehow spotted the weight. Criminalists found David Hargis's blood, hair follicles and tiny patches of his scalp still clinging to the weight.

Teri Depew went to trial first—in November 1977—in Superior Court Judge William T. Low's courtroom. She wore a leather jacket that hid her tattoos, but her hair was shorter than most men's. Her testimony matched the taped confession she had given to Joe Cellucci and Fred Balmer. In a low monotone, she confessed to killing David Hargis. "But if it hadn't been for Carole, I would never have touched the man. . . . I couldn't bring myself to hurt him. He looked so peaceful, lying there sleeping. I walked out of the bedroom and Carole said, 'It's got to be done tonight.' I took some pills and drank some beer to relax. I entered the room. I said, 'I'm sorry,' and, without realizing it, I hit him. I kept on hitting him."

Teri said David had called out for his wife after she left the bedroom. But Carole hadn't gone to him. "I rested my head on Carole's shoulder and I was crying,"

Teri testified. "But Carole said, 'Don't worry. Everything's going to work out okay.' I went back and hit him again. . . ."

Teri told the jury the terrible details of the "bloody mess" and of how awful the drive through the night to dispose of David's body had been. When Teri decided to plead guilty, Judge Low discharged the jury.

Low asked Teri if her words on the confession tape were true. "Is that how it happened?"

"Yes, it is," she said almost in a whisper. And then Teri Depew pleaded guilty to murder. She would go to prison, but she would not face the death penalty.

Carole Hargis went to trial in December 1977. Her makeup was perfect and her hair was soft and feminine. She wore a flower-patterned blouse and pastel slacks as she sat demurely next to her attorney.

Carole's defense was that Teri was a psychopathic liar and a lesbian who wanted her only for sex. "My client is innocent," her lawyer said. "She is innocent of this murder because Teri Depew controlled her mind."

Carole said she was afraid of Teri because of her sheer physical strength. Her attorney said that he had located a number of lesbians who were so afraid of Teri that they refused to testify in Carole's defense—for fear she would hurt them, even though she was in prison. But Carole had a kind heart. She felt sorry for Teri, he said, and had tried to befriend her.

"Teri came out of the bedroom, laughing," Carole said, tears in her voice, testifying about the immediate aftermath of her husband's murder. "I grabbed the telephone to call the police, I guess. I was dazed. . . . Teri waved that thing [the sash weight] at me to remind me that I had kids in the bedroom. I took it to mean my sons would be next if I called the police. I was scared."

Carole said she had cleaned the blood up "because I didn't know what I was doing."

Deputy District Attorney Lou Boyle didn't buy Carole's helpless act. He asked her why she didn't call the police after she knew Teri was in custody and no longer a threat to her. Carole answered that she was afraid they wouldn't believe her—she was still very frightened, not only of Teri but of the police, too.

"Why did Teri Depew attack your husband?" Boyle asked.

"I don't know why."

"Was sex the answer, perhaps?"

"I don't know. Teri just made the remark that she liked my body. It was just off and on, so I ignored it."

"You didn't encourage her?" Boyle asked skeptically.

"No."

In court, Carole was the epitome of a weak and fragile woman, frequently bursting into tears. But then Boyle introduced a fascinating tape into evidence. Carole had called the police on July 21, all right, and she had indeed sobbed as she reported her husband missing. But she hadn't realized that she was still being recorded while the 911 dispatcher kept her on hold. During those moments, Carole had a perfectly calm conversation with Teri. From the expression in her voice, she might have been ordering something from a department store or gossiping cheerfully over the back fence. At one point she said to Teri, "Where *are* those idiots? Are we still on hold?"

When the operator came back on the line, Carole started to sob again, sounding like an anxious wife.

"It's clear she's an actress," Boyle told the jury. "Sobs, then a normal conversation, then sobs again."

That tape fascinated the jurors, but not as much as a surprise witness the San Diego County prosecutor called. Carole had often hired a seventeen-year-old baby-sitter to stay with her boys. The girl said that she looked upon Carole Hargis as almost a mother, and it was apparent that she hated having to testify against her.

But testify she did. Teri and Carole were so accustomed to having the baby-sitter in the house that they had freely discussed their plans to kill David in front of her. "Carole said she could get a lot of money from David if he died," the girl testified in a tremulous voice. "She said she ought to put the spider in his bed and say the boys accidentally left the cover off the terrarium."

The girl had overheard the two women discuss a number of deadly plans that would rid them of Carole's husband so they could be rich.

On rebuttal, Carole Hargis told the jurors that her baby-sitter was an inveterate liar. "She lies all the time. . . . She was a habitual liar."

The jurors deliberated only a little over two hours, and they decided who the liar was. On December 19, 1977, Carole Hargis was convicted of murder in the first degree and sentenced to life in prison for the murder of her husband.

Because of The Slayer's Act, which prohibits convicted killers from benefiting financially as a result of their victim's death, she did not collect a penny on David's insurance policy.

In that same July of 1977 when David Hargis died, another restless wife was hatching a similar plan for instant wealth. Some 1,300 miles north of San Diego,

Sandra Treadway* was no longer happy with her marriage. Unlike Carole Hargis, however, she didn't have a willing girlfriend who was ready to help, and she didn't think she could physically pull off a murder by herself.

Sandra Treadway lived in Tacoma, Washington. She was forty-eight years old and still quite good-looking. When she did a good job with her makeup and put on heels and hose, she was often asked to dance at the local watering holes, where dim lights and a couple of martinis made her irresistible to the lonely men at the bar. Sandra longed for romance. She and fifty-two-year-old Burt Treadway had been married for many years, but for the last several it had been a marriage of convenience. Working together, they had amassed a considerable inventory of mortgage-insured real estate. Burt had taken out $150,000 in life insurance with a double-indemnity clause in case of his accidental or violent death. He named Sandra as the beneficiary of all the policies.

Burt and Sandra Treadway agreed that their marriage was more of a business arrangement than a love match. Some years earlier, they had chosen open marriage as a way to handle their boredom. Burt was allowed to see his women friends and Sandra could have her men friends, and they would share the community property. They had children—his, hers, theirs—and there seemed to be no reason to end their marriage.

It was probably inevitable that the arrangement wouldn't work forever. Burt Treadway found a woman with whom he wanted to share his life, and he asked Sandra for a divorce. Sandra wasn't particularly upset that Burt had fallen in love with another woman—but she was very upset that he wanted a divorce. If they split up legally, their assets would be divided and she would lose a great deal of money. She would no longer be Burt's beneficiary and they would have to sell their jointly owned property before it reached its peak value. She certainly didn't want to share her financial assets with some Jenny-come-lately who hadn't worked for any of it. Burt was about to ruin everything just because he'd fallen in love.

Sandra soon had a steady boyfriend herself, a man some years younger than she. She'd met him in a bar a few months earlier. As their relationship progressed into an affair, she confided to Sam Bettel* that she didn't love her husband. She really didn't even like him. In fact, she said, she would like to see him dead as soon as possible.

Sam was used to hearing women say that they didn't like their husbands; very few women who did like their husbands chose to pick up other men in bars. But none of them had ever told him that they wished their spouses dead.

"Why do you want him dead?" Sam asked, amazed.

"There's quite a bit of life insurance money at stake," Sandra said. "If he were dead, it would all come to me."

Sam assumed that Sandra had simply had one too many drinks. But once she brought the subject up, she wouldn't let it go. She asked him if he thought he could find someone who would kill Burt Treadway for her.

The conversation made Sam nervous, and he hoped he'd heard the last of it. When the bar closed at 2:00 A.M., they walked out into the soft June night. Who could think about murder on a night like this? he wondered. He managed to change the subject, and when he left Sandra, he was sure it had just been liquor talking.

But on July 3, Sandra spoke again about having her husband killed. "Have you found anyone to do it?" she demanded.

Sam shook his head. Fooling around with a man's

wife was one thing; finding somebody to kill him was a whole other story.

Sandra Treadway, however, was obviously obsessed with the idea. There was just too much property involved, not to mention all that insurance money. She pleaded, cajoled, and wheedled. She laid out arguments, which seemed to make sense. Sandra offered Sam a large share of one of the insurance policies if he would help her. She wanted to arrange a contract hit, something Sam knew nothing about. He realized that Sandra was really set on having her husband killed and that if he didn't help set it up, she would find someone who would. He didn't want to get involved in this at all, but he knew he wouldn't be able to live with himself if he allowed a man to be killed.

Sam talked it over with a policeman friend. "She's determined, and I don't know what the hell I should do," he said. "I went along with her for a while because I thought she was just fantasizing, that she wasn't really serious, but now I'm getting scared. If that man ends up dead and [the police] find out that she's been seeing me, I'm likely to be number one on the suspect list."

The officer advised Sam that he had good reason to be worried, and suggested he call the Pierce County Sheriff's Office.

It wasn't much of a moral struggle for Sam. He had long since lost interest in Sandra. On August 2 he called Detective Walt Stout at the sheriff's office and outlined Sandra Treadway's plans for her husband's death. "I don't want anything to do with it," Sam said, "but somebody's going to look at all that money she's offering and kill the guy."

Stout agreed that such a thing might happen, and he received a promise from Sam Bettel that he would co-

ANN RULE

operate with the sheriff's office in heading off a murder before it ever happened.

Walt Stout, whose job it was to catch murderers, would now play the undercover role of a hired killer. "The next time she brings up hiring a killer," he instructed Sam. "Tell her you think you may know of someone."

"No way. I don't know any contract men."

"Yes, you do," Stout corrected him. *"Me.* Not for real, but just to head the lady off before she actually finds someone to do it."

Sam Bettel left the sheriff's office a little relieved— but concerned now that he wouldn't be able to pull off the ruse. Sandra had an uncanny knack for reading people, and he was afraid she would see it in his face when he lied to her. But he was going to give it a try.

It was only a day or two before Sandra Treadway called him to ask if he'd found someone to kill her husband. This time, Sam said that he had located someone who might possibly do the job, but only if the price was right.

"Great!" she said. "I want to meet with him tonight."

Sam said he would try to arrange a meeting, but warned Sandra that it might take a few days. He hung up and called Walt Stout. Stout would be walking a narrow legal ledge. He could not suggest anything to Sandra because that would be construed as entrapment; he could only follow her lead in a death-plot conversation.

At 9:00 p.m. on August 5, Stout met Sam Bettel at his office and Sam phoned Sandra. "I've got him to agree to talk with you," Sam said. "I'm with him now."

"I want to meet him right away," Sandra said. "But it's got to be in the right place—I don't want to be seen talking to him in public."

"You say the place."

"Behind the Yorktown," she said, mentioning a restaurant they both knew well. "Out back in the parking lot. What's he look like?"

Sam's eyes raked over Walt Stout, as he tried to figure a way to describe him. "Oh, in his forties, six feet, 185 pounds, brown hair. Big old mustache. Tough-looking—you'd figure that." Stout grinned.

"Okay," she said. "I'll meet him behind the Yorktown, say, in fifteen minutes."

Walt Stout wore casual clothes and drove a five-year-old white Chevrolet convertible. He hoped devoutly that he didn't look like a cop as he followed Sam's car. He pulled into the parking lot behind the Yorktown Restaurant. A Ford station wagon was parked in a corner, away from the other patrons' cars.

Sam got out of his car and walked over to the station wagon. Stout could see a woman sitting behind the wheel and he saw her talking with Sam Bettel, but he couldn't hear what they were saying. At length, Sam raised his arm and pointed toward Stout's car. Then he walked toward the detective.

"She still wants to go through with it. She wants to talk to you. I told her your name was Doug."

The parking lights on the Ford wagon went off, and the woman known to Stout as Sandra Treadway slid out of the driver's seat and headed toward him. She had thick ash-blond hair, cut in layers and swept back from her face. She would have been pretty, except for the deep lines around her mouth and the hard look on her face. She peered into Stout's car, and then climbed in beside him.

"This is Doug," Sam said. "I'll let the two of you talk." Sam hurried to his car and drove away. He had done his part.

Sandra told "Doug" that they couldn't talk where they were because her husband and his lady friend often frequented the Yorktown. He suggested they drive a few blocks to a Safeway supermarket parking lot.

"I understand you have a job you want done," Stout began when they reached the Safeway lot. That was as much as he dared say.

But Sandra, who was no blabbermouth, cautiously answered, "Yes."

"Just what is this job?"

"I think you know."

"Your friend says you want someone taken care of."

"That's right."

"Well, what do you mean by 'taken care of'?" Stout pressed, pretending to be unaware of what she really wanted of him, although the phrase "taken care of" wasn't that difficult to decipher.

Exasperated, Sandra blurted, "I think you know perfectly well what I mean!"

"You mean you want someone killed?" Stout exhaled as if he was shocked at the thought, but she was nodding her head.

"Yes . . . my husband."

For almost an hour, Sandra talked to the man she believed to be a hired killer. She wanted him to know that she wasn't a jealous woman. She wasn't at all upset about the other woman in her husband's life. He could have all the women he wanted; she just didn't feel that a divorce would be financially feasible for her. "He's got a triple-indemnity insurance policy—if he dies accidentally, that is—and all the money goes to me, his legal wife."

Stout listened quietly, appearing to consider the job. He sighed and shook his head. "A job like that wouldn't come cheap—it's risky. That would cost you in the neighborhood of five thousand dollars."

Sandra didn't flinch.

"It would have to be twenty-five hundred up front," Stout said, explaining that no hired gun in his right mind would pop someone for nothing. What assurance would he have that she wouldn't run and spend her insurance payoff in some foreign country?

Sandra nodded.

"And it would have to be twenty-dollar bills."

From what she'd read in books and seen on television, this was the way it was done, and she nodded eagerly. After all, if her husband was killed, she would have the insurance, and two homes. She could easily afford the $5,000. It was a bargain. "But it will take me a week or so to get twenty-five hundred together," she explained, "and I don't know if I can get it all in twenties, but I'll try."

Now that she felt the financial terms were set, Sandra began to set her ground rules. As for the murder itself, she didn't want her husband killed in their home. "I have children at home," she said, "and Burt's hardly ever home alone. I wouldn't want them to see it."

She had a plan, however. Her mother had died recently and left Sandra and Burt a home in the Oakbrook section of Tacoma. The house was full of valuable antiques. It was a sitting duck for burglars, so the family made sure someone was there all the time. Sandra's daughter, Claudette, had lived there for a while but had recently moved out. To protect the antiques, Sandra and Burt had been taking turns sleeping there until they could find a trustworthy tenant.

"I'll see that it isn't rented again until Burt is killed," she promised Walt Stout. That would make it very convenient for Burt to be taken care of on one of the nights when he was sleeping at the Oakbrook house. "We can drive by there now," she said, "so you'll know where it is, and you can get familiar with the floor plan."

Walt Stout, who knew every inch of Pierce County by heart from his days on patrol, pretended to need Sandra's directions to find the Oakbrook neighborhood. It must have been Sandra's night to sleep there because the house was empty. She led him through the rooms that were indeed packed full of armoires, fragile-looking chairs, tables, paintings, china, and figurines. Stout wasn't an expert on antiques, but the stuff looked valuable. He wondered to himself if she was going to warn him not to accidentally put a bullet hole in any of these treasures when he shot Burt.

Even though Walt Stout had been in law enforcement for many years, it felt almost surreal for him to be in this house, which still had the sense of the old woman who had lived here and who had obviously cherished it. Listening to Sandra Treadway outline her plans, he found it hard to believe that she could be plotting her husband's violent death so casually and coldly.

There was no doubt in Stout's mind that Sandra Treadway intended to have her husband killed. She told him she would have the money by August 15, and they agreed to meet again at the Villa Bowl in the Villa Plaza. She promised to bring along a picture of Burt Treadway and detailed information about him so "Doug" could begin his plans to murder him.

Walt Stout breathed a sigh of relief. For the time being, at least, Burt Treadway was safe. Until the fifteenth, anyway. Sandra believed she had hired a real killer.

Their next meeting was set for 10:00 P.M. on the fifteenth. Early that evening, Stout met with Chief Criminal Deputy Henry Suprunowski, whom his men called Ski, and Detective Terry Murphy, at the Pierce County West Precinct. They would coordinate their movements so there would be three witnesses to Sandra Treadway's plan to kill her husband.

Stout would drive the Chevy convertible, the same car he'd used during his first meeting with Sandra. There was a relatively thin barrier between the trunk compartment and the backseat. Detective Terry Murphy would hide in the trunk where he would be able to hear every word of the conversation between Stout and Sandra Treadway.

Suprunowski would park a short distance away where he could observe the car. On Stout's signal—a light touch on his brake lights—Suprunowski would be alerted to the fact that the money for the hit had actually been exchanged, and Ski would then move in for the arrest.

At a quarter to ten, Stout and Murphy pulled up behind a hardware store near the Villa Bowl, and Murphy crawled into the car's trunk. Then Stout drove to the meeting place where Sandra Treadway would be waiting—if she hadn't changed her mind.

At 10:00 P.M. Sandra drove up in a Ford LTD and parked facing Stout's convertible, their front bumpers almost touching. Stout saw her set a thick envelope on the dashboard of the car. Then she picked it up and walked over to sit in the passenger seat of Stout's car.

"I didn't know whether you'd be here or not," she said.

"Well, you showed up," Stout replied. "That must mean you still want your husband killed."

"That's right," she said. "I have the money right here in my lap. It's all in twenties, but it might be one bill short. If it is, I'll make it up to you. You can count on it."

"Did you bring his picture and info about the places he hangs out?"

Sandra Treadway was canny. He could see that she was wary of leaving her fingerprints on something. She handed Stout a piece of paper and pen and told him that he could write down the information she dictated. "You ask what you want to know," she said. "I'll tell you and you can write it down." She dictated a description of Burt Treadway's car, gave Stout the license plate number, and told him about her husband's general physical appearance.

"I have decided I want it done on Wednesday night, the seventeenth," she said briskly. "I've got the schedule all figured out. If he dies on Wednesday, I'll have the memorial service here on Saturday and then ship his body back to Michigan for burial on Sunday." Sandra said she planned to fly to Michigan on Sunday morning and be gone for about a week. "I might have the other twenty-five hundred for you before I go . . . but I'll have it for sure by the time I get back."

She had thought about other locations, but now she was sure she wanted her mother's house in Oakbrook to be the scene of the killing. Wednesday was Burt's night to house-sit there, and he would be alone—he understood that Sandra didn't like him taking his girlfriend to her mother's house. "He probably won't get there until late, though, because he spends most evenings with his girlfriend," she added.

She cautioned Stout that there might be a few hitches in her plan, but she felt she had most of them covered. "There might be a little problem because my daughter wants to spend some time in that house earlier in the evening," Sandra explained. "But I'll be baby-sitting for her, and I'll just tell her she has to pick up her baby by ten P.M."

"Do you have a key to the house I could have?" Stout asked.

"Yes . . . I'll give you one."

"How about if I call you Wednesday evening at your house, just to check and see if your daughter's back home?"

"Sure," she agreed. "That would be better." Sandra handed Stout one of her cards, which read, "Sunrise Enterprises Firewood," and told him he could reach her any time at the phone number on the card. Then she gave him a picture of Burt.

"Will you count out the money for me?" Stout asked, but Sandra refused and told him to do it himself. He took the money, which was in an envelope inside another envelope. She had done everything possible to keep her prints off any of the paper. He counted the bills out loud, laying them on the seat of the car. There was only $2,480 there, and Sandra reached in her purse and gave him a single twenty to make it an even $2,500, as promised.

For the first time, Sandra questioned her own motivation and murmured, "I guess I'm not a very nice person for doing this?" And then she chuckled and commented, "But then, you're not any better for agreeing to it, are you?"

The deal was set, the money had changed hands, and Sandra Treadway was about to have the surprise of her life. Walt Stout lightly pressed the brake pedal of his car to signal Suprunowski.

Ski slowly pulled his car up beside Stout's, so close

that Sandra Treadway couldn't open her door wide enough to get out. She looked up, startled, and blurted, "What's this? What's going on?"

"I'm not really Doug," Stout said quietly. "I'm Walt." He identified himself as a sheriff's detective and showed her his credentials. "You're under arrest, Mrs. Treadway."

Suprunowski removed Sandra from the car and advised her of her rights, while Stout let Detective Murphy out of his cramped hiding place in the trunk. Sandra Treadway, red with indignation and shock, refused to say anything at all as she was driven to the West Precinct.

There the detectives counted the money again. There were 125 twenty-dollar bills, half-payment to end a man's life. Sandra Treadway was transported to the Pierce County jail. She was allowed to call her attorney and was then booked for criminal intent to commit murder in the first degree.

Burt Treadway was at the Oakbrook house when the phone rang. It was Sandra, calling to tell him that she was in jail for attempting to have someone killed.

The astonished man asked, "Who?"

"You."

When Walt Stout interviewed the bemused Burt Treadway later, he acknowledged that it was true that his marriage was one of convenience rather than devotion, and that he did have a great deal of life insurance with triple-indemnity clauses. Sandra also stood to inherit two homes with mortgage payoff clauses that would be covered by insurance in case of his death.

But Burt Treadway had had no idea that Sandra wanted him dead. He told Stout that she had tried to persuade him to put off their divorce, giving various excuses for the delay. He had put it down to sentiment on her part, wondering if she really loved him after all. "Now I think I'll file for divorce as soon as humanly possible," Treadway said. "Like yesterday."

Sandra Treadway was released on bail to await trial. On November 13, 1977, however, her own life almost ended in what some might call poetic justice. She had been spending the evening at home with her daughter, Claudette*—the same daughter that Sandra had wanted to be sure was not in the Oakbrook house back in August.

Claudette was separated from her husband, Benny Bowes,* and the rift was far from friendly. Benny Bowes was terribly jealous of Claudette and he hated her new boyfriend with a passion. They had all noticed Benny's car circling the house several times during the early evening. As Sandra sat eating her supper, Claudette ran to the window and cried, "He's here—he's coming up to the door!"

Claudette ran to throw her weight against the door and Sandra joined her, the two women desperately trying to keep Bowes from coming in. But he shattered the door with one kick and strode in through the splintered wood. He had a gun in his hand. Claudette and her new boyfriend ran for the back door, leaving Sandra to face Benny alone. She tried to get away, but Benny Bowes caught her and knocked her to the floor. Screaming epithets, Bowes fired directly at Sandra's chest, and she writhed on the floor bleeding, crying "Benny, you've shot me!"

The gunfire wasn't over. Now Bowes aimed at Claudette's new boyfriend, who stood in the kitchen, hurling bottles at the gunman. Then he ran into a rear bedroom and cowered there. Bowes kicked open the doors of all the bedrooms until he came to the locked room where his rival hid. He fired two shots through the door, and then walked in, shouting, "Take your glasses off, you bastard—I want to shoot you right between the eyes!"

The gun roared several times. The would-be home wrecker wasn't shot between the eyes, but he was shot almost every place else. As his latest victim lay bleeding, Bowes put the gun to his own temple—but he didn't shoot. Benny was still standing with the gun to his head when sheriff's deputies arrived. They were braced for a standoff, but Benny's suicidal gesture had been only that. The deputies quickly wrestled the gun away from him.

Sandra Treadway and the wounded man were rushed to the hospital, where her chest wound was found to be serious but not fatal. Claudette's new boyfriend was in critical condition, however.

Ironically, Sandra had wanted to kill her husband for money. Jealousy hadn't even entered into it. Her son-in-law, however, had attempted murder out of jealousy alone. They were rapidly becoming the poster family for the old joke: "The family that slays together stays together."

Sandra recovered in time to plead guilty to a reduced charge of solicitation to commit murder in the second degree and was sentenced to serve ten years in the women's prison at Purdy, Washington. Purdy is one of Washington's plusher prisons, but it is still a far cry from the life Sandra had planned for herself once she got her hands on $150,000 in insurance money.

Claudette's boyfriend almost died of his wounds, but he eventually recovered. Benny Bowes pleaded guilty in the shooting and went to prison.

*   *   *

The Gentler Sex

Not all females are as inept as Carole, Teri, and Sandra. An intelligent, determined female sociopath is as dangerous as any black widow spider. Women kill for different reasons than men, and they employ dissimilar methods. There are really only two reasons why the vast majority of women kill: for love—very broadly defined to include passion, revenge on a faithless lover, jealousy, or a desire to clear away obstacles to an affair—or for money. The promise of riches tends to bring out wickedness in some women. Whether it be for love or money, women plan murder with far more care than do men. They seem to be able to delay gratification longer than their male counterparts. One might say that, even in homicide, women enjoy more foreplay than men.

Perhaps all marital insurance policies should read, "And to my beloved wife, the proceeds of my life insurance . . . with the express exemption that this policy is null and void if she kills me."

The Conjugal Visit

The social science *of penology has come a long, long way since prisons were hellholes unfit for any living thing. No rational person today would wish that another human being should serve out a sentence with torturous punishment, in cells that are filthy and dark, and yet questions remain as to just how comfortable and civilized is too comfortable and civilized for those who deserve to be locked up. There are three main reasons to lock someone behind bars: (1) to punish him or her for a crime; (2) to protect society from the criminal; (3) to rehabilitate her or him. In our enlightened era, there are prisons where convicts enjoy a lifestyle some free men might envy. Prisons now have gyms and libraries. Cells have bars, but they also have television sets and radios, and prisoners may hang whatever posters and "art" they like on the walls. A number of penal institutions provide quarters—often mobile homes—where married and engaged prisoners may enjoy conjugal relations with their wives and lovers.*

Keeping a prisoner in touch with his family isn't necessarily bad, and it keeps a lot of paroled felons from returning to a life of crime when they are released. But there are cases where too much compassion for convicts ends in tragedy. A handsome prisoner named

*Carl Cletus Bowles played such a progressive system
as if it were a fine old fiddle and he a fresh bow. Bowles
serves as a sobering example of what can happen when
concern for a prisoner's sensitivities blinds authorities
to potential danger. This consummate con man hood-
winked some of the most experienced prison adminis-
trators in the country. A little luck, a disregarded
warning, and a beautiful woman willing to throw away
her life for him, and Bowles walked free of the bars
meant to hold him for life. In retrospect, anyone who
believed Bowles's promises needed a refresher course
in abnormal psychology.*

Carl Cletus Bowles was born in Amarillo, Texas, in 1941. He was a wild boy and teenager who always walked just at the edge of the law, sometimes slipping over it. He wasn't very tall, but he was handsome, with a full head of wavy blond hair and perfectly aligned features. Girls and women were always drawn to Carl, and he was a lusty young man. He began his serious criminal career at a young age. He was just past twenty when he served time in Colorado for larceny. Barely free from jail in Colorado, he was convicted for a larceny and breaking-and-entering rap in Oregon in the early 1960s. At the Oregon State Penitentiary, he formed an unlikely liaison with Norbert Tilford Waitts, a man six years his senior. Waitts was a native of Brunswick, Georgia, but his criminal activities had afforded him a tour of the inside of America's jails. He had done time in New York State and was sentenced to prison for assault with a deadly weapon during a robbery of a motel in Tigard, Oregon.

Neither Carl Cletus nor Norbert took well to the rehabilitation aspects of imprisonment; they merely bided their time until they could get out and make up for the lost years. Waitts got out first, on June 1, 1965. He waited impatiently for Bowles's release four weeks later. It was Monday night, July 5, and wisps of leftover smoke from Sunday's fireworks still floated in the air.

The woman working the desk at the same Tigard motel Norbert Waitts had robbed before—which had landed him in prison—was startled to see a customer walk in so late. She thought to herself that he was one of the homeliest men she had ever seen in her life—bald with a long, dour horse face. His arms were covered with garish tattoos. He didn't want a room, he explained, as he stuck a pistol in her face. She handed over the twenty-five dollars in the cash register, but that wasn't all he wanted. She looked desperately around for someone she could cry out to for help, but the parking lot was quiet and the people in the units that spread out from the office had long since gone to sleep. The man with the gun raped her, but he apologized, saying, "I'm sorry to force you to do this . . . but I haven't had a woman in two years."

When he left, she called the police. She was upset, but she gave a good description of her attacker and she remembered his explanation for raping her. Hearing that, they knew where to look; there is only one place, short of a desert island, where a man is forced to go two years without a woman, and that is prison. Detectives checked descriptions of recently released inmates at the Oregon State pen and came up with a balding, horse-faced man with tattoos on his arms: Norbert Tilford Waitts.

They didn't know where Waitts was, but they didn't have to wonder for long because he surfaced again at 1:40 P.M. the next day. Two men held up the 42nd Street Branch of the First National Bank in Portland. The man holding the shotgun was handsome, in a baby-faced way, and looked to be in his early twenties; the man who actually collected the stacks of money while he held a pistol was older and taller and far less attractive. He hadn't bothered to put a hat over his bald head or a mask over a face that was a study in misalignment. When he reached for the money, his shirtsleeves slid up and the tellers noted his tattoos. He picked up $15,514 in cash and beckoned to his partner to move out of the bank.

The two bank robbers slipped out into the street and disappeared into the crowds in downtown Portland before the first police arrived.

Waitts's description was becoming familiar, and it wasn't hard to find out whom he had buddied with in the penitentiary: Carl Cletus Bowles. They certainly made an unlikely pair, but prison officials said they had been good friends—who had, incidentally, been released within a month of each other.

The bank employees picked out Waitts and Bowles from the lay-downs—the glossy sheets that showed photographs of six other men mixed in with the true suspects. Witnesses were positive that this was the pair who had robbed the bank. Within hours, a two-state search was under way for Waitts and Bowles. Both were charged with bank robbery, and Waitts faced an additional charge of rape.

It was 11:15 that night in Springfield, Oregon, some 110 miles south of Portland, when Lane County Deputy Carlton E. Smith patrolled on his first night shift. He was in a one-man car, something departments try to avoid but are sometimes forced to resort to due to a shortage of manpower.

Smith was thirty-three years old. He had a wife, four children, and a stepchild to support, and he'd chosen police work because it gave him an income while he studied to become a teacher. He had served two years on the Eugene, Oregon, Police Department, and then had resigned to drive a dairy route because the money was better. But Smith couldn't get all the credits he needed to be accredited as a teacher in night school. He'd already taken a number of night courses in education at the University of Oregon, and now he needed to attend day classes in order to get his degree. So he'd gone back to police work, working 8:00 P.M. to 4:00 A.M. and attending classes during the day. Somehow he would find time to study.

The Lane County sheriff's dispatcher heard Smith's voice on the police radio: "This is fifteen at Goodpasture and the Delta Interchange. I have a 1959 Triumph, license 9F 6773. 2–10." It was a routine call. Something about the sports car had alerted Smith; maybe the driver was speeding or had a headlight out. The next communication would normally be his request for a wants-and-warrants check. Instead, Smith's voice said, "Fifteen to thirty-three. Can you come?" He was asking for backup.

Thirty-three was Watch Commander Sergeant Howard Kershner. Kershner was not alarmed when he heard the call. Smith sounded calm, and it was standard operating procedure to request a watch sergeant in certain situations. Only later would Kershner wonder if Smith had some inkling of the danger he was in and had really been calling for help. Before Kershner could respond to Smith, he heard the most dreaded words any policeman can hear "Oh, my God!" Smith cried. "I'm shot."

As Kershner sped to Smith's location, he held his mike in one hand, broadcasting the description of the Triumph, instructing all law agencies in the vicinity to set up roadblocks. If the shooter had slipped through the dragnet, he could be on the I-5 freeway, which was a straight shot south to the Mexican border, or a straight shot north to Canada.

Kershner was the first officer to get to Smith. A

passerby was already bent over the deputy, who lay sprawled on his back beside his patrol car. "I think he was alive when I drove up," the white-faced man said, "but I'm afraid he's dead now."

Two men from a nearby home said they heard shots and ran out to see the stopped patrol car and a red sports car racing away.

Carlton Smith hadn't had a chance. An autopsy revealed that he had taken the full blast of a shotgun at close range in his left side. Just to make sure he died, his killer had pumped seven bullets from a handgun into his body as he lay helpless.

There appeared to be no motive except pure evil, unless the gunman needed to make sure that he would never be identified. Whoever drove that red Triumph must have had more than a traffic stop on his mind.

Two Eugene police officers spotted the Triumph in south Eugene and gave chase, but they lost it. They later recalled that they had never wanted so badly to stop a car, and they'd felt searing frustration as they watched the powerful car pull away from them. But the investigators did have the Triumph's license number. Carlton Smith had given it to the sheriff's dispatcher when he radioed in. The Oregon Motor Vehicle Department in Salem, the state capital, always had someone on duty, and the night clerk checked the records and told the Eugene investigators that the car had recently been taken in on a trade by a car dealer in Salem.

The sleepy dealer answered his phone at 3:30 A.M. "Yes," he said groggily. "I know that car. In fact, I just sold it tonight—last night now, I guess. I was just getting ready to close at nine P.M. These two fellows walked in, looked the car over, and bought it for $895 in cash money. They gave me mostly twenty-dollar bills and this one guy said he'd been saving up his money to buy a good sports car."

The buyer's name? Norbert Waitts. The salesman identified mug shots of Waitts and Carl Cletus Bowles as the men who had bought the red Triumph. Buying the car was a clever move because if they were stopped, Waitts would have proper legal registration for the vehicle. But they were stopped, and something had gone terribly wrong.

What had made them shoot Carlton Smith? Had they simply panicked at the sight of a uniform? Or were they such confirmed cop-haters that their reflexes took over? No. It was most likely they knew they would be in trouble from the moment Smith picked up his radio to check on wants and warrants. If there was a "want" out on them for the bank robbery that afternoon, Waitts's name would have brought an immediate hit. Their names had not been broadcast on civilian radio stations yet, so they couldn't be sure that they were wanted—but they hadn't taken that chance.

Their new car was useless to them now. Waitts and Bowles realized that, and officers found it abandoned in a field adjoining a residential area only an hour after Deputy Smith died. That probably meant they were on foot. Police, sheriff's deputies, and FBI agents covered the area like an army of ants on a sand hill, and yet the two killers evaded them again. Searchers realized that they must have stolen a car or hidden in some house in the neighborhood next to the field.

Lane County Sheriff Harry Marlowe was of the opinion that the fugitives had somehow gotten ahold of a car. At eight the next morning, a young girl called the police to say that her mother and brother weren't in the house. Elizabeth Banfield and her twelve-year-old son had simply disappeared during the night, leaving four other children alone in the house. The Banfield home was only three blocks from the site of the abandoned Triumph.

The child who had alerted the police said her mother would not leave her children at home alone without at least telling them where she was going. The child had a vague memory of voices in the night, but she had rolled over and gone back to sleep, believing that she was only dreaming. "Then when I got up this morning," she said, "I found the lights on in the kitchen and my mother and brother were gone."

Her father, Larry Banfield, was working far away from home on a dam project in northeastern Oregon. When he was notified that his wife and son had disappeared, he was just as dumbfounded as the rest of the family. The Banfields' five-year-old Ford Thunderbird was also missing.

There was good reason to worry. Elizabeth Banfield was described to lawmen as an extremely attractive redhead. In light of the attack on the Tigard motel clerk and the vicious killing of Carlton Smith, there was no reason to think that she would be safe. Her twelve-year-old son's fate might be even bleaker. Once the youngster had been used to slide past roadblocks and was no longer of value to them, police feared that Bowles and Waitts would dump him.

Teletypes were sent to all eleven western states, and police up and down the West Coast were alerted to watch for the Banfields' T-Bird with Oregon plates. Radio and television news flashes warned people, "Do not attempt to stop this car. Ascertain the location of the vehicle and report it at once to your local police."

That Wednesday morning passed with agonizing

slowness, and then, at noon, the stolen car was found. It was located 125 miles northeast of Eugene, ditched in a remote logged-off area high in the Cascade Mountains along the Santiam Pass. The two loggers who spotted it approached it slowly. They had heard the news broadcasts and they half-expected to find the bodies of the missing woman and her son inside. But the car was empty.

The Oregon State Police expressed grave concern for the safety of the woman and boy when they saw the car; there was no longer any doubt that they had been taken as hostages by the ex-cons, but where were they now? The car had been driven to its resting spot along a rugged logging road. When the road came to a sudden end, the driver had obviously made an effort to turn it around but it had become hopelessly stuck in the soft sand; the tires had dug in so far that the back portion of the T-Bird's frame actually rested on the ground. "Whoever left it here had to walk out," one officer muttered. The unspoken question was whether the woman and boy had walked out, too. The area had been logged off, but acres and acres of waist-high brush had overgrown the fir stumps that dotted the area. Beyond that, the densest of forests soared skyward. If the hostages had been left here, they could easily die in the wilderness before being found. Worse, if they'd been gunned down like Deputy Smith, their bodies might never be found.

Scores of human and canine searchers scoured the wilderness along the Santiam Pass. The dogs didn't pick up a trail of any distance, and they kept circling back to their handler, M. D. Obenhaus. "There had to be another car here," he said. "I'm sure of it. Whoever left the T-Bird must have gotten into another vehicle.

They're gone—otherwise my dogs would have picked up their trail."

He didn't voice what they were all dreading. Most dogs will not home in on dead bodies; only specially trained necro-search dogs are adept at that. It was far easier to believe the hostages were still alive, even if they were being held captive in a car now miles away. But the question remained: how had the kidnappers found another car up here in the wilderness? They had to wonder if the fleeing killers had stopped a passing car and taken even more hostages.

Roadblocks were set up on all likely escape routes in Washington, Idaho, Montana, Utah, Colorado, Nevada, and California. Elizabeth Banfield and her son had been missing for more than twenty-four hours, and the fugitives could have crossed several state lines by now.

At one o'clock in the morning, two full days after the Banfields' disappearance, a deputy stationed in their home answered the phone and heard a tired woman say, "Are my children all right?" It was Elizabeth Banfield. She was alive and calling from Woodland, California. She told the deputy that both she and her son were safe in a motel there—along with other hostages. Yolo County authorities in Woodland, which is not far from Sacramento, were contacted and asked to take all the hostages from the motel and into protective custody. Elizabeth Banfield told the California deputies and FBI agents about her ordeal. Before she could stop him, her son had answered a knock at their kitchen door at about eleven-thirty on the night Deputy Smith was killed. Two men asked to use the phone to call for help because they had an emergency. Then they pushed their way into her home and held her and her son hostage at gunpoint. They told her they had just killed a police officer and had to get out of town in a hurry. "You'll drive us in your car," they ordered.

She protested that she had four children asleep in the house and couldn't leave. But the men insisted that she and her son leave with them. "One kid's enough," the tall, homely man said. "It will keep the cops from shooting at us if they should spot us. A flock of kids would be a mess."

When the men said they wanted to go to Idaho, Elizabeth Banfield directed them to take a route that ran past the dam where her husband was working. She held the faint hope that her husband might recognize the car and rescue her and her son. It was one chance in a million, and her heart sank when they passed close to the dam and she realized no one even saw their car.

Her kidnappers knew that the Banfields' car would soon be identified on both police and civilian radio broadcasts as a stolen vehicle, so they were anxious to dump it. Near Marion Forks, they came across a truck with an attached camper parked along the road. Inside, they found Mr. and Mrs. Rudolph Sternberg of Renton, Washington, their fourteen-year-old son, and his friend.

Sternberg, a civil engineer for the Boeing Airplane Company, was no stranger to conflict. He was a veteran of the Latvian Army, and he had lost an arm in World War II when the Germans pressed him into military service against the Russians. It took him only a moment to realize he dared not resist the armed men who commandeered his camper; he had his family to consider.

It was decided that Bowles would drive, with Sternberg sitting beside him. Waitts herded the five other hostages into the back of the camper and held a gun on them. Carl Bowles turned the camper south toward the California state line.

The hundreds of miles between Salem, Oregon, and the California line passed slowly. Bowles monitored the radio news intently and kept Waitts informed through an intercom system Sternberg had installed in the camper. They learned that Deputy Carlton Smith had died and that the police believed the two ex-cons had abducted the Banfields.

As they rolled up to the California state line, the hostages and their captors alike froze as a border inspector approached the truck. "You ready back there?" Bowles asked.

"Ready," Waitts muttered. "You keep the intercom on. I'll know what to do."

"Carrying any fruit or vegetables?" the inspector asked, his trained eye scanning the rig.

"No, sir," Bowles said, and Sternberg shook his head too.

"Any animals? Anyone in the back?"

"No. Just me and my buddy here," Bowles said, smiling.

"Have a good day," the border guard waved them on.

Luckily for both the border agent and the hostages inside, he didn't suspect that the camper held anything but a couple of fishing buddies.

The odyssey of fear continued for another eighteen hours. During the trip, Bowles and Waitts pulled into truck stops twice and bought hamburgers, coffee, and milk for the hostages, but there was never any possibility that the hostages could cry out for help. If they did, someone would be shot.

Late in the evening, Bowles announced that he had heard on the radio that the Banfields' Thunderbird had been discovered. It was time to get rid of the camper; authorities were now so close on their tail that it was only a matter of time before the camper would be marked as a hot car, too. They allowed their captives to leave the camper to relieve themselves in a field.

The hostages noted that their captors seemed disorganized; neither had slept since Monday night and it was now midnight on Thursday. The kidnappers couldn't really sleep with six captives to watch. The best they could do was take turns with catnaps. The Sternbergs' teenage son watched Bowles and Waitts as they tossed their two shotguns into a pond outside Marysville, California; the boy pretended to be looking up at a nearby hill, but he was actually memorizing everything he could about the area. He saw exactly where the guns splashed into the pond. If he survived this ordeal, he figured he could lead FBI agents right back to the spot.

This was one of the most demoralizing moments of the endless trip down the interstate freeway. The hostages wondered if they would be dumped next. If their captors no longer wanted to be linked to their shotguns, it wasn't likely they wanted to leave any witnesses. The hostages were afraid that their bodies were about to join the guns in the pond. Or maybe the kidnappers were going to stuff them all into the back of the camper, shoot them, and leave them there.

The backs of their necks prickling with apprehension, the Banfields and Sternbergs followed Waitts's directions and walked back toward the camper, waiting for the crack of a pistol. But the shorter man—the one who looked like actor Robert Conrad—ushered them all back into the camper and got behind the steering wheel and they took off again. Even in the middle of the night, it was beastly hot, more so because the camper wasn't big enough to hold six people.

At 8th Avenue and J Street in Sacramento, the

camper slowed to a stop. In the wee hours of Friday morning, the streets were virtually empty. The men they knew only as Carl and Norbert stepped out of the vehicle. And then, miraculously, Carl told Rudolph Sternberg: "Drive this camper away from here for the next two hours and don't call the cops."

Norbert Waitts added, "And don't make no mistake about it. We may be following you in another car. You goof it up and somebody will get hurt." Still unable to believe they were free, Sternberg peeled out. He drove the camper fourteen miles to Woodland. He kept watching the rearview mirror for headlights and saw none. Finally convinced they were truly free, he stopped at the motel where Elizabeth Banfield called home.

Bowles and Waitts knew they were high on the Wanted list of every cop in Oregon and California. They needed another car, but this time, even though they still had money, they didn't dare buy one. They trudged on foot for four miles, looking for a vehicle that would be easy to steal.

The ex-cons happened onto an unlikely—and unfortunate—target. Sacramento is the capital of California, and the men and women who run the state live there most of the time. Ted Wilson was the finance director for the state of California—the highest appointed office in the state. He and his wife, Joan, their ten-year-old son, and their nineteen-month-old baby girl lived in a very nice house. There was a brand-new Ford Galaxie parked in their driveway.

· Joan Wilson was scheduled to play golf the next morning with a good friend, the wife of the deputy director of motor vehicles in California. But Joan Wilson wasn't at home when her friend came to pick her up at

9:00 A.M., and her home was in a state of confusion. The Wilsons' ten-year-old son and a thirteen-year-old cousin had woken up to find no one else in the house. No one had gotten them up for school.

A baby-sitter who was supposed to care for the Wilsons' baby while Joan played golf arrived, but the baby wasn't there, nor were the Wilsons. Ted Wilson had already missed an important business conference and a long-distance call from a congressman. The phone kept ringing for him, but no one knew where he was. The boys said they had bunked out on a porch during the night and hadn't heard anything all night until they answered the phone when the congressman tried calling Wilson.

When the California State Patrol investigators learned that Carl Cletus Bowles and Norbert Waitts had dropped off their hostages only four miles from Ted Wilson's house, they had a pretty good idea what happened to the state official. They only hoped that the kidnappers didn't know they were holding a very important person.

A bulletin was issued to city, state, and federal agencies listing the Wilsons' green Ford Galaxie, LDG 311, as the latest getaway car. As soon as he heard the news, Governor Edmund "Jerry" Brown returned to Sacramento and took personal charge of the case. "I'm the baby's godfather," he told his troopers. "I don't want any harm to come to her or her father and mother."

Wherever they were, Carl Bowles and Norbert Waitts were getting themselves deeper and deeper into trouble. A federal grand jury in Portland was called into special session and returned an indictment charging both men with bank robbery and set bail at $150,000 each. In Lane County, Oregon, they were charged with the first-degree murder of Deputy Carlton Smith. Federal authorities were also preparing kidnapping charges against them. The only good thing any law enforcement official had to say about them was that they hadn't killed the Banfields and the Sternbergs. That gave them hope that the Wilsons might survive, too. In California, every state trooper, fish and game official, forestry officer, and even highway work crew member was sent out along back roads to look for the Wilsons' car. But the search was fruitless all that day and into the evening. By midnight on Friday, July 9, Bowles and Waitts had gone another twenty-four hours without sleep, and a crisis was brewing. They were headed toward the hamlet of Tonopah, Nevada, which is halfway between Reno and Las Vegas.

Deputy Thomas Wilmath spotted a green Ford stopped beside the road about four miles out of town. The plates were familiar; they'd been etched on every lawman's brain over the last twelve hours. But the Wilsons' car was empty. Wilmath figured that the occupants were out in the brush relieving themselves or that the kidnappers had ditched the car when they found a less recognizable vehicle.

Wilmath walked quietly over to the car and was bending over to look inside just as two men stepped out of the brush with drawn guns. "Don't try anything, cop," an icy cold voice said. "You'll get it, and so will the people with us."

The people with them were the Wilsons and their baby girl. Wilmath had no choice; if he resisted, the Wilsons might be killed. So instead of risking their lives, the deputy sheriff became the duo's tenth hostage. In a move that must have made sense to them at the time, the desperadoes crowded everyone into the police car. They used the squad car's police radio to contact the Nevada State Highway Patrol headquarters.

The man on duty was Dispatcher Dave Branovich. The sixteen-year patrol veteran swallowed his shock when he heard Waitts's voice on the police radio. He listened as Waitts told him they wouldn't kill the hostages if they got what they wanted. What they wanted first was relatively simple—or seemed so; they wanted food and ammunition. Their plan was for Deputy Wilmath to go into a club in Tonopah and get sandwiches while Bowles and Waitts waited outside with the hostages. There were seventy people in the nightclub when the deputy strolled in with elaborate casualness. He waited for the sandwiches, which were delayed because the kitchen was so busy, and he was prepared to leave without saying a word.

Every law agency within a hundred miles had been notified that two of the most-wanted criminals were now in a county squad car, along with a deputy, the finance director of the state of California, and his wife and baby. The roads surrounding Tonopah were beginning to bristle with patrol cars. The net was tightening. But the word was "Do nothing that might jeopardize the hostages."

Carl Bowles and Norbert Waitts were getting jumpy, and they didn't trust Deputy Wilmath. They grew restless waiting for him to come back with food. They stood in the doorway of the club for a while, with one eye on Wilmath and one on the hostages. Then, without warning, they began firing into the club at random. Patrons hit the floor and scrambled under tables when Carl and Norbert shouted that they were coming in for food and that nothing could stop them.

Predictably, those inside who were still standing raced for the exits in a panic. A card dealer pulled a revolver and started firing back. Wilmath yelled at him to hold his fire because there were hostages just outside in the car. But it was too late. Bowles and Waitt made a dash for the squad car, and three of the shots fired at them pierced the police car, one of them smashing the rear window as the car careened out of town.

"Come in . . . come in," Dispatcher Branovich pleaded over the radio. "Has anybody been hurt?"

Bowles answered, "This guy Wilson has been shot."

Although Branovich tried to cajole Bowles into taking Wilson to a hospital, the fugitive refused. "Don't tell me what to do," Bowles spat. "I'm telling you. We're a couple miles out of town. There's a service station on the left side and it's closed. We'll leave him there, and you can pick him up. He ain't bad hurt. We're taking the woman and the kid with us. If you try to stop us, you know what's going to happen to them."

Wilson begged to stay in the car with his family, but Bowles pushed the bleeding man out of the car at the gas station. Deputies who picked him up a few minutes later were relieved to see that his thigh wound wasn't as serious as it looked; he waved away medics and agreed only to minor first-aid treatment. He was taken to the Mineral County sheriff's headquarters to await news of his wife and baby.

The hostage situation was becoming more volatile with every passing minute. Half crazy with lack of sleep, the two gunmen had gotten spooked just because they had to wait for sandwiches. There was no telling what they might do as the pressure on them increased. The Wilsons' baby had to be screaming from hunger and exhaustion by now, and Joan Wilson was probably worried to death about her husband.

Dispatcher Branovich continued to urge the fugitives to release Mrs. Wilson and her baby. "You make the terms," he said convincingly. "We'll do it any way you say."

But Bowles and Waitts were having none of it. "I wouldn't trust a cop any further than the end of my gun," Waitts snarled at Branovich.

The stolen squad car had a conga line of police vehicles following it now, but no officer dared try to force it off the road or take a shot. For more than an hour, the strange procession rolled down the road. When they reached Coaldale, the army of officers trailing Carl Bowles watched incredulously as he parked and walked into a bar. They could have shot him easily enough, but they knew that Norbert Waitts was in the car holding a gun on Joan Wilson and her baby. If they brought Bowles down, they had no doubt that Waitts would shoot to kill.

The parade of official cars, their light bars flashing red, blue, and yellow, stopped and waited. Their frustrating convoy would one day be the inspiration for a critically acclaimed Goldie Hawn movie called *Sugarland Express*. But *this* real drama was terrifying, galling, and fraught with danger.

Finally, Bowles emerged from the bar, got back into the stolen squad car, and the procession of police vehicles continued down the road.

As they crept along Highway 6, perhaps fortified by alcohol from the bar, Carl Bowles came up with a deal: "We'll leave the woman and kid in the car if you'll give us a half hour on foot."

Dispatcher Branovich quickly agreed. If Bowles kept his promise, it would be the best possible scenario for getting the woman and baby to safety, but he wouldn't believe it until it happened.

Actually, the sleep-deprived killers had another

scheme in mind. They had spotted an empty pickup truck along the road and they planned to steal it. With a half-hour head start, they could slide into Vegas where they would be swallowed up by the crowds and bright lights. Odd that men without honor expected the police to honor them, to keep a promise to two ex-cons who had killed one of their brothers in cold blood.

Bowles and Waitt walked away from the squad car and headed back toward the pickup. They planned to hot-wire the truck, but Special Deputy Jerry Minor had a gun on them before they ever got the engine to turn over. They took off running through the brush on foot. Minutes later, California Highway Patrolmen Bill Rich and Howard Hoffman from Bishop, just across the state line, spotted the pair.

The outlaws surrendered meekly.

The officers on the scene approached the stolen police car, afraid of what they might find inside. As they drew closer, they heard a sound and saw someone sit up. Joan Wilson and her baby were alive.

Reunited with her worried husband, Joan Wilson told him that Carl Bowles had made a bizarre final gesture. "He tossed $900 in my lap when he left the car," she said. "And he told me, 'You don't need to tell your old man where you got the dough. I don't think I'm going to have a chance to spend it, so go out and have a ball on a spending spree.'"

Carl Cletus Bowles went to a federal prison first, serving nine years at the McNeill Island facility on Puget Sound. Surrounded by water as cold and rough as it is beautiful, the prison is an island unto itself both figuratively and literally. No one escapes from McNeill, although a few hapless convicts have tried. But the churning current pulled them under, trapping them in a watery prison forever.

Seven years later, when he was thirty-one years old, Bowles was transferred to the Oregon State Penitentiary in Salem to begin serving concurrent state and federal sentences. According to Judge Edwin Allen's sentencing warning, Bowles was never to be considered a candidate for parole. His file at McNeill Island showed he had received seven disciplinary transfers in seven years of incarceration before he came to the Oregon State pen. A parole coordinator had written: "Bowles is extremely dangerous. He has committed crimes of extreme violence on more than one occasion, culminating in the brutal slaying of a police officer."

But when he came to the state penitentiary in Salem, Carl Cletus Bowles seemed to have turned over a new leaf. Psychologists there noted that Bowles now said he felt his crimes, including the murder of Carlton Smith, had not been justified and that he felt remorse. However, the interviewer suspected Bowles was only trying to earn an early release by saying what he thought parole board members wanted to hear.

As the first year passed, however, Oregon prison officials were surprised to find that Bowles was handling imprisonment "exceptionally well." Like most sociopaths, he was an ideal prisoner, charming and apparently eager to get an education and change his behavior. He was a very handsome man, something that all too often blinds observers to what is really going on behind a wonderful facade and clear, friendly eyes. All of us tend, unconsciously perhaps, to view beautiful people as positive and good, and homely people as negative and suspicious. And because Bowles was small in stature, he seemed somehow less threatening than a six-footer would have.

Hoyt Cupp, the superintendent of the Oregon prison, took a personal interest in Carl Bowles and became a leading advocate for his rehabilitation. In Cupp's defense, this was in an era when inhumane prison conditions were being blasted by critics, and Cupp had done much to renovate the sections of the Oregon prison that were run-down and shut off from the light. Most states had outlawed the death penalty, and rehabilitation was the philosophy of the day. Cupp saw something in Carl Bowles that he thought merited an attempt to save him, and the warden believed the crimes of his wild youth didn't necessarily mark Bowles forever a criminal. No one knew for sure which of the two parolees had shot Deputy Carlton Smith, and all of the hostages they had taken as they sped toward California had been released unharmed. Ted Wilson was shot, yes, but his wound could have come from friendly fire when the police shot at the stolen police unit. Hoyt Cupp was certainly no novice when it came to dealing with prisoners. He had an unblemished three-decade record in prison administration. And on May 17, 1974, Cupp was in Arkansas presiding over the Western Wardens Association meeting. His innovative techniques and his concern for the rights of both victims and prisoners made him the natural choice to oversee the organization.

One new concept being implemented in the Oregon prison system was that of conjugal visits, the theory behind it being that if men were cut off from the women they loved for endless months and years, they would never be able to fit into their families or society again. Conjugal visits between prisoners and their wives had been tried first in a prison in Parchman, Mississippi, in the late sixties, and the results had been good. Half a dozen years later, a number of prisons were providing trailers and cabins on the penitentiary grounds where prisoners with good records could be alone with their spouses. The Oregon State Penitentiary did not yet have this kind of facility, so the prisoners who qualified for the program were allowed, in rare instances, to visit their loved ones at the women's homes, but always under the watchful surveillance of corrections or probation officers.

Carl Bowles didn't have a wife, but he did have a fiancée. Jill Fina* was in her early twenties, a slim woman with huge dark eyes and full lips. She had begun to write to Bowles, although no one knew for sure where she had heard of him; she would have been only thirteen or fourteen when he and Norbert Waitts made their marathon run through Oregon, California, and Nevada.

Nevertheless, Jill Fina visited Bowles at least a dozen times between August 1973, and May 17, 1974. At the prison, she was known as his fiancée. Superintendent Cupp and Ted Winters, the assistant ombudsman for the governor's office, visited with Jill several times and found her to be a "responsible, concerned type of individual," someone who would be a good influence on Bowles. And he certainly needed it. He wasn't in prison for life—not yet—and having someone like Jill to bond with might make all the difference in the world for him.

Jill Fina really was concerned about Bowles, and she had shown responsibility in her life, but she also had a wild side, and unbeknownst to Cupp and Winters, she was not who she said she was.

She was born Jill Onofrio in Lubbock, Texas, and had run away from home at thirteen. From that time on, she lived with foster parents in Oklahoma. Although she was alienated from her parents, Jill had an uncle who became a kind of hero to her, and she felt more related to him than she did to her immediate family.

Jill was smart. She graduated from high school in Felt, Oklahoma, in 1969, and for the next three years she worked as an accountant at banks in Oklahoma City. She married a man named Fina and they moved to Monrovia, California, where they bought a house. Her husband was a skilled carpet layer for a Los Angeles firm, and Jill worked as an assistant bookkeeper for an acoustics company in Pasadena. Her boss would remember her as a very good employee who was capable of doing the work of three people. "She was a little wild in her attitudes," her employer said, "but then, she was only twenty-three."

Somewhere along the line, Jill became estranged from her husband and began to focus all of her attention on Carl Bowles. Her letters and monthly visits seemed to give him new optimism, and the pair made plans for a future together when he was paroled. Bowles confided to Warden Cupp that he and Jill were engaged, and he put in a request for a conjugal visit.

There was a long wait, but eventually Carl and Jill were granted those visits. Jill's residence of record was a Motel 6, not a house in Salem, not even one in the section closest to the prison known as Felony Flats because so many parolees and prisoners' families lived there.

Bowles was given a "social pass"—the euphemism for a conjugal visit—on February 17, and he returned to the prison after several hours, right on time. On May 17 he asked for a thirty-six-hour pass, which was refused. He settled for another four-hour pass, which was granted.

At 8:15 on that Friday evening in May, Carl Bowles

left the prison in the company of a young corrections counselor, more of an escort than a guard. He wasn't in handcuffs or leg irons, and his escort wouldn't go into the motel and sit outside the door of Jill's room—he would wait in the parking lot to drive Carl back to prison shortly before midnight.

They drove to the sprawling pink-and-green Motel 6 on the outskirts of Salem. There, Bowles was taken to the room of his twenty-three-year-old fiancée to begin several hours of a social visit. The concept was kind of romantic when you thought about it, with roses and lilacs blooming all over Salem and a lonely prisoner united for only a few hours with his true love.

While Carl and Jill were inside her room making love, his counselor waited discreetly in the motel parking lot, but in a spot where he had a good view of the exit. At 11:00 P.M. he tapped quietly on the door of Jill's room. He waited. There was no answer. He tapped louder. Finally he got the motel manager to open the door with a passkey.

The room was deserted. The escort knew it even as he poked futilely in the closet and slid back the shower curtain. Both his prisoner and Bowles's fiancée were gone—and probably long gone, from the looks of the room. The bed had not been used, the soap in the bathroom was still wrapped, and the paper band across the toilet seat had never been broken. That meant that the pair had at least a three-hour head start. The prison escort told the manager he didn't understand how they had escaped without his seeing them; he'd been watching the exit constantly.

"That's the front way in," the man said. "You didn't know there was a back door?" The chagrined officer shook his head. "I knew, but I thought it had an alarm on it."

"Not until after midnight."

When the press got word that Carl Cletus Bowles—cop-killer, kidnapper, repeat felon—had been allowed a conjugal visit in the Motel 6 and had managed to easily dupe his guard and escape, there was hell to pay. Governor Tom McCall called Hoyt Cupp home from the wardens' conference and demanded an explanation. Cupp explained that he had indeed authorized short leaves for Bowles so that he might have some hope and some ties with the outside community. Cupp said he believed Bowles would not resume his criminal career when he was released.

McCall was a no-nonsense governor and a decisively fair man. He withheld judgment until an initial investigation was conducted. Then he docked Cupp's pay by $1,000, and gave him a fourteen-day suspension, saying he hoped he wouldn't have to give him more than this "mild" reprimand because of Cupp's long and distinguished career. But he hinted that Cupp's job could be in jeopardy if anyone was injured because of Bowles's escape.

The question arose immediately: Who was Jill Fina? A check into her background brought some startling news. Jill Fina, née Onofrio, had been only fourteen years old when Bowles and Waitts ripped a path through Oregon, California, and Nevada. But she remembered it well. She was not, it seemed, a stranger who had begun to write to Bowles, nor was she his fiancée. She was Carl Cletus Bowles's niece, the daughter of his sister! She was the wild little girl who saw her uncle as a hero.

Ironically, an urgent message had been teletyped to

authorities at the Oregon State Penitentiary in September of 1973 by Amarillo Detective Jimmy Stevens. It read: "Bowles and his girlfriend, Jill Onofrio, are planning to break him out in some way."

However, Warden Hoyt Cupp never saw that message, and it was never entered into Bowles's file. One explanation for this gross oversight was that, at the time of Stevens's warning, there was an uproar in the prison because one convict was holding another hostage with a knife at his throat and was demanding his own release.

Detective Stevens said that his source had reported that Jill was "scared to death of Bowles," but that made no sense. If she was frightened of him, why had she visited him so often? Why had she left her home, her husband, and a good job to journey a thousand miles once a month to visit him, to talk with his warden and his counselors, even to pretend so convincingly to be his fiancée? All they could deduce was that Bowles had some kind of Svengali-like influence over Jill or that there might be an incestuous relationship between the young woman and her uncle. Or perhaps they had both inherited the "danger gene"; like her uncle, Jill Onofrio Fina yearned for excitement and danger and a walk on the wild side. Now she had it. She was somewhere out there with an escaped felon.

In Eugene, the widow of Deputy Carlton Smith, now remarried to another officer in the Lane County sheriff's office, was shocked to hear that Bowles had been given a conjugal pass. "I never would have thought a pass would have been issued to someone of Carl Bowles's nature," she said. "It's especially difficult to explain to my four children, who range in age from nine to seventeen, how their father's killer managed to escape. It's pretty hard to explain what a conjugal pass means. If he had been issued a supervised pass to visit a sick mother or to go to a funeral, that wouldn't be so hard to take. But how do you tell a child that they gave him a pass to visit a girlfriend in a motel?"

Bowles's escape sat hard with other prison inmates, too. They worked hard to earn privileges, and the notoriety of this escape brought a clampdown on all prisoners, even those who really did want to go straight. In 1973 some 30,000 social leaves and work releases were granted, and only .023% of the prisoners failed to return on schedule. There were 24,941 passes for work release for one to twelve hours, 1,800 work-release passes for more than twelve hours, and 3,839 unescorted passes for social reasons—for visiting families or for job interviews.

But never before had a pass been issued to a man with a record like Bowles's. Governor McCall pleaded with Bowles to return for the sake of the warden who had trusted him. But wherever he was, Bowles didn't give a hoot about Warden Cupp.

Six days after the couple disappeared from the motel, Jill Fina's Thunderbird was found on the Reed College campus in Portland, 47 miles north of Salem. Three other vehicles had also been stolen in the immediate area, and their descriptions were put on Teletype wires as possible getaway cars for the fugitive duo.

No one knew where the couple had gone. They had not shown up in Texas to visit Carl Cletus's mother. They had seemingly gone to earth, just as a wily fox hides from mounted hunters. Investigators didn't know if they were still together, or if Jill was even still alive; she might merely have been an expedient way out for Bowles, an adoring niece who had now become expendable.

There probably had never been a manhunt in Oregon that was as important to the officers who now looked for Carl Cletus Bowles for the second time. None of them had forgotten the fallen deputy in Eugene. They knew that any cop who approached Bowles faced the same danger.

It was almost a month after Bowles's escape when he finally made headlines again. On Thursday, June 13, a pretty young woman entered a mom-and-pop grocery store in South Eugene and carried half a rack of beer to the checkout counter. She was asked for proof of age and presented a driver's license bearing the name Jill Fina—in Eugene, of all places, where the names of Carl Bowles and Jill Fina were familiar to almost every man on the street! The son of the store owner sold her the beer and then attempted to follow her when she left the store. When he lost sight of her, he ran back to call the police. They had been waiting for this call, and already had a contingency plan. Stealthily, a cordon of local officers and FBI agents positioned themselves around a fourteen-block area. The search moved into high gear when the sun rose the next morning. At 8:00 A.M., two federal agents in a stakeout car spotted a man who looked remarkably like Carl Bowles at the corner of South 34th and Willamette Street. They approached him to ask for his I.D.

He showed his identification all right; he waited until they were thirty feet away from him and then opened fire with a handgun. The agents returned fire as they ducked behind a parked car, but Bowles escaped by running between houses into a thickly wooded area. The Eugene-area task force was made up of seventy-five officers, including FBI agents, Springfield and Eugene city police, Oregon State Police, and Lane County deputies. They began a house-to-house search. When residents of the area tried to return to the streets where they lived, they were stopped and told to stay away; it wasn't safe to go home. Those who were at home were urged to keep their doors and windows locked and open them only to law enforcement officers with proper identification.

Shortly after the search began, Jill Fina was spotted in a guest house behind a residence in the neighborhood. She didn't resist arrest. She was subsequently charged with hindering prosecution. The woman who owned the guest house was not at home and had no idea that her cottage had been appropriated by the fugitives.

Jill, in custody after her abortive escape honeymoon, seemed to have tired of adventure and danger. She had huge dark circles beneath her eyes as she told the FBI that she and Bowles had been in the Eugene area for seventeen days. She named two men who had assisted them by driving them to a commune-type residence on May 28. There they were outfitted with camping equipment and driven to a rural area outside Eugene. They had stayed out in the woods until one of the men picked them up and drove them to the house where she was arrested.

Jill admitted that she had been in on Carl's escape from the beginning. Prior to the actual escape, she had coordinated the arrangements with the Eugene contacts. She either did not know or would not say where her uncle-companion was at the present moment.

The two men who allegedly helped the escapees were charged with willfully and knowingly harboring an escaped prisoner. The charges were soon dropped on one of the men, however.

Two days later and 500 miles away, Carl Bowles surfaced again. Somehow he had evaded the tight net that lawmen had dropped over Lane County and had headed east. Kootenai County, Idaho, Sheriff Thor Fladwed would eventually be able to reconstruct Bowles's zigzagging travels.

Sometime during the morning hours of Sunday, June 16, Carl Bowles commandeered a mobile home owned by an elderly couple in Kingston, Idaho, by threatening them with his gun. This location was about fifteen miles east of Coeur d'Alene, well into Idaho. For reasons known only to him, Bowles was heading west at that point, toward Washington State. The trio had driven along Interstate 90 to a spot west of Coeur d'Alene when the elderly man refused to go any farther. Bowles "slapped them around a bit," but left them alive when he fled.

A short time after that, he stopped an automobile driven by a resident of Post Falls, a hamlet of 3,000 just inside the Idaho state line. With an armed Bowles beside him, the driver drove only a few miles before he smashed into a utility pole. Either he was so frightened that he lost control of his car or he hit the pole deliberately. At any rate, Bowles took off on foot.

Next Carl Bowles wrestled a motorcycle away from a young man who came riding down the road. But the police were closing in. Bowles leaped off the motorcycle and headed for the Spokane River. Three Post Falls officers, led by Police Chief Del Larson, were right behind him. They didn't know who he was, beyond the fact that he had abducted at least four motorists at gunpoint. The fugitive jumped into the river, and when officers ordered him to halt he turned and raised his pistol.

It was one of those moments that seemed hours long. Post Falls Patrol Sergeant Jim Guy had the man in the river in his gunsight and ordered him to drop his weapon. But Bowles lifted it and aimed it at Guy. Guy pulled the trigger.

Carl Cletus Bowles—who until now had walked away from every encounter with the law without so much as a scratch—fell into the river. The water turned red from the severe wound in his abdomen.

Jim Guy had never shot a man before and wasn't happy about having done so now. The sensation of watching blood bubble from another man's belly sickened him. "The FBI told me I did everyone a big favor," he said later, "but that still doesn't make me feel any better."

It was ironic. Bowles, who had slipped through the fingers of some of the most skilled big-city officers in the West, had been shot by a small-town policeman. He was rushed to Kootenai Memorial Hospital where he underwent six hours of emergency surgery to repair extensive damage to his colon. Surgeons speculated that the tough little con would live, barring infection or hemorrhaging.

But the incredible saga wasn't over yet. The Teletype that went out to law enforcement agencies early on the morning of June 17 was phrased in the taut language of such communications, yet it was ominous indeed:

Wanted: Federal fugitive. Vehicle involved. Carl Cletus Bowles, fugitive. Currently hospitalized in Coeur D'Alene, Idaho, after being shot resisting arrest. Investigation at Eugene, Oregon, reveals Bowles at residence of E. C. Hunter and wife subsequent to Friday, 6/14 last. Mr. and Mrs. Hunter, ages sixty-two and sixty respectively, together with 1971 Chevrolet coupe, currently missing from residence. Whereabouts unknown. Bowles advised Hunters and car in Yakima, Washington. Car described as 1971 Chevrolet coupe, tan over beige, Oregon license JHS 772, VIN 16447LCL79284. All law enforcement agencies be alert for information re Hunters and vehicle.

And later in the day:

Urgent. Locate vehicle and missing persons. Possible homicide. Earl C. Hunter, 6'3", 235, black hair, wears glasses. Last seen wearing blue checked sport coat, blue slacks, white shirt, and tie. Wife "Vi" Hunter, 5'6", 150, brown, blue. This department has reason to believe this couple was abducted by Carl Bowles after exchanging gunfire with FBI agents in this city. Request all police agencies check the areas of their cities where vehicles have been stolen in an attempt to locate the above vehicle. It is urgent that if the vehicle is located, notify the Eugene Police Department immediately to process the vehicle. This request is urgent. Notify Lt. Lonnecker immediately or Sergeant Moreland, Eugene, Oregon. Lt. Lonnecker, E.P.D.

Back in Eugene, Earl Hunter had left work early at 3:30 in the afternoon on Friday, June 24, after telling fellow workers that his wife was upset by the news that an escaped killer was loose near their home. That was the last time he and Vi Hunter were seen. Police checked their empty home after neighbors became alarmed. They found that three of the four single beds in the house had been slept in, leading them to believe that Bowles might have held the Hunters captive overnight. There was also evidence that someone had shaved off a heavy beard in the bathroom sink. Vi Hunter's glasses were found on the floor of the garage and their car was gone.

Recovering in the Idaho hospital, Carl Bowles admitted that he had abducted the Hunters and used their car, but he insisted that he had let them go in Yakima, Washington. He said they had told him they had friends in Yakima, and would enjoy the trip. Their children, who lived in Seattle, told police that their parents had no friends or relatives near Yakima. They said that Bowles's explanation made no sense at all to them.

If the Hunters had been released unharmed, surely they would have contacted their worried relatives or the police. But their silence was ominous. Days passed, and despite massive searches neither the Hunters nor their car turned up in the Yakima area.

Hoyt Cupp flew to Bowles's bedside and talked to him for two and a half hours in an attempt to learn what had really happened to the Hunters. "I uncovered no significant facts," Cupp said wearily. "He still insists that he left the Hunters safe in Yakima, and that there was no bodily harm. He said he hitchhiked from Yakima to Coeur d'Alene. I do not feel he has been truthful."

The eastern half of Washington baked under temperatures in the mid-nineties as the fruitless search for the Hunters went on. The couple's son went to Carl Bowles's bedside and begged him to tell him where his parents were. But Bowles only said in a convincingly sincere voice that they were perfectly fine when he got out of their car in Yakima. Nothing could shake him from his story.

On Friday, June 21, the Hunters' Chevrolet was

found on a quiet residential street in Spokane, 250 miles east of Yakima. All that nearby homeowners knew was that the car had been there for about a week. No one had seen anyone get into or out of the car. FBI agents processed the vehicle and found a wallet and two pair of men's glasses in the trunk. "But there was no indication there had been any bodies in there."

Hope for the safe return of the Hunters faded rapidly. Investigators who had contacted the oil company the missing couple had patronized for years found that their credit card had been used at a Yakima self-service gas station on June 15, but station attendants could not remember who purchased the fuel.

Lane County detectives proceeded with their investigation as if it were a double homicide. Only the missing couple's son held out hope. "It's my objective opinion," he said, "that he did not shoot them. I think he left them somewhere, probably where they can't escape." There were lots of spots in the broad plains, dry deserts, and sweeping hills between Yakima and Spokane where the missing couple could have been left. They might have been locked in some deserted barn or stranded on some rattlesnake-infested wasteland miles from help.

Finally the bodies of a very tall man and a woman were found in a densely wooded area on farmland about 20 miles south of Spokane. Dr. Lois Shanks, the Spokane County Coroner, said that postmortem exams showed that Earl Hunter had been shot in the chest and head, but there was no definitive cause of death for Vi Hunter.

Earl Hunter had been almost a foot taller than the tiny escapee and outweighed him by close to a hundred pounds. But Carl Bowles had a gun. Why he chose to shoot the Hunters after driving them hundreds of miles from their home would forever remain a mystery. He had let everyone else he'd ever captured go free. Perhaps Earl Hunter rushed him for the gun and he panicked. No one will ever know.

Federal charges were filed against Bowles for kidnapping and murder. It became obvious that he had never been rehabilitated, for all the kindness shown to him. He was as dangerous as a lion in the streets. Indeed, when Judge Edwin E. Allen had sentenced Bowles to life back in 1965, he meant life. "The defendant in this case should at no time be considered for parole, work release . . . or any type of program thought up in the future. For the protection of society, he must be imprisoned for the rest of his natural life."

Carl Bowles was only twenty-four years old, a handsome, almost baby-faced young man, when he heard this sentence pronounced. His name has faded from the headlines, but the ten people Bowles took as hostages will never forget him nor will the wife and four children of the lawman he killed or the descendants of the Hunters.

Bowles is now fifty-eight years old. After pleading guilty to three counts of second-degree murder on June 27, 1974, at a special court session held in a conference room at the Kootenai Memorial Hospital in Coeur d' Alene where he was recovering from his wounds, he was transferred to the Idaho State Penitentiary to begin serving a seventy-five-year sentence.

When federal charges were added to his long list of felonies, Carl Cletus Bowles was moved to a federal prison. He lives there today, in one of the most escape-proof prisons known to mankind. Bowles, who was given extraordinary consideration and who laughed in the face of prison officials, spends his days and nights in a federal prison that is built seven floors beneath the earth. It is doubtful that he will ever see the light of day again.

Norbert Waitts, meanwhile, was found guilty and sentenced to life in prison for the Wilson kidnappings and the murder of Deputy Carlton Smith. He ended up in federal prison in Leavenworth, Kansas, where he is still serving his term. Waitts's first possible date of release will be November 14, 2040. If he is still alive then, he will be ninety-nine years old.

Jill Fina went to jail for a relatively short time on charges of harboring and concealing an escaped prisoner. She is almost fifty now, and does not find danger nearly as titillating as she once did.

Killers on the Road

In American *criminal folklore, there have always been roving killers who travel the freeways and back roads. Jim Morrison wrote a hit song about them: "There's a killer on the road." The Woody Harrelson movie* Natural Born Killers *explored the same concept. I don't know why the mindless sacrifice of perfect strangers should fascinate us so much. Maybe it's because we all harbor a certain nagging fear that we may meet one of these traveling maniacs one day. They don't fit the profile of serial killers, who always look for a specific victim type. The roving killers have no patterns at all, beyond the fact that they kill unpredictably. Maybe little seeds of violence lie dormant in their brains, only to blossom suddenly, bringing with them the coldest manner of murder.*

Why? I don't know why. . . .

This was the first trial in my career as a fact-detective writer, but it wasn't just that milepost that stamped it in my memory. In the years since, I've attended over a hundred trials but this one keeps coming back to me. The judge, the jury, and everyone in the gallery of the Snohomish County courtroom actually slipped for a time into the consciousness of a murder victim. We all saw what she saw and heard; we all went with her to the place where she would die. There was no way, of course, that we could actually feel her terror and despair, but this was as close as I ever came to gazing through the eyes of a murder victim. To say this was disturbing and unsettling doesn't even begin to describe what everyone in that courtroom felt.

The first-degree murder trial of Thomas Eugene Braun and Leonard Eugene Maine in Superior Court Judge Thomas G. McCrea's courtroom had been a long time coming. More than three years had passed since the brutal crime they were accused of had occurred. Now, finally, these two young men, their skin faded to a greenish-white jail pallor, were charged with four felonies: first-degree murder, first-degree kidnapping, grand larceny by possession, and robbery. The jury would not know that they were also accused of other crimes in other jurisdictions. What they would learn, however, was chilling enough.

Deanna Buse was born toward the end of World War II and turned twenty-two on August 19, 1967. Had she not met up with two strangers on that summer day so long ago, she would now be almost fifty-five and probably a grandmother. She was a very pretty young woman with delicate features and a halo of soft brown hair. She was a newlywed, married to Denton Buse, a longshoreman, for less than a year.

Deanna worked for the United Control Company at their Redmond, Washington, location. In the late sixties, Redmond was still a sleepy rural town northeast of Seattle where the residents knew one another and where there were far more pastures for horses than office buildings. No one in Redmond had ever heard of computers or software. The concept that would make Microsoft revolutionize communication had not yet bloomed in the brain of Bill Gates, who was still in grade school. There were no condominiums or shopping malls or fast-food restaurants in Redmond. It was a different world then, a safe place to live and work. So were most of the other little towns in the area—Issaquah, North Bend, Monroe, Snohomish.

Deanna and Denny lived in Monroe, and they both worked hard so that they could one day have the house and family they wanted. During the week, Deanna worked from eight until five, and on Saturdays she went in for an early morning shift. She usually left home at 4:00 A.M. and was through by 2:30 P.M. She always went to her mother's home after work on Saturdays to do her laundry, and she always arrived by 4:00 P.M.

But on August 19, she never made it to her mother's house. This was totally unlike her, and her mother began to worry before five. She knew Denny was working, so Deanna couldn't be with him.

Deanna had gone to work that day, and her coworkers remembered walking with her to her car in the company lot a little after 2:30 P.M. Deanna drove a dark maroon two-year-old Buick Skylark, which she kept immaculate. As far as any of her co-workers recalled, Deanna was happy that day. If she had been worried about anything, she didn't let it show. She was smiling at them as she drove away shortly before 3:00 P.M.

Denton Buse was a handsome, muscular twenty-six-year-old. He was very concerned when he learned

Deanna had not arrived at her mother's house. When he got home from his job at 9:00 P.M. that Saturday, everything was as they'd left it. Nervously, he waited there for Deanna to come home. She had to be visiting friends or relatives. He tried to tell himself that she must have mentioned it to him and he'd forgotten, but he couldn't remember that she'd had any plans. Denny Buse called every acquaintance and all of her family but no one had seen or heard from Deanna after she left work.

Surely, if she had been in an accident, someone would have been notified. There were some lonely, heavily wooded spots on the road between Redmond and Bellevue as it meandered along Lake Sammamish, but the road between Redmond and Monroe was well traveled. It seemed impossible that an accident would have gone unnoticed.

"We grew more and more worried," Denny Buse would recall, "and finally, at 12:15 A.M., after calling all the hospitals and the state patrol and not finding out anything about an accident, we called the sheriff's office and reported Deanna missing."

At the first light of day, Buse and his father-in-law drove back and forth over Deanna's usual route from their home two miles north of Monroe to the United Control plant. They scoured the areas on either side of the road fearing that they might spot the Buick Skylark crashed there. They searched for several hours—and found nothing.

Snohomish County officers, led by Chief Criminal Deputy Russ Jubie, scoured the county for some trace of Deanna Buse. Four days after she had vanished, their hopes for her safety faded. Either Deanna Buse had reasons of her own to disappear—which her family said was impossible—or she was being held captive. Or worse, she was dead.

Susan Bartolomei and Deanna Buse never met; in fact they lived almost a thousand miles apart. Only a terrible kind of synchronicity placed both of them in the path of two strangers within a short time frame.

Were it not for the unbelievable courage of seventeen-year-old Susan Bartolomei, there might never have been an answer to what happened to Deanna Buse.

Susan was supposed to disappear, too, on the Monday night following Saturday, August 19—the day Deanna vanished.

Howardine Mease and her family were driving along Route 120 in the evening of August 21. They had visited their daughter in Clear Lake, California, and then headed south on a meandering vacation path back to their home north of Santa Barbara. They had planned to drive straight through the night, but as the hours wore on, their brakes overheated from the strain of too many hills along the road. Rather than risk a runaway wreck, the Meases pulled over to a wide spot in the road where they spent an uncomfortable—but safe— night, bundled up in sleeping bags on folding lawn chairs. "We woke up about ten minutes to six," Mrs. Mease recalled. "We packed up our sleeping bags and chairs and drove off. We hadn't gone more than a mile when we saw a person lying in the road that bisected 120. We stopped, and my husband reached the person and called to me to bring a mat right away. I ran back with the mat and saw that the person was a young girl."

They thought at first she must have been hit by a car, and she seemed to be dead. "She was lying facedown on the road. She was motionless, but when I held her wrist, I found she had a faint pulse. My husband stood by the road to flag down a car to go for help. Two pickup trucks came by and they both said they'd call the authorities."

Helpless to do much, Howardine Mease knelt beside the young woman, and talked to her, assuring her that help was coming. "I asked her her name," she said, "and she said it was Susan Bartolomei and that she was from Ukiah. She gave me her parents' phone number. She told me that she and her boyfriend had been hitch-hiking because of car trouble." Ukiah, the injured girl's hometown, was more than 200 miles from this isolated spot. Mrs. Mease wondered if the girl was delirious.

The girl, Susan, gasped that "they" had killed her boyfriend and shot her, but she said she didn't know the shooters. "I asked her who they were, and she said they were two teenage youths, about eighteen, named Mike and John and they were driving a '67 green Mercury with Oregon plates. I asked if they were from Oregon and she said no, they were from Oklahoma. No town. [She just said] 'all over Oklahoma.' "

California Highway patrolman Lloyd Berry got the first call for help at the Moccasin Cut-Off and Highway 120. It came over his radio as an accident call first and was designated "high speed." Halfway to the site, the radio operator informed him that the "accident" was actually a shooting but that he should proceed as fast as he could because no sheriff's car from Tuolumne County was available to respond.

Berry got to the lonely spot in the foothills of the Sierra Nevada just before an ambulance arrived. The dark-haired girl had lapsed into unconsciousness; it seemed to have taken the last of her strength to tell Mrs.

Mease about the two men who had shot her. She was rushed to Sonora Community Hospital.

Howardine Mease gave Trooper Berry the scant information she had gleaned from the victim about her assailants. Evidently a teenage boy had been shot too, and the girl said he had been killed. Berry picked up his radio microphone and relayed the message to the dispatcher that two white males driving a 1967 green Mercury were wanted as suspects in the shooting of a girl.

For the next two hours, the sketchy description of the assailants was broadcast repeatedly over all California law enforcement channels, alerting officers on both outgoing and incoming shifts. They didn't know where the victim had encountered the gunmen, or where her boyfriend might be. There were so many roads between Ukiah and Tuolumne County. It seemed an impossible task.

Someone in the Mease family had spotted some shell casings glinting in the early morning sun on top of a steep embankment next to the road. Police investigators recognized them as jackets from .22 caliber bullets. They could have fallen from the injured girl's clothing, or might have landed there when they were ejected from a gun.

Susan Bartolomei might have been shot on the road and then thrown over the embankment by her attackers. They probably believed she was either dead or so near death that she couldn't identify them—if indeed she knew who they were. As he looked over the bank, Berry could see the impossible route the grievously injured girl had to take to reach the road and any chance of help. The vegetation was crushed 75 to 100 feet down the incline. Green leaves and wildflowers were stained scarlet along the path where the slender girl had crawled. In this desolate section of the motherlode country, there were no houses. No one would have heard the wounded girl's faint cries for help. Her only hope had been to pull herself up the steep slope to the road—and she had done just that.

Doctors at Sonora Community Hospital found it hard to believe that Susan Bartolomei had made that climb. She had four bullets in her brain and one in her chest, and her condition was very critical. She was unconscious and unresponsive to treatment and her vital signs were deteriorating.

Susan's family rushed to her side. They knew who her missing companion was. He was Tim Luce, the son of the district attorney of Lake County, California. The young couple had left Ukiah the previous afternoon, August 21. Tim, age seventeen, had planned to drive to nearby Hopland to purchase parts for an old pickup truck he was rebuilding. Hopland was barely ten miles south of Ukiah on Highway 101. He and Susan should have been home for supper, and when they still weren't home by dusk, their frantic parents had called the police. Their concern grew as a whole night passed with no word from them.

Where was Tim? The rescuers who had clambered down the bank to where Susan was found didn't find any sign of him. It was likely he had been pushed out of the abductors' car or that he was still with them. Susan had been nearly unconscious when she said he had been shot, too. Maybe she was hallucinating. He was a young, strong male. If he had been shot, they hoped against hope that he, too, had survived. If they pass through soft tissue, .22 caliber bullets don't necessarily do fatal damage; the danger occurs when they strike a bone. Then the small slugs tend to tumble and do terrible damage. Tim could still be alive but injured and trapped somewhere in the more than 200 miles between Hopland and Chinese Camp.

All hope for Tim's safe return vanished when the investigators learned that an amateur archaeologist searching for arrowheads near Hopland had wandered into a vineyard adjacent to Highway 101. His eyes sweeping the ground, he had spotted a patch of color that stood out against the green of the grapevines. Moving closer, he saw it was the clothing of a young man who lay sprawled face up on the ground. A halo of blood surrounded his head, and there were dark stains on his shirt. Like a cruel afterthought of his killers, the imprint of automobile tires crisscrossed the boy's chest.

Tim Luce had obviously been killed shortly after he and Susan accepted a ride from someone, but Susan was held captive as the vehicle in which she rode headed south and then east.

Mendocino County sheriff's officers who worked the scene could see that someone had methodically fired small-caliber bullets at close range into Tim Luce's skull and then run over him, probably several times, in a heavy vehicle.

It seemed to be a singular incident, unconnected with other homicides in California. Tim Luce's body was discovered just after sunrise in the early morning of August 22, long before word of Susan Bartolomei's plight reached the Mendocino authorities.

They soon made the tragic connection, however. Patrol officers in Mendocino County came across an old car abandoned about five miles from the vineyard where the young male victim was found. Checking the plates, they learned the car was registered to Timothy Luce. The car, like so many owned by teenagers, was held together by spit, bailing wire, and luck, and something had cracked or blown or boiled over. The car wasn't drivable when officers found it. The question that kept playing over in the investigators' minds now was "Why?" Susan had told Howardine Mease that she and Tim Luce were hitchhiking because of car trouble. Anyone bent on robbery could have done a lot better than two teenagers. His parents were sure Tim only carried enough money to buy some used auto parts from a junkyard.

It wasn't long before investigators found the motive, though. Acid phosphatase tests indicated the presence of semen during Susan's vaginal examination. She had been raped, probably several times. Two predators had given the young hitchhikers a lift. Tim would have recognized the danger they were in early on, and he probably fought to protect Susan from the men who called themselves Mike and John. Tim had become an impediment to their plans. How sad that while his father successfully prosecuted killers, Tim had become a victim of murder.

California officers wanted to find Mike and John. Anyone who would kill so ruthlessly could be expected to do so again. State Highway Patrol Lieutenant William Endicott and Tuolumne County Sheriff's Lieutenant Robert Andre headed the search team. They had one thing in their favor; the killers probably assumed that both Tim Luce and Susan Bartolomei were dead. And if they believed their victims were both dead, there was no reason for the killers to leave the Sonora area. The information that Susan was still alive was deliberately withheld from the media.

Jamestown, known locally as Jimtown, was a picturesque one-block hamlet three miles from Sonora. It was a railroad town back in 1897. It was eleven o'clock in the morning when Constable Ed Chafin arrived in town, after making his customary early morning rounds. He had heard the police radio call regarding two fugitives and had checked passing cars that morning with a little more care than usual. Chafin knew which cars belonged to locals and which belonged to tourists; there weren't that many of the latter lately.

He spotted a green 1967 Buick parked on Jamestown's main street in front of the hotel. It was unoccupied, and it bore Oregon plates. There was a car parked in front of it, and Chafin pulled in behind it, deliberately nudging its bumper so the Buick could not be driven away. He got out and walked around the car, studying it. Something wasn't right. The girl who had been shot had gasped that her attackers had driven a Mercury.

And yet . . .

He had a feeling. "Sometimes when you've been in law enforcement long enough, that happens," he recalled. "I knew in my gut that I was looking at the getaway car. It was dirty and dusty, but on the trunk I saw two perfect handprints in the dust—from small hands—as if maybe the girl had been forced to lean against the car."

The car sure looked road-worn and the interior was cluttered. There were broken crackers, crumpled cigarette packs, an old blanket, and a small man's jacket on one seat. Chafin radioed Bob Andre and Bill Endicott to tell them about the car. The color and the plates were right; it was close enough to take a second look.

The highway patrol officers called for backup to meet them in Jamestown. Trooper Lloyd Berry, who had just delivered emergency blood to the Sonora hospital for Susan Bartolomei, headed for the scene.

When the lawmen checked the guest register in the local hotel, they realized they weren't looking for criminal masterminds. The names Mike Ford and John Ford were scrawled on the page. They hadn't even bothered to change the names they had used with their victims.

"You know them?" Chafin asked the clerk.

"Nope. They're strangers."

"What do they look like?"

He shrugged his shoulders. "Young, messy, wild hippie hair. Both of 'em could do with a shave and a change of clothes—and a night's sleep."

"Are they upstairs now?"

"I think so. In rooms 19 and 26."

Within a matter of minutes, Andre and Endicott had cleared the lobby and the area surrounding the hotel. They were given a master key and they headed up the staircase to the second floor. Trooper Berry, armed with a shotgun, waited at the rear exit of the hotel while other deputies and highway patrolmen, who had sped to Jimtown, surrounded the building. Room 26 was at the top of the stairs while number 19 was near the end of the hall. The lieutenants bypassed number 26 and walked quietly to the more distant room. Endicott carried a shotgun while Andre held a handgun. Andre slipped the key into the lock of room 19, and the door swung open, but only a few inches; it was secured by a chain. Through the crack in the door, they could see a figure sleeping on the bed. Andre pushed his gun through the opening and said, "Put your hands up—come over here and unlock this chain." The man on the bed hardly seemed dangerous. He followed Andre's orders meekly, sliding the chain along its slot and letting it hang free. He was a small man, and young—probably a teenager. He wore only sagging undershorts and he seemed bewildered. He put up no resistance as they instructed him to lie down on the hall floor while they handcuffed him.

The next stop was room 26. Again the chain lock held. "Kick it open," Endicott ordered urgently. He could see the second suspect lying facedown on the bed, but his hands were hidden under the pillow. If he was only feigning sleep, he would have the opportunity for a clear shot at the officers through the door opening. As the chain snapped, Endicott shouted, "His hands— watch his hands!"

Andre was beside the bed in an instant, grabbing the man's hands before he had a chance to go for a gun. The second suspect was taller and more muscular than his partner but they hadn't given him a chance to fight back.

The two had been sleeping soundly. They must have believed that Susan Bartolomei was either dead or so near death that she would never identify them. They were caught only twenty miles from the spot where she was found.

Lieutenant Andre entered room 19 and emerged with a brown plaid plastic bag—the type used to carry car blankets. He'd found it very heavy when he lifted it and he checked its contents. In the bottom lay two hand weapons; a fully-loaded automatic .22 caliber Ruger, and a Frontier Colt single action .22 caliber pistol, also fully loaded. The drawers in the nightstands in both sus- pects' rooms had .22 caliber hollow-point bullets rat- tling around in them. Constable Chafin and Lieutenants Andre and Endicott led the surprised suspects from the hotel to waiting patrol cars. They were transported to the Tuolumne County sheriff's headquarters in Sonora. They didn't look like desperadoes, but they did look nervous as they underwent intensive questioning.

They finally admitted that they were not Mike and John Ford. Nor were they from Oklahoma as they had told Susan Bartolomei. They were from Ritzville,

Washington, a little town of 1,500 residents that sat on a lonely stretch of I-90 west of Spokane. The taller, rather-studious-looking member of the duo gave his name as Thomas Braun. He wore thick, dark-rimmed classes. His slight, wispy-mustached partner said he was Leonard Maine.

The California authorities checked with the sheriff of Adams County, Washington. Surprisingly, neither suspect had a criminal record. Braun had been employed at a service station in Ritzville while Maine, married and the father of a three-month-old baby, worked in a local cement-mixing plant. The two had left Ritzville on August 17 in Braun's recently purchased Borgward sedan. They were both eighteen years old.

If they were guilty of killing Tim Luce and raping and shooting Susan Bartolomei, no one who knew them in Ritzville had ever had any reason to expect such violent behavior from them. They seemed to be ordinary guys living ordinary—if boring—lives in a little town that baked hot in the summer and froze in the winter. Sometimes it seemed that if Ritzville wasn't being blasted by sandstorms, it was being pelted by blizzards.

As the questioning continued, the local officers were joined by John B. Smoot of the California Investigation and Identification Department. Tom Braun admitted to Smoot that he had raped and shot Susan Bartolomei, killed Tim Luce, and killed a woman near Seattle and a middle-aged man in Oregon. The admitted mastermind of the killing spree calmly agreed to help detectives in those states locate the bodies of the victims.

Leonard Maine confirmed Braun's story. Maine, however, insisted that he had been an unwilling pawn who was terrified of Braun and that he continued on the journey only because Braun would have killed him if he didn't. The men questioning him wondered why—if he feared for his life—Maine hadn't crept out of the hotel in Jamestown and escaped instead of falling asleep with a fully loaded gun in his possession.

California I.D. men compared the .22 caliber bullets taken from the bodies of Tim Luce and Susan Bartolomei with the bullets in the suspects' Ruger and Frontier Scout and in the drawers in rooms 26 and 19 of the Jamestown Hotel. They all proved to be from the same lot and the same manufacturer. More significant, the tool marks on the casings on the road where Susan was found indicated that the bullets had been fired by the Ruger and the Scout. No other guns could have made those exact markings.

The lawmen in Tuolumne and Mendocino Counties hoped they had apprehended Maine and Braun in time to prevent other killings; they hadn't reckoned with the possibility that their cases came at the end of a murder spree. Now the word coming back from Snohomish County, Washington, and Portland, Oregon, seemed to confirm Braun's and Maine's stories: their killing spree had obviously begun in the North.

Braun and Maine had described a murder up near Cannon Beach, Oregon, that had not yet been discovered. There, they said they had encountered "an old guy" on a logging road where they had detoured to take a look at the Pacific Ocean. Oregon salesman Samuel Ledgerwood, fifty-seven, had apparently had a successful day's fishing and was heading home when he came across the two suspects, who were changing a tire on the side of the road. He pulled over to help them. It was the last act of kindness he would ever perform.

Within a very short time, Ledgerwood lay dead on the isolated logging road with two .22 caliber slugs in his head. Tom Braun and Leonard Maine had still been driving Deanna Buse's car when Ledgerwood stopped to help them, but now they set it on fire—they didn't need it anymore. They headed toward California in their latest victim's green Buick. Perhaps it was Ledgerwood's newer model Buick that tempted the killers and led to his death. Or perhaps murder just for the hell of it had been their goal all along when they rolled out of Ritzville. They didn't know any of their victims and the victims themselves were different ages, different sexes. The only thing they had in common was that they were there when Braun and Maine roved along roads and freeways.

Oregon officers had a Missing Report on Sam Ledgerwood, but they hadn't found his body yet. Even as they headed out to the spot Leonard Maine described—a wooded area off a logging road near Cannon Beach—a report came in. A hunter had just discovered the remains of a man in that area, and there were indeed two bullet wounds in his head. It was Ledgerwood.

Nearby, the Oregon investigators found Deanna Buse's Buick Skylark. The car was a charred hulk, and they could see bullet holes in the gas tank. It's VIN was still quite readable; the clumsy suspects had thought the flames would obliterate all connections to the missing Washington bride, and once again they were wrong.

With directions relayed from Tuolumne County, Detectives Russ Jubie and Tom Hart of Snohomish County, Washington, left headquarters at 11:00 P.M. on August 22. Deanna Buse had been missing for three days and now, though they dreaded what they might find, they had their first clue to her whereabouts.

Following the directions that Braun and Maine had given the lawmen, Jubie and Hart headed for the densely wooded area surrounding Echo Lake, eight miles south of Monroe, Washington, then down Highway 202 and east on the Echo Lake Road, where they eventually turned off and traveled half a mile down a gravel road. Finally, they came to a one-way lane leading into the woods. Even in the middle of an August day, the woods were a dark and inky green, shut off from the sun by evergreens that grew so close together it was hard to tell where the branches of one tree ended and another began. Now, at midnight, the woods were absolutely pitch dark.

Carrying a high-powered light, the officers walked into the morass of brush and fir trees; the only sound was their boots crunching on the forest floor. Some twenty-five yards from the end of the lane, Tom Hart found Deanna Buse.

It was obvious that the pretty young housewife had not had even the slight chance of survival granted to Susan Bartolomei. Had she been left grievously wounded, there was no way Deanna could have crawled out of the deep woods. She lay on her back, her arms crossed over her chest. She was nude, and her clothes were folded meticulously and left in a neat pile beside her body. From what the detective sergeant could tell in the artificial light, she had been shot beneath her left eye and just below her ear. While Snohomish County detectives began their night-long investigation at the scene, representatives from the sheriff's office undertook the sad task of informing Deanna Buse's relatives that she had been found.

Dr. Alexander G. Robertson performed the autopsy on Deanna's body the next morning, August 23. He found five "projectile entries"—five entrance wounds from .22 caliber bullets. Several of them would have been instantly fatal. Any assailant who aims for the head of a human being is intent on killing that person. There was only small comfort for her husband and family. Deanna had been forced to remove her clothes out there in the deep woods; folding them neatly may have been a desperate attempt to delay the inevitable. She had not been raped, however; perhaps something had spooked the two men who took her there, or maybe her pleading had dissuaded them.

Morning papers all over the West Coast headlined the monstrous results of Thomas Braun's and Leonard Maine's flight from Washington to Oregon to California. There was little doubt that the deadly pair would be tried for murder in each of the three states. They were swiftly indicted in California and arrangements were made for their trial for the murder of Tim Luce and the shooting and sexual assault of Susan Bartolomei.

Miraculously, Susan was still alive. She had made it through intricate brain surgery, although the extent of the damage to her brain wouldn't be known for some time. The brain, which feels no pain, swells tremendously when it is insulted, forcing it against the hard surface of the skull where it is crushed and bruised. If surgeons aren't present to cut the skull away temporarily, the human brain begins to die. Susan had lain unattended for hours with bullets in her brain.

The murder of Tim Luce had inflamed public opinion against the defendants. Because of all the publicity, their California trial was moved to San Jose in a change of venue. This first trial was carried out in two phases; only during the penalty phase did the prosecution bring out the cases of Deanna Buse and Samuel Ledgerwood. Susan Bartolomei, the girl neither defendant ever expected to see alive again, was carried into the courtroom on a stretcher. There, painfully, slowly, with the use of hand signals, the brave girl proved to be a devastatingly damaging witness against the men who had meant to kill her.

The San Jose jury found Braun guilty and recommended the death penalty. He was sentenced to the gas chamber and transferred to death row in San Quentin. Maine, who steadfastly insisted he'd been an unwilling accomplice, was found guilty but sentenced to ten years to life. He began that sentence in the prison at Tracy, California, immediately following the trial.

Still more trials lay ahead. In Everett, Washington, the Snohomish County seat, Leonard Maine and Thomas Braun now went on trial for Deanna Buse's murder.

There were two phases of the trial—one to decide the guilt or innocence of the accused, and one to set the penalty for Braun and Maine should they be found guilty. Testimony from California authorities during the first phase of the trial was restricted to facts pertaining to the youths' arrest in Jamestown.

Spectators packed the second-floor courtroom each morning as testimony began. This would be the first time that Washington trial watchers would hear the entire story of the murderous duo's trail of death and destruction.

Judge McCrea issued an order to the news media weeks before the trial. The three-page document drawn in open court on October 8, 1970, decreed that reporters could not disseminate to the public any testimony given in the absence of the jury, judge, court reporter, defendants and counsel for all parties. Cameras and recording devices were banned from the second floor of the Snohomish County Courthouse. Sketches would be allowed, but only if they were "non-inflammatory" in nature.

Judge Thomas McCrea had good reason to caution newsmen. The Braun-Maine trial was expected to last four to six weeks, so he decided not to sequester the jury. He doubted that the attorneys could choose a representative panel from the pool of potential jurors if they learned they would be separated from their families for such an extended time. Without McCrea's gag rule, jurors who went home each night might hear, and be influenced by, comments and testimony that was off the record.

At that, selecting a jury whose members were not familiar with some aspect of Thomas Braun and Leonard Maine's crimes would prove difficult; the Ritzville pair had cut a swath of violence across three states three years earlier, and that was difficult to forget. Ordinarily, jury selection lasts a day or two. In the Braun-Maine trial, it took almost two weeks before Defense Attorneys Richard Bailey (for Thomas Braun), Samuel Hale (for Leonard Maine), and Prosecutors David Metcalf and Bruce Keithly were all satisfied with a jury of seven men and five women, plus three alternates.

Judge McCrea instructed the jury, "Don't let sentiment, pity, passion, sway your judgment. You will be judging these men on the axiom of reasonable doubt. You will not be judging them by whim or intuition."

It was 2:00 P.M. on an uncommonly bright October day when Deputy Prosecutor Metcalf rose to make his opening statement to the jury. As he spoke about the murder of the victim, Deanna Buse, Thomas Braun and Leonard Maine listened to the state's damning statements with no change of expression. Braun wrote constantly on a yellow legal tablet—as he would do throughout the trial. Both wore conservative suits, and their haircuts bore no resemblance to the wild "hippie" locks they had affected at the time of their arrest. If there was one clue to the fact that they had, indeed, been in jail for the past three years, it was their dead-white prison pallor. They looked as if they'd been underground for a long, long time.

"Each piece of this trial is part of a puzzle," Prosecutor Metcalf told the jury. "On Tuesday, August 22, Deanna Buse was found nude in the vicinity of Echo Lake. She had been shot five times in the head; there were four .22 caliber bullets in her brain and one beneath her body. The state will prove that Thomas Eugene Braun and Leonard Eugene Maine are guilty of this killing." Metcalf outlined the testimony he would present to the jury as the trial moved ahead. Most of this information was new and unfamiliar to those present in the courtroom, including the media. The prosecutors and the Snohomish County Sheriff's investigators had deliberately guarded the facts in the Buse case against the day when Braun and Maine would answer to them in court. In doing so, they had managed to avoid a change of venue.

If there are such things as ghosts, there were ghosts in that brightly lit courtroom. Timothy Luce, Susan Bartolomei, and Samuel Ledgerwood had never known Deanna Buse, but they had all faced the same terror in the last moments of their lives. Only Susan had lived to speak of it.

True to his opening statement, Prosecutor Metcalf presented dozens of witnesses who retraced the fatal journey of Braun and Maine.

First, Denny Buse described his wife's last day on earth. The young husband was dismissed as a witness after he identified pictures of Deanna and their Buick Skylark. As Buse left the courtroom that day, the prosecution submitted pictures of the victim taken as she lay dead on the ground near Echo Lake. The defendants' attorneys, Bailey and Hale, argued vociferously that several of them should be kept from the jury because they were "inflammatory." The pictures, showing the nude victim with her eyes closed and visible bullet wounds to her head, were admitted by Judge McCrea with a few reservations. Hale next argued that "in the interests of good taste" the pictures should be cropped so that the victim's pubic area would not be shown.

This motion was denied, and the pictures were shown. Braun and Maine were allowed to see the pictures, and the courtroom quieted as they glanced at the startling photos. Neither defendant showed any emotion.

Jurors and spectators then experienced an eerie sensation as they watched a seven-minute movie. The showing of the film in the darkened courtroom was prefaced by testimony from Chief Criminal Deputy Ross Jubie, who told of receiving word through the Seattle Police Department that two suspects in Tuolumne County, California, had confessed knowledge of Deanna Buse's murder. Jubie testified about a telephone conversation he had with Leonard Maine. During that call, Maine had described to him what had happened to the missing woman.

After finishing her shopping in Redmond, Washington, the young wife had headed for her mother's home in Monroe along Route 202. Braun and Maine, driving the Borgward, had pulled up beside her and signaled to her that she had a tire that was about to blow out. According to Maine, Mrs. Buse eased her car over to the side of the road. The suspects then pulled in behind her. After walking around her car and finding all her tires in good shape, the young woman turned to face the two strangers with a questioning look, only to be met by the sight of a gun in Braun's hand. He then ordered her back into her own car, got in with her, and instructed Maine to follow them in the Borgward. Slowly, the two-car caravan proceeded, under Braun's direction, onto less and less traveled roads until the trio pulled up at the end of the dirt lane leading into the woods near Echo Lake.

Maine alleged that Braun then disappeared into the woods with his helpless captive. Minutes passed and then Maine told Jubie of hearing five shots ring out in the wilderness. Braun returned to the car alone.

The film shown to the jurors retraced the route Deanna Buse was forced to drive at gunpoint. Following Maine's directions, a sheriff's patrol car drove that route while a deputy sat on the hood of the car with a camera. Those watching the film could not help but put themselves in the place of the terrified woman as the film showed first a well-traveled highway and then focused on side roads and finally on deep woods. The wooded scene—the last thing Deanna saw before she was killed—lingered in the courtroom as the film ended.

According to Maine, both cars were driven from the scene of the murder but the ancient Borgward had become excess baggage, so they abandoned it on a busy Seattle street. The two men were seen by witnesses removing articles from the Borgward and transferring them to a maroon Buick Skylark.

Sergeant Tom Hart told the jury that he searched the Borgward, which had been impounded by the Seattle Police Department, on August 23, 1967. Hart found five .22 caliber shell casings in the black foreign car.

After a weekend recess, the first witness to be

heard on Monday morning, November 9, was an uncle of co-defendant Leonard Maine. The uncle, a resident of Fife, Washington, twenty-two miles south of Seattle, told about a visit from his nephew and a friend during the afternoon of August 19, 1967. The two arrived in a 1964 or 1965 Buick and asked him the quickest way to get to Portland, Oregon. The uncle could not identify Maine's companion during the visit.

The next witness shed some light upon the frame of mind Leonard Maine was in on that grim Saturday. The pretty woman who lived next door to another uncle of Maine's and who told the jury she had been dating Maine for about a year, described a phone call she received from him at about nine o'clock that evening while she was baby-sitting in the uncle's home.

"We talked for about five or ten minutes—just a casual conversation. But then he said to come out on the porch or he would start shooting!" The witness said she did not go out on the porch but instead hung up and called the Seattle police. The murderous duo left the area then and headed south. On the Oregon coast, according to one motel manager, they attempted to register at his establishment but when they gave him incomplete information, he asked the wild-haired pair to leave. Although the Snohomish County jury would not hear the name Samuel Ledgerwood until the penalty phase of the defendants' trial, it was just after this incident that the kindly salesman met his killers.

Weeks of testimony in the first phase of the trial were coming to a close. Neither Hale nor Bailey called any witnesses for the defense.

Prosecutor Metcalf summed up his case by reviewing the voluminous testimony presented, and then said,

ANN RULE

"By use of force and fear, this girl was kidnapped, killed, and robbed. The state has proved its case. The defendants are guilty as charged."

Bailey, the attorney for Braun, challenged the prosecution by saying, "There was no motive for this killing. Thomas Braun didn't even know Deanna Buse. You must decide if he intended to kill her."

Samuel Hale, in defense of Leonard Maine, hit hard at the concept that Maine had been a frightened, unwilling pawn in the hands of his traveling companion. He recalled testimony where Maine told California officers that Braun had pointed a gun at him just before the two stopped Deanna Buse's car.

On rebuttal, Prosecutor David Metcalf deplored Bailey's argument that there had been no motive. "I don't know *why* murders are committed. I don't know *why* kidnappings are committed. I don't know *why* robberies are committed." He stressed that the reason for Deanna's brutal murder did not matter; it had been committed. Hale's contention that Maine had acted under duress and fear for his own life prompted Metcalf to point out that Maine had many opportunities to get away from Braun, yet had remained with him.

On November 19, after twenty-seven days of testimony, the jury retired to deliberate. In seven hours, they returned with a verdict. Thomas Braun and Leonard Maine remained stoic as they heard the decision of their peers. Ten times the word "Guilty" was repeated. Each of the defendants was found guilty of first-degree murder, kidnapping, robbery, grand larceny, and possession of a dangerous weapon during the commission of the murder, kidnapping, and robbery.

Judge McCrea polled the jury as the defendants sat stone-faced. All of the jurors affirmed their decisions.

After a weekend's rest, the case moved to the penalty phase. For Braun, already under the death penalty in California, his sentence seemed academic. He could only be executed once. If he was given the death penalty in Washington, a successful appeal to the Supreme Court on the California death penalty still wouldn't save him. For Maine, whose much lighter sentence in California made the Washington trial crucial, the jury's decision could be disastrous.

Now all the evidence and testimony previously barred concerning the crimes against Susan Bartolomei, Tim Luce, and Samuel Ledgerwood was placed before the jury, beginning with a chronology of events that linked the attacks.

Snohomish County had taken the missing persons report on Deanna Buse on Saturday, August 19. Then word had come from Portland that Sam Ledgerwood, an automobile salesman, had failed to return from a fishing trip to the Oregon coast. The last call from him came on Sunday, August 20. When his body was found days later, the police also found Deanna Buse's burned Buick. Next came the kidnapping of Susan Bartolomei and Tim Buse in Hopland, California, on Monday. The time line was unassailable.

In addition, the jurors heard testimony from a Seattle hotel proprietor who told of events on the Friday evening of August 18, 1967, the day before Deanna Buse was murdered. The hotel owner described a young man who had requested a room. "But then I saw a shadow in front of me," she recalled. "I looked up and he was pointing a gun at me. Then I screamed and stepped into an adjoining room and shut the door."

She identified Thomas Braun as the man who had threatened her with the gun.

California Superior Court Judge Arthur E. Broaddus took the witness stand to read lengthy portions of a transcript of an interview he had with both Braun and Maine as they were questioned following their arrests in Jamestown.

Broaddus, at that time the Tuolumne County district attorney, read the damaging statements concerning the savage attacks on Tim Luce and Susan Bartolomei. Attorney Hale then asked Judge Broaddus to read sections of the transcript where Maine said he felt sorry for the victims and that he was afraid of Braun, who usually had a pistol in his possession or nearby.

Further testimony during the penalty phase brought out the shocking magnitude of the defendants' antisocial feelings. A former cell mate of Maine's in Ukiah, California, told of being forced to commit sodomy by the defendant, who threatened him with a straight-edged razor. Braun hadn't been the ideal cell mate either. A twenty-one-year-old inmate of the Snohomish County jail testified that Braun had threatened him while the two shared a cell. In the ensuing scuffle, the witness was injured and had to be treated at an Everett hospital.

Tension in the courtroom mounted during the final phase of the trial. Twice Leonard Maine told Judge Mc-Crea that he was too ill to continue and court had to be recessed while he was examined by a county physician, who found nothing seriously wrong with him. Braun's attorney asserted that his client wasn't responsible for his acts because of mental irresponsibility, although such a plea had already been ruled out in this trial. He detailed the defendant's wretched childhood and told the jury that Braun's mother had died after having an illegal abortion; Braun's father, an alcoholic, according to the defendant, routinely locked Braun and his sister in his truck and left them for hours while he visited taverns.

A Seattle clinical psychologist, Dr. Ralph Hirschstein, who interviewed Braun twice and conducted psychiatric tests, told the jury that he considered the defendant a "pseudo-psychopathic schizophrenic"—a "bright man" who had been out of contact with reality during August of 1967.

Virtually the same opinion was given by Paul Handrich, a clinical psychiatrist from Ukiah, California. Handrich defined a psychopath as a person who has no conscience and a schizophrenic as a person who has a conscience but does not know how to use it. "Schizophrenia is characterized by disturbance of emotions, marked ambivalence, and loose associations of thought. This man is genuinely perplexed." Braun's sister recalled the pathetic and trauma-fraught childhood they had endured. Alternately neglected and abused by a punishing father, she said her brother had once been forced to shoot his own dog because the animal had killed chickens. Hale's plea for Leonard Maine also hit hard at the mental irresponsibility of his client. He called Maine's parents and wife, who had been in the courtroom since the beginning of the trial. They described the diminutive defendant as a man continually beset by feelings of inferiority because of his borderline intelligence.

"He was a good boy," Maine's mother recalled, "who had a record of good behavior in school. His two main interests were cars and horses. It hurt him that he couldn't keep up with the other children in school." She told of Maine's being held back in the third grade and of how he finally dropped out of school just before his ninth grade year was over because the struggle to keep up had been too much.

Dr. Fariborz Amini, a California psychiatrist, testified regarding his examination of Maine. He said that the defendant viewed himself more "as a victim . . . than as a participant in the crimes. Maine has an inadequate personality with some characteristics of passive dependency, accentuated by below-normal intelligence." He said his examination of Maine showed that the defendant's IQ was somewhere between 80 and 90. "In August of 1987," Dr. Amini said, "Mr. Maine was under severe stress, which made him unable to deliberate. Given Maine's need to be dependent on others, he is not able to act on his own when under heavy emotional stress." Cross-examined by Deputy Prosecutor Metcalf, Dr. Amini was asked if Maine knew the difference between right and wrong during the events of August 1967. "If you're asking me if he had absolute knowledge, no. If he had an awareness, yes."

Leonard Maine himself took the stand briefly to testify regarding the alleged sodomy assault in the Ukiah jail. He agreed that he had been in the cell with two other prisoners but denied having participated in, or even witnessed, any sexual attacks.

That Braun and Maine did kill is known. Why they killed is not. One officer who worked on the case says, "I don't know that they had murder in mind when they started out from Ritzville, but I think after they killed their first victim, they continued to seek out victims for nothing more than the sheer pleasure of killing."

Only one person who faced the guns of Thomas Braun and Leonard Maine remains alive: Susan Bartolomei, whose grievous wounds changed her from a sparkling teenager to an invalid. Although Susan was able to talk with Howardine Mease on the morning after her night of horror, the damage done to her brain robbed her of speech. There was only so much doctors could do, and she spent her days in a wheelchair and lived with extensive paralysis and impaired vision.

But Susan Bartolomei *did* survive in spite of the tremendous odds against her, and she lived to see the men who shot her convicted of their crimes. Had it not been for the courage she summoned up as she inched her way up the steep bank to the road on that scorching day in August 1967, law enforcement officers can only imagine how many more victims might have been added to the list written in blood by Thomas Braun and Leonard Maine.

At 3:40 P.M. on Friday, December 18, the jury once again retired to consider a verdict. The longest capital punishment trial in Snohomish County was at last over. The jury voted unanimously to impose the death sentence upon Thomas E. Braun on both counts of first-degree murder and first-degree kidnapping. They voted not to inflict the death penalty upon Leonard Maine; this meant he would receive an automatic sentence of life imprisonment.

A Dangerous Mind

The third week *in June 1981 was a macabre, albeit informative, time for me. Along with a few hundred detectives and physicians, I attended King
County Medical Examiner Dr. Donald Reay's seminar
on death investigation. After forty hours of lectures
and slides detailing death by fire, gunshot, strangulation, bludgeoning, and drowning, and studying the parameters that denote lust murder, I was more than
ready for a vacation from violence. Even though homicide detectives and crime writers spend their working
hours in a world where a knowledge of the patterns of
death is essential, we can still be shocked and sickened. Indeed, if we are not sensitive to the pain and
pathos of unnatural death, we shouldn't be in the ca-
reers we have chosen.*

*But some times are rougher than others. On the last
day of Reay's seminar—Friday, June 19—six Seattle
homicide detectives in the audience were working the
kind of case that can bring the toughest investigators to
their knees. The victim was a child, a tiny seven-year-
old girl. This case predated the JonBenét Ramsey case
in Boulder, Colorado, by almost two decades, but the
details were almost identical: a pretty blond child murdered in her own home during the dark hours before*

dawn. As in the Ramsey case, there was no sign at all that someone from the outside had broken in.

At each coffee break during the medical examiner's seminar, the Seattle detectives checked in with their office to see how the case was progressing. They were grateful they had not been on duty when that call came in. Although they had not been summoned to the initial crime scene, they were responsible for finding the killer.

It would take four months for the full story of the murder of Jannie Reilly* to unfold, and with its denouement, it would trigger even more tragedy. Lives were destroyed and hearts broken. When the last chapter was written, it became all too clear that misguided kindness had ended in murder. Good people had offered hospitality to someone whose promises meant nothing. But at least, unlike JonBenét's murder, there were answers and the killer was caught and taken to trial.

The Joseph Reillys seemed to have the safest home possible. Joseph had once been a priest and his wife, Lorraine, was also a devout Catholic. After realizing that the calling was not right for him, Joseph had left the priesthood, but he and Lorraine maintained close connections to their church.

Joseph and Lorraine had met sometime after he rejoined the secular community. They fell in love, married, and adopted two children. Jannie was seven years old in June of 1981; her brother, Max,* was six months younger. The Reillys lived in a pleasant white frame house in the Magnolia Bluff section of Seattle. They had a dog and plenty of neighbor children for Jannie and Max to play with. The children's bedroom was in the basement, close to Lorraine's sewing room, conveniently near the door that opened into the big backyard. The Reillys slept upstairs.

Joseph Reilly was educated by the Jesuits, the scholars of the Roman Catholic priesthood, and he made a solid, comfortable living working for a furnace company. Lorraine was involved in the community, devoted to her adopted children and her extended family in Oregon. She had a warm and forgiving heart, but she was, perhaps, naive. She believed in giving people endless second chances and she felt that love and acceptance could cure most of the ills of the mind and spirit.

Despite the serenity of the Reilly home, something unspeakable happened there during the night of June 18. One of their neighbors awakened sometime that night. She would be the first person outside the Reilly home to sense that something horrible had happened.

Just before the summer solstice in Seattle, it stays light until 10:00 P.M. and the sun rises again a little after 4:00 A.M. The Reillys' neighbor was unsure of the time she woke, but she was positive it was full dark when she heard voices outside. She pulled back the curtain next to her bed and saw two figures walking on the street, but she thought little of it; the neighborhood was close to Discovery Park, a sprawling greensward that ended abruptly at a dizzyingly high bluff overlooking Puget Sound. There were people in the park at all hours of the day and night.

The Reillys' restless neighbor finally fell back to sleep, but something woke her again near dawn. She looked at her bedside clock, noting that it was 4:00 A.M. She heard a car door slam shut, or perhaps it was a house door. Peering out at the street again, she saw Lorraine Reilly's brother, who was visiting from Oregon. Lorraine had told her that her brother, Arnold, was twenty-four, but somehow he seemed much younger. Now he was standing anxiously at the curb, apparently waiting for someone. As she watched, she heard the wail of a siren and saw a fire department aid unit pull up next door. It was followed almost immediately by a Medic One rig. The neighbor's first thought was "heart attack." The Reillys were barely middle-aged, but such things did sometimes happen.

She could not have imagined what had occurred inside the protective walls of the house next door. Even the paramedics, who are used to tragedy, were shocked when they saw their patient. A small girl lay on the living room couch, her body covered with a blanket. Her face was suffused with a deep cherry-red flush, something they knew was characteristic in cases of suffocation or carbon monoxide poisoning.

Jannie Reilly was unresponsive to stimuli, and the paramedics could detect no heartbeat or pulse. Still, they tried to resuscitate her. They lifted her to the carpet and cut away the red, white, and blue shirt she was wearing over a pair of red panties. They attached leads from their Life-Pak to her chest to monitor any sign of heart activity and then began CPR.

Nothing.

They started a peripheral I.V. and slid an endotracheal tube down her throat to force oxygen into her lungs.

Nothing.

With permission from a supervising M.D. at Harborview Hospital, they attempted to start her heart with an injection directly into the heart itself. It was too late. In truth, they had known it was too late going in, but it was so hard to believe that a child so young was beyond help, even when they saw that her pupils were fixed and dilated. And she had not been dead long; her flesh was still warm.

While her agonized parents and her uncle stood by, the paramedics stopped their efforts and marked the time of death at 4:14 A.M.

Seattle Police Patrol Officers Ty Kane, Jon Mattox, Garry McLenaghen, and J. G. Burchfield had been dispatched moments after the call for help came from the Reilly home. Now the paramedics beckoned them over and pointed out the angry scarlet crease on the child's neck. It was an obvious ligature mark. Jannie Reilly had not died of natural causes.

Unlike the Ramsey investigation in Boulder, Colorado, this crime scene was immediately sealed to all but the police. The patrol officers cordoned off the home and yard with yellow crime-scene tape and sent for a homicide team.

While a police radio operator was alerting the on-call sergeant, Don Cameron, the officers inspected the exterior doors and windows of the home. There was no sign of forced entry, and Joseph Reilly assured them that the doors and windows had been locked when the family went to bed the night before. He had double-checked them himself.

Understandably, the Reillys were nearly overwhelmed with shock and grief, and their priest hurried over to give what comfort he could to the family who were now confined to the kitchen while the police began their investigation. Lorraine Reilly's brother, Arnold Brown, crouched on his heels next to the refrigerator, his large brown eyes fixed on the opposite wall. Antsy and tense, he made several trips to the bathroom to wash his hands.

Nobody was acting normal—but it was a far from normal situation. Only Jannie's little brother, Max, slept on, unaware that his world had changed forever.

It was 4:36 A.M. when Don Cameron called his crew—Danny Melton and John Nordlund—at home. Then he left for the crime scene. The three detectives arrived at the Reilly home shortly after 5:00 A.M. and tried to make some sense of what had happened. The house was warm and homey, but the Reillys were obviously not at all wealthy. Why would someone choose their home to invade?

Cameron asked the Reillys what they remembered

of the previous night. Had they heard or seen anything out of the ordinary? Shaking his head as if waking from a nightmare, Joseph Reilly said that everything had been completely routine the night before—until Arnold woke him in the wee hours of the morning. "He said he had walked past Jannie's room and she wasn't there," Reilly recalled. "We immediately began to search for her."

He and Arnold had hurried to the backyard, accompanied by the family dog. "Our dog immediately went to the right with his tail wagging, and then he went to the corner of the fence," Reilly said. "I looked over the fence, and that's when I saw Jannie over on the other side of the fence, lying on the ground."

Reilly said he scaled the fence and ran to his daughter, who was lying on her side in a fetal position. He lifted her and carried her in his arms, while Arnold wrenched a section of the fence out with his bare hands so that Reilly could bring Jannie through. She felt warm and soft, like herself, and he thought she had only been walking in her sleep. But he couldn't figure out how she had gotten over the fence.

He tried to fight down the panic that kept bubbling up. Jannie's body was very still, and she wasn't making a sound. The horrified father called out to his wife as he ran toward the house, shouting for her to call 911. They laid Jannie on the couch and covered her with a blanket while Arnold ran out to watch for the paramedics.

Arnold Brown explained to the trio of detectives that he was not a regular member of the Reilly household; he had arrived only three days earlier and was visiting from Eugene, Oregon, where he lived with his parents and his other sisters. "I'm only going to stay and visit. about ten days," he said.

Arnold said that he'd spent the previous evening at the Reillys' house, except for a short stroll from 10:30 to 11:00, when he took their dog for a walk. After that, he stayed up late watching television while the Reillys went to bed.

"How was it that you noticed Jannie was missing?" Don Cameron asked.

"Well, I watched TV upstairs until about two-thirty and then I went down to my room to watch on my set there," he answered. "I got thirsty and started upstairs to get a glass of water, and I noticed that Jannie wasn't in her bed, but Max was there. That's when I went and woke up my sister and brother-in-law and we started to look for her. I helped Joseph over the fence, and then went to where I thought there was a gate, but there wasn't any, so I just pulled the fence apart."

Dr. John Eisele, assistant King County medical examiner, arrived to examine the victim's body at 7:15 A.M. He agreed with the investigators that the reddish purple mark on her neck indicated that some kind of ligature had been tightened around her throat with terrific force.

There was very little in the way of physical evidence. Eisele found a few single hairs inside the victim's red panties. They appeared to be pubic hairs and they were much darker than her blond hair. John Nordlund bagged these into evidence.

The detectives took hair samples from members of the household. Arnold Brown was asked to supply samples from his head and pubic area and he did so without argument.

They noted what appeared to be blood spatters on the wall of Brown's room, which was located directly across the hall from the children's bedroom on the ground floor. Both rooms were close to the back door that led out to the yard. The detectives photographed the spatters before they carefully lifted blood samples from the wall with swabs moistened with a sterile water solution.

Something about Arnold Brown niggled at them; they sensed that he was experiencing something more than grief. He was nervous, but that was to be expected. He looked young for twenty-four. He still had that gawky, unfinished look that teenagers have. He was medium-tall, medium-built, brown-haired. He had just lost his niece, a child he said he was very fond of, but his reactions were slightly off, and his demeanor was flat. Still, people deal with grief and shock differently. Maybe they were looking at Arnold so closely because he was the one new element in the household's composition; he had been visiting for only three days.

When they questioned him more closely, Arnold Brown grudgingly revealed that he was in Washington State on a travel permit from the Oregon State Department of Corrections. "I'm on probation," he said quietly.

"For what?" Nordlund asked.

Arnold said he had a conviction for first-degree burglary because he'd been found inside a roller rink after it was closed.

Nordlund knew that it took more than that to be convicted of first-degree burglary, but he said nothing. "Anything else?" Nordlund asked.

Arnold admitted that he also had a juvenile record because of an assault, but he declined to be more specific. Nordlund didn't press him—they would check on his record later.

Arnold's hands were scratched and they had curious red pressure marks on them, creases that were not quite bruises.

"Where did you get those?" Danny Melton asked.

He stared at his hands and said finally, "I must have gotten those from the blackberry bushes."

John Nordlund took pictures of Arnold's hands; they would be part of a growing photographic record of the scene where Jannie Reilly had lived and died. Among the photos were shots of the house, the yard, and the body of the victim.

Asked what clothes he wore the evening before, Arnold said he had on his Movin' On jeans when he walked the dog, but had changed into the cutoffs he wore now. He readily agreed to turn over his cutoffs and jeans to the detectives so they could be tested in the crime lab. He couldn't find his jeans in his room, but then he finally dug down into his backpack and pulled them from the bottom. "If they have blood on them, it would be Jannie's from her getting hurt at the playground today," he said.

They knew that Jannie Reilly's body had no cuts or abrasions on it—nothing beyond the mark on her neck. Arnold was protesting too much.

The homicide detectives had yet to find the weapon of death—some cord or rope that might have caused the deep groove in Jannie's neck. They searched the backyard in the gray light of early morning, scanning it for anything that looked out of place. Eventually, they found a wire cord near the fence. They thought it might match the cruel indentation on the small victim's neck. But Dr. Eisele looked at it and shook his head. No match.

It seemed more and more unlikely that someone could have crept into the Reillys' house during the night. The windows were either locked or had screens firmly in place, with enough dust and spiderwebs to show they hadn't been removed and then replaced. The doors were locked with dead bolts. The killer almost certainly had known where Jannie and Max slept. In most homes, the children's bedrooms are upstairs rather than in the basement, so someone had to know the layout of the Reillys' home.

The early suspicions of Don Cameron's crew only grew stronger as they worked the crime scene. It was too coincidental that Arnold Brown just happened to go upstairs for a glass of water during the night and discover that Jannie was missing. In the dark of the children's room, how could he have seen that? Further, if a stranger had entered the home during the night, why hadn't the Reillys' dog barked?

The focus of the investigation kept swinging back to Arnold Brown. His manner was oddly wooden as they questioned him. Even when he was asked to accompany detectives to the homicide offices for more questioning, he displayed little emotion. And he went along willingly.

Sergeant Cameron and Detective John Nordlund talked with Arnold Brown in one of the interview rooms at headquarters. They asked him to remember everything he could about the night before. Shortly after 9:00 A.M., he agreed to give them a statement. He recalled that his sister had gone out to a meeting the evening before. The children were eating supper with a neighbor's family, and Joseph left a little before 8:00 P.M. to pick up Lorraine.

"He told me to have the kids get into their pajamas when they got home from the neighbors' and get them to bed," Brown related. "The kids came home about fifteen minutes after Joseph left and they got ready for bed."

Arnold said he watched some musical on pay television with his brother-in-law until about 10:00 P.M., then he walked the family dog. "I like dogs," he said, his eyes fixed on the wall of the interview room. "I have my own dog, Queenie, in Eugene, and I miss her."

He repeated that he watched television alone upstairs until about 2:30 A.M. and then he went downstairs and noticed that Jannie was missing when he walked by her room. He stressed that he had hurried to tell his brother-in-law so they could look for her.

Asked bluntly if he had anything to do with the death of his niece, Brown said he didn't want to talk anymore. "I had nothing to do with Jannie's death," he finally said. "This is a true statement."

While Cameron and Nordlund talked with Arnold Brown, Detective John Boatman placed a call to Lane County, Oregon, to see what background information on the suspect he might find. He learned that Arnold Brown was *very* familiar to Oregon authorities, and they gave Boatman a chilling criminal history of the meek-looking man in the interview room.

Arnold Brown was the slow child in a family of high achievers. Tested at age sixteen, he was found to have the mental capabilities of a fifth grader. His IQ was about 77. Normal IQ is 90 to 110; and 77 would place Brown in the "dull-normal" range.

Arnold had a great deal of trouble learning to read, and he was easily frustrated. Early on, he had problems with anger, and he reacted with violence when he felt frustrated. He could not keep up with his high school classes and dropped out of school so he could apply for admission to the Job Corps program. On June 6, 1973, he learned that he would not be admitted to the current Job Corps' class; he would have to wait until there was space. He had looked forward to learning a trade, something where he could use his hands. Always easily frustrated, he could not cope with the delay.

Arnold Brown had been very angry on that summer day years earlier. Convinced that the odds were against him and that he would never get to do what he wanted, he headed toward the bank of the Willamette River. He carried with him a hunting knife with a ten-inch blade.

In Seattle, John Boatman scribbled notes rapidly as a Lane County, Oregon, detective went on with Arnold's criminal history. Thirteen-year-old Maria Coleman and her eight-year-old brother Jimmy were also at the river's edge that long-ago day. They were looking for crawfish and tadpoles and they scarcely glanced up when Arnold approached. They did nothing at all to provoke him, but in a sudden spate of horror, Arnold stabbed both Maria and Jimmy in the chest. He plunged his hunting knife into their helpless bodies again and again. Miraculously, the youngsters survived, but the Oregon investigator described the knife as being "bent like a corkscrew" afterward.

Arnold Brown was arrested, and a juvenile hearing was held. Detectives James Wolcott and Martin Deforest testified that Arnold admitted stabbing the Brown children "because I wondered what it would feel like to knife someone."

A psychiatrist testified that Brown told him he only remembered walking near the Willamette River and passing two young children. He explained that he had a blank space in his memory until he recalled running from the area. He could not remember stabbing anyone. The psychiatrist hadn't believed him; he diagnosed Arnold Brown as having an antisocial personality. "He feels no guilt at all, no responsibility."

As they always had, Arnold's family defended him

vehemently, claiming that the detectives had misled him by promising him that he could still join the Job Corps even if he was found guilty of stabbing the two children. The Oregon investigators were adamant that they had made no such promises.

It ended in a draw. Brown's confession was ruled inadmissible because the judge felt Arnold had been read his rights under Miranda too rapidly for him to understand them. He was made a ward of the court and committed indefinitely to the Parrot Creek Boys' Ranch in Oregon City. He stayed there only eighteen months and then moved back to his family home in Eugene.

Arnold Brown *was* slow, but his borderline IQ didn't cause his rage. There was something else—something either genetic or environmental—that contributed to his losing control when he didn't get his way. The treatment he received at Parrot Creek didn't change his basic personality structure at all. Psychiatrists have long agreed that the antisocial personality is probably the most resistant personality disorder to treat. Most children develop a conscience around the age of three and a half. When that doesn't happen, it is next to impossible to acquire a conscience and to develop empathy and compassion for others. The child grows tall; his conscience shrivels.

Released from the boys' school, Arnold was angry, frustrated, and, worse, possessed by unfulfilled sexual cravings.

He was a time bomb.

Arnold applied for admission to the National Guard that summer. He was rejected in his efforts to find a place where he would be "accepted as a man." But he was turned down not so much because of his lack of intellect as because the National Guard interviewers found him lacking in maturity and empathy for others.

A month later, Arnold strolled toward the Willamette River to go fishing. Five-year-old Summer Rogers lived near the river too. She was a pixyish little girl with dark eyes and pigtails. She wore a bathing suit on this hot summer day. Her mother was fixing supper inside the house, and she told Summer to stay close because they were going to eat in fifteen minutes. The child nodded and ran outside to play.

Summer's stepfather came home and called her to come in to supper, but she didn't respond. Her parents assumed she had gone next door to her friend's house to play, as she often did; it was still sunny and light out and they weren't worried. They went ahead and ate dinner, saving a plate for her, and then called Summer, again. But their voices hung in the air. There was only silence in response. Frightened now, they scoured the neighborhood for Summer, asking everyone they met if they had seen her.

Arnold Brown walked by as they searched, and Summer's mother asked him if he'd seen her little girl. He shook his head and walked on. By sunset, the parents were frantic. As night fell, they notified the police.

Summer Rogers was the second five-year-old girl to disappear in the Eugene area that summer. When more young girls were found murdered in the Salem area forty miles north, it began to appear that a serial killer—referred to back then as a mass murderer—was roving in central Oregon. Because Eugene detectives were aware that Brown had stabbed Maria and Jimmy Coleman on the bank of the Willamette three years earlier when he was sixteen, Arnold Brown became their prime suspect in the disappearance of Summer and, tangentially, in the decapitation killing of another child, whose murder was still unsolved.

They soon found witnesses who had seen Summer walking with Arnold toward the Willamette River. But they didn't find anyone who had seen Summer walking back. They found traces of blood on Arnold's tackle box and on his pants; he explained that it was from his dog, who was in heat. In that era, the samples were too minuscule to test for blood type classification or even to verify that it was human blood, so they had no way to disprove his statement.

After hours of interrogation, Arnold Brown gave a statement admitting that Summer had accompanied him down to the river. Lane County District Attorney Pat Horton recalled Arnold's version of what happened: "He admitted seeing her fall while she was wading, and hitting her head on a rock. He said she looked dead and he panicked. He thought he would be in a lot of trouble because of his background. After she was dead, he said he simply pushed the body off into the current and watched it drift downriver. But there was never any admission that he caused her death. Basically, he said he had done the wrong thing by pushing the body in the river, but that the girl just slipped, fell, and was killed in front of him. That he wasn't responsible."

Arnold Brown's story seemed incredible, and Horton wasn't happy with the progression of the case. The Eugene detectives were convinced that Brown had deliberately crushed Summer Rogers's skull with a rock and then disposed of her body in the fast-moving river. But they had no body and no physical evidence to take to court. Many bodies are lost forever in the Willamette. The police realized that they might never find Summer.

The Willamette River *did* give up Summer's remains ten weeks later, but the body was so decomposed that it was at first misidentified. Today DNA would be used to identify her small torso, but when Summer died, they retrieved only shreds of clothing and enough blood to type. Even in the year 2000, cause of death of a body that long in a river would be difficult to determine. There was nothing left of the little girl but a decaying torso with ragged bits of a blue-and-white bathing suit clinging to it. The head and extremities were gone forever. Pathologists could not determine cause of death or say for sure if the head, arms, and legs had been cut off or had simply fallen away as the result of decomposition.

If Arnold Brown's life was frustrating, it was nothing compared to the agony of detectives who were sure that a desperately dangerous man was walking free in their community. There was not enough left of the victim to arrest Arnold; they had only their terrible suspicions. The Oregon investigators kept an eye on Arnold, but they didn't have the manpower to trail him all the time, and his family closed in around him in fierce protection. He was cleared in the murder of the second child after another Eugene resident confessed.

The Eugene detectives remained angry and bitter. "I could write a book about Arnold Brown," one muttered years later. "We know all about him, and it makes us sick."

So there it was. Arnold remained free for two years after Summer Rogers died. He was arrested once more on February 16, 1978—but not for murder. He was convicted of stealing $45,000 from the roller rink. He went to the Oregon State Penitentiary with a twenty-year sentence. The prosecution brought up the death of Summer Rogers in the burglary trial, and Circuit Judge

Helen Frye gave Arnold the maximum twenty-year sentence.

Not surprisingly, Arnold Brown's lawyers immediately filed an appeal, the basis of which was the admission of the testimony regarding Summer Rogers's death. Legally, Arnold's attorneys were on sturdy ground; he had never been charged in what was only presumed to be murder. In a convoluted legal tangle, his sentence was struck down in February 1980. He was given a suspended sentence for the roller rink burglary and placed on probation. Once again he walked free.

Arnold Brown went back to his family and his pet dog. He lived in the old neighborhood where all the crimes he was suspected of had occurred. He often visited the Reillys in Seattle, and their young children adored him.

But none of his deep-seated problems were gone; they only lay festering. In March of 1981, Arnold began making reports to the police about "people" who were "bugging" him. On March 26 he reported that someone had damaged a boat on his family's property. A day later he claimed that strangers had assaulted him while he walked Queenie. On March 29 he reported that someone had damaged their boat further and had also cut the phone lines to his family's residence.

The police doubted his claims; they suspected that Arnold himself was doing the damage. But when they asked him if he would take a lie detector test, he refused. They weren't sure why he was getting restive, but it worried them. Was Arnold sending out signals that something bad was going to happen again? Or was he only enjoying the attention he got when he cried wolf?

Few clever con men have walked away from as

many suspicions, charges, and convictions as deftly as Arnold Brown, despite his lack of intellect. The family who loved, protected, and cosseted him from the law and from responsibility did so at unspeakable cost. And now their refusal to allow him to be punished for *anything* might have led to tragedy in their own family.

John Boatman, voluminous notes in hand, knocked on the door of the interview room on the fifth floor of the Public Safety Building in Seattle and signaled to his sergeant to come out. And then he told Don Cameron about Arnold's background.

They weren't dealing with a twenty-four-year-old man who just happened to be present in a house on the night his niece was murdered; they were questioning a man whose life had been laced with violence and suspicion for eight years. And most of the incidents had involved harm to children.

Arnold Brown's family had supported him, believed in him, hired lawyers to get him out of prison. And he had been taken into the Reilly home as a welcome guest. He was allowed to baby-sit for Jannie and Max, and he slept in a bedroom only steps from theirs.

Now, in the Seattle Police Homicide Unit, Arnold held out his hands so detectives could take fingernail scrapings. Then he was placed under arrest.

Three hours later he faced Cameron and Nordlund again. He had sent word from his jail cell that he wanted to talk more about Jannie's death. He was ready to give another statement.

His story of the evening of June 18 began just as it had before. He watched television upstairs until 2:30 A.M. and then went downstairs, where he peeked into the children's room. In this version, though, he admitted that he saw Jannie sleeping in her bed.

John Nordlund looked at him and said quietly, "I think you are a sick person, and that you killed Jannie. You probably belong in a mental hospital."

"I probably do."

"Arnold, where did you kill her?" Nordlund asked quietly.

"The sewing room."

"Did you rape her?"

"Yes."

Arnold said that he had picked Jannie up from her bed and carried her, still sleeping, into the shop area of the basement where he found a single-braided rope. He then carried her to the sewing room behind his bedroom, but Jannie, who weighed only 66 pounds, began to wake up, stirring slightly.

"I placed the rope around her neck . . . Then I pulled."

As Jannie's breath was cut off, Arnold admitted that he placed his finger in her vagina. Although any forcible penetration of a body orifice for sexual purposes is considered rape by Washington State statute, it was clear that Arnold Brown understood very little about sexual intercourse or the human body. He insisted if his niece's vaginal vault had semen in it, it must have been from her; he thought both males and females produced semen.

Jannie Reilly had suffered trauma to her vagina, but it was questionable whether she had been raped in the traditional sense of the term.

"And then what did you do?" Nordlund asked.

"I carried her outside and lowered her over the fence next door. I think her heart was still beating. I didn't mean to kill her."

The terrible danger that walked with Arnold Brown had come, finally, to an end. He was returned to jail, while Cameron and Nordlund went to the Reilly home to search for the braided, tasseled rope that Brown had described as the murder weapon. They found the hemp rope lying against the backyard fence on the east side of the property. They took it to Dr. Eisele, who said it fit exactly into the indentations on the dead child's neck.

Arnold Brown was placed in a cell with an inmate who was in jail for violation of probation on a theft charge. The twenty-one-year-old prisoner asked him the usual question: "What are you in for?"

Arnold lied and said he was in for manslaughter for hitting a woman with a car. But his cell mate's father had read of Jannie's death and informed his son about the real charges against Arnold Brown. In jails and prisons, there are crimes that prisoners cannot stomach; molestation and cruelty to children top the list. Arnold's cell mate, an expectant father, did not relish sharing a cell with him. He confronted him with what had really happened, pointing out that he was aware of the real charges against him.

"You did it, didn't you?" he demanded of Arnold.

Arnold admitted to him that he had strangled his niece—for a reason that was both shocking and unfathomable to a normal man. He said that he had never had sex with a woman and he resented other men who had. The sight of Jannie in her nightclothes had "infuriated" him, reminding him that he had missed out on sexual experience. And so he had placed the rope around her neck and taken what he wanted.

The other prisoner was filled with revulsion. He saw tears in Arnold's eyes, and asked him why he didn't just go ahead and cry.

"Tears are there," Arnold said, "but they just don't want to come."

Once Arnold started to confess to his cell mate, his words bubbled over. He also admitted killing Summer Rogers. He said he was angry at Summer because she wore only a bathing suit that day. That, too, reminded him that he had never had sex.

"He told me he hit her on the head with a rock and then cut off her head and arms and legs with his fishing knife," Arnold's cell mate told the Seattle detectives. "He said, 'They had to let me go in Oregon due to lack of evidence . . . thank God.'"

The informant begged to be moved to another cell; he could not bear to look at Arnold, knowing what he knew. His request was granted. The man had never heard of Summer Rogers and he couldn't have known the details of her death unless Arnold had told him, but when Don Cameron and Danny Melton talked to Arnold about Summer's murder, he denied having any part of it. "She fell on a rock and hurt her head, and she stopped breathing," he insisted stubbornly.

Melton asked him about his true motivation for killing his niece. *"Was* it because you have never had sexual intercourse?"

Arnold nodded. "I get angry when people talk about sex, because I've never had it myself. I don't know why it makes me angry to see kids with hardly any clothes on."

"How could you see she only had panties and a shirt on?" Melton pressed. "Wasn't she in bed, covered up?"

"The blankets were kicked off."

"Did you ejaculate during the time you were choking her with a rope?"

Arnold shook his head. He didn't want to talk about it.

"And Summer Rogers? You say you didn't hit Summer?"

"No. She fell on a rock. I only feel it was my fault because I should have gotten help. And I didn't cut her up. If you give me a lie test, you'll see I didn't!"

Arnold said he felt sorry and depressed because of what he had done to his niece. He said he couldn't eat. Still, he seemed calm and his voice remained flat and void of emotion.

Arnold Brown was charged with aggravated murder in the first degree, a capital crime in Washington State. There were many legal battles ahead, and his family stuck by him as always. Even his sister and brother-in-law, Jannie's parents, sent word that they were behind him. Once more, he was forgiven for having committed an unthinkable crime. The family retained Tony Savage, one of Seattle's top-ranked criminal defense attorneys.

Preliminary hearings began before King County Superior Court Judge Liem Tuai in mid-September 1981. The crux of the defense's argument was that the statements given by Arnold's cell mate, his own oral and written confessions, and his previous criminal history should not be admissible evidence. King County Deputy Prosecutor Rebecca Roe held that all of the above were part and parcel of the case at hand. They showed who Arnold Brown really was and what his obsessions were.

Judge Tuai ruled that the conviction for the stabbing of the Coleman children would not be admissible during the trial phase, but that Arnold's statements made to his cell mate would be, notably the alleged admission that he had killed Summer Rogers. It took five days to select a jury of eight women and five men. It would be a bifurcated trial: if the jurors found Arnold Brown guilty, there would be a second part of the trial, where they could decide whether he should be sentenced to life in prison without possibility of parole, or whether he should die by hanging or lethal injection.

Arnold sat throughout his trial with one hand to his face, which remained vacant of emotion as the prosecution presented devastating evidence against him. The proceedings took only two days: Defense Attorney Tony Savage presented no witnesses. He didn't deny that Brown had killed Jannie Reilly. He attempted only to remove the premeditation portion of the charges and thus save Arnold Brown from death.

The jury returned a verdict of guilty. The penalty phase of the trial began. In the second segment, prior bad acts committed by Arnold Brown were admissible. His long record of vicious crimes against children spilled out. Some jurors showed shock as they heard Arnold's history of sexually aberrant offenses. They even heard from some of his victims.

Maria Coleman, who had survived the thrusts of Arnold's hunting knife, was twenty-one now, but she broke into tears as she described what had happened to her and her younger brother, Jimmy. "We went down to the Willamette River to get some crawdads for Jimmy's show-and-tell at school," she said softly. "My little brother found a hatchet in the river, and I carried it for him when we walked through the woods on the way home."

It was clear that Maria was reliving the terror of that day. "We heard some noise in the bushes," she told the jury, "but there were always birds and animals in there, so we kept walking. All of a sudden, everything went really blurry. I was just standing there and I saw this figure in front of me. I threw the hatchet at it. I remember yelling, 'Please stop!' I looked for my little brother and I ran to the house that was nearby. I collapsed there and people came out to help. Then my mom came down, and I remember the ride to the hospital. I was in the hospital for about a week." The knife had been plunged into the children's bodies so swiftly that they had no warning. It was a scene reminiscent of the movie, *Psycho*.

Jimmy Coleman—eight years old at the time of the attack—told the jury much the same story. He remembered only "a flash of silver" before he and Maria ran blindly to a house where he remembered a woman who began to scream when she saw the blood on their chests.

Summer Rogers's mother took the stand to recall the day her five-year-old daughter vanished. Stoically, she identified the remnants of the bloodstained blue-and-white bathing suit found on Summer's torso.

One of the few times Arnold Brown showed any emotion came when his former cell mate took the stand. He was visibly startled when the man recounted the confession Arnold gave him in the King County jail a few days after Jannie's death.

"He said he was going fishing and had seen Summer Rogers," the witness said, "and she asked him where he was going. He said 'Fishing' and she asked to go along . . . She went, and they were down by the river, and she wasn't looking at him, and he hit her in the head and cut her up—cut her head off, and her arms and legs off. . . . He [said] he threw the knife away in the rapids and then went fishing in another part of the river."

But there was still no way to prove that Summer Rogers's killer had actually dismembered her; Jim Pex, a forensic expert from the Oregon State Police Crime

Lab, testified that the loss of Summer's head and limbs was consistent with advanced decomposition of a body immersed in water for a long time.

Of all the testimony given in the effort to spare Arnold Brown's life, the most heartrending came from his sister and brother-in-law, Jannie's adoptive parents. Lorraine Reilly could not bring herself to testify in person; her image appeared on videotape. She begged the jury to save Arnold's life, not because he was her brother but because she did not believe in the death penalty: "If the jury takes his life, Jannie will have died in vain. I can't live with that."

She said she did not want her son to grow up knowing that the uncle he loved, who had always been so good to him, and who had killed Jannie "in sickness," was to be killed himself.

Her plea made little sense. Jannie Reilly *had* died in vain, no matter what became of the uncle who had killed her.

Joseph Reilly told the jury that as long as there was life, there was still hope that good could come of it. He too pleaded for Brown's life and wept when he finished his statement.

But Arnold Brown sat stonily, as he had throughout all the proceedings. He scarcely glanced at his brother-in-law. The Reillys had demonstrated the ultimate in turning the other cheek. But the vital question hung in the courtroom: If Arnold Brown had not been forgiven and released so often, how many lives might have been spared horrible physical and emotional damage? How many victims might have been spared?

Many, many individuals with IQ's in Arnold's range are able to marry, raise families, work successfully at jobs, and bring credit to their communities. They feel guilt and pain and empathy for others. It would take a team of brilliant psychiatrists to explain why Arnold Brown's psyche developed in such a warped fashion and why he struck out at helpless children when he felt frustrated. Arnold Brown knew right from wrong, but he had been allowed to think that he was special, and he had soon learned that there were ways around the law. His family paid a terrible price for their indulgence.

If Brown was to receive the death penalty, the jury's decision would have to be unanimous. After much deliberation, ten jurors voted for the death penalty. The other two could not. On October 23, 1981, Arnold Brown was sentenced to life in prison without the possibility of parole. The majority of the jurors expressed sympathy for the Reillys' pleas for mercy but said they could not spare Brown on that basis alone. Their deeper sympathies lay with the little girl who had died at the age of seven, strangled by the hands of a man she had loved and trusted.

As Judge Tuai meted out the life sentence, he looked at Arnold Brown and said, "Consider yourself a very fortunate young man, having received this sentence rather than the alternative."

Clad in the bright red jail coveralls worn by high-risk felons, Arnold took the sentencing quietly, shifting from one foot to another. Asked if he wished to say something, he shook his head.

"You realize this is your last chance to talk to me?" Judge Tuai asked, but Arnold still refused to speak. He had never murmured a word during the trial, and he would not talk now. He was removed from the courtroom and placed in one of seven single cells in the jail's mental health unit in the Public Safety Building, a precaution because he had been harassed by other inmates in the general population. He was interviewed by a psychiatrist and a psychiatric social worker and found to be subdued but basically stable emotionally.

He was not.

Arnold Brown had been incarcerated before, but this time he probably knew that his chances of surviving inside the walls after the other convicts learned of his crimes were slight. He must have known he was a pariah. Perhaps he could not bear the thought of never going free, of never seeing his dog Queenie again; he seemed to find something in the companionship of animals that he never realized with people.

There may well have been ghosts haunting him in his cell, memories of the children he had injured and killed.

Prisoners in the jail's mental health unit were looked in on every fifteen minutes, but Arnold took advantage of seven minutes of solitude. Eight minutes after a check, he fashioned a noose from the sheet on his bed and hanged himself. Paramedics could not revive him.

Arnold Brown left several suicide letters—to his attorney, to a Catholic priest, to his parents, and "To Whom It May Concern." The contents of those letters are sealed and will never be revealed in their entirety, but some of his thoughts were published in the newspaper. He wrote, "I didn't mean for her to die, but when that feeling came over me, I somehow couldn't control myself."

Although he didn't know the terms that described his sickness, in his own words Arnold admitted in his last letters that he was an addicted pedophile. He had seen a picture of children in a magazine, and his eyes had gone out of focus as he was seized with a terrible headache, "something a little worse than a migraine," he wrote. "That's when it started to happen."

A Dangerous Mind

It may be that Arnold Brown was born without the restraints that normal humans have; he may not have possessed the ability to resist a strong impulse. In the end, he gave himself the sentence that a jury could not bring itself to hand down. If only he had confided his bizarre fantasies to the many psychiatrists who tried to understand his behavior while he lived, he might well have provided a key to treat other pedophiles—but he left only those last vague letters. With his suicide, a deadly siege ended. Arnold Brown, at least, would do no further harm.

To Kill and Kill Again

A decade before Arnold Brown was sentenced to life in prison, a similar drama played out in the King County Courthouse. The nineteen-year-old defendant in this case was an exception to the long-held belief that multiple murderers tend to stalk similar victims, repeatedly seeking out the same kind of quarry. This killer did, however, represent a frightening category of murderers who kill simply for the sake of killing. Because he varied his choice of victims, he was all the more difficult to trap. Nothing connected his four victims, save for the fact that each of them vanished suddenly and inexplicably. They were seen, and then they were not seen, until their bodies were found in wooded areas.

Although the media are quick to publicize profiles and categories, it's always a mistake to describe murderers too narrowly. Aberrant behavior can never be forced into a box with tight parameters, no matter how many criminologists try to predict what a particular subject will do. By its very definition, aberration means "a deviation from the norm."

Among the felons I have written about, I never found one as unpredictable as this one. Anyone could have been his victim—anyone who was alone and unaware of who was following.

It was a hot August day in 1969 Seattle and the sun was shining on Elliott Bay as the ferries crisscrossed the sparkling water, heading for Bainbridge Island, Vashon Island, and Bremerton. Only four blocks up the hill from the bay, in room W-863 of the massive gray King County Courthouse, Judge David W. Soukup was presiding over a trial that was drawing more spectators than any procedure in the past two years. The proceedings cast a pall of loss and pathos over officers of the court and spectators alike.

The selection of any jury is a tedious procedure, but the senseless killings of four young people in Renton, Washington, had received so much television and newspaper coverage that it seemed unlikely that thirteen registered voters—one of whom would be an alternate juror—who hadn't already formed an opinion about the defendant's guilt or innocence, could be found. Indeed, over a hundred prospective jurors were questioned before a full jury panel was chosen.

Compared to Seattle, Renton is a small town in King County. Even so, its population burgeoned over the years, mostly because of the number of workers drawn by the Boeing Airplane Company plant located at the edge of Lake Washington. Renton is an unpretentious suburb, much of it built on hilly land rising for miles to the east above the lake, or spilling south on flat land that drifts toward the Green River Valley. There used to be coal mines southeast of Seattle, and there are still abandoned mines near Renton, but the ore veins ran out many decades ago. By 2000, there would be 46,000 people in Renton; when the horrific crimes took place, there were half that many. The biggest distinction Renton had in the seventies and eighties was its loop, which drew high school drivers who circled for hours on weekend nights. Second to that was the Renton Public Library, part of which was actually built over the rushing Cedar River.

But beginning in December 1969, Renton took on another—very unwelcome—distinction. Its citizens moved through a holiday season chilled with dread. Even while Christmas lights swung in the wind over the downtown streets, a killer moved like a wraith among them, leaving victims along isolated pathways. There were scant clues for Renton police detectives to follow up. In truth, they didn't know if they were looking for one suspect or several.

Carole Adele Erickson was nineteen years old on December 15, 1969. She was a pretty girl with huge aqua-colored eyes, long shiny hair, and a slender figure. Carole worked in a local restaurant to help pay for courses in food preparation at the Renton Vocational School. On that chilly, dank evening in December, she left a note for her roommate, saying that she planned to do some research on a school project at the Renton Library. She said she would probably be home early.

Carole went to the library—there was no question of that. She was seen there by the librarians who knew her. But when one of her former boyfriends, who was home on furlough from the army, went there to surprise her, he couldn't find her. He got to the library a little after 7:00 P.M. and walked through the entire building looking for Carole. He even zigzagged between the stacks, where she sometimes preferred to study.

Assuming she had left for home, he went to her cottage to wait for her. He sat there making polite conversation and then strained conversation with Carole's roommate as the minutes ticked by. He was really anxious to see Carole, but hours passed and there was no sign of her. Finally he and her roommate decided she must have had a date. The young soldier finally left. "Tell Carole I'll call her before I go back," he said.

Carole's roommate went to bed only moderately concerned. She fell asleep quickly, unaware that the night was passing and Carole had not come home.

Well before daylight the next morning, two fishermen drove onto the rutted road that ran along the bank of the Cedar River north of the library building. The road ended abruptly and became a gravel footpath. They parked their vehicle, grabbed their fishing gear, and walked about twenty-five feet up the path, squinting through the murky light. Suddenly they stopped as they saw a motionless figure lying several feet off the path. It was half hidden in some brush and looked like a store mannequin. Moving closer, they could see that it was a partially clad young woman. She appeared to be either dead or unconscious. The fishermen ran to their car, drove to a nearby service station, and telephoned the police.

Renton Patrol Officer Dave Smith responded to the call. He touched his fingertips to the fallen girl's neck and felt no reassuring pulse in her carotid artery. Her skin was as cold as the ground beneath her. She was dead, and probably had been for several hours. Smith called the detective division of the Renton Police Department and reached Detective Don Dashnea, who had just reported for duty. Dashnea hurried to the death scene, which was only a few blocks from police headquarters. By 7:30 A.M. a complete crew of Renton detectives had joined him.

The dead girl lay on her back, her legs spread-eagled, her arms thrown above her head. Fresh scuff marks in the dirt formed a trail between the path and her body, suggesting that she had been dragged to where she lay. She wore only a long-sleeved yellow sweater, a bra, and white socks. A single scarlet stain was visible on her white bra and in a startlingly macabre touch, leather shoelaces were wound tightly around her neck.

While waiting for King County deputy medical examiners to arrive, the officers searched the immediate area meticulously. Detective Arnold Huebner found a school notebook. Inside it, someone had written directions for the preparation of an international dinner. There was also a letter, written in the same neat hand, which was dated only the night before and signed "Carole." It was addressed to another woman, who said she was "in the library doing homework."

The Renton detectives located a pair of rain-soaked women's jeans and some panties in the brush near the body, along with a pair of women's shoes. The shoes had no laces.

It wasn't long before they found a wallet, as sodden with rain as the clothing was. It contained pictures and a driver's license for Carole Adele Erickson. The picture on the license resembled the face of the dead girl, but it was difficult to be positive.

The officers thought they knew who she was; they had no idea how she had come to be abandoned on the riverbank.

Don Dashnea and E. A. McKenney drove to the address listed on the license but found no one at home. Another officer said he knew the Erickson family—the man who lived there was probably at his job as a custodian in a nearby factory. There was a teenage girl in the family. They found the father at work and told him they needed someone to identify the body of a young female. The anguished man accompanied the detectives to the King County morgue. There he nodded silently as he looked at the body of the victim. It was, indeed, his nineteen-year-old daughter, Carole Adele.

He gave the detectives a studio portrait of his daughter. Seeing a clear image of Carole, several detectives were startled to realize that they recognized her; she had often served them at lunches hosted by the foods preparation department at the vocational school. Because the students were graded on how well they cooked and on their presentations, the lunches were popular with the police department—great food for a reasonable price.

One of the detectives recalled Carole: "She was very vivacious, always friendly, with a smile for everyone."

Neither her father nor her roommate could imagine any reason why someone would want to kill Carole. Her roommate knew that Carole routinely used the riverside path to reach their cottage from the library because it was an easy shortcut.

Don Dashnea read again the last letter Carole had written and looked up to say, "She wasn't afraid of anything; she had no idea in the world what lay outside. This was a letter to a close friend. If she was worried or afraid about anything, surely she would have mentioned it. Instead, all we've got here is a rough timetable of the last few minutes of her life. She finished this letter and then she took the shortcut home."

Arnold Huebner walked the path between the library and Carole's cottage and checked his watch. At a reasonable pace, the walk took seven minutes. Although many people used the shortcut, several nearby residents said they considered it dangerous because the path was hidden from view by dense underbrush. They had, in fact, asked the city to clear the brush away. The detectives already knew that; with grim synchronicity, a work crew had arrived that morning to chop down the underbrush, only to find detectives already there, processing the murder scene. If they had cut down the thicket a day earlier, the young woman might still have been alive.

It was almost impossible for the investigators to cast plaster moulages of tire marks on the path because of the gravel surface. But they did note that a car—probably a foreign model with very small tires—had been near the body site. They cast those tracks the best they could, hoping they might one day have a suspect's car to compare them with.

At eleven o'clock that morning, Dr. Gale Wilson, medical examiner for King County, performed an autopsy on Carole Erickson's body. Carole was 5 feet 6 and weighed 126 pounds. Oddly, she had suffered only one severe injury. Someone had plunged a knife into the middle of her back, causing a deep, thrusting wound that had severed her seventh rib and pushed the rib into her chest cavity. The knife then penetrated the lower lobe of her right lung and entered the right atrium of her heart. According to Dr. Wilson, such a wound would have caused her to collapse at once and die within five minutes.

There were two constriction marks caused by the leather shoelaces tied around her neck. They were deep enough to cut into the flesh, but the larynx beneath had not been fractured. Save for a small abrasion on her upper lip, there were no other wounds on the victim's body and no defense wounds to indicate that she had fought her attacker.

The vaginal examination indicated evidence of rape and the presence of viable sperm. "It could have been deposited there just before—or just after—death," Wilson said.

Dr. Wilson set the approximate time of death at 9:00 P.M. on December 15, fourteen hours before the postmortem examination. It looked as if someone had dealt Carole Erickson a fatal blow as he came up behind her on the path. If he had approached her from the front, surely she would have fought him, but there was no evidence that she had. She was slender, but she wasn't a small girl; she could have put up a fight. Sexual intercourse had taken place—but it had not been consensual intercourse.

Women reading about Carole's murder were afraid. How terrible to be walking along a dark path where no one could help you, where the sound of the river would drown out screams. Even after the brush was cut down, the shortcut to the library no longer attracted walkers; they now preferred to take the longer—safer—route.

The Renton detectives launched a massive manhunt, following up on leads they obtained from Carole's school and work associates. A picture of Carole was printed in local papers along with a request for information from anyone who might have seen her on the day she died. There were many responses, but most of them were from people who meant well but who had little useful information.

Some of the people who worked at the restaurant with her recalled that Carole had argued with her current boyfriend on the very day she died. She told her co-workers that they had had words when he drove her to work that afternoon. Dashnea and Huebner were very much interested to learn that Carole's current boyfriend drove a small foreign car. They questioned him about his activities on December 15. Regretful now that his last moments with Carole had been angry, he explained that their quarrel was brief and over something silly. He said he'd been with several friends throughout the evening. When the detectives checked, they found that he was telling the truth.

Even more interesting was a fellow student of Carole's at Renton Vocational Tech. Her friends described him as "very shy, afraid of girls." He apparently had a crush on Carole. "He got up his nerve once," one girl told Dashnea, "and he wrote her a really corny note, like 'Meet me tonight. I'll be wearing a white carnation.' That kind of thing. She didn't go, but he still acted like he was spaced out about her."

Investigators found the lovesick student. He was certainly nervous and very unhappy about Carole's death, but he assured them that he had nothing at all to do with her murder. He was appalled that they would think he would ever hurt her. He agreed to take a polygraph examination to back up his claim. The test, administered by Seattle Police polygraphist Dewey Gillespie, supported his protestations of innocence. He was telling the truth.

With the cooperation of the Renton Library, the detectives began a tedious search. With no other clues to go on, they could only wonder if someone had seen Carole in the library and decided to follow her down the gravel path when she left. Now they copied down the names of every patron who visited the library on December 15. They found that *eight hundred* people had passed through the library on the day Carole was killed. Was the killer somewhere on that list?

Their meticulous backtracking eased—if only for the moment—when a man came forward in response to an appeal for information. "I think it's possible that I saw that girl's killer just before it happened," he said. "My son and I were driving along the river at dusk on December 15."

Huebner and Dashnea showed him a photograph of Carole Erickson, and he was sure she was the girl he had seen on the path. But he had also seen a man—a man who was walking several feet behind her. "I doubt that she even knew he was there," the eyewitness recalled. "He was an adult, I think. Over twenty-one, anyway. He was a white man with dark hair combed straight back and a pompadour in front. He wore a long-sleeved windbreaker jacket and 'Beatle' boots that came up over his trouser cuffs. I'm sure he was aware of me because he ducked his head and turned his face away when he saw me."

The man regretted now that he hadn't warned the girl, but he had no idea she was in danger. Working with a Seattle Police Department artist, he described the man he'd seen on the river path. Gradually, a composite sketch emerged. It was done in profile, the angle at which he'd seen the man. That was all he could recall, at least consciously. He readily agreed to submit to a session with a hypnotist in the hope that there was more information locked in his memory that he might be able to tap into. Disappointingly, the hypnosis elicited no further information.

Working on the theory that murderers seldom report for work the day after their crimes, the Renton detectives obtained absentee reports from the Boeing Company for December 16. Their murder investigation took place well before the computer era. A computer would have made their search much easier, but the principle of winnowing out non-suspects was the same. First, they eliminated all females, then non-Caucasians, and finally individuals whose age didn't match that of the man on the path. The names that were left were matched against the eight hundred library patrons. Names that popped up on both lists were examined and culled. In the end, they questioned more than two hundred individuals and arranged for ten polygraph examinations.

Despite their efforts, the name they were seeking didn't drop out of the mass of information. A sad Christmas passed, and the identity of Carole Adele Erickson's slayer remained a mystery.

All through the spring and summer that followed, the investigation continued with no tangible results. By fall, reports on the investigation of Carole Erickson's murder were relegated to occasional newspaper updates. For everyone but those who had loved her, her murder was old news—but the Renton detectives still followed every possible lead that came their way.

Seventeen-year-old Joann Marie Zulauf, who lived just outside the Renton city limits, felt no trepidation about taking a late Sunday afternoon walk by herself on September 20. The pretty teenager waved to a neighbor before she turned onto a deeply wooded path, one of many that crisscrossed a ravine in the Renton Highlands that led down to Honey Creek. The neighbor watched the blue-jean-clad teenager disappear into the trees, waited a few moments, and then himself headed down one of the sylvan trails. He didn't see Joann, but he didn't think anything about it; the area was a jungle of blackberry bushes, alder saplings, and evergreens as the path meandered down to the creek.

In fact, he didn't think of Joann again until hours later, when her worried parents began to search the neighborhood and asked him if he had seen her. The Sunday dinner hour had come and gone and the tiny brunette girl had not come home. The night passed and the sun rose without anyone finding any sign of Joann. Her mother and stepfather and neighbors searched steadily for twenty-four hours.

King County Police Deputy Les Moffett talked with her family and was convinced that this was more than a typical runaway-teenager case. He talked to his patrol sergeant, George Helland, who agreed that the sheriff's office should get involved. Search-and-Rescue Explorer Scouts arrived in teams, along with search dogs whose handlers would work them in grid patterns throughout the ravine area.

"It was like a maze," one of the searchers said. "The dogs would run again and again to a dead end. Once my dog began to howl and sniff up in the air. I even looked up in the treetops, but there was nothing."

He was relieved that there was nothing there. Experienced search dog handlers know that sometimes dead things on the ground send odors into the trees. When dogs look up, it is usually bad news.

Thirty hours after Joann began her walk in Hidden Valley down to Honey Creek, the search ended. Clyde Reed, a member of the Washington search-and-rescue group, followed his bloodhound's throaty whoops, his mind full of dread because he knew what the sound meant.

Joann Zulauf lay sprawled in a depressed wash area next to the path she had taken on Sunday afternoon. She was naked, but oddly someone had piled her neatly folded clothing on top of her.

The sheriff's deputies and detectives were summoned from where they were combing other areas of the ravine. Les Moffett arrived first. Knowing that it was useless, he nevertheless checked for signs of life and found Joann's body "very, very, cold." He backed away and summoned Homicide Detectives Ron Sensenbach and Robert Schmitz.

It was full dark now, and the detectives had to use their flashlights to see the dead girl. The sweep of the lights gave them enough illumination to see that her face was grotesquely swollen and purple. In all likelihood, she had been strangled. They could see bruises on her forehead and dried blood in her hair on the right side of her head.

It was after midnight in the tangled woods and there was little they could do in the pitch-black ravine but guard the scene and wait for the first rays of daylight.

Deputy Michael Temcof stood by the body all night in the chill rain. It was a bleak and lonely vigil. The roped-off area had to be kept sacrosanct; they didn't dare risk missing some vital bit of evidence that even the high-powered auxiliary lighting might have missed.

At dawn, the King County detectives processed the scene thoroughly, searching it literally inch by inch. But they found no leads to the slayer's identity. They cut blaze marks into the surrounding trees for the triangulation measurements that would allow them to pinpoint the precise site of the body long after it was removed.

The postmortem examination of Joann Zulauf's body seemed to substantiate the detectives' first impression. The autopsy indicated that she had succumbed to asphyxiation, probably manual. Like Carole Erickson, Joann had sustained an injury from some force behind her. Dr. Gale Wilson discovered a V-shaped laceration on the back of her head just below her right ear.

Although Joann had been a virgin with an intact hymen, the pathologist noted bruising at the vaginal entrance where rape was attempted. She had apparently been dragged for some distance, probably by the arms, just as Carole had. It wouldn't have taken much effort to drag Joann: she was only 5 feet 2 and weighed 113 pounds.

Now, eight months after the investigation into Carole Erickson's murder, another urgent plea went out to the public; the police needed information—anything, even if it seemed unimportant. And again there were precious few useful responses. Some tips verged on the bizarre. A woman called Renton detective Wally Hume to say that she had talked to a mystic on a Puget Sound ferryboat on the afternoon of the Sunday Joann disappeared. The man had suddenly become very agitated. "Then he told me that there had been another murder in Renton!" she reported.

The man might have been clairvoyant, or he might have been putting on an act to impress the woman. Or he might have been a 220, as Seattle area detectives call mental cases. At any rate, the man was many miles away from Renton when Joann Zulauf was killed. There was no way he could have committed the murder himself, and the woman on the phone didn't even know his name or how to find him.

Homicide detectives grow weary of psychic reports that come in after the details of sensational crimes have been published in the newspapers. While most good detectives will consider *any* avenue that might help, it is the rare seer who is able to offer precise details that will allow them to find a killer—or a body.

King County Police Sergeant George Helland was placed in charge of the investigation. He talked to Joann's relatives and friends, but he could find nothing at all in her life that might have marked her as a target for violence. She was only seventeen; she had no enemies; she'd been in no arguments. She was a lovely young woman, all alone in the woods. *That* was probably what had made her a target for someone who hid and watched her from the shadows. She had the great bad luck to have crossed a murderer's path when he was in a killing phase of his aberration.

Joann's mother went through the ordeal of checking the clothes found with her daughter's body. The clothes she had been wearing when she left for her Sunday walk were all there, but her watch was missing. It was her sixteenth birthday gift—a white metal watch, with the brand name Lucien Perreaux. Her mother was positive Joann had been wearing the watch when she left for her last walk. She never went anyplace without it.

Helland issued a bulletin to area pawnshops in an effort to locate the missing watch. It did not turn up.

The investigation continued—just as the Erickson investigation had never really stopped. All of the police agencies in King and neighboring counties pooled their information on the two cases but their leads ended in midair.

Fall and winter passed and by the third week in April trilliums, forsythia, and dogwood dominated the woods and fields of western Washington. April 20 was a school holiday in Renton due to a teachers' conference. In the southern end of town, two six-year-old boys, who were fast friends and spent most of their waking moments together, began their day. Bradley Lyons got up at eight and ate the bacon and eggs his mother prepared for him. He rode with her and his sister to the lumberyard to pick up some boards for a home project. Then he changed into black rubber boots and a quilted green jacket and headed for his friend Scott Andrews's house.

Scott, who had wanted only a bowl of Alphabits for breakfast, waited impatiently for his socks to come out of the dryer. Then he too donned black rubber boots and a jacket much like Bradley's and headed out to play. He was back in at eleven to ask for cookies "for the kids," then left again with a handful of them.

The boys played for a while on a dirt pile near Scott's house and then left to go to the Lyons's backyard. It was a fascinating yard for six-year-old boys because it disappeared into a woods rife with trails, potholes, and marshy areas.

A little before noon, Scott's mother called Brad's mom to ask her if she had seen the boys. Their laughter had carried on the air all morning, and their mothers had watched them from their kitchen windows, but now they were nowhere in sight. The mothers looked around the usual spots, but they were not frightened yet; they both expected Brad and Scott to come running around the corners of their houses at any moment. Theirs was a family neighborhood full of kids who ran between the streets and cul-de-sacs all the time. They were a long way from fast roads and commercial areas.

But the boys didn't come home for lunch. Now neighbors passed the word that they were missing, and those who were home hurried out to help look for them.

Before long the police were notified and a full-scale search was organized.

Once again, the Explorer Scouts, tracking dogs, helicopters, and police and sheriffs' patrols gathered. They combed six square miles for the missing boys. Residents in the neighborhood were asked to check boats and trailers, car trunks, sheds, abandoned refrigerators—anyplace where the youngsters might have become trapped. Along with a growing number of civilian volunteers, forty members of the Spring Glen Fire Department joined the massive search.

But that Tuesday night passed without a trace of Brad or Scott, and the search teams continued around the clock. Wednesday and Wednesday night went by and the first graders were still missing. There is no way to even imagine the terror in their families' hearts. The friendly woods seemed menacing now. The spring storms had flooded swamps and potholes deep enough so that a child could drown. Even though Brad and Scott had been warned over and over not to go near creeks and ponds, the searchers checked virtually every deep puddle, with negative results.

Two days after the boys were last seen and two miles away, weary searchers came upon a child's clothing: shirt, jeans, undershorts, and socks, but their frantic parents could not identify the clothing as belonging to either Bradley or Scott. Next, someone spotted small footprints leading to an abandoned gravel pit a mile away. And yet, when the flooded pit was dragged, they found nothing at all.

Much of the search area was choked with wild evergreen ground cover: salal, sword ferns, vine maple saplings, huckleberry bushes, and deadfall logs encircled with bindweed and blackberry vines. Just beyond the recently constructed homes the woods were almost as impenetrable as they had been when the pioneers first came to the Northwest. It was tough going for volunteers but none of them quit as the days dragged by at an agonizing pace.

It was early evening on Thursday, April 22, when a volunteer fireman spotted something that made him catch his breath; it was what they had all feared. A small boy clothed in a striped T-shirt lay as if asleep in a shallow dip in the woods. The firefighter called his team leader, who signaled the group to stay back as he walked carefully around the depressed area. Both of the missing boys lay in front of him, partially covered with ferns and soil. He felt the youngsters' chests for any signs of life. There were none.

The firefighters secured the area and put out a radio call to both the King County Police and the Renton Police Department. Sheriff's Deputy Richard A. Nicholiason arrived first, followed shortly by Sergeant Helland. The gully where the boys lay was determined to be within Renton city limits and the Renton detectives who had investigated Carole Erickson's death responded. Don Dashnea, Arnold Huebner, Harold Caldwell, and I.D. expert Joe Henry hurried to the tragic scene in the woods.

Both bodies were partially nude. Bradley Lyons lay on his back, the striped T-shirt pulled up under his chin, his trousers lying across his chest. A venetian-blind cord, used as a ligature, was knotted tightly around his neck.

Scott Andrews was lying facedown, his Jockey shorts twisted around his ankles. A bloodstained T-shirt had been knotted around his neck. What looked like knife wounds marked his chest and neck. It was apparent the boys had been dead for some time.

As daylight faded, floodlights were brought in. Dashnea and Caldwell removed the items of clothing found at the scene and placed them in sealed plastic bags. Joe Henry took a series of photographs leading from the entrance to the trail down to the body site.

Assured that searchers had not approached the bodies closely except for the team leader's one cautious check for signs of life, the detectives were intrigued by a set of large footprints left in a distinctive circular pattern around the bodies. They immediately made moulages of the prints.

They began an intensive search for a knife or other weapon that might have been used on Scott Andrews, but neither their eyes nor metal detectors located one.

Early the next morning, the detectives from Renton attended the postmortem examinations on the small victims. The investigation of the murder of a child is always the hardest assignment any homicide detective can have. The cops braced themselves and tried to think clinically, fighting back the normal emotions that any father would have felt in the same situation.

Six-year-old Bradley Lyons had died of asphyxia secondary to ligature from the venetian blind cord. He also had bruises on his lips. Based on the contents of his stomach and the progression of rigor mortis in the body, Dr. Wilson estimated that Bradley had died between 12:30 and 1:30 P.M. on April 20, the last day he was seen. Although there were no overt injuries to his genitals, Dr. Wilson found a twig and a hair in the rectum.

Scott Andrews had contusions on his forehead, left cheek, and lips. There were fabric imprints on his neck from the knotted T-shirt, but the underlying tissue had neither hemorrhaging nor constriction enough to cause suffocation. He *had* sustained three knife wounds. One, just beneath the left collarbone, had penetrated only 1.5 centimeters. The other two wounds, however, were fatal wounds where the knife had slashed through the lung and heart to a depth of 4½ inches, ending at the vertebrae just below the skin of the boy's back.

Death would have been virtually instantaneous. There was no evidence that Scott had been sexually molested. Like Brad, he had been dead since shortly after noon on Tuesday.

With the massive media coverage that followed the discovery of the two six-year-olds, tips flooded in. Doctors in the ER at Valley General Hospital in Renton reported that a rather bizarre forty-year-old man with a long beard had presented himself to the emergency room on the afternoon of April 20 and asked for help with mental problems. He feared that he "might harm children" and told a rambling story where he compared his emotional problems to Charles Manson's.

ER personnel said the man had numerous scratches on his arms, lower legs, and forehead. He explained that he had scratched himself while running through the brush. Still, at the time, he seemed harmless enough. He was released from the hospital and he vanished. Was he the killer or was he just another compulsive confessor?

After yet another request for help from the public, Renton detectives learned that the bearded suspect had asked for a drink of water at a home and at a business some three to five miles from the body site around 4:30 P.M. on April 20. Then he had checked into the ER at 5:22 P.M.

He seemed the perfect suspect in a pedophiliac homicide. Detectives located him in Tacoma. His name was Antoine Bertrand,* and he was forty years old. Bertrand was interrogated about the murders of Brad and Scott, but either he truly knew nothing about them or he had experienced a complete memory block. He looked baffled and said he had no idea what they were talking about. He hadn't seen any little boys.

The King County prosecutor's office charged Antoine Bertrand with two counts of murder, based on a mass of circumstantial evidence, his proximity to the crime scene at the time Scott and Brad died, and his own feeling that he might hurt children. However, any prudent prosecutor wants physical evidence, and there was nothing concrete linking Antoine Bertrand to the young victims.

The search for the knife that had caused Scott's death continued. On April 28, an Explorer search-and-rescue scout, Emmett Husa, age seventeen, combed the ravine on his hands and knees some 150 feet from the spot where Scott and Bradley were found. And there it was—a bowie knife with a heavy curved blade—nestled beneath the salal and vine maple leaves. The handle of the knife was wrapped with black friction tape.

Renton detectives examined the handle. They could barely make out a name scratched lightly into the surface. They contacted the young man whose name was on the knife.

"Yeah, I used to own that knife," he said. "I bought it for a dollar fifty and kept it until August of 1970. Then I sold it to a friend of mine."

Officers Wally Hume and Jim Phelan talked to the friend. He said he owned the knife for only a couple of months. "I traded it to this guy."

"Who?"

"Some guy. He gave me a pea coat for it."

Wondering how long this trail was going to be, Hume and Phelan located yet a third teenager.

"Yeah, I had a bowie knife," he said. "But I only had

it for about two weeks. Around Christmas of 1970 I left it in my friend's truck."

"What's his name?" Hume asked wearily.

"Gary Grant. He gave me a ride and I absentmindedly left it on the seat of his truck. When I asked him about it, he said his father had found it in the truck and put it in his room and that he couldn't get it back right away. I never did get it back."

On April 30, Hume and Phelan drove to the trailer park where nineteen-year-old Gary Grant lived with his parents. Gary wasn't there. His mother said he was getting a haircut.

"We want to talk to him about a knife he owns."

"He'll be home pretty soon. You can wait for him if you want to."

It wasn't long before a pickup truck pulled in front of the mobile home. A tall, skinny teenager stepped out and walked toward the detectives.

"You're Gary?" Jim Phelan asked.

"Yes, sir."

"We understand a friend of yours left a bowie knife in your truck not too long ago," Phelan said.

Grant nodded a little nervously. "I had it, but I guess I left it out in the woods—out back of the park here."

He was neither cooperative nor antagonistic, but the pimply-faced teenager wasn't sure if he would be able to find the knife in the woods. He did, however, agree to go to Renton Police headquarters to talk with the detectives about it.

Once there, Phelan pulled out a photograph of the bowie knife where it lay in the underbrush near the crime site.

"That look like yours?"

Phelan and Hume watched the suspect's face as he

stared at the photo. "It looks like that knife I had," he said finally.

Gary Grant was wearing tennis shoes. Jim Phelan tried to appear casual as Grant rested one foot on his knee and the sole came into view. It had a circular pattern that was very similar to the prints found surrounding Brad's and Scott's bodies.

The configuration was close enough for Phelan to ask Gary Grant to take his shoes off so they could be compared to the moulages locked in the evidence room.

Wally Hume advised the quiet teenager of his constitutional rights and asked Grant if he recalled April 20. Grant said he remembered it because it was a school holiday. Odd that he would recall that, since he was no longer in school himself. He said he worked that morning at his part-time job at a Renton golf course. "After that," he said, "I stopped in to see one of my girlfriends."

"After that?"

"I went looking to buy some shoes. I must have been to about three stores. Didn't find what I wanted."

From there Grant said he walked along the Cedar River. Wally Hume studied Grant. He was kind of an ungainly kid, slow-talking and average-looking except that he slicked down his dark hair with water or hair cream and combed it straight back from his forehead without parting it.

Grant said he also remembered that day in April well because he had a close call. "I was standing close to the river to watch the salmon, but it was really muddy on the bank and I slipped and fell in. I floated down the river for about forty feet until I could get my footing and climb on shore. I was soaking wet and I stopped at the grocery store and called home. I wanted a ride, but my mom said my dad was taking a nap and told me I had to walk home. So I did."

Wally Hume was a thirteen-year veteran of the Renton Police Department. Amiable and soft-spoken, he was a deceptively low-pressure interrogator. He talked to Gary Grant about why they were interested in his lost knife, quietly moving closer and closer to the vital questions. Approaching the subject from varying angles, Hume asked Gary Grant four or five times if he knew anything about the deaths of the two boys.

Gary Grant was adamant that he did not. He insisted that he was very fond of children and would never hurt them. He didn't even know Brad and Scott and he seemed shocked that anyone would think he would kill two little boys.

They were at an impasse. Hume asked Gary if he would be willing to take a lie detector test, and he said he would.

Dewey Gillespie was respected as one of the most accurate polygraphers on the West Coast. Called at his Seattle Police Department office, he told Hume that he would give Gary a polygraph examination if they would bring him into the city. Wally Hume, Jim Phelan, and Gary left at once for Seattle, but when they got there, Gillespie sent word that he would be tied up in an emergency session for some time.

The Renton detectives felt they were at a breakthrough point with Gary Grant and they certainly didn't want to turn him loose now, so Hume and Phelan headed for a restaurant, where they ordered hamburgers for all three of them. Gary ate heartily. Spinning out the time, they drove out to the University of Washington and through the Arboretum. They might have been three friends out for a pleasant drive. Neither detective

ANN RULE

brought up the subject of the double homicide. Instead, they spoke of innocuous things—the weather, sports. The next questions should come from Dewey Gillespie.

By the time they returned to the waiting area outside Gillespie's office, the two detectives could see that Gary was nervous and apprehensive. Several times he murmured half aloud, as if arguing with himself: "I couldn't have done something like that."

Hume and Phelan were thinking only of the murders of two little boys. Even though Antoine Bertrand was already under arrest for the killings, there was something about Gary Grant and his missing knife that made them wonder if they had arrested the wrong man. If Gary was holding something back, Gillespie would know. The polygraph machine was a formidable device for anyone to face. To the uninformed, it looked as if it could zap its subject with a jolt of electricity if it detected a lie. Leads would measure respiration, blood pressure, pulse, galvanic skin response, perspiration. A number of people are convinced it can somehow read human thought. It is certainly an intimidating machine.

Gary Grant was far from sophisticated, and he was already sweating and mumbling.

When the tests were evaluated, however, it would be the detectives who were shocked. They had no idea when they brought Gary in for a lie detector test that they had netted a much bigger fish than they could have imagined.

In the jargon of the polygrapher, Gary Gene Grant "blew ink all over the walls."

When the information he gave Dewey Gillespie was followed up by more questioning from Renton detectives and a careful reconstruction of his whereabouts in the prior eighteen months, they realized that one man and one man alone was probably responsible not only for the murders of Scott Andrews and Brad Lyons but also for the violent deaths of Carol Adele Erickson and Joann Marie Zulauf.

Grant was not a flamboyant suspect, and that may have made it easier for him to move about Renton without being noticed. He was not in the least memorable. He was something of a loner who had few close friends and who worked at a low-profile job. What rage he carried within himself—and he did carry rage—he kept carefully hidden.

After his encounter with Dewey Gillespie and the polygraph, nineteen-year-old Gary Grant was charged with four counts of first-degree murder. As far as the public knew, he was initially arrested and held only as a material witness in the tragic murders of two six-year-old boys. They would have to wait until his trial to learn the whole story.

In the meantime, charges against Antoine Bertrand, the bearded and rambling man who had walked into the ER at Valley General Hospital, were dropped.

Grant's trial was set for July 6, 1971. Because neither he nor his parents could afford to retain criminal defense attorneys, two of King County's most able lawyers were appointed to defend him. One was C. N. "Nick" Marshall, who had been the senior deputy prosecuting attorney in the King County prosecutor's office until six months before. He was now a partner in his own firm. Marshall had successfully prosecuted some of the most infamous homicide cases in Washington State. The other was James E. Anderson, also a former deputy prosecutor with a solid conviction record. Now the onetime prosecutors would be on the other side in a very challenging defense case.

Judge David Soukup would preside over the trial. His black Abraham Lincoln beard made him look very judge-like, but spectators were sometimes surprised to see him *before* court began as he jogged to trials from his home. Racing through the marble halls of the courthouse in shorts and Nikes, Judge Soukup looked more like a marathon runner than a superior court judge.

Gary Grant's trial was a battlefield of legal experts all trained in the same school. Besides Marshall and Anderson, Judge Soukup, and both prosecuting attorneys—Edmund P. Allen and Michael T. Di Julio—were all either current or former deputy prosecutors. There was an expectant air in the courtroom as the gallery waited to see how the five men, trained to work together, would act in their new roles.

Gary Grant was noticeably thinner than he had appeared in early press photos, and he sat stoically beside Nick Marshall as the prosecution built its case against him. He was gaunt and pale. He gulped silently, his breathing rate increased, and he would occasionally lower his forehead to his hands.

A great deal of the testimony in the Grant trial was painfully explicit. The prosecution produced witness after witness who detailed the last hours of each victim's life. As they spoke, the victims came alive in the courtroom, and the enormity of their loss brought tears. Even Defense Attorney Marshall, who had a five-year-old son of his own, walked quickly from the courtroom during a break and ducked into one of the myriad marble niches to hide the tears streaking his face.

Over the defense's strong objections, the prosecution introduced graphic pictures of the victims' bodies. Medical Examiner Gale Wilson's testimony was lengthy, and Nick Marshall cross-examined him vigorously, particularly on the alleged sexual motivation of the killer. In the Carole Erickson case, he disagreed with Wilson on how precisely the age of sperm can be pinpointed. Wilson replied that it could be done within certain limitations, but he was adamant that viable sperm *can* be present in the vagina from thirty-six to forty-eight hours after intercourse.

In an attempt to suggest to the jurors that Carole had intercourse with someone else before she went to the library the December evening she died, Marshall asked, "Then how can you say whether these sperm found in the Erickson girl were there just before or just after death?"

"If they had been there sometime before death they would have migrated further up the vagina," Wilson said flatly.

"How many did you find?"

"Five or six . . . on the labia at entrance [to the vagina]."

"Could they not have been deposited up to twenty-four hours earlier?"

"No. They would have been further up."

"Then how could you classify this as rape with so few sperm deposited?"

"Imperfect penetration," Wilson answered succinctly.

It seemed a fine point—and it was—but Nick Marshall was trying to save his client from the death penalty; murder committed because the killer had rape in mind tended to influence a jury far more than murder with other motivation.

Again, Marshall took particular issue with Dr. Wilson's statement in direct testimony that Joann Zulauf had succumbed to "asphyxia and attempted rape." He asked for a mistrial because Wilson had included the rape attempt as a cause of death. Judge Soukup denied the mistrial, but during cross-examination Dr. Wilson qualified his statement by saying that the attempted rape was a "condition associated with death."

The most dramatic aspect of Gary Grant's trial was the admission of lengthy taped interviews between Jim Phelan, George Helland, and the suspect. Grant had been informed that his statement was being recorded, but during pretrial hearings, Marshall and Anderson had fought to have these tapes excluded. In a surprising reversal, the defense attorneys themselves introduced the tapes. It was a calculated risk on their part; they wanted to present the defendant as emotionally disturbed but still, Marshall told the jury, "a human being."

The courtroom was hushed as the tapes played for over three hours. Most people never actually hear what goes on during a police interrogation and certainly this jury never had. Hearing the recorded voices of the detectives and the defendant somehow had more power and immediacy for the jury than what was actually going on in front of them in the courtroom.

Wally Hume told the jury that he and Jim Phelan had waited while polygraphist Dewey Gillespie talked with Grant, preparing him for the polygraph. But Gillespie told them that Grant had pulled back and blurted that he didn't want to take the test at all. He would rather tell them what had really happened than be hooked up to all the leads and wires.

"Detective Gillespie walked to the door," Hume recalled. "He said, 'I think this is your man.' "

In his expanded statement on the tape, Grant began his story of the events of April 20 exactly as he originally had told Gillespie. This time, however, he added more to his story.

Gary Grant's voice on the tape explained that after he shopped for shoes, he had somehow found himself on a wooded trail. He began following two small boys, five or six years old. Because he ducked behind trees and foliage, the children were totally unaware that he was behind them. When they came to a "level area," Grant recalled that one of the boys stopped to examine something on the ground while the other walked on ahead. Grant stepped out from the tall brush and told the boy to take off his clothes. The child started to cry and refused. At that point, Grant said he pulled out his knife and the little boy obeyed him, removing his clothes down to his undershorts.

Then Grant said, "I thrusted [*sic*] my knife into him."

The other boy, who had gone on ahead, doubled back on the trail and saw his friend lying on the ground. Grant said he pulled a cord out of his pocket and wrapped it around the second boy's throat until he was dead. Grant's voice shook as he admitted that he had stripped the boy's clothes from his body. He also recalled hitting "the lighter-haired boy in the face."

He then told of throwing the knife away, walking along the river, falling in, and calling home for a ride. Everything was the same, except that, when he was first questioned, he had completely left out his deadly encounter with Scott and Brad. He insisted that he had no memory of interfering with either youngster sexually. And his recall of the actual killings was somewhat dreamlike. He insisted that, after the murders, he didn't remember killing them. "I asked my daddy if I could go and look for them while they were lost," he said, "but he wouldn't let me."

Phelan and Hume had asked Gillespie to question

Grant about the death of Carole Adele Erickson. They gave him pertinent details of that homicide and Gillespie said to the suspect: "Can you recall any like incidents? I will only mention three items—a girl, a riverbank, and a shoestring."

Grant responded with three questions: "Was she stabbed in the back? Was it at night? Did she have long, dark hair?"

And then he began to cry. When he was calmer, Jim Phelan took over the questioning, and it led to Grant's finally giving a statement on the Erickson case. His queries and Grant's answers echoed in the courtroom, the tape amplified by microphones.

"Do you recall a girl walking along a riverbank somewhere around Christmas?"

"I was walking behind her. I saw her walking along the river. She had on blue jeans, a green jacket, some sort of leather tie-on shoes. I followed her for ten or twelve feet. Then I walked up behind her and thrusted [sic] the knife into her back. I untied the shoelaces and put them around her neck. I dragged her on her back and pulled her by her hands into the bushes—the stickers. Then I heard a couple on the bridge and I was afraid they'd see me, so I ran."

When Jim Phelan asked him if he had tried to rape the dying girl, Grant began to cry and answered over and over: "I don't know . . . I don't know . . . God, I wish I did."

"Was she a pretty girl?"

"Yes."

"Did you remove her coat . . . her sweater?"

"I'm not sure."

"Do you remember her pants? Did you do anything to her?"

"I don't know. I can see her. She's lying on her back. Her shoes are off and one [sleeve] of her coat is off."

"Gary, did you do anything to her sexually?"

"I didn't."

"Did you want to?"

"I suppose I wanted to, but I don't remember doing anything sexual or touching her clothes in any way."

After his confession to yet a third murder, Gillespie spoke with Gary once more. As they talked, suddenly the gaunt teenager put his head in his hands and murmured in horror, *"My God! There's another one!"*

The jurors and spectators flinched—as if they were hearing the confession firsthand and not on a tape that was months old.

It was as if Gary Grant had buried the murders so deep in his subconscious that he really did not remember them until the investigators asked him to focus on them. And they, of course, had no idea that he was connected to either the Erickson or Zulauf cases when they began to question him about the two little boys.

In truth, they were as shocked as Grant seemed to be when he moved on to describe what had happened to Joann Zulauf. At that point, Wally Hume had put in a call to Detective George Helland, who joined them outside the polygrapher's office.

The interview that followed was also taped, with Grant's permission, and lasted nearly two hours. Grant had difficulty remembering just when the Zulauf killing occurred. He said he didn't know if it had happened two months or two years before.

Once again the defendant's voice bounced off the courtroom walls as he responded to George Helland's questions.

"It was in a green time of year because there were

leaves on the trees and foliage," Grant said, trying to come up with the month he killed Joann Zulauf. "I came down into a woods and I saw her ahead of me. She didn't see me. . . . I had a rock or whatever, and I hit her in the back of the head. She fell down. She started to say something and I choked her until she was dead."

"Gary," Helland said, "if we are going to believe you, we'll have to have more particulars—more details."

"I want it to come out," Grant said, his voice choked with sobs. "I did something wrong, I want it to come out. I can't hold it inside me anymore."

"Did you remove her clothing?"

"I don't know—I don't know whether I did or not." Here an incredulous tone came into the defendant's voice on the tape. "Up until I saw her in front of me on the path, I don't remember anything else. I just remember being on the trail and the sun seemed to be out—sort of cloudish, maybe somewhere around three or four in the afternoon."

Grant responded to Helland's questions, recalling that the girl was small, with shoulder-length curly reddish brown hair. He said she was wearing an army jacket and blue jeans. His voice became breathier and more tearful as he described the scene. "When she hit the ground and I grabbed her, she swung around on me. She saw me then. I just used my hand on her throat. She was on her knees. Her back arched and she beat me with her hands and arms, but I kept choking her until she was quiet."

Again, Gary Grant said he could not remember any sexual approach to his victim. "It's like the two little kids—I come to one point and then, *Bam!* I'm at another point. That's just it. I don't know what I've done. Like I heard about the little kids and I wanted to go and look for them . . . but then when I do remember, I see up to one point and no further."

The prosecutors tied up their case by introducing into evidence Gary Grant's tennis shoes and the moulages taken at the death site of the two small boys. They matched, right down to the small nicks and scratches that had come with wear.

A girl who had once dated Grant testified that he had given her a present for her birthday, which was two weeks after Joann Zulauf's murder. She said he had presented her with a used woman's wristwatch. "It was made of white metal, and the brand name was Lucien Perreaux." She testified that she used to tease him by asking him why he didn't get paid more for the work he did, since he never seemed to have any money. "When he gave me the watch, he said, 'See, I do get paid for the things I do.' "

As Nick Marshall and James Anderson began their defense, it became apparent that they would make no attempt to deny their client's guilt in the homicides but would, rather, strive to show that Gary Grant was desperately ill—a stunted, warped personality who possessed Jekyll and Hyde characteristics. Gary Grant could be a gentle, accommodating friend who displayed no violence at all, but he could also be possessed by a terrible "unconscious rage."

Friends testified regarding the "good" side of Grant's personality, and two psychiatrists gave some insight into the tremendous anger that sometimes gripped him.

Psychiatrist Dr. Robert Anderson labeled the killings "senseless" and said they might have made sense only if the victims represented hated persons from the defendant's past. He speculated that "Grant may have had no more control over the personality who committed the murders than we do over our dreams at night."

Dr. George Harris classified Grant as "emotionally ill." Both psychiatrists testified that Grant considered sex "dirty and shameful." Through interviews with friends and relatives, the psychiatrists learned of a background riddled with violence. Grant's navy career was short-lived; he could not adjust to what he considered harsh treatment of fellow recruits by superior officers and was discharged as "unfit for service."

Relatives described Gary Grant as a quiet child who was very disturbed by family fights. Often he was pushed to the breaking point by domestic altercations. The "good" Gary was reduced to tears by the death of a pet kitten and a lizard, which he tried to nurse back to health with tender care. At the mention of the death of the lizard, the defendant's eyes filled with tears as he sat in the courtroom. It was hard to see him as an obsessed killer.

After weeks in trial, the time had come for summations by both the prosecution and the defense. Special Prosecutor Edmund P. Allen faced the jury and calmly related the sequence of events in all four murders. The soft-spoken prosecutor recalled pertinent parts of Grant's confessions and said, "We have an answer for everything. The only real issue in this case is whether or not to invoke the death penalty. I submit, if ever—*if ever*—an appropriate case existed for the death penalty, this is it."

Nick Marshall rose to plead for Gary Grant's life. The red-haired former FBI agent was most accomplished at legal rhetoric. He was one of the more persuasive attorneys around.

"You will recall," he began, "that I warned you the evidence in this case would make you cringe—that your emotions would be right there in your throat. I will not offer you facts; I will offer you perceptions. I offer you no magic, but I appeal to you as human beings. Four lives have been lost; nothing will bring them back. Now another life hangs in the balance. It is in your hands. You've heard the statements. Nine pages. Six pages. Three pages. In human misery, hopelessness and despair . . .

"You have heard that Gary Grant was gripped with unconscious rage, that he had no more control over his actions than you do over a dream at night. These crimes were not thought out or premeditated, because he was emotionally ill."

The Grant jury retired at 5:00 P.M. on Monday, August 23. Almost forty-eight hours later, and after eighteen hours of steady deliberation, the jurors sent word that they had reached a verdict. They found Gary Grant guilty of murder in the first degree on all four counts. They did not, however, recommend the death penalty. Instead, they recommended that on each count, Gary Grant was to serve a minimum of thirteen years and eight months and a maximum of his natural life. Judge Soukup ruled that the four sentences were to run consecutively.

Almost three decades later, Gary Grant still resides in the Washington State Prison at Walla Walla. His parents have died, and he has little connection to the world outside. He is fifty and his first parole hearing will be in 2048. At that time, should he still be alive, he will be ninety-eight years old.

Carole Adele Erickson would be fifty now. Joann Zulauf would be forty-seven. Scott Andrews and Brad Lyons would be thirty-five.

Three decades later, we are still a long way from understanding the psychopathology of the sexual predator. We know only that they are desperately dangerous and almost impossible to rehabilitate. Gary Grant and Arnold Brown both seemed to be gentle people. Their actions and demeanor instilled trust in the people they met. The only promises they ever kept were to the animals they loved so devotedly. When it came to human beings, *they* were the animals.

The Stockholm Syndrome

There is a time-worn belief among lay people that murder will out—that all homicides will eventually be solved and that killers will eventually be prosecuted and found guilty. That is perhaps a comforting thought, but it isn't true.

Two bizarre and inexplicable deaths in an isolated forest in Oregon were almost written off as accidental. It was only through the efforts of some of Oregon's top criminal investigators and prosecutors that the killer was found and convicted.

The investigation began with a paucity of physical evidence, a witness who had been brainwashed, and two deaths that certainly appeared to be tragic accidents. But when it was over, a team from the Oregon attorney general's office uncovered a story of horror and violence that made even the most experienced detective's flesh crawl.

Until the Patty Hearst kidnapping, the mass suicides of Reverend Jim Jones's followers in Guyana, and, more recently, the cult deaths in Waco and southern California, people thought of brainwashing as something that happened only in Korean or Vietnamese prison camps. It's easy to be smug and confident in the safety of one's own living room or at a cocktail party and say, "I could never be programmed to do something like that. There are just some things I would never do."

But the mind is an incredibly complex entity and, given the right circumstances, virtually any mind will crack and begin to believe that black is white, that wrong is right, and that reality no longer has any validity. Brainwashing can take place in an hour or over many days. It is a strategy used in many hostage situations. When ordinary people are held prisoner in banks or planes, some of them will eventually begin to think their captors are good and kind people *simply because they haven't killed them.* When their plans are interrupted, captives move from outrage to fear to passivity and finally to a belief that their captors must possess at least a few tender places in their hearts. When they survive, many hostages feel they owe their lives to the bank robbers or skyjackers. This curious phenomenon is known as the Stockholm Syndrome.

For brainwashing to occur, a human being must be exposed to four basic elements:

1. A severe traumatic shock
2. Isolation—being taken away from the people and surroundings where the person feels secure
3. Programming—hearing what the mind controller wants the subject to believe, over and over and over and over
4. The promise of a reward—often the subject's very life

When all four of these components come into play, the stage is set. Every one of these elements is vital in unraveling the story of Robin* and Hank Marcus* and their seemingly benign meeting with a stranger in the woods.

It was Thursday, July 22, 1976, when Robin and Hank set out from their home in Canby, Oregon, for a camping trip along the Clackamas River near the foothills of Oregon's majestic Mount Hood. The trip was to be a celebration of their first wedding anniversary. Robin was only sixteen, her husband five years older, but they were so much in love that her family didn't object when their beautiful raven-haired daughter wanted to marry. They knew Hank loved Robin and would take care of her. The young couple's happy first year of marriage showed everyone that their decision had been the right one. The trip into Oregon's idyllic wilderness would be like a second honeymoon for the couple.

Hank and Robin lived on a shoestring. They had only sixty dollars to spend on their trip; that immediately eliminated motels and restaurants. They would have to sleep out under the trees or in their car and cook over a campfire. At first they planned to leave Rusty, their collie, with Robin's grandmother, but she was ill. They certainly couldn't afford to put him in a boarding kennel, so they decided to take him along.

A sense of fatalism would run through all of Robin's eventual recollection of the events of that bizarre weekend. Call it karma, destiny, or what you will. If they had made even some small decisions differently that weekend, Robin's and Hank's lives might have gone on without incident for another fifty years.

Robin initially wanted to go to the Oregon coast, where she and Hank had spent their honeymoon, but Hank chose Austin Hot Springs in the Oregon mountains instead. He wanted to teach her how to fish; it was one of his passions, so she finally capitulated. That made him happy, and they could always go to the coast another time.

But Robin had terrifying dreams the night before their trip. Something indefinable frightened her and she woke knowing only that her nightmares had something to do with their planned outing in the mountains. The next morning she mentioned her fears to a girlfriend, who suggested she take her Bible with her on the trip. "If you have your Bible with you," she said, "you know everything will be all right."

Robin tucked her much-read Bible into her backpack, but she was still afraid. She told Hank about her dreams, and he too admitted that he felt a presentiment of danger, something that was totally unlike him. Just to be on the safe side, he suggested they stop and ask a friend of his to go along with them for the weekend, but the friend wasn't home. They left him a note which read, "We were by to ask you to go to the mountains with us. Sorry you missed the fun!"

The sun was shining, the weather was perfect, and

Robin and Hank tried to shake off their forebodings. They bought fishing licenses and canned food, and they gassed up their car. That left them with about twenty dollars to cover any emergencies.

They drove the twenty miles from Molalla to Estacada, and headed south. Somehow though, they missed the turn leading into the Austin Hot Springs campground and turned instead into the road leading into Bagby Hot Springs. They drove deep into the wilderness before they realized they were heading in the wrong direction. "This road is so much spookier than I remember it," Hank commented when he failed to recognize any landmarks. "In fact, it's so spooky, it gives me the creeps. It's like no other road I've ever been on."

Once they realized they'd taken a wrong turn, they retraced their path. By then they had used up a quarter of a tank of gas, they were running late, and they finally arrived at the Austin Hot Springs campground just as the gates were being locked for the night. All the camping spots were taken.

The park ranger told them they could park outside and walk back in. "You can cook your supper, take a dip in the hot springs, and you can fish, just so long as you don't camp inside the park tonight."

Robin and Hank cooked dinner, laughed at some people who were skinny-dipping, and took Rusty for a walk in the woods. They felt better and their spooky feelings now seemed silly.

Still, they didn't want to camp alone; they wanted to park near other campers, and they finally found an enclave of Russian families and parked their sedan close to them. They slept in the car with the doors locked. They were having a restless night with Rusty jumping on them and whining. They finally got up, made their way down to the Clackamas River by flashlight, and gave the dog a drink of water. Then they returned to the car and settled down for the night.

They woke at six the next morning. It was Friday, July 23. The park ranger said there was a spot available inside the park now and he directed them to the campsite. Robin cooked breakfast while Hank fished. But he had 'no luck, and they swam in the hot springs instead. There were people all around them, including the families they'd met the night before, and Robin felt safe enough when Hank headed farther upriver to try his luck again.

The only bad moment she experienced was when a man yelled at her for letting Rusty swim in the springs. "They're for people, not dogs," he complained. "You could get slapped with a $500 fine."

"He's probably cleaner than you, most likely," she'd called back, as she tugged the collie out of the water.

Hank was gone fishing a long time, at least two hours, and Robin began to worry. When he finally showed up, he was grinning and soaked to the skin. "You almost lost me," he laughed. "I was helping some of those Russians ford the river with a rope and I hit a sinkhole and started going under some white water—until I grabbed a branch and got my footing."

Robin had been so worried that she was mad at him at first, but she relented. "I'm sorry I yelled at you," she apologized. "I thought something had happened to you, and I got scared."

Hank Marcus was a big man—6 feet tall, 185 pounds. He was fully capable of taking care of both of them. He soothed Robin, pointing out all the people around them, saying there just wasn't anything for her to be so afraid of. She was timid without him, though, and tended to worry far more than she needed to.

It was a good afternoon. They frolicked in the hot springs and talked to the Russian families. One of the men made a pass at Robin as he carried her across the river and she deliberately stepped on his boat, swamping it. Later, Hank laughed when she told him what she'd done. He wasn't jealous of her; he had no need to be.

But Hank was disappointed with the trip so far; he still hadn't caught any fish, so they broke camp and headed up the road to give it another try. Robin cooked a late lunch while Hank tried out the new fishing spot. They said grace before they ate, as they always did.

That evening, while it was still light out, they drove farther and farther downstream looking for signs of fish in the river. They passed a lone man fishing and asked him if the fish were biting. He shrugged and said, "I haven't caught anything all day." So they kept on driving.

They came upon another fisherman, who told them he had only caught three fish all afternoon, "and they weren't keepers." But he told them he'd heard that a truckload of fish had been dumped into the Colawash River earlier in the week. "Ask about that up at the ranger station," he suggested.

Hank and Robin were undecided whether to stay or head home. Their gas was getting dangerously low now, and they hadn't found any good fishing at all. For Hank's sake, Robin suggested they try just one more spot before going home.

The road they chose took them deep into the woods as the long shadows of evening closed over them. They came upon a small boat-launch area near the North Fork Dam and stopped to watch some children playing in the river. They were parked at the side of the road when a red pickup pulled up. It was an old truck, road-worn and mud-covered, with a broken tailgate and a crumpled bumper. The lone occupant was a short youngish man. He left his engine running as he got out and ran up the fish ladder.

Hank Marcus went over to talk to the stranger. Robin waited in their car; the windows were open, and she could hear snatches of their conversation. Hank was telling the man that the fishing prospects seemed to be nil in the area. "All we found were a couple of suckers," he said.

The stranger didn't even turn to look at Hank. He mumbled something and kept staring out at the river. But when Robin got out of the car and walked toward the two men, the man turned to look at her and she felt his eyes burning into her. "It was almost as if he'd never seen a woman before," she recalled. "He lit up like a Christmas tree."

Suddenly he smiled and turned back to Hank. "I know where they just dumped a whole truckload of fish," he said. "I was just up there working when they dumped them off the bridge. That's where I'm headed."

Since the other fisherman had also told them about the fish dump, it seemed reasonable that this stranger, who said his name was Tom, was telling the truth. Hank was really tempted, but he worried about his nearly empty gas tank. Tom told them that it wasn't that far—they had more than enough gas to make it, adding, "Besides, I can go to town in the morning and bring back gas if you run low."

They decided to follow Tom to the place where he said he'd seen the fresh dump of fish. The two-vehicle caravan wended its way slowly down the deserted road. At one point, Tom pulled the truck over and suggested that they ride with him so that they wouldn't run out of gas, but Robin shook her head, and Hank shrugged. She wanted to stay in their own car; the feeling of uneasiness that had plagued her for the past two days had returned.

"Just where is this spot?" Hank asked.

"Just beyond the Bagby Hot Springs Road."

Hank and Robin looked at each other; that was the road that had frightened them when they'd taken it by mistake the day before. It had given them both goose pimples on a hot day. They whispered to each other about turning back, but they finally decided to go on. "It's silly for us to be afraid of a road," Hank reassured Robin.

They passed a man and his daughter they'd camped with the night before, and Robin felt better; they were nice, normal people and seeing them here on this road allayed her fears.

Hank looked over at Robin and grinned. "See, things always work out. It's neat that we met Tom. If we hadn't been at the dam at that precise minute, we wouldn't have had this chance to catch some fish. We probably would have just gone home and lost the whole weekend."

Up ahead, Tom turned onto an old dirt road that was bumpy and deeply rutted. They could no longer see much of the landscape because the sun had dropped below the horizon, and it was that time of evening between dusk and full dark. They pulled in behind the glowing taillights of Tom's red pickup.

They lit a fire, and Tom pulled out a bottle of liquor and offered them a drink. To be polite, they each took a little sip. Then Tom pulled something out of his truck. It was a milk carton with a dead bird in it. "See this?" he bragged. "I picked it off on the way down here."

Robin felt her stomach turn over. "We don't believe

in killing things for sport," she murmured. "Not unless you have to—for food."

"Oh, don't worry," Tom said. "I plan on eating it."

After they ate, Tom grabbed a rifle from his truck and called to Hank and Robin to join him on a walk. They came to a clearing in the midst of the lowering pine and fir forest and Tom told them that this was where he did his hunting. "If we got a deer, we could eat only the hindquarters. We could be wasteful masters," he said. It was an odd term. Robin had never heard it before.

"That's illegal," Hank said.

Tom only laughed and shrugged.

They shared Tom's binoculars, and there was just enough light to see a deer foraging in the clearing and, farther on, some bear cubs playing. Tom raised his gun, sighting in on them, but he didn't shoot. Robin heard him cock the gun, and she quickly turned her back in disapproval and horror. She tugged on Hank's arm and pleaded, "I want to go back to camp right now. If he shoots a cub, the mother will kill all of us!"

Tom smiled, his teeth white in the dusk, and lowered the gun. They made their way back to the campfire.

Hank and Robin prepared to sleep in their car again.

"I'll rap on your hood in the morning when I get up," Tom said, "about five."

Alone in their car, with Rusty tied outside, Robin told Hank she didn't like Tom. "He seems to enjoy killing for its own sake," she whispered.

Hank held her close and said softly, "You just have to understand everyone in his own way, honey."

Hank was like that. He didn't judge people—he accepted them, but Robin felt an overwhelming rush of fear that she couldn't shake. She clung to Hank all night. While she watched him as he slept, she had a

ANN RULE

numbing thought. What would she do if something took him away from her? She loved him so much, but she knew that sometimes there was nothing she could do to stop whatever Fate had planned for them.

At dawn on Saturday, July 24, they awoke to Tom pounding on the hood of their car. They'd slept in their clothes, and now they hurriedly pulled their shoes on. The three of them agreed they would fish before breakfast and Tom drove them in his truck deeper into the woods to a large clearing. He had trouble finding the trail, and Robin found this odd since he'd told them that he came here to hunt every weekend.

They finally found the path and headed up the overgrown trail. Robin ran ahead with Rusty and waited for Tom and Hank to catch up. The sun was shining now, and there were field daisies and wildflowers growing everywhere. The night's dread began to recede.

They had to climb over logs and rocks to reach the riverbank. Once there, Robin and Hank sat on a rock, and Tom stayed behind them. They all threw lines in, but their luck was no better here than it had been anywhere else. None of them caught anything.

Suddenly Robin felt prickles running up and down her spine and she sensed that Tom was pointing his gun at them. But when she turned to look, he was staring elsewhere, his gun cradled carelessly in his arms.

They decided to go back to camp and fix breakfast. They wouldn't have the fresh fish they'd counted on, but Robin would manage to throw something together. They were tired from tromping through the thick woods and climbing over deadfalls, and so they rested on a log along the trail. Robin whistled, and a bird flew close to them, checking to see if she was a bird, too.

She started to make a joke about her name being appropriate when Tom's rifle roared. He fired repeatedly at the birds all around them. Eerily, the more he fired, the closer the birds came.

"Why do they do that?" Robin asked. Tom seemed to have some weird aura about him.

"They're curious about the sound," he explained.

"Haven't you got better things to do than try to kill poor little birds?"

Tom didn't answer. In the sunlight when he squinted, he had eyes like a fox or a ferret; they seemed to see everything between his half-closed lids. He finally stopped firing at the birds, but he held his gun so that it appeared to be pointing at Hank, who didn't notice. Now Tom looked at their Rusty. He was stroking the dog as he said, "There're only two things wrong with Rusty," he said. "He's alive and walking."

It was a sick joke, and neither Hank nor Robin laughed.

Robin studied Tom. She couldn't figure him out. When he'd first seen her, his eyes had practically undressed her and he'd smiled broadly. She recognized male interest, but he'd barely glanced at her since, talking only to Hank.

Still, Hank told her he didn't trust Tom around her. When they got back to the truck in the thick early morning heat, Robin unbuttoned her blouse, revealing her bikini top, and Hank quickly told her to button it up again. Then Hank gave her a kiss, smiled, and walked away with Tom. They each carried a gun and were headed back toward the clearing.

Robin was alone now. She could hear the birds chirping and Rusty panting in the heat. She knew she should fix breakfast, but she was immobilized with a dread that was much worse than before. She tried whistling loudly but no one responded, not even the birds.

And then she heard the shot. Only one shot. It reverberated through the woods until the echoes diminished into dead silence.

She waited, wondering what the men had shot at. After a time, Tom came strolling back. "We got us a deer," he said laconically. "I need a knife to gut it out."

Something wasn't right. Hank would have been the one to come back and tell her. He wouldn't have sent Tom back. With Rusty close beside her, she began to run toward where she'd heard the shot.

Tom's gun roared again behind her and she looked back to see Rusty falter and fall dead in the path, his blood staining his silky sable fur. Horrified and sobbing, Robin turned toward Tom with a question on her lips. But now Tom was leveling the rifle at her.

"You shot my dog!" she screamed.

"Yeah, I know," Tom smiled. "I shot your husband, too."

Tears coursed down her face, and she pleaded, "Oh, God . . . please don't hurt me!"

She believed Hank was dead. She knew Rusty was dead. Robin Marcus was sixteen years old, and she was alone in the wilderness with a killer. She fully expected to die, but it didn't seem to matter much at that point; she had lost the two beings who were closest to her.

It would be three days—Saturday, Sunday, and Monday—before Robin would get the chance to tell anyone what had happened up there in the woods near the meadow. When she did, she appeared rational—in shock, certainly—but basically lucid.

The detectives and attorneys who listened to her

story took her at her word. They didn't understand then that they might as well have been listening to a programmed robot.

On Tuesday, July 27, Robin Marcus and Tom Brown entered the offices of an Oregon City attorney, James O'Leary. O'Leary, who had served as Tom Brown's attorney in the past, listened while Tom and Robin explained that Brown had accidentally killed Robin's husband in the Bagby Hot Springs area on Saturday, July 24. Robin sobbed as she recalled witnessing the accident. She said that she wanted to go with Brown to talk with the Clackamas County sheriff about the incident. She didn't want him to be blamed for something that wasn't his fault.

O'Leary contacted Detectives Hank Reeves and Lynn Forristall and they listened to the incredible story that Tom Brown and Robin Marcus gave. On the face of it, it seemed to be a tragic story about the accidental discharge of a gun. According to Brown, he and Hank Marcus had been looking for deer when they decided to exchange rifles. Brown said that one was a Winchester lever action and the other a .22 caliber high-power Savage. As they had passed the guns between them, Brown said one of the guns had gone off, fatally wounding Hank Marcus in the head. He died in an instant.

Tom Brown said that after Hank died, the Marcuses' pet collie, Rusty, went wild and attacked him. Robin nodded as Tom explained that he had no choice but to shoot Rusty. In the shocked aftermath of what happened, he said he and Robin wandered the wrong way in the forest and lost their bearings for three days.

Brown admitted that he had an extensive prior record, and conceded that this made him reluctant to report the accident. But then Robin promised to go to the authorities with him and confirm what had happened.

She told him she would explain to the police that she had witnessed her husband's death, and she would verify that Tom was telling the truth.

The cops separated the strange pair, and each gave a formal statement. The two statements matched in every detail. Then Robin, exhausted and covered with scratches and insect bites, was driven back to her home in Canby. Tom Brown agreed to accompany the Clackamas County investigators into the wilderness to show them where the bodies of Hank and the dog lay.

Medical Examiner Ken Dooley would join the detectives for a cursory examination of the bodies. It was 5:45 p.m. on July 27 when the group left headquarters; they reached the Buckeye Creek Road at 8:20. It was dark and they needed high-powered flashlights as they moved along the trail looking for the dead man and his fallen dog. They found the remains of the trio's campsite, and 200 yards farther on, they came across Hank Marcus's body.

Fully clad in jeans and hiking gear, the dead man lay 30 feet from the logging road, his body partially covered with ferns. From the position of the body, it appeared that he had rolled over an embankment and landed 8 feet below. He lay on his face as if asleep, his left arm tucked under him. According to Tom Brown and Robin, Hank Marcus had been there for almost four days in the baking July heat. Decomposition was advanced, particularly in the area of the head wound.

The investigators took photographs in the twilight of that Tuesday night, and Detective Forristall placed stakes at the edge of the road to mark the probable site of the actual shooting, where dried blood stained the earth about four feet from the edge of the bank.

Tom Brown had voluntarily turned over the Savage

rifle, saying it was the gun he had used to kill Rusty, the collie. He told them he had discarded the other weapon— the one that had fired unexpectedly, killing Hank Marcus. He didn't know if he'd be able to find it again; it was in a heavily wooded area much farther away.

They found Rusty's body along the trail. The huge collie was also covered with vegetation and he too had suffered a single gunshot wound in the head. Someone had apparently made an attempt to protect the two bodies. Or perhaps to hide them.

Tom Brown, age twenty-nine, seemed both cooperative and contrite as he told the investigators about the fatal accident. They put him up in a motel for the night, and he agreed to come to sheriff's headquarters the first thing in the morning to help them find the missing rifle.

Detective Sergeant Bill Werth and Forristall and Reeves, met with Thomas Brown early the next day. They went with him again into the Mount Hood National Forest in the Colowash River area to recover the gun.

They took more photos of the campsite, the Marcuses' car, and the scene where Hank had died. Then they hiked into the wilderness beyond. They crashed through underbrush for a mile to the banks of the Colowash, where they walked upstream for three miles, then crossed the river and came to a smaller stream. There Werth noted footprints that appeared to match Brown's shoes and much smaller footprints in the soft sand. Both sets were headed in the opposite direction from where Brown was leading the investigators.

In the heat of the day, the pace was rapid and wearying. The group walked three more miles upriver and then cut away from the riverbank again and moved into the woods in a northerly direction. They were now so deep into the forest that civilization seemed not to exist at all. Indeed, the terrain here had changed little since pioneers first came to Oregon almost 140 years before. Lost in these woods, a novice hiker might never find his way out. It was easy to understand why Tom Brown and Robin Marcus had become disoriented. But now Brown led the group, pointing out landmarks as they moved along. All of this was beginning to look familiar to him.

He pointed to a very heavily vegetated area. "We spread our sleeping bags out here on the night of the twenty-fifth," he said. "There it is! There's my rifle. It's a .22 high power with lever action. I had about eleven bullets left in a plastic bag. I tossed them out into the brush."

The gun was there all right, but even when they dropped to their hands and knees and searched through the undergrowth, the detectives could not find the bullets. To preserve any latent prints, they fashioned a sling in which to carry the rifle.

Back down along the creek bed, Brown showed them where he and Robin had dumped a sleeping bag when they had finally found their way to the trail head. The sleeping bag was literally torn to pieces from being dragged through the underbrush.

The exhausted search party got back to the campsite at 9:35 P.M., after more than ten hours of slogging through the forest. Packing the two bodies out along the trail for postmortem examination was extremely difficult. When they returned to the sheriff's office, the investigators secured the .22 rifle in the property room to await ballistics tests and dusting for fingerprints. They had also retrieved blood samples from the dirt near Hank's corpse, and from Rusty's body.

On July 29, Tom Brown gave a more detailed statement of the accident. He explained he hadn't known either of the Marcuses before he met them near the dam; they decided to join up for a fishing trip. The next morning he and Hank Marcus took a hike before breakfast.

"Hank and I walked up to the clearing the morning of the twenty-fourth. He was looking through my binoculars and he spotted a deer. He handed the binoculars to me so I could see, and I handed the rifle over to him at the same time. Then, after I got a bead on the deer, I gave the glasses back to Hank and he handed the gun back. As it was being passed to me, I grabbed it by the balance with my finger on the trigger. It fired . . . and the bullet hit Hank in the head."

"And his wife saw this?"

Brown nodded. "Like she said, she was standing a couple feet behind us. Hank fell to the ground, and I scooped up both the rifles. Robin started screaming. I ran toward the campsite."

Brown said that Rusty had been asleep back at the site and came running toward him, snarling as if he was about to attack. "I had to shoot him."

Brown said he'd been in shock. He sat around the campsite for several hours trying to decide what to do. "I finally knew I had to split—that no one would believe me. I told Robin she could do what she wanted, but that I was going to head to the mountains. She said I couldn't leave her there, that I had to take her back to civilization, but I said, 'No way. I'm going.' I told her she could go with me if she wanted, but she'd better hurry and get her stuff together."

It was obvious that Brown lacked gallantry, but it was easy to imagine that Robin Marcus, lost in the woods, in deep shock after seeing her husband killed, *might* have chosen to stay with the only other human being around.

497

She told the investigators she had witnessed the accidental shooting. And then, she said, Brown told her that he was afraid no one would ever believe him—not with his record. He was panicking and determined to head up and over the mountain. He said he knew the woods; she didn't. She decided, Brown said, to go with him rather than wander around in the wilderness where she probably would have died of fatigue or starvation or as prey for a bear or a cougar.

Brown acknowledged that he had dragged the collie's carcass off the trail and that he'd rolled Hank's body off the bank and then covered both bodies with sword ferns to deter the ravages of animals. That stamped him as a novice in the woods, the detectives thought. A few ferns wouldn't keep animals away, but they might hide the bodies from a human hiker.

So Tom Brown took off into the deep woods, with Robin trailing behind. He said he spent the next three days trying to calm himself down, and he finally decided the best thing to do was to turn himself in. Robin promised him that she would stand by him, and tell the cops she was a witness to her husband's death. "Then we headed back to Oregon City."

On July 29, a polygraph expert from the Oregon State Police gave Tom Brown a lie detector test. All the tracings of his body's reactions indicated that he was telling the truth. The victim's own wife was supporting Brown's story, all the evidence had been turned over by Brown himself, and he passed the polygraph test. It was tragic that the young husband should have died on his first wedding anniversary, but it clearly wasn't a homicide.

Tom Brown vacated the motel room and disappeared. There was no reason to require him to stay around.

The postmortem examination of Hank Marcus confirmed that he had died of a single gunshot wound to the head with the bullet entering the right cheek and traveling out the left side of his neck. The path of the bullet had been almost horizontal, indicating that he was standing next to someone of similar height when he was shot. Unfortunately, because of the extreme decomposition of the tissue, there was no way to determine if there had been any blotching or stippling of powder burns around the wound. That eliminated their chance to establish how far the shooter had been from the victim.

However, because the Oregon State Crime Lab was doing a special study on lead traces in bullet wounds, two fragments of Hank Marcus's tissue—each no more than an inch or so in diameter—were excised from the site of the entrance and exit wounds so they could be examined under a scanning electron microscope equipped with a laser beam.

Because of an oversight, Rusty's body was buried before the direction of the wound to the dog's head could be determined. And he wasn't buried in a single grave, but in a mass grave at the city dump with several other dogs.

Hank Marcus was buried, too, and Robin and their families tried to pick up the loose threads of their lives.

Everyone thought Robin was going through normal, predictable grief. In truth, Robin Marcus was suffering through her own private hell, something far beyond normal grief. There was something just below the surface of her mind that kept bubbling up, no matter how hard she tried to keep it submerged. As the days passed, it grew stronger and stronger.

Her memory was playing games with her. It was very odd. She could remember everything about preparations for their trip, remember the day they spent before they met Tom, and even recall how she'd been afraid of him at first. But the three days after Hank and Rusty were shot were all a blur. For the life of her, she could not pull those memories into focus.

She liked Tom. She *thought* she liked Tom. She could remember riding to the sheriff's office with Mr. O'Leary, Tom's attorney, and telling him Tom was a nice person. They asked her a lot of questions in the Clackamas County sheriff's office about why she'd gone up into the woods with Tom. Could she have escaped from him? She said yes—yes, she could have. She could have left when they got to Mr. O'Leary's office, but she promised Tom she would stick by him and tell them about how he'd shot Hank accidentally. The gunshot haunted her. She kept hearing the *boom* in her head and seeing Hank's blood. And it frightened her. But she couldn't bring the actual shooting back. When she talked to the detectives, she believed she had seen it. But now she could not remember it.

Although she didn't realize it, Robin Marcus was beginning to come down from the intensive brainwashing she had undergone for three days after Hank's death. Whenever she began to go over the events in her mind the way Tom told her they happened, a very clear picture kept getting in the way—a picture that warred with Tom's words. She kept seeing his smile as he told her that he had shot Hank as well as Rusty. Why *did* he smile? It was such an odd smile, like the grimace on a devil's mask. But then she recalled that Tom had smiled when he was talking with detectives, too. Even though tears were running down his face when he told them about the accident, he'd had that same peculiar grin on his face. Maybe that's just the way he was.

As the days passed, Robin began to remember what had happened more and more clearly. She'd told the detectives what Tom wanted them to hear; she'd even told her family and Hank's that his death had been an accident. And she had believed it herself. Now she no longer did; her memory was coming back.

On August 2, Robin and her parents appeared at the sheriff's office again. "I want to tell you what really happened," Robin blurted. "It wasn't an accident. Tom Brown killed Hank."

She seemed so positive about what she was saying that the detectives immediately ushered her into an interview room where she gave a second statement. There were to be five more statements as her memory fought its way to the surface.

Robin explained that she had gone with Tom after Hank was killed, but only out of fear for her life. Tom had not been her savior in the woods. He had raped her again and again. She still didn't understand how but Tom had somehow managed to convince her that she was there when Hank died, that the killing had been an accident, and that she should return to town with him to verify his story. At the time it seemed the most natural thing in the world.

This new version was hard to swallow, and the detectives interviewing her looked at each other doubtfully. Robin Marcus was given a polygraph exam—and failed.

Indeed, Robin Marcus would fail more lie detector tests, but the investigators came to believe her even though they couldn't say why. She agreed to talk with a psychiatrist in the hope that it would help her explore which memories were real and which had been planted there by Tom Brown.

The forensic psychiatrist talked with Robin at length and reported his findings. He explained that Tom Brown had played such tricks with her mind that it would be a long time before she would be able to remember exactly what had happened. She wasn't lying; she had been very skillfully brainwashed.

At this point, the Clackamas County sheriff's office didn't have much of a case to take into court. Conflicting statements. Conflicting polygraphs. Nothing tangible to work with. Worse, Tom Brown was gone. He was a drifter; he could be anywhere. He might never be found.

The case, however, was taken to a grand jury, which would decide if the death of Hank Marcus had been a murder or an accident. The case remained there for some months. In the interim, Brown's lawyer, James O'Leary, ran for district attorney of Clackamas County and won. Even if the grand jury decided that Brown should be charged, there was no way O'Leary could prosecute a case in which he had originally been the defendant's lawyer.

The grand jury ultimately agreed that Tom Brown should be tried for the murder of Hank Marcus. An indictment charging Thomas Brown with murder, forgery, and car theft was handed down by the grand jury in late December, five months after Hank Marcus died; it was not going to be an easy case to prosecute. (The latter two charges were from another state, and both crimes had occurred before the events of July 24.)

James A. Redden, Oregon's attorney general, maintained a special Criminal Justice Division. It was manned by assistant attorneys general and investigators who were available to help county D.A.s prosecute cases if they requested assistance. Small counties often had complicated cases that required more manpower than they had on staff. Most of the attorney general's lawyers and several of the investigators had years of experience in criminal investigation. The investigators were once the cream of the detectives in the departments from which they were recruited.

Assistant Attorney General Stephen Keutzer was from the Lane County district attorney's office in Eugene, and Assistant Attorney General Robert Hamilton had once been on staff in the Marion County D.A.'s office in Salem. Between them, they had a great deal of experience in prosecuting homicide cases. Now they responded to Clackamas County's request for help in the investigation and prosecution of Tom Brown.

Robin Marcus's many statements suggested that she might be a good candidate for Sodium Amytal (truth serum) and the grand jury requested an examination by Dr. J. H. Treleaven, head of the Psychiatric Security Unit of Oregon State Hospital, to see if the drug might unveil hidden areas in her mind.

Treleaven's conclusion was that the young widow would probably reveal nothing more under truth serum. He determined that she had been subjected to classic brainwashing during the time she was held captive after her husband's murder. All the elements were there: psychic shock, isolation, programming, the promise of reward and, for Robin, the need to alleviate her guilt that she had been responsible for Hank's death.

The shock of hearing her husband was dead and seeing her dog shot before her eyes would have been profound. The wilderness of the Mount Hood National Forest was as isolated as a place could get. And over the three days Robin was held captive, Brown systematically programmed her to believe whatever he told her about the "accident." Robin's promised reward was that she might escape with her life. Perhaps more important to her, she wanted to believe it had all been accidental. That would relieve her of the burden of knowing Hank had died because this stranger desired her sexually and was willing to kill to get her. In her mind, she would have felt responsible for the death of the man she loved more than anyone on earth.

Robin Marcus was, after all, only sixteen years old. She was suggestible and pliable. Before her ordeal, she had been an exceptionally trusting person. She was deeply religious, and she had only her Bible for protection against the stalking killer.

Now Keutzer and Hamilton and their team of investigators would start from the beginning, reviewing all the evidence on the case, the conflicting statements, and the circumstances of the killing. Optimally, a homicide case is easier to prepare when the prosecution team has been at the crime scene within hours of the event, just as the time element in solving a murder is so vital. The more time that passes after a killing takes place, the less likely investigators are to solve it.

Hank Marcus's family was distraught, crying for justice. Robin Marcus only wanted to forget. What she had experienced was so disturbing that she could not bear to go over it again. She was distraught that she had been asked so many questions, and forced to relive her terror so many times. She was jittery at the thought of testifying before a jury.

Robin had been hammered with questions and linked to the leads of lie detectors so often because her original statement was in direct opposition to what she had later told the Clackamas County detectives. They had no choice but to keep questioning her. Predictably, she was not the most cooperative witness a prosecuting team could hope for.

One of the first things the team from the attorney general's office did was to review the past record of Thomas Brown. When he said he had a long criminal history, he hadn't been exaggerating. Brown had an incredible background of violence—seemingly for its own sake. He had first come to the attention of Oregon lawmen when he was barely sixteen years old, after a wild shooting incident. The Clackamas County sheriff's office had been called after a young man was critically wounded by a gunshot while he was standing in the window of his own home. Witnesses had identified the gunman as Tom Brown, who was arrested almost immediately by a deputy who saw Brown as he was getting out of a pickup truck with a rifle in his hand.

With Brown in custody, the deputy raced to the house of the victim, who was only nineteen. He was still standing, but his hand was pressed tight over his stomach in a vain attempt to hold back the blood that gushed out between his fingers. The wounded man was taken to the hospital while Brown was questioned.

"Did you shoot him?"

"Yeah," Tom said. "I wanted his car, and I was willing to kill to get it."

Tom said that he and a friend had decided at school that day that they needed some money. Brown borrowed a rifle and five bullets from a friend, picked up the sixth at home, and the teenagers headed for a gas station near a junior high but "there were too many people there for a single-shot weapon," the cocky kid explained.

Then they headed for Canby, Oregon. They only had

a little gas, so they ran a woman motorist off the road, demanding money when they ran up to the car. The quick-thinking woman quickly locked her doors, but the two teenagers fired anyway. "The expression changed on her face," Tom said, smiling at the memory. "We thought we'd hit her."

They had run into the woods, but they came back to where the woman had abandoned her car and run for help. Their plan to find someone else to shoot ended when they saw a police car approaching with the colored beacons on its light bar circling.

"Jim hit the gas pedal," Tom had told the deputy. "I told him to turn off at Clackamas. I knew we could make a standoff because there was only one cop. We hit a truck, slid sideways, and flipped. I was in the backseat, aiming out the back window, and let the cop have it. The next thing I knew I was out in the weeds."

Luckily, Tom's shot missed the officer—but the two wild teenagers weren't done. They were going to show the world.

Next, Tom ran along a log boom and approached a man, demanding his car keys. The man said he didn't have any. Then Tom had gone to a nearby house and threatened a girl there. Panicked, she ran across the street to the house where the nineteen-year-old shooting victim lived. "I ran to the girl's house. There were windows in every room and I figured if a cop came after me, I could pick him off."

It was at that point that Tom Brown shot the man in the stomach, and commandeered a pickup truck to make his escape. "But there wasn't enough room in the cab to aim my rifle—that's when you got me," he finished, evidently proud of his shooting spree. He believed he had shot at least two people. In truth, he had critically injured just one man, who eventually recovered.

Tom Brown was sentenced to the MacLaren School for Boys, Oregon's reform school. The man who liked to shoot birds and cubs and deer out of season—the "wasteful master"—had started his violent career fourteen years before he met Robin and Hank Marcus.

Upon his release from the MacLaren School, and after an interim period of petty crimes, Tom Brown committed a crime that sounded like a rehearsal for what he'd done to the Marcuses. He had been going with a woman who had two young children, and she'd rejected him. He kidnapped her and her children at gunpoint and took them into the mountains, where he kept them overnight.

After he released his hostages, Tom told police: "I was going to have her one way or another. I would have burned down her house, used a gun, whatever it took, so no one else would ever have her either."

That Milwaukee, Oregon, case never went to trial. The woman victim refused to file charges, grateful for her life and afraid of reprisal from Tom Brown.

After that kidnapping incident, Brown had gone to Nebraska, where he worked on a farm. His boss allowed him to use a red GMC pickup truck. One day in early summer, Tom said he was going into town. He just kept on going all the way to Oregon, however, taking the truck and his employer's rifles with him.

Brown's Nebraska boss was considerably disappointed in the man he'd trusted. He filed a stolen car report, and that warrant out of Nebraska was still in force. Several other friends in the Clackamas County area were also disappointed when they had cashed checks for Brown and they came back bouncing.

This was the man Hank and Robin had met in the

woods. Although he was now indicted for murder, it might be months, even years, before Tom Brown could be arrested and brought to trial. Bob Hamilton and Steve Keutzer went ahead and built the foundation of their case. They would be ready whenever Brown resurfaced.

And then, surprisingly, Tom Brown himself strolled into the Clackamas County sheriff's office one day. He said he'd heard there was a murder warrant out for him and he "wanted to get it all straightened out." He didn't seem worried or even mildly upset. He looked, indeed, for all the world like a man who had an ace up his sleeve. He was booked into jail to await trial.

The Oregon State Police Crime Lab's study of gunshot residue turned out to be a godsend for Keutzer and Hamilton. It gave them solid physical evidence they badly needed. Laser evaluation of the two tiny exemplars of the tissue from Hank Marcus's wounds revealed no gunpowder residue at all. That meant that Hank could not have died the way Tom Brown said he did. He said they were exchanging rifles when the gun went off. For this to be true, the rifle would have been so close to Hank's face that his wound would be near-contact and gunshot residue would certainly have been present. The crime lab tests proved that Tom Brown must have been standing at least a foot and a half away from Hank when the gun went off, and probably even farther away.

Secondly, if the shooting happened the way Brown described it, the trajectory of the bullet would have been at an upward angle. It was not; autopsy findings indicated that the wound was almost horizontal, with a variation of only an inch or so from a straight, flat path.

Unfortunately, Rusty was long buried in a mass

grave, and they would never be able to find out whether the bullet had entered the dog head-on, as Brown said, or from the rear, as Robin claimed.

There were no bullets to test, only fragments. Bob Hamilton spent two weeks trying to find similar ammunition for the near-antique 1932 rifle and finally came up with a precious few from a gun buff. Their makeup matched the fragments found in Hank's neck.

Robin Marcus's polygraph tests had gone from "failed" to "inconclusive" to the point where she passed cleanly. After profound brainwashing, psychiatrists explain that memory returns slowly, but it *does* come back. Finally, Robin knew exactly what had really happened. But how would a judge or jury react to the information that it had required a series of polygraph tests to elicit the truth from Robin? And even if she did make a believable witness, she had not actually seen the killing; she had only heard the gunshot that killed her husband.

Jim Byrnes, one of the attorney general's criminal investigators, was given the task of obtaining the seventh, and final, statement from Robin Marcus. Byrnes was the chief of detectives of the Marion County sheriff's office when he was asked to join the A.G.'s staff. He was a highly skilled interrogator, and if anyone could gain Robin's trust, it would be Jim. He knew he would have to spend days with her as he explained why it was essential she give just one more statement.

Finally he hit on the right approach. "Robin, I won't ask you to give me a statement," he said. "I want you to write it out yourself. Take as much time as you want. You write exactly what happened, everything you remember, and when you're ready, call me."

Robin had not been in control of her own life for a

long time. And Byrnes believed that, for a time, she had actually allowed Tom Brown to take over the thought patterns in her very brain. By letting her write her own statement, he was allowing *her* to ask herself the questions and to pick the time when she was willing to hand her statement over to Jim Byrnes. She liked him—he had daughters close to her age. She wanted to trust him, but it was hard for her to trust anyone anymore.

Byrnes had guessed right. Robin Marcus wrote an eighteen-page statement from her own memory and it was one of the most frightening and incredible statements Jim Byrnes, Bob Hamilton, and Steve Keutzer had ever read. Robin Marcus had forgotten nothing. The truth had been locked up in her subconscious mind and now came spilling forth. Her statement detailed exactly how her husband's savage killer had brainwashed her, causing her to forget her ordeal.

Robin wrote how she begged Tom to leave her in the woods after he killed Hank and Rusty, but he answered, "If I leave you here, it won't be alive."

Then he forced her to drag Rusty off the trail and wipe the dog's blood off her hands with dirt and ferns. She thought Rusty might still be alive because his feet were still moving, and she wanted to take care of him. But Tom told her, "Those are his reflexes. I never have to shoot anything more than once. I don't like to see anything suffer."

Tom told Robin it wouldn't do her any good to run. His gun could shoot 500 yards. She didn't know anything about guns, and she believed him. She pleaded with him not to kill her, but all he did was smile that same odd grin. He then explained he couldn't trust her and had to tie her hands. Then he led her to her husband's body.

"Don't look. You wouldn't want to see him," he

warned, leaving her tied a short distance away. He returned with Hank's watch. "Now," he ordered. "You're not allowed to cry. I'm going to tell you a story. You'll have your time to cry, but I'll tell you when it's time."

He washed any residual blood off her hands with a bottle of water and then took a swig of water as he began his story.

"You and your husband were dumb to believe I was a logger who worked up here. You can see my truck's from Nebraska. I've killed five or six people, and I'm wanted for murder in several states. My name is Kent, not Tom, and I'm a hit man for the Organization, but I've killed one man too many, and now they're after me. I had to kill your husband because I wanted to take you into the mountains to live with me. I need companionship.

"If they come after us, you are to run in one direction and I'll run in another so I'm the one who'll be killed."

He explained that he had been watching her and thought she was fit enough to make a mountain woman. She stared at him, dumbfounded. He was like someone from another planet to her. She could barely believe what he was telling her. "Now, now," Tom said, "you can cry."

Finally, Robin let her sobs out, crying brokenheartedly. When she was empty of tears, she tried everything she could think of to convince him that he didn't want her. She told him she was really a city girl who couldn't last on the mountain trails. She told him she was sick; she would be a drag on him. She even told him she was a "slut who gets it on with everyone," hoping this would turn him off and make him afraid she might infect him with something. But he only kept smiling that fixed grin. "I was so afraid to be up there with him," she wrote. "He tried to comfort me and hug me, but I wouldn't let him."

Then Tom instructed her to gather her belongings and some food and follow him. He allowed her to take her Bible. She pleaded with him to let her leave a note for her family, but he said they couldn't leave a trail.

Laden down, they headed into the woods. When the trees closed off behind them Tom had her change into army pants so that she would be camouflaged from the "hit men who are after us." She went into the bushes to hide herself from him as she changed. Strangely, Tom dumped articles along the trail as they went. At first, she thought he was being careless, but then, when he cut through the brush, she knew he was leaving a false trail. They went down a steep rocky bank to the river's edge, and headed upriver. "If you see an airplane or a helicopter, duck," he warned, "that will mean they've found us."

Robin wrote, "He was bossy and always telling me to hurry. He told me only to step on rocks—never mud, sand, moss, or bark or anything else that would leave footprints. He said we were going way over to the other side of the mountain, and if anyone did come across us, I was to keep quiet and pose as his wife."

Robin recalled that a small plane flew overhead and they'd hidden. Then they cut over to the smaller tributary of the river. She asked Tom if they had brought her grandmother or their friend along, would he have killed them too? He said, "Yes, but I don't really like killing. We do it only if we have a good reason."

He didn't look like a hired assassin, she thought; he was slightly built and his swaggering seemed to be an act, but he certainly talked like a member of a sinister organization. And he had the cruelest eyes she'd ever seen, deep-set and full of hate. After hours of crashing through the brush, Tom told her they could take a rest.

He lay on the sleeping bag while she went into the water to cool off.

"I went in the water in my bikini with my back to him. I wasn't even thinking of sex, so I figured he wasn't either. All of a sudden, I felt him staring at me. He ordered me to come over to him. I got out of the water with my hair over my cleavage, and then he told me to take my top off. I begged him to wait a few days. I said, 'You've just murdered my husband. Please don't do this.' "

Tom took the knife from his belt and put it on the ground next to him, and said, "Remember what I told you?"

She took off her top, but left her long black hair covering her nakedness.

"Now take off the bottoms and pull your hair back," he ordered. Trembling, she was forced to stand naked in front of him.

Tom expected romance because he had chosen her to be his woman, his companion in the woods, but Robin broke into tears of fear and embarrassment. Her terror didn't bother him at all. He forced himself on her and raped her.

When he finished, he allowed her to get dressed. Robin begged Tom again to just leave her in the woods, telling him that she would somehow find her way out. But he refused.

They continued along the river, climbing over logs and rocks. Tom grudgingly helped Robin over difficult spots when she couldn't keep up with him. That night they made camp and ate. Robin felt like gagging on her food, but she knew she had to keep up her strength. Tom bragged to her that he could have killed Hank with a knife or with his bare hands since he was trained in hand-to-hand combat. "But of course, a gun is much less messy and painless," he finished, "if you know how to use it."

Robin told him she'd been ill and that Hank had considerately avoided having sex with her. Tom shrugged and said, "I was going to kill him last night, but I thought I'd be a sport and give you one more night together."

Tom explained to Robin that *he* was trying to protect her. After all, he hadn't killed Hank in front of her. "I tried to make it easy for you."

"How did you kill Hank?" she asked.

"I just pointed at something and gave him the binoculars, and I stepped back and fired."

As Robin's long, handwritten statement continued, a reader could track the points where her mind had gradually began to bend under the combination of grief, fear, guilt, and the persuasive words of her captor. She submitted to more sex acts, things Hank had never asked her to do. She learned to turn her mind off and not think about what he was doing to her. She just wanted to get it over with, and now she no longer fought him. "I cried myself to sleep," she wrote. "I've never felt so alone before. The next morning I woke up, forgetting that it wasn't Hank beside me but the man who had killed him. It was a nightmare. I didn't want to believe he was a murderer, though, because he was the only person on earth I had to talk to."

The brainwashing process intensified. The world Robin knew was far behind her, and she was so frightened. All the time, Tom talked on and on and on. The second day wasn't as bad for her; she began to get used to plunging mindlessly through the woods. Whenever they rested, she read her Bible and prayed.

"I used to be religious myself," Tom commented, "but God gave up on me a long time ago."

Robin assured him that God didn't give up on anyone, not even him.

Tom shook his head. "I've killed too many people— a lot in the army and five or six for the Organization. That's all I know how to do."

Tom embellished his story of Mafia connections. He told Robin he had been betrayed by a girlfriend who was in the Organization, and Robin believed him. She knew he could kill, and she believed now that he was an expert in survival. Now he was letting her see the pain he had known in his life. It was important for her to see him as something other than a murderous monster.

Tom didn't like to see Robin cry. "You should be getting over it by now," he complained. But Hank had only been dead for twenty-four hours. How could he expect her to get over it so soon? She would *never* get over it.

"He was hard to figure out," Robin wrote. "One minute, he'd be rough and mean, and the next he'd be kind and gentle. We talked about the human mind a lot. He said the mind contains a lot of little doors and that you could open and shut them when you wanted to. He said, 'When I kill someone, I open a door.' He said someday the doors in his head might all open and let the bad things loose and he might go crazy, but until then he had no guilt feelings."

Robin read the Bible aloud to Tom until he asked her to stop. It helped her to hear the words aloud. When she began to cry again, Tom got angry and yelled at her.

All along, he assured Robin that he was her protector. She had to remember that he was saving her from the men who were hunting them.

"Why didn't you just tie Hank up," she asked. "Then you could have taken me away."

He explained why he hadn't done that. "That would have been mean," Tom said. "[To leave him] In the hot sun with no food or water."

His reasoning was bizarre, but somehow he made it seem believable. He said he had killed Rusty out of kindness, too, because the dog would never have made it in the wilderness with them. It was far better to eliminate him humanely. "Rusty never knew what hit him."

Robin was getting mixed up. There was no one but this man beside her, and she wanted so much for him to tell her it had all been a terrible accident. She couldn't bear to think Hank had died only because Tom wanted her.

They camped out for a second night.

"What will you do if you tire of me?" she asked.

"I don't see how I could. You're the only person here."

They talked about books and movies. He told her he admired Adolf Hitler. She asked him about his family and he said he hated them. She had to be careful about the subjects she brought up. Things could make him so angry in an instant. Gradually, however, Robin's fear lessened and she prayed, asking God to somehow allow her to get home.

The next day, July 26, they didn't travel at all. Tom was sick, coughing and pale. He thought he might have pneumonia. He ranged around, checking the area, asking her how far away she could spot him. He wanted to be sure they would see anyone looking for them so they wouldn't be ambushed. He came back and asked for some paper, and he then sat down to write three notes to friends in which he apologized for the "accident."

"I'll probably be dead soon," he said.

Robin started to cry, and suddenly Brown began to

cry, too. "I knew that one of those doors in his head had finally opened," she wrote. "He told me that if I would mail the letters for him, he would tell me what had really happened. He told me that killing Hank was an accident. When he said that, it was just what I needed to hear. He said he didn't remember how it happened."

Seeing Robin coming around to his thinking, Tom pressed on, telling her the sad story of how the woman he loved had rejected him. He said he'd gone to Nebraska to forget her, and he was treated well there. He admitted his name was really Tom, after all. He promised to walk Robin to the river and let her make her way home. He even went so far as to take her there, telling her that he was sick and was better off dying alone in the woods.

"I felt so sorry for him," Robin wrote. "Deep inside, I knew it was no accident, but I told myself he was telling the truth. I couldn't just let him die up there. After all, he was nice enough to spare my life and let me go."

Tom was now all generosity. He offered her the sleeping bag and the water, and he told her sadly that no one would ever believe him about the accident. He had no choices left.

"And you're sure it was an accident?" Robin asked.

"Yes. I'm sure."

"If you're sure," Robin said, "I'll go to the police with you and tell them I saw it."

Tom smiled then, as if this was exactly what he wanted her to say. He led Robin all the way back to the camp she and Hank had set up—how long ago? The days were beginning to blur. She knew she could easily find her way out of the forest from here. Then Tom told her that he was heading back into the woods. "All I ask is one hour."

Robin's essay for Jim Byrnes continued, detailing her day with Tom. She wrote that she hated the thought of leaving a sick man all alone deep in the woods. She insisted she would be his alibi. At this point, she'd honestly believed he was a nice person, that he was a victim of a terrible mishap. Her brainwashing was complete. He allowed her to "persuade" him to accept her help. Finally he agreed to go with her so she could explain that she had seen the shooting, that it had all been an accident.

Tom went to where Hank's body still lay and brought back his wallet. Meekly, he asked if it was all right that he'd taken two dollars out for gas, and Robin said it was. She didn't want to see Hank dead. The sun was setting by the time they reached Tom's truck.

They headed for Estacada, and Robin noticed that Tom was driving erratically. He actually *was* ill and had a high fever, so she told him they should wait until morning to go to the police. They spent the last night in a park, going to Tom's lawyer's office to talk to James O'Leary the next morning.

Although Robin had not seen Tom shoot Hank, it seemed now that she had. Tom had explained it to her often enough. "He told me how it was supposed to have happened, what to say, and I believed that story. I heard it so often, I really believed it was true."

And, according to Dr. Treleaven, she did indeed believe the story she had told the Clackamas County sheriff's detectives was true. At that time, she had been methodically and thoroughly brainwashed.

Tom Brown was now in jail. Criminal Investigator Paul Keller spoke with him, and he glibly went through the same story he'd told before. The shooting was an accident, and Robin had seen it. That was all there was to it. If the dead man's wife backed him up, he couldn't understand why the police were harassing him. Then, on the advice of his lawyer, Tom stopped talking. He had nothing more to say.

As Tom Brown's trial approached, Steve Keutzer and Bob Hamilton acknowledged that they had some problems with their case. They were absolutely convinced that Brown was a merciless killer, but would a jury believe the victim's widow? The defense would certainly bring up the undependability of her memory. Was the evidence enough? And would a jury understand the gunshot-residue evidence?

Knowing Brown's potential for violence, they didn't want him out on the streets. Could they gamble on a win in court? It might be safer to agree to a plea bargain, allowing him to plead guilty to a lesser charge. That would ensure he was locked up for a little while at least.

The two state attorneys were conferring with Brown's defense team about the possibility of reducing the murder charge to negligent homicide when a grinning detective walked up. "Don't agree to anything," he whispered. "I've got somebody you might like to talk to."

At this point in the case, a colorful witness named Wendell Stokeberry* came forward. He had never been known for his cooperation with the police; Stokeberry had a rap sheet that went so far back that even he wasn't sure just what he'd done and what he hadn't done—although if he was pinned down, he could usually sort it out. He was bright and silver-tongued, and he would make one of the best—and one of the most flamboyant—witnesses Hamilton and Keutzer had ever brought into a courtroom.

Wendell Stokeberry was currently a resident of the Clackamas County jail and had recently renewed a friendship with Tom Brown, an old schoolmate from the MacLaren School for Boys. Brown was so positive that he was going to walk free that he had spent hours bragging to Stokeberry about how he had convinced Robin Marcus to go to the police with him.

Jim Byrnes taped Stokeberry's statement. Stokeberry wanted little in return. He wanted a simple escape charge erased from his record, and he wanted to be sent to an out-of-state prison after he testified. That wasn't unreasonable; snitches didn't live long inside the walls. Jim Byrnes knew Stokeberry was risking more than he might gain. Still, he agreed to give information without any promises being made to him. Even with his many walks on the wrong side of the law, Stokeberry felt Tom Brown was too dangerous to be turned loose on society.

"I been knowing this cat since the early sixties, even before we went to MacLaren," Stokeberry said. "Once we got there, we were in the same cottage. We was good friends. So I get booked into jail here, and there he is. I tell him what I'm in for and he tells me he's in for first-degree murder and a couple of sex things."

"Did you ask him any questions?" Byrnes asked.

"Yeah, about the murder charge."

Tom Brown had explained who the Marcuses were but had not given their names. He just told Wendell Stokeberry he'd met them only the day before the killing. "He said they all went fishing and that they had a big collie with them. He said he shot the guy in the face."

"Did he say it was an accident?"

"He said, 'I killed him,' but that his story to the police was that it was an accident that happened when guns were being exchanged. He said he had used an odd kind of gun. The casing of the bullets was extra long with a heavier powder charge than usual."

"Did he tell you the reason for killing this man?"

"Later he did. He said he was paid to kill him, and he said the police didn't have a case against him, because of the girl involved. He says it's just his word against hers, and he said the girl wasn't even there. Then he said he just leveled the gun down and blasted the dog. Then he said he got together with the girl for four days. He said he was going to beat the case because the girl was so nervous and the jury wouldn't believe her. Then he said he was going to kill her, too, as soon as he got out."

"Did he say why?" Byrnes asked, keeping his voice calm. "Yeah, because she won't corroborate the lie he made her tell police in the first place. He told me how he beat the polygraph. He said you just have to tell yourself the same story over and over, and then you get to believe it yourself. Then you have no worry, no stress at all when you take it yourself. Then he showed me how to breathe and all when you take it."

Stokeberry said that Tom was sure a jury wouldn't believe Robin because she looked about twenty-four or twenty-five. "She's a Jezebel type," he says. "They won't believe her."

Tom added that he'd been 8 or 10 feet away from the victim when he shot him. "Tom says powder burns won't show from that far away, and he's worried about that now."

"Did he say why the girl gave the wrong statement?"

"Yeah. He says he convinced her that the police wouldn't believe her." Then Brown explained to Stokeberry how he'd worked on the girl's mind until she believed him.

Jim Byrnes knew there was no way Stokeberry could have known certain details about the case unless

Tom Brown had told him. No one beyond Robin and the investigators knew all these details. Wendell Stokeberry was clearly telling the truth.

With the added impact of this witness, Steve Keutzer and Bob Hamilton felt they had more than enough to go ahead with a first-degree murder charge against Tom Brown. There would be no jury. The case was to be heard in front of a judge only—Judge Winston Bradshaw.

Two days before the trial, Tom Brown scraped up enough money for bail and walked out of jail. He had threatened to kill Robin Marcus, so the attorney general's office put her into a motel under guard until the trial. She was petrified with fear even though they assured her that Brown couldn't find her. She was registered under a fake name and a police officer would always be there to ensure that no one could approach her.

When the time came for trial, the smug defendant wasn't nearly as confident as he had been. As the eight-day trial progressed, Robin testified for a day and a half. Wendell Stokeberry testified, too, although he drew giggles from the gallery as he swaggered to the witness chair. He adeptly parried defense efforts to discredit him by saying, "If you say I got busted for something, then I guess I must have. My record is *ex*-ten-sive."

He might not have been a law-abiding citizen, but he was telling the truth—and it showed.

Prosecutor Bob Hamilton presented expert testimony on the fact that there were no lead particles in the tissues around Hank Marcus's wounds. Using a long wooden dowel, he demonstrated just how far the killer had to have been away from Hank so that a shot wouldn't leave gunpowder stippling on his skin. There was no way that it could have happened as Tom Brown said.

Hamilton showed the judge the angle of the wound. Again, it contradicted Brown's version. Brown had even forgotten which side of the victim's head the bullet entered.

After hearing his story riddled with errors, Tom Brown insisted on testifying. Now he gave a different version of his recall of the gun exchange, but his efforts were feebly transparent.

Over defense objections, Judge Bradshaw allowed testimony on the mechanisms of brainwashing into the record. This was a major coup for the prosecution. As Dr. Treleaven explained it, the brainwashing of Robin Marcus was a classic example of mind control. Her mind literally became evidence in the case.

As the trial wound down, it was apparent that the attorney general's prosecutors, Bob Hamilton and Steve Keutzer, had presented a brilliantly organized case—a case that had begun with all the earmarks of a loser.

Judge Bradshaw retired to make his decision. Three days later, he came back with a verdict of guilty. Thomas Leslie Brown was sentenced to life in the Oregon State Penitentiary. His motion for a new trial was denied on July 19, 1977.

The testimony in the Marcus-Brown case on brainwashing was something of a landmark in legal precedent. Bob Hamilton pointed out that, although such testimony is generally not admissible, furtive conduct to cover up a crime is evidence of guilt. In this instance, the evidence that Tom Brown covered up was Robin Marcus's memory. If he could have permanently changed the "computer" of Robin's brain, the crime

might never have been discovered, much less successfully prosecuted.

The long ordeal of Robin Marcus seemed to be over.
At the time Hank Marcus was murdered, however, life
sentences in Oregon were not what they seemed to be.
Some lifers got out in ten to twelve years. And by the
late 1990s Tom Brown began to appear periodically before the parole board, asking to be released.

The victims or the victims' families usually appear
at these hearings, standing in a small room with the
felon who terrorized them as they give their reasons
why the prisoner should *not* be released. To protect
Robin, Bob Hamilton stands in as the victim. "It would
be too hard on Robin to have to see Tom Brown again,"
Hamilton explains. "So I'm there in her place, and
Brown and I engage in what's basically a long staring
contest."

Thus far, Brown has failed psychological tests that
would indicate he was safe to move about in society.
He is still in prison, but he will continue to come up for
parole, and it's quite possible he will one day be released from the Oregon prison system.

Robin Marcus is over forty now; she has remarried
and has children. In her new, happy life she now lives
thousands of miles away from Oregon. Only a handful
of people know where she is and what her name is, and
she is grateful for that. She is still afraid of the man
who hunted humans rather than animals, and she
dreads the day he is paroled.

Epilogue: Empty Promises

Steve Sherer left the King County Jail in a "chain" of prisoners headed for the Washington State Penitentiary in Walla Walla. The man who had lived the first thirty-eight years of his life in hedonistic self-indulgence could look forward to a life behind bars. He would be ninety-eight years old if he survived his sentence. There would be no alcohol except for the "pruno" prisoners manage to brew from scraps of fruit and vegetables smuggled out of the penitentiary's kitchen. No drugs, save for the minuscule amounts that sometimes were brought in. No more women to charm with his smooth lies. A man of his small stature might well be a target himself for convicts looking for a sex partner in a world without females.

Sherer didn't lose his arrogance as he bragged that he would be out in no time when his appeal was granted and the verdict overturned. His family had money and prestige, he commented, and he wasn't like other men behind bars. And while he waited for a new trial, he quickly found a way to meet women—if only by mail. For under thirty dollars a year, convicts can sign up for an Internet dating service with businesses like Friends Beyond the Wall or Prison Pen Pals.

The premise is much like other personal ads: Prisoners looking for love or friendship or sex can advertise their availability. They post photos of themselves online, usually wearing muscle shirts, and give their vital statistics and their philosophy of life. Most prison online dating services don't have any requirements about full disclosure of *why* their subscribers are in correctional facilities in the first place. Fortunately, convicts do not have access to computers and must have an intermediary who will pass on responses to their ads. After that, inmates can write directly to those who are intrigued about writing to them. There have been marriages resulting from the prison personal ads, even in cases where prisons have no conjugal visits and there is little chance these marriages will ever be consummated.

Steve Sherer purchased the most expensive option with Prison Pen Pals, a "platinum" membership, and he also signed on with Friends Beyond the Wall.

His ad on January 29, 2002, in the latter shows him in jeans and a muscle shirt and in a business suit with a tailored shirt and tie.

Friends Beyond the Wall Presents . . .
Steven Sherer
DOB: 11-04-61
RACE: Caucasian
HEIGHT: 5'9"
WEIGHT: 170
HAIR: Brown
EYES: Blue
EXPECTED RELEASE: 02-2051 (Case on appeal)

"How does a person in my position attract another to write?" Sherer began. "If you're willing to look past the charge I'm being held for, which I did not do, then write me and let's see where it goes.

"With that out of the way, a little about me and what I'm looking for. I've been married once and have a 13-year-old son. I love my son more than anything. Kids are so much fun, and since I'm a big kid at heart, I get along with all kids. I've lived in the Seattle area most of my life. I was born in California and lived in Arizona as recently as 1998. I'm a sun and outdoors type which is the reason for the moves. I also enjoy sports a lot, but would rather participate than watch. I've had season tickets to the Mariners in the past, which my son and I enjoyed—along with Monster Truck shows and amusement parks. For quiet times, I enjoy a good movie or when I'm alone a good suspense novel. Most of the time I like to be busy but most importantly, just happy.

"I'm looking for someone to be a friend while I'm in this place. My case is currently under appeal and I hope for a reversal. It would be nice to have some new friends on the outside when that happens . . . and I believe it will.

"So, now it's up to you! Did you like what you read or what you saw? (Pictures from 1998.) If so, write me and enclose a photo of yourself, but be sure to write my name and #929130 on the back of each photo you send. In return, I will send a recent photo of myself.

"I'm limited in what I can say here, so I hope you will write if you want to know more. Thanks for taking the time to read this. I hope to hear from you soon!

"Sincerely,

"Steven."

Sherer failed to mention that his marriage had ended in the complete disappearance of his wife, or that he was in prison because he'd been convicted of murdering her. That might have put the kibosh on any "new friends" who were waiting out there to write love letters to him.

He most certainly forgot to mention that he had other secrets. Steve Sherer was a man who held on to a grudge the way a bulldog holds on to a bone, and he especially resented women who got in the way of what he wanted to do. At the top of his list was his ex–mother-in-law, Judy Hagel. She had testified against him, and he blamed her for his conviction. He blamed King County Assistant Prosecutor Marilyn Brenneman, too. How he had hated both of them as he sat in Judge Anthony Wartnik's courtroom. If he had his way, both Judy Hagel and Marilyn Brenneman would pay with their lives, and their families' lives, for what they had done to him.

As always Sherer believed that a persuasive story and the promise of money could make anyone do almost anything. He had been in the Walla Walla penitentiary for a little more than a year when he came up with a plan in mid 2001 *and* someone who could carry it out for him. His cell mate was a young man who was easily manipulated. Jed Turner* was only 21, despite the fact that he was in prison after being convicted of attempted kidnapping. Even though he had bungled that, his intentions to abduct someone were enough to land him in the penitentiary. Still, he was scheduled for parole in early 2002.

Sherer bombarded Turner with his protestations that he was an innocent man who had been railroaded into prison by vindictive women for something he hadn't even done. He swore he would never have hurt Jami.

If Jed Turner didn't totally believe that, Sherer offered more compelling reasons to enlist the help of a man who was within months of being free. Jed needed money, and Steve assured him that he could pay him for a "job" that would never be traced to Turner. Sherer said that he knew where at least $17,000 worth of his mother's jewelry was hidden. If Jed did what he asked, he could have all of it.

Although Steve was still looking at sixty years in prison, Jed Turner was getting out soon, and he was going to need money. Sherer spent hours talking to his cell mate, tempting and cajoling him, something he had always been good at.

Neither prisoner realized that there was a "snitch" in their cell block, or, rather, a "plant"—a person who was not a prisoner at all but someone in the justice system willing to do that dangerous job. In fact, Sherer had already approached that man and tried to hire him to carry out a plan he'd formulated in his mind. This first man he contacted had pretended to be interested, but then he'd backed out. He recalled later how Sherer, unaware that he was talking to a police informant, had bragged about getting away with Jami's murder. "I did everything right," he said, apparently ignoring the fact that he was sitting in prison as he boasted.

What Steve Sherer really wanted was shocking, although even he realized that he couldn't tell Jed Turner the whole truth. This man whose ads in the pen pal columns hastened to say that he loved his son "more than life itself" was obsessed about getting back at Jami Hagel's parents, especially Judy Hagel, and he didn't care who else might get hurt in the process. He wanted Jed Turner to set fire to the Hagels' house. His own son lived there, and might well perish in the fire, too.

Once Sherer had Turner persuaded to carry out the arsonous fire, he gave Turner an address in the Lake Hills neighborhood in Bellevue. "There's a guy who lives there who testified against me," Sherer said. "He needs a lesson."

But the address wasn't for some anonymous man. It was the Hagels' address. When Steve Sherer got the proof that their house had burned, he said he would give Turner the address of his mother's house. The jewelry was buried in a crawl space under a porch there. It would all belong to Jed Turner and he could break it up and sell it and realize at least $17,000 profit.

After Sherer heard about the fire and was convinced of his cell mate's loyalty, he said there would be more assignments for the 21-year-old parolee. He wanted Marilyn Brenneman and her whole family killed, and there were others who had betrayed him. He might be sitting in prison—in fact, it would be *better* that he was in prison when it all went down—but he would put the fear of God into anyone who had ever messed up his life. And since he would be tightly locked in his cell when it happened, he would have the perfect alibi.

Jed Turner was scheduled to leave the walls in February 2002. Shortly thereafter, he would begin to carry out Sherer's plans.

What Steve Sherer was unaware of was that Washington investigators had been tipped off to his alleged revenge plots in December 2001 by someone *inside* the prison. His conversations with his cell mate were being recorded and his phone calls tapped. His chosen hit man didn't know either that they were being watched and overheard constantly, and that the newest revisions of their plans were being duly reported to detectives.

Confident that he was smarter than the stupid police and the King County prosecutors who put him behind bars, Steve Sherer was operating on many fronts. His mother continued to pay his legal fees as he appealed his conviction to the Washington Court of Appeals. A 151-page appellant brief was filed, citing alleged errors made by the prosecution in Sherer's 2000 trial. He was now represented by defense attorney Lenell Nussbaum, who raised nine issues of objection, beginning with the contention that a man shouldn't be convicted for the murder of someone whose body had never been found, who, indeed, was probably still alive someplace.

The appellant's case demanded physical evidence that might prove Jami Sherer was really dead, and Nussbaum asserted that there was no body, no blood, no weapon, nothing at all to show absolutely that a murder had occurred. For all anyone knew, she was living a sweet life somewhere, happy that Steve was behind bars.

The defense argument got complicated and it contradicted itself. First, they suggested that Jami was alive. But then they attempted to blame her demise on someone other than Steve. Nussbaum had objected to Judge Wartnik's allowing testimony and evidence about Steve Sherer's violent behavior in the past into the trial. But Sherer's new attorney said that Lew

Adams had had at least two domestic violence convictions, and that the court should have let the jury know that—asserting that Jami's lover was just as likely to have killed her as her husband.

But Lew Adams hadn't been angry with Jami. Not at all. Steve Sherer had been furious with her, and she herself had told Judy Hagel that she was leaving her husband for good—that she would be at her parents' home in a short time. And she had been with Steve at the time—not with Lew Adams.

Marilyn Brenneman and Kristin Richardson had their own brief refuting Nussbaum's arguments, and theirs was 174 pages long.

As for the fact that Jami had never been found, Marilyn Brenneman said, "It would be nice to have a body or a weapon—but you don't reward people for doing a good job of disposing of a body."

Further, if Steve Sherer had wanted to implicate another man as a suspect in Jami's murder, he could have taken the stand and testified about his suspicions regarding Lew Adams. But Sherer had declined to testify.

"Every state in the country has ruled that *circumstantial* evidence is just as important as direct evidence," Marilyn Brenneman pointed out. Contrary to what most laymen believe, a body isn't necessary to prove murder, Richardson and Brenneman argued, citing one of Washington State's most infamous homicide cases. Ruth Neslund was the onetime housekeeper—and later, wife—of a ship pilot named Rolf Neslund. Rolf had already made Northwest headlines some years earlier when he fell asleep at the wheel of his ship and crashed into supports of the West Seattle

Bridge, closing down the vital access to commuters for a long time.

Ruth had been considerably younger than her 80-year-old husband. In 1980, neighbors realized that Rolf had vanished from his San Juan Island home. His body was never found, although regional lore said that Ruth and her brother had shot Rolf and then fed his body parts into a meat grinder. Ruth insisted he had voluntarily returned to his native Norway, and it wasn't her fault if she didn't have an address for him.

She was eventually convicted.

The defense appeal reached far afield to suggest other scenarios that might explain why Jami had never been found. At the time, a man named Robert Yates had been arrested in Spokane and accused of being the serial killer who had murdered a number of prostitutes there. Eerily, one victim's body was actually found buried in the yard of the house where Yates lived with his wife and children. Nussbaum wondered if Yates might have killed Jami Hagel Sherer.

It was a strange connection.

Jami was *not* a prostitute, not by any stretch of the imagination; she had been a respected secretary at Microsoft. And Spokane was almost three hundred miles east of Seattle. Beyond that, the prosecution brief pointed out that Robert Yates had been in the army in Europe when Jami disappeared.

The Court of Appeals gave Steve Sherer thirty days in which to come up with another appeal brief. At that time, both sides would be allowed to give oral arguments.

In the meantime, Sherer and Turner were completely oblivious to the fact that Sherer's phone calls had been tapped, and that every step of their scenario to burn down the Hagels' house was on cassettes listened to by King County sheriff's detectives. Full of bravado, Sherer saw rainbows for himself everywhere. He expected to get a new trial and that he would soon be free. But first he would have sweet revenge on Judy Hagel and probably Marilyn Brenneman, too. He reportedly had no preference about whether the Hagels or his son were in their Bellevue house when it was torched. If they died, they died.

Jed Turner was paroled from prison in February 2002, and he boarded a bus for Seattle. He was glad to be out of prison, but hesitant about setting fire to the house in Lake Hills. That indecision was taken care of when he arrived at his destination. He had only a brief glimpse of the free world as he looked out the bus window between Walla Walla and Seattle. King County sheriff's investigators met his bus and took him to their offices for questioning.

When Turner learned that the police had been aware of Sherer's plans for a couple of months, he rolled over. He was willing—even eager—to tell them everything. He hadn't actually committed the crime of arson or murder for hire, yet. He saw a chance to enjoy his freedom, and he had no particular allegiance to Steve Sherer.

They asked him how Sherer would know whether he had carried out his instructions, and Turner said he was supposed to send him some kind of proof: "I had to take pictures or something—somehow—to let him know the house was burned down."

And so the King County Sheriff's Office formulated a plan of their own. If Steve Sherer wanted a fire, he would get one. With the help of the Bellevue Fire Department and after a warning to the Hagels, the investigators "staged" a fire. It looked real to their neighbors on March 22 as sirens screamed and the street was blocked by fire trucks. Smoke poured from the Hagels' roof and out the back of their house, although it wasn't caused by real flames; it came from a smoke bomb.

After the firefighters "extinguished" the fire, they anchored heavy blue tarps on the roof, a standard procedure to protect the interior of any partially burned building.

As far as anyone knew, the Hagels' house had come close to burning down. It seemed too cruel a blow for this family to suffer after they'd already been through so much. Their neighbors rushed to offer housing to them, and brought casseroles and cakes. Judy was embarrassed that she had to fib to them about "the fire," but it was vital that she and her family go along with the plan to deceive Steve.

The investigators and the fire department had notified the *Eastside Journal* (now the *King County Journal*) about what they were going to do, afraid that the paper's reporters might inadvertently expose their plan to trap Sherer.

In a decision that would draw criticism from journalistic purists, editor Tom Wolfe and his staff discussed what they would do. They knew that Steve Sherer had a master plan that would end with the deaths of a number of people—including Judy Hagel, his own son, Marilyn Brenneman and her family—and that he wanted their homes burned. Could they erase the bottom line of journalistic ethics, the stipulation that newspapers should always print only what they knew to be true? Could they indeed participate in a falsehood and print a story that said the house had been burned? If they did, that would serve as Steve Sherer's proof that his orders had been carried out.

In the end Wolfe decided that the *Journal* would take the heat for printing an untruth.

". . . We have a responsibility to the community and that weighed heavily in our decision," he said. "The targets identified by the investigation were the children of a prosecutor, his own son, and the mother of the wife he killed. Right there, you have a pretty exceptional situation. We thought it was important; we thought we had a good purpose. . . . One thing we determined from the beginning: We had no desire to blow their cover."

The *Journal* printed a succinct seven-sentence article about the house fire in Lake Hills, gave the address where the Hagels lived, and stated that officials felt the fire had been deliberately set. They didn't comment on the amount of damage, but noted there was heavy smoke pouring out of the back of the house.

Detectives sent the article to Steve Sherer anonymously. According to witnesses in the penitentiary, he was "very happy" to read it. His master plan was working.

Had Jed Turner gone ahead with the plan, Sherer had promised he would mail him Sherri Schielke's address and a map to help him find it and the expensive jewelry that was his payment. It wasn't Jed who searched the crawl space, it was the detectives. There was no jewelry there, and there probably never had been. Why would Sherer's mother have buried her jewels? She was a sensible woman who would have put them in a safe-deposit box or a safe—if she ever had them.

Steve Sherer was willing to cheat anyone, and he must have known that Jed Turner wouldn't dare contact him after committing arson—and, perhaps, murder. He sat in his cell, smiling to think that he had once again pulled off a perfect caper, still ignorant of the fact that the police had been tracking him for almost four months.

It would be more than a year later that Sherer got a rude shock. On April 16, 2003, prosecutors charged him with criminal solicitation to commit murder. Once more he was convicted of a felony, and sentenced to many more years in prison.

He no longer had a cell mate. He was moved to the Intensive Management Unit at the Walla Walla penitentiary, where prisoners are kept in their cells for twenty-three hours a day, and let out in a I.M.U of pen to exercise by himself. Inmates in the I.M.U. sometimes swear at guards, throw feces through the bars of their cells, and go into intense rages. For a time, Steve Sherer had a new neighbor; the cell next to his was occupied by Gary Leon Ridgway, the Green River Killer.

Plots and plans became almost impossible for Sherer. His mother has sold her lovely home and moved on. When Steve Sherer screamed at Jami Hagel Sherer's family that he hoped they "rotted in hell," his words bounced back and he found himself in a kind of hell.

Recently, Sherer has been moved to a Clallam Bay

correctional facility in the far northwest corner of Washington State.

He still advertises for women to write to him. Does he still have hopes of appealing for a new trial? Only he knows.

Jami is still missing, but her parents are raising her son lovingly.